BAKUMAN。

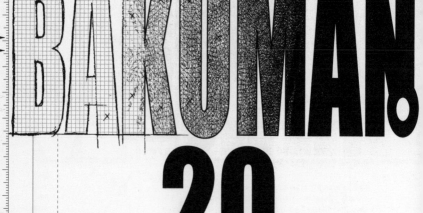

20

DREAMS and REALITY

STORY BY
TSUGUMI OHBA

ART BY
TAKESHI OBATA

SHONENJUMP MANGA

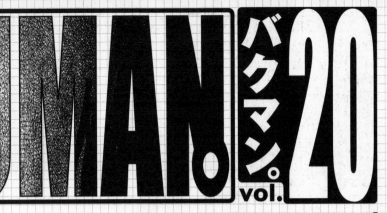

バクマン。 vol. 20

D
C
B
A
LOVE

EIJI
Nizuma

A manga prodigy and Tezuka Award winner at the age of 15. His goal is to create the world's best manga.

Age: 25

KAYA
Takagi

Miho's friend and Akito's wife. A nice girl who actively works as the interceder between Moritaka and Azuki.

Age: 24

AKITO
Takagi

Manga writer. An extremely smart guy who gets the best grades in his class. A cool guy who becomes very passionate when it comes to manga.

Age: 24

MIHO
Azuki

A girl who dreams of becoming a voice actress. She promised to marry Moritaka under the condition that they not see each other until their dreams come true.

Age: 24

MORITAKA
Mashiro

Manga artist. An extreme romantic who believes that he will marry Miho Azuki once their dreams come true.

Age: 24

*These ages are from March 2018.

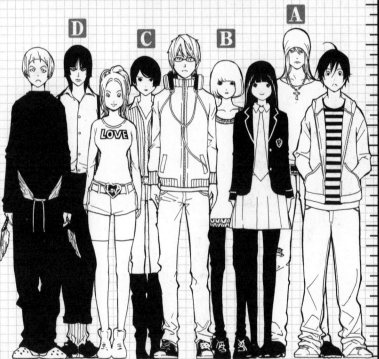

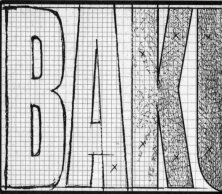

STORY In order to attain the glory that only a handful of people can, two young men decide to walk the rough "path of manga" and become professional manga creators. This is the story of a great artist, Moritaka Mashiro, a talented writer, Akito Takagi, and their quest to become manga legends!

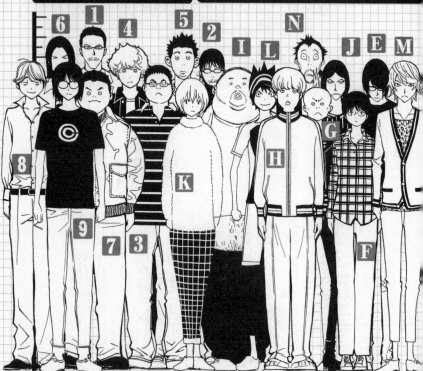

WEEKLY SHONEN JUMP
Editorial Department

1. Ex-Editor in Chief Sasaki
2. Editor in Chief Heishi
3. Deputy Editor in Chief Aida
4. Yujiro Hattori
5. Akira Hattori
6. Koji Yoshida
7. Goro Miura
8. Masakazu Yamahisa
9. Kosugi

The MANGA ARTISTS
and ASSISTANTS

A. SHINTA FUKUDA
B. KO AOKI
C. AIKO IWASE
D. KAZUYA HIRAMARU
E. RYU SHIZUKA
F. NATSUMI KATO
G. YASUOKA
H. SHOYO TAKAHAMA

I. TAKURO NAKAI
J. SHUICHI MORIYA
K. SHUN SHIRATORI
L. ICHIRIKI ORIHARA
M. TOHRU NANAMINE
N. MIKIHIKO AZUMA

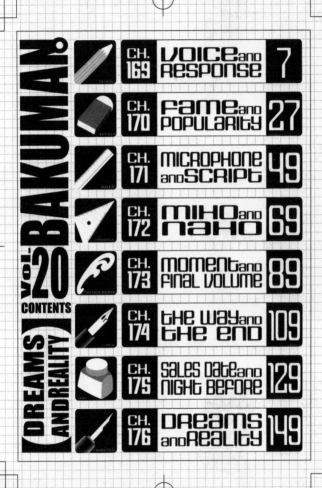

BAKUMAN。 VOL.20
CONTENTS
[DREAMS] [AND REALITY]

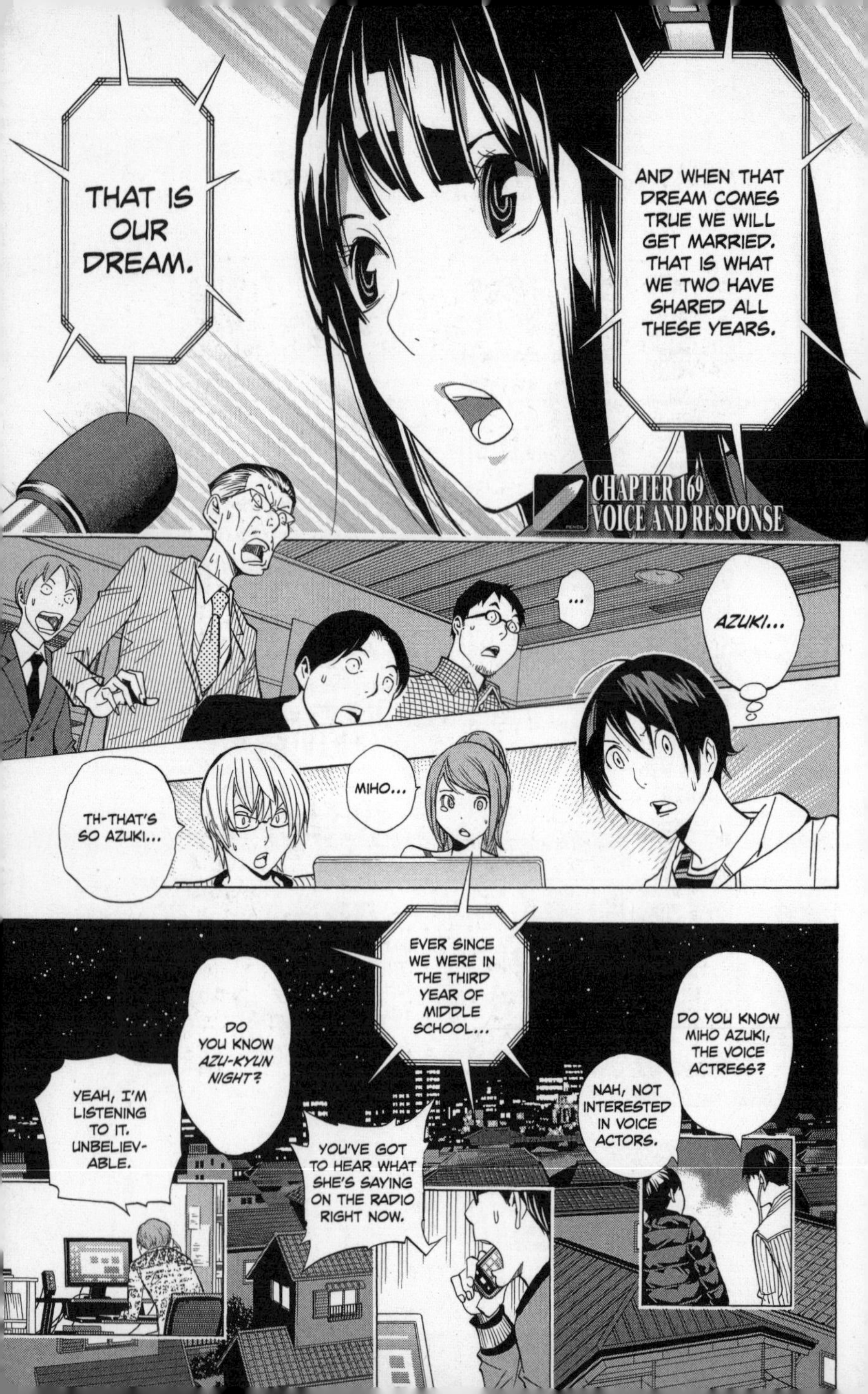
AND WHEN THAT DREAM COMES TRUE WE WILL GET MARRIED. THAT IS WHAT WE TWO HAVE SHARED ALL THESE YEARS.
THAT IS OUR DREAM.
CHAPTER 169
VOICE AND RESPONSE
AZUKI...
...
MIHO...
TH-THAT'S SO AZUKI...
DO YOU KNOW MIHO AZUKI, THE VOICE ACTRESS?
NAH, NOT INTERESTED IN VOICE ACTORS.
EVER SINCE WE WERE IN THE THIRD YEAR OF MIDDLE SCHOOL...
YOU'VE GOT TO HEAR WHAT SHE'S SAYING ON THE RADIO RIGHT NOW.
DO YOU KNOW *AZU-KYUN NIGHT*?
YEAH, I'M LISTENING TO IT. UNBELIEV-ABLE.

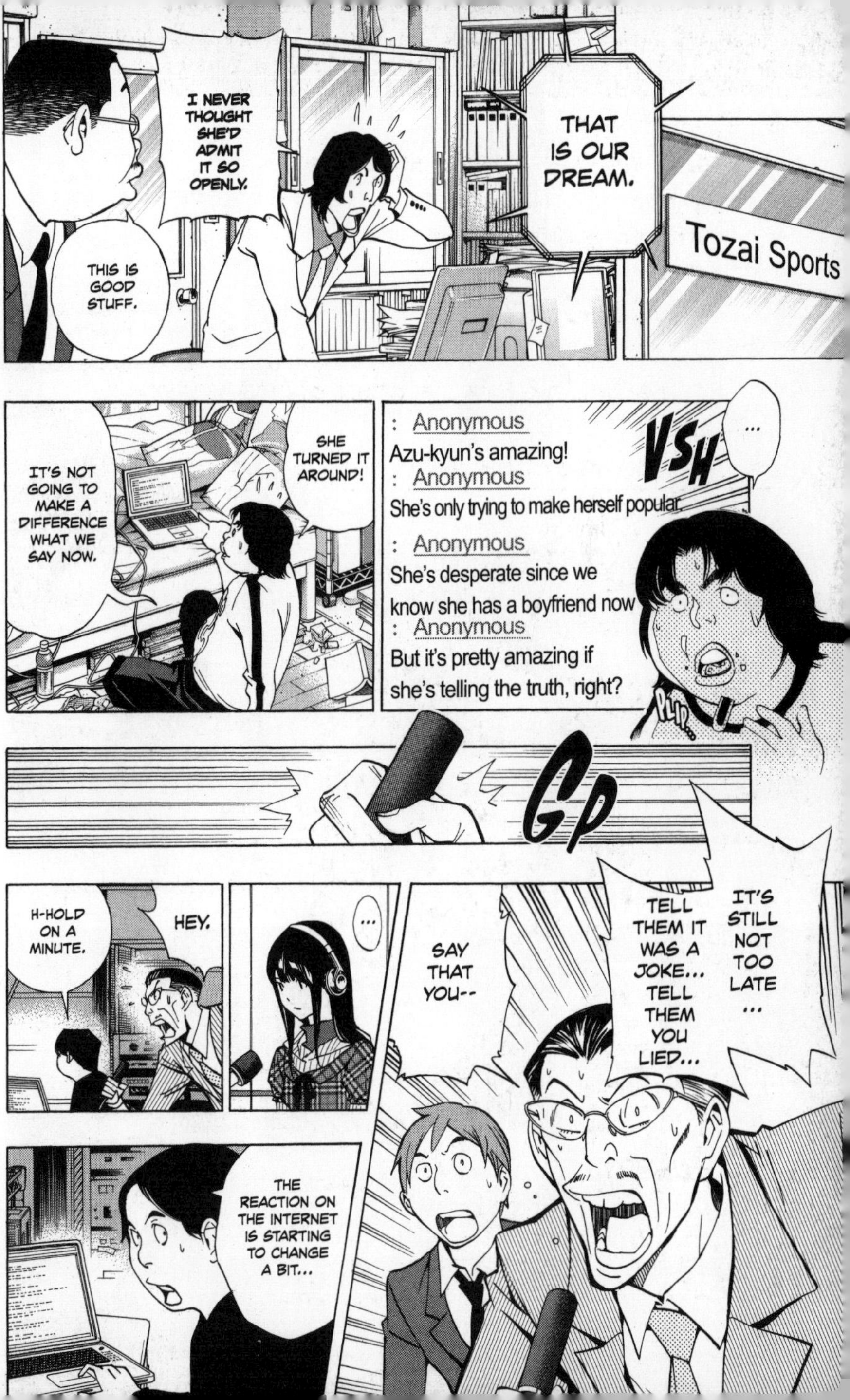
THAT IS OUR DREAM.
Tozai Sports
I NEVER THOUGHT SHE'D ADMIT IT SO OPENLY.
THIS IS GOOD STUFF.
...
VSH
: Anonymous
Azu-kyun's amazing!
: Anonymous
She's only trying to make herself popular.
: Anonymous
She's desperate since we know she has a boyfriend now
: Anonymous
But it's pretty amazing if she's telling the truth, right?
PLIP...
SHE TURNED IT AROUND!
IT'S NOT GOING TO MAKE A DIFFERENCE WHAT WE SAY NOW.
GP
IT'S STILL NOT TOO LATE...
TELL THEM IT WAS A JOKE... TELL THEM YOU LIED...
SAY THAT YOU--
...
HEY.
H-HOLD ON A MINUTE.
THE REACTION ON THE INTERNET IS STARTING TO CHANGE A BIT...

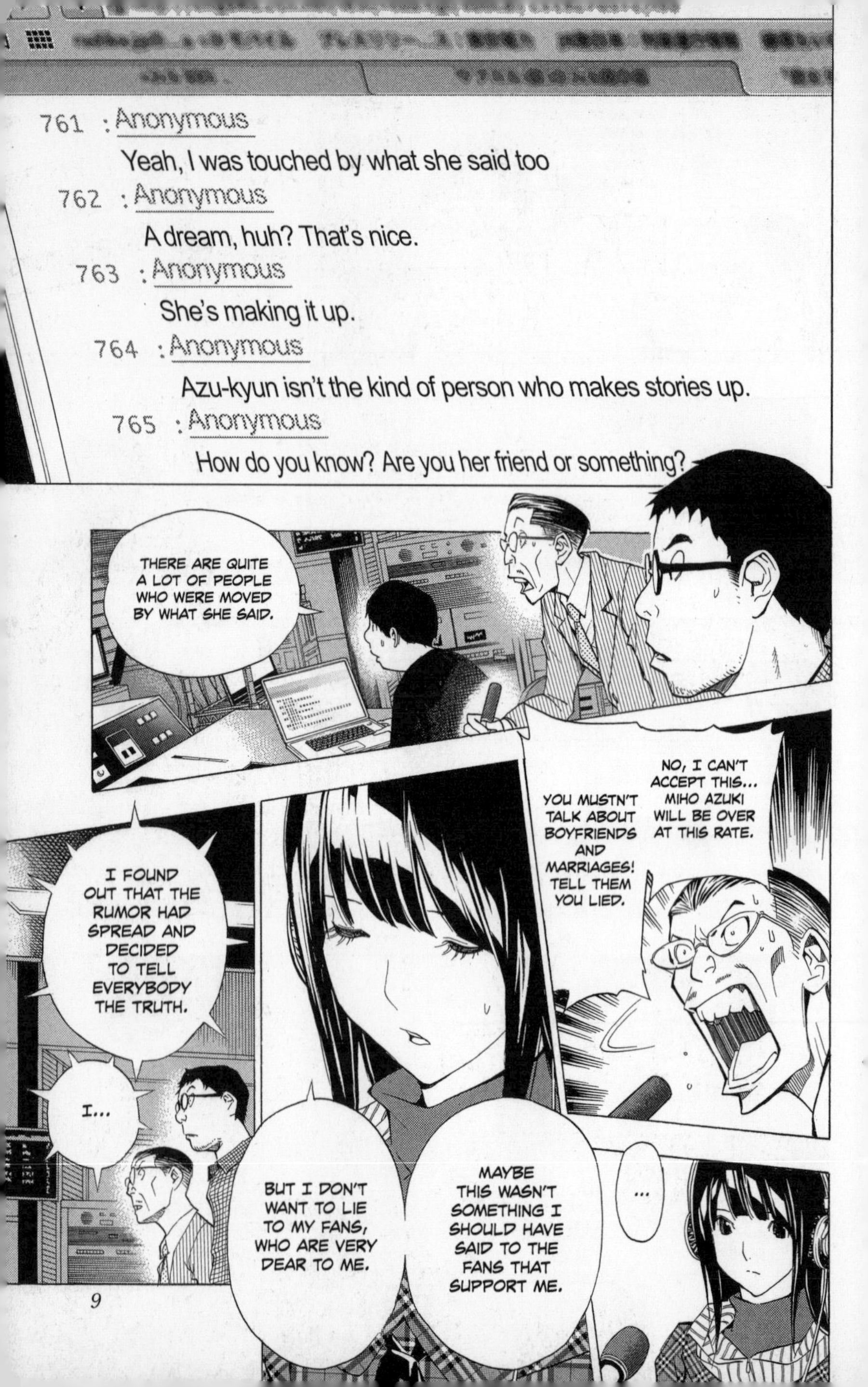
761 : Anonymous
Yeah, I was touched by what she said too
762 : Anonymous
A dream, huh? That's nice.
763 : Anonymous
She's making it up.
764 : Anonymous
Azu-kyun isn't the kind of person who makes stories up.
765 : Anonymous
How do you know? Are you her friend or something?
THERE ARE QUITE A LOT OF PEOPLE WHO WERE MOVED BY WHAT SHE SAID.
NO, I CAN'T ACCEPT THIS... MIHO AZUKI WILL BE OVER AT THIS RATE.
YOU MUSTN'T TALK ABOUT BOYFRIENDS AND MARRIAGES! TELL THEM YOU LIED.
...
I FOUND OUT THAT THE RUMOR HAD SPREAD AND DECIDED TO TELL EVERYBODY THE TRUTH.
I...
MAYBE THIS WASN'T SOMETHING I SHOULD HAVE SAID TO THE FANS THAT SUPPORT ME.
BUT I DON'T WANT TO LIE TO MY FANS, WHO ARE VERY DEAR TO ME.

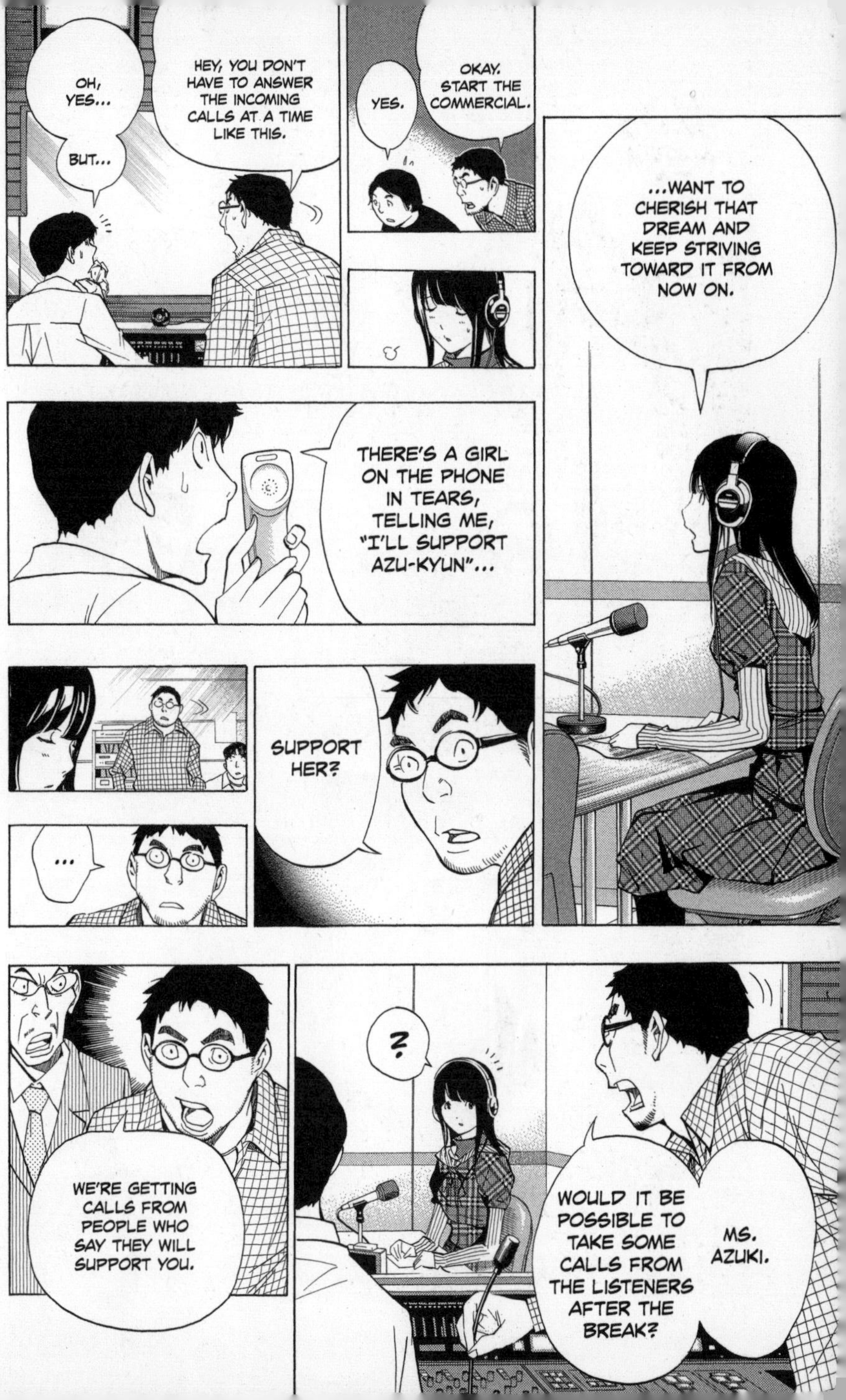
...WANT TO CHERISH THAT DREAM AND KEEP STRIVING TOWARD IT FROM NOW ON.
OKAY. START THE COMMERCIAL.
YES.
HEY, YOU DON'T HAVE TO ANSWER THE INCOMING CALLS AT A TIME LIKE THIS.
OH, YES...
BUT...
THERE'S A GIRL ON THE PHONE IN TEARS, TELLING ME, "I'LL SUPPORT AZU-KYUN"...
SUPPORT HER?
...
MS. AZUKI.
WOULD IT BE POSSIBLE TO TAKE SOME CALLS FROM THE LISTENERS AFTER THE BREAK?
?
WE'RE GETTING CALLS FROM PEOPLE WHO SAY THEY WILL SUPPORT YOU.

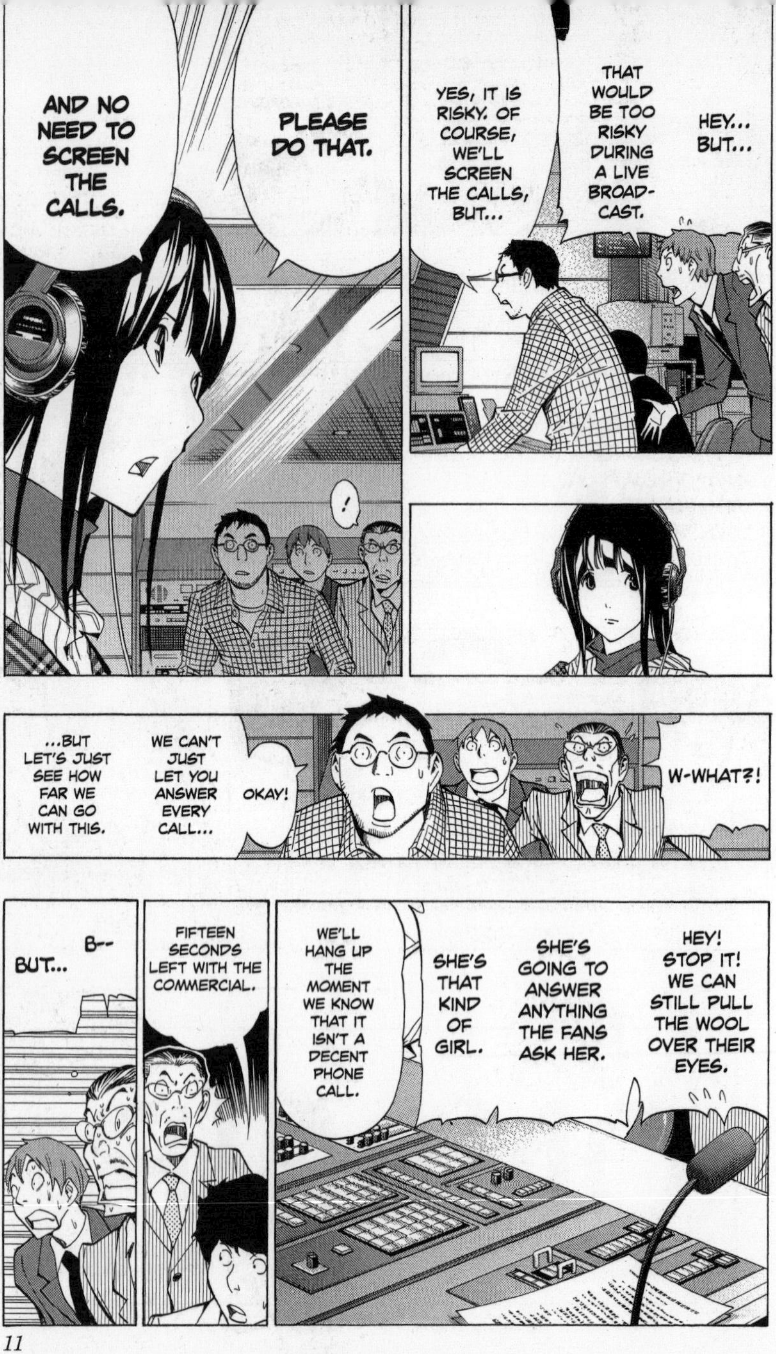

HEY... BUT...
THAT WOULD BE TOO RISKY DURING A LIVE BROAD-CAST.
YES, IT IS RISKY. OF COURSE, WE'LL SCREEN THE CALLS, BUT...
PLEASE DO THAT.
AND NO NEED TO SCREEN THE CALLS.
!
W-WHAT?!
OKAY!
WE CAN'T JUST LET YOU ANSWER EVERY CALL...
...BUT LET'S JUST SEE HOW FAR WE CAN GO WITH THIS.
HEY! STOP IT! WE CAN STILL PULL THE WOOL OVER THEIR EYES.
SHE'S GOING TO ANSWER ANYTHING THE FANS ASK HER.
SHE'S THAT KIND OF GIRL.
WE'LL HANG UP THE MOMENT WE KNOW THAT IT ISN'T A DECENT PHONE CALL.
FIFTEEN SECONDS LEFT WITH THE COMMERCIAL.
B-- BUT...

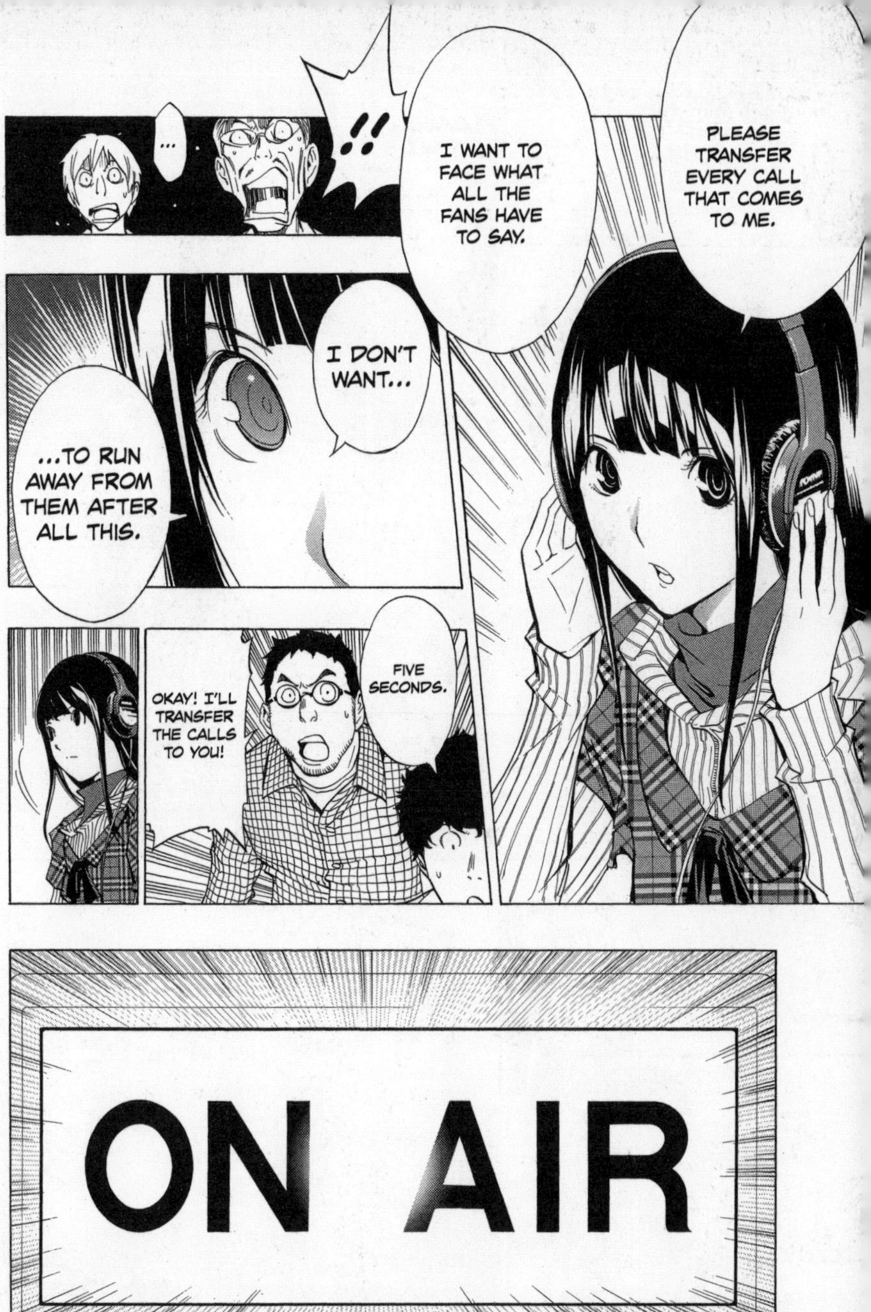
PLEASE TRANSFER EVERY CALL THAT COMES TO ME.
I WANT TO FACE WHAT ALL THE FANS HAVE TO SAY.
!!
...
I DON'T WANT...
...TO RUN AWAY FROM THEM AFTER ALL THIS.
FIVE SECONDS.
OKAY! I'LL TRANSFER THE CALLS TO YOU!
ON AIR

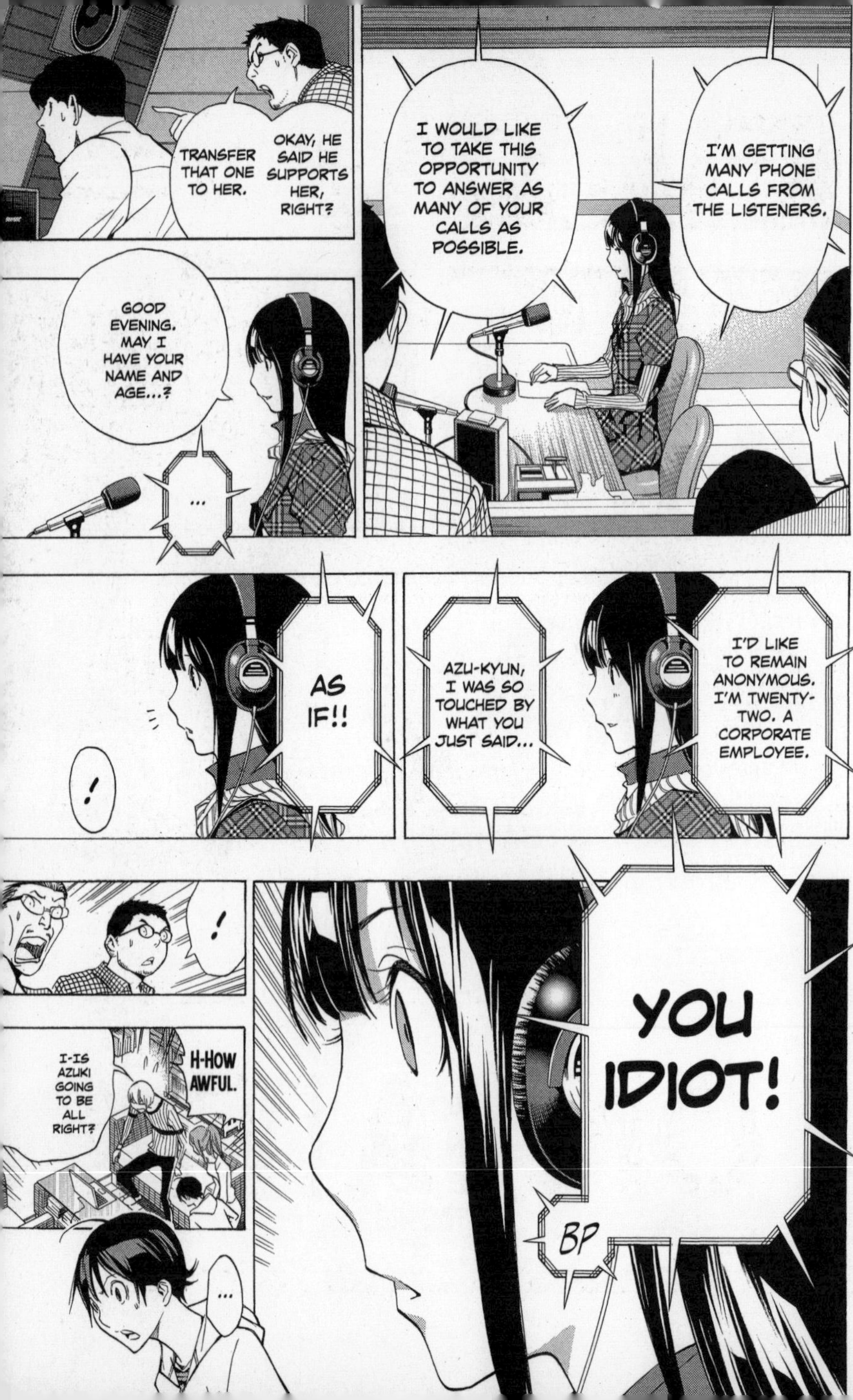
I'M GETTING MANY PHONE CALLS FROM THE LISTENERS.
I WOULD LIKE TO TAKE THIS OPPORTUNITY TO ANSWER AS MANY OF YOUR CALLS AS POSSIBLE.
OKAY, HE SAID HE SUPPORTS HER, RIGHT?
TRANSFER THAT ONE TO HER.
GOOD EVENING. MAY I HAVE YOUR NAME AND AGE...?
...
I'D LIKE TO REMAIN ANONYMOUS. I'M TWENTY-TWO. A CORPORATE EMPLOYEE.
AZU-KYUN, I WAS SO TOUCHED BY WHAT YOU JUST SAID...
AS IF!!
!
YOU IDIOT!
BP
!
H-HOW AWFUL.
I-IS AZUKI GOING TO BE ALL RIGHT?
...

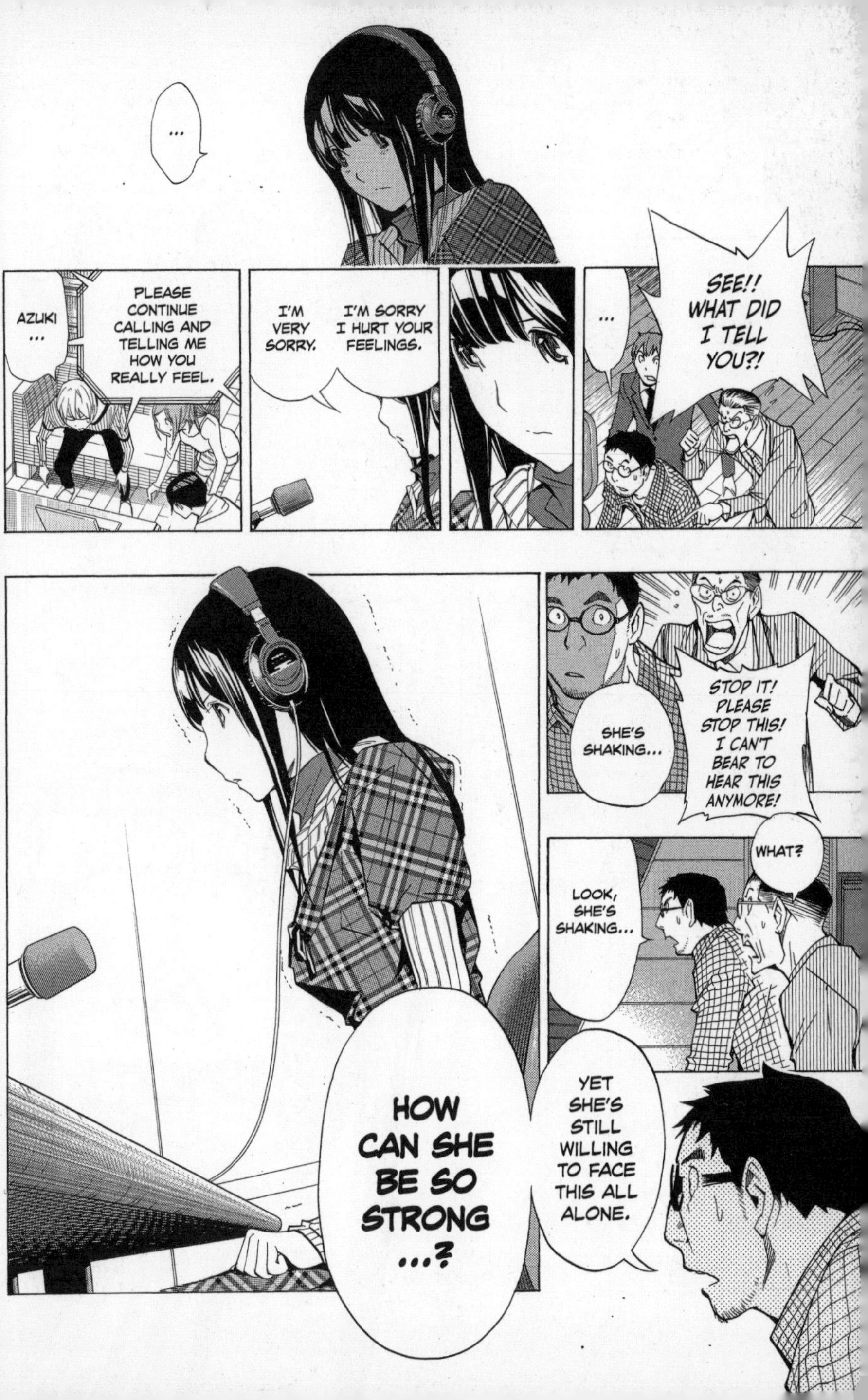
...
SEE!! WHAT DID I TELL YOU?!
...
I'M SORRY I HURT YOUR FEELINGS.
I'M VERY SORRY.
PLEASE CONTINUE CALLING AND TELLING ME HOW YOU REALLY FEEL.
AZUKI ...
STOP IT! PLEASE STOP THIS! I CAN'T BEAR TO HEAR THIS ANYMORE!
SHE'S SHAKING...
WHAT?
LOOK, SHE'S SHAKING...
YET SHE'S STILL WILLING TO FACE THIS ALL ALONE.
HOW CAN SHE BE SO STRONG ...?

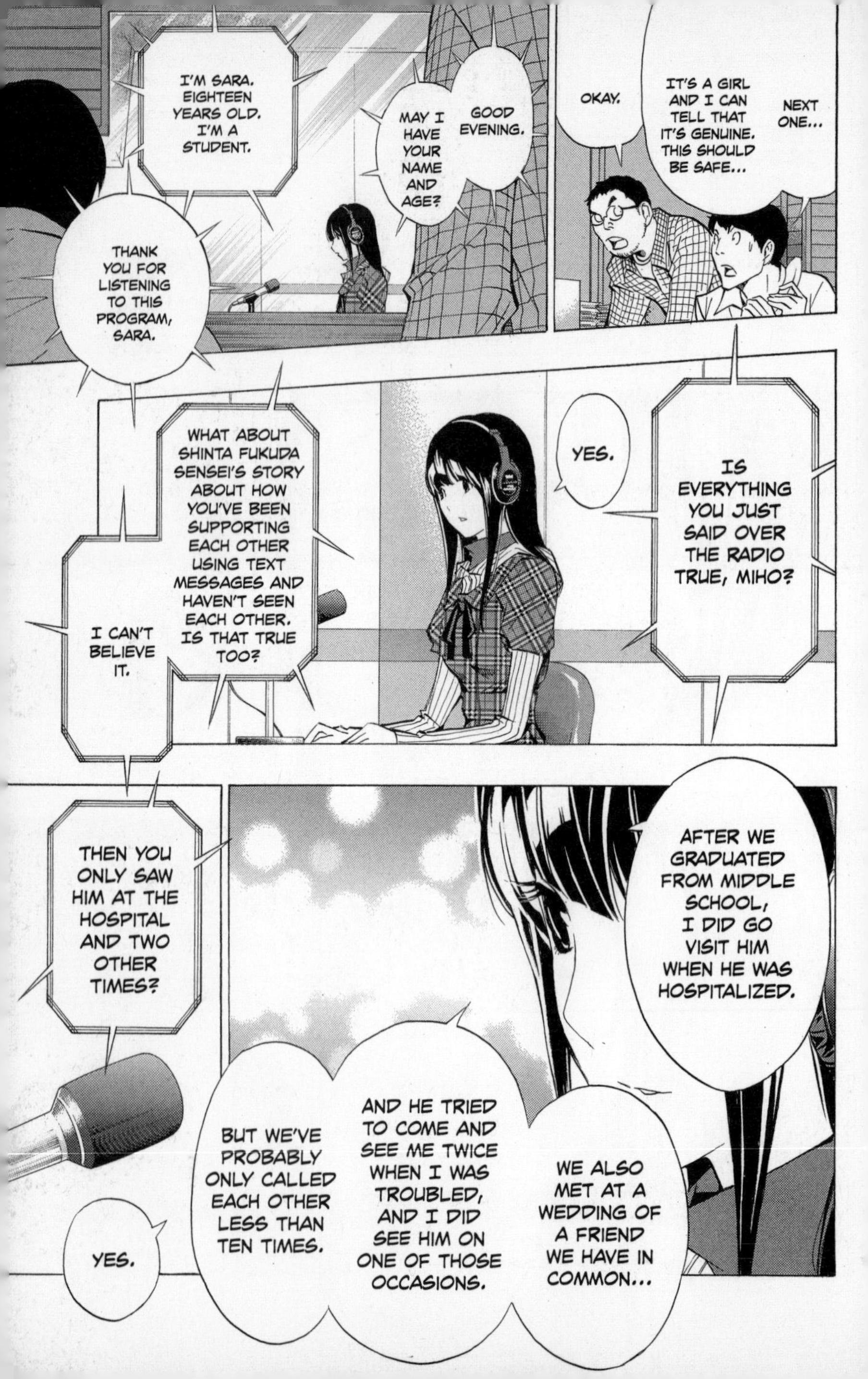
NEXT ONE...
IT'S A GIRL AND I CAN TELL THAT IT'S GENUINE. THIS SHOULD BE SAFE...
OKAY.
GOOD EVENING.
MAY I HAVE YOUR NAME AND AGE?
I'M SARA. EIGHTEEN YEARS OLD. I'M A STUDENT.
THANK YOU FOR LISTENING TO THIS PROGRAM, SARA.
IS EVERYTHING YOU JUST SAID OVER THE RADIO TRUE, MIHO?
YES.
WHAT ABOUT SHINTA FUKUDA SENSEI'S STORY ABOUT HOW YOU'VE BEEN SUPPORTING EACH OTHER USING TEXT MESSAGES AND HAVEN'T SEEN EACH OTHER. IS THAT TRUE TOO?
I CAN'T BELIEVE IT.
AFTER WE GRADUATED FROM MIDDLE SCHOOL, I DID GO VISIT HIM WHEN HE WAS HOSPITALIZED.
WE ALSO MET AT A WEDDING OF A FRIEND WE HAVE IN COMMON...
AND HE TRIED TO COME AND SEE ME TWICE WHEN I WAS TROUBLED, AND I DID SEE HIM ON ONE OF THOSE OCCASIONS.
BUT WE'VE PROBABLY ONLY CALLED EACH OTHER LESS THAN TEN TIMES.
THEN YOU ONLY SAW HIM AT THE HOSPITAL AND TWO OTHER TIMES?
YES.

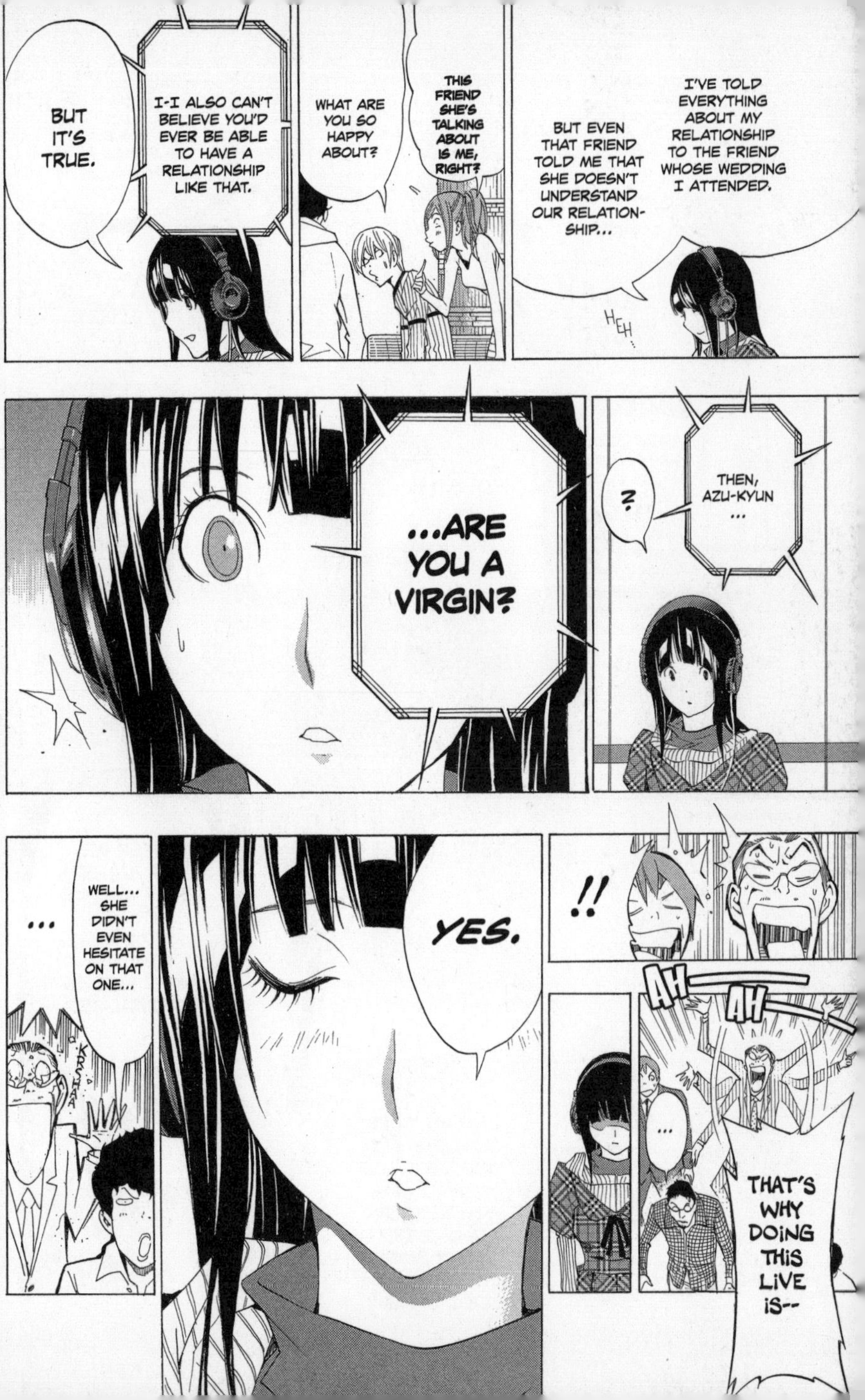
I'VE TOLD EVERYTHING ABOUT MY RELATIONSHIP TO THE FRIEND WHOSE WEDDING I ATTENDED.
BUT EVEN THAT FRIEND TOLD ME THAT SHE DOESN'T UNDERSTAND OUR RELATIONSHIP...
HEH...
THIS FRIEND SHE'S TALKING ABOUT IS ME, RIGHT?
WHAT ARE YOU SO HAPPY ABOUT?
I-I ALSO CAN'T BELIEVE YOU'D EVER BE ABLE TO HAVE A RELATIONSHIP LIKE THAT.
BUT IT'S TRUE.
THEN, AZU-KYUN ...
?
...ARE YOU A VIRGIN?
!!
AH—— AH——
...
THAT'S WHY DOING THIS LIVE IS--
YES.
...
WELL... SHE DIDN'T EVEN HESITATE ON THAT ONE...
KRSHAA

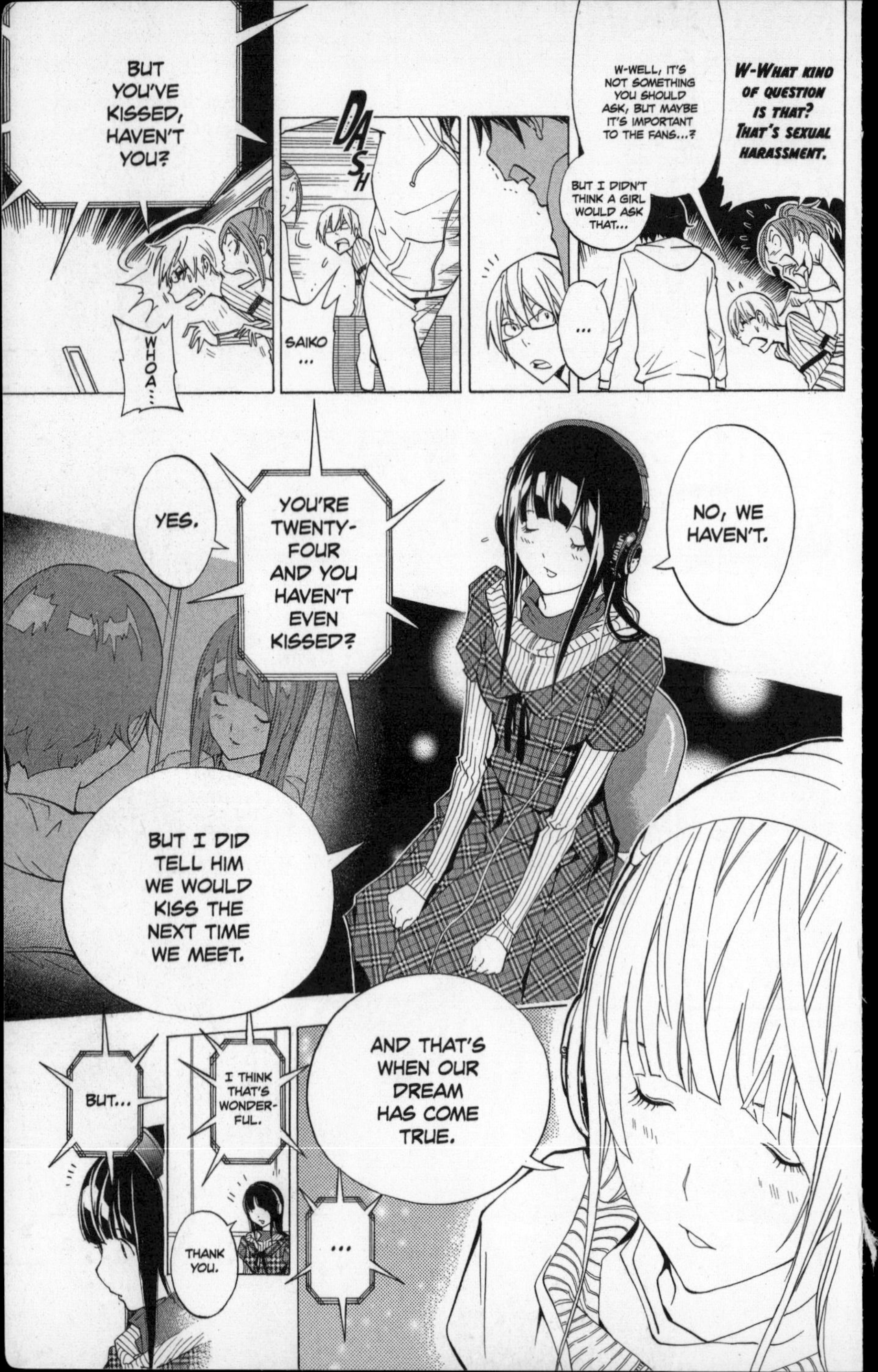
W-WHAT KIND OF QUESTION IS THAT? THAT'S SEXUAL HARASSMENT.
W-WELL, IT'S NOT SOMETHING YOU SHOULD ASK, BUT MAYBE IT'S IMPORTANT TO THE FANS...?
BUT I DIDN'T THINK A GIRL WOULD ASK THAT...
...
DASH
SAIKO...
BUT YOU'VE KISSED, HAVEN'T YOU?
WHOA...
NO, WE HAVEN'T.
YOU'RE TWENTY-FOUR AND YOU HAVEN'T EVEN KISSED?
YES.
BUT I DID TELL HIM WE WOULD KISS THE NEXT TIME WE MEET.
AND THAT'S WHEN OUR DREAM HAS COME TRUE.
I THINK THAT'S WONDERFUL.
...
THANK YOU.
BUT...

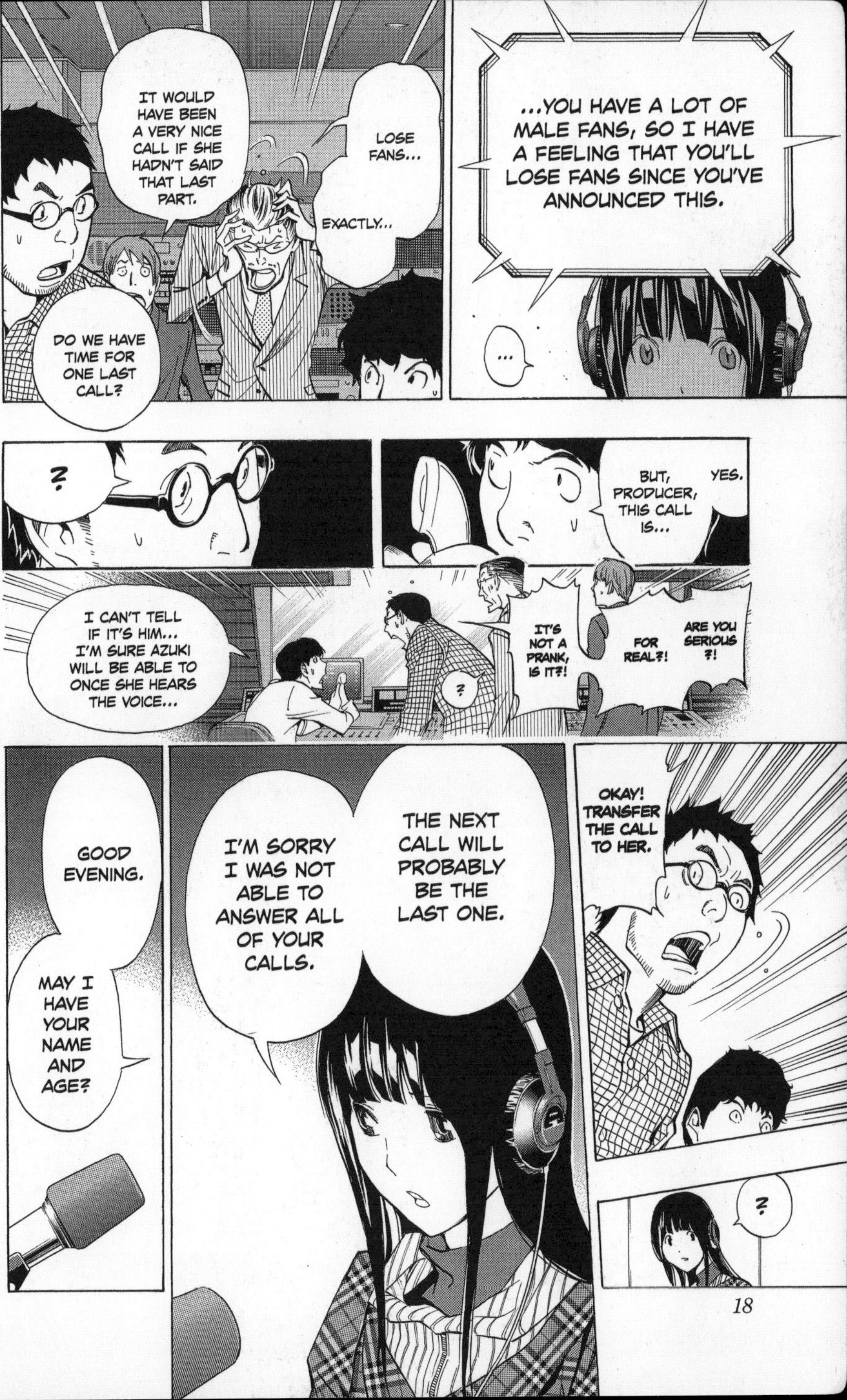
...YOU HAVE A LOT OF MALE FANS, SO I HAVE A FEELING THAT YOU'LL LOSE FANS SINCE YOU'VE ANNOUNCED THIS.
...
LOSE FANS...
EXACTLY...
IT WOULD HAVE BEEN A VERY NICE CALL IF SHE HADN'T SAID THAT LAST PART.
DO WE HAVE TIME FOR ONE LAST CALL?
YES.
BUT, PRODUCER, THIS CALL IS...
?
ARE YOU SERIOUS?!
FOR REAL?!
IT'S NOT A PRANK, IS IT?!
?
I CAN'T TELL IF IT'S HIM... I'M SURE AZUKI WILL BE ABLE TO ONCE SHE HEARS THE VOICE...
OKAY! TRANSFER THE CALL TO HER.
?
THE NEXT CALL WILL PROBABLY BE THE LAST ONE.
I'M SORRY I WAS NOT ABLE TO ANSWER ALL OF YOUR CALLS.
GOOD EVENING.
MAY I HAVE YOUR NAME AND AGE?

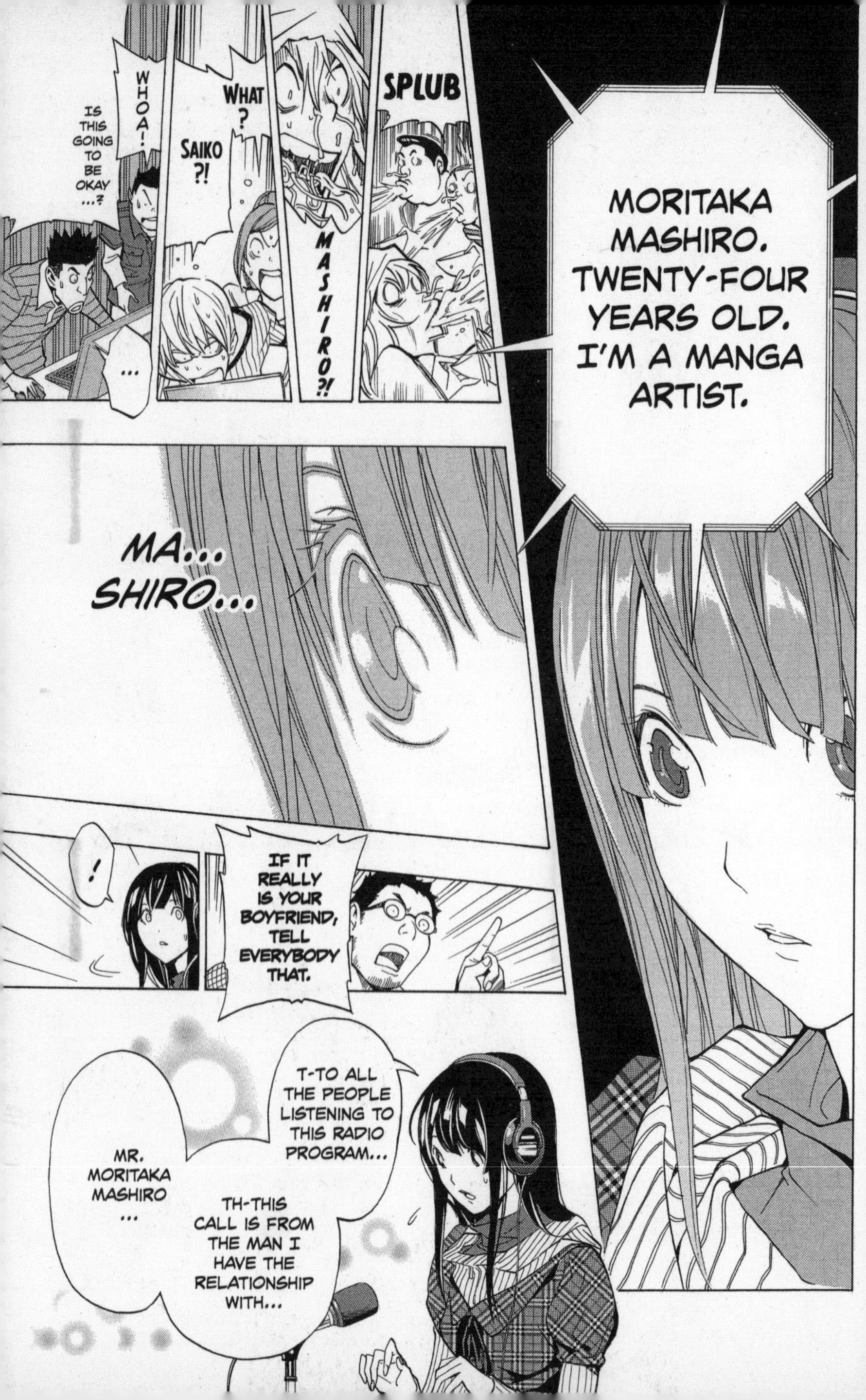
MORITAKA MASHIRO. TWENTY-FOUR YEARS OLD. I'M A MANGA ARTIST.
SPLUB
MASHIRO?!
WHAT?
SAIKO?!
...
WHOA!
IS THIS GOING TO BE OKAY...?
MA... SHIRO...
IF IT REALLY IS YOUR BOYFRIEND, TELL EVERYBODY THAT.
!
T-TO ALL THE PEOPLE LISTENING TO THIS RADIO PROGRAM...
TH-THIS CALL IS FROM THE MAN I HAVE THE RELATIONSHIP WITH...
MR. MORITAKA MASHIRO...

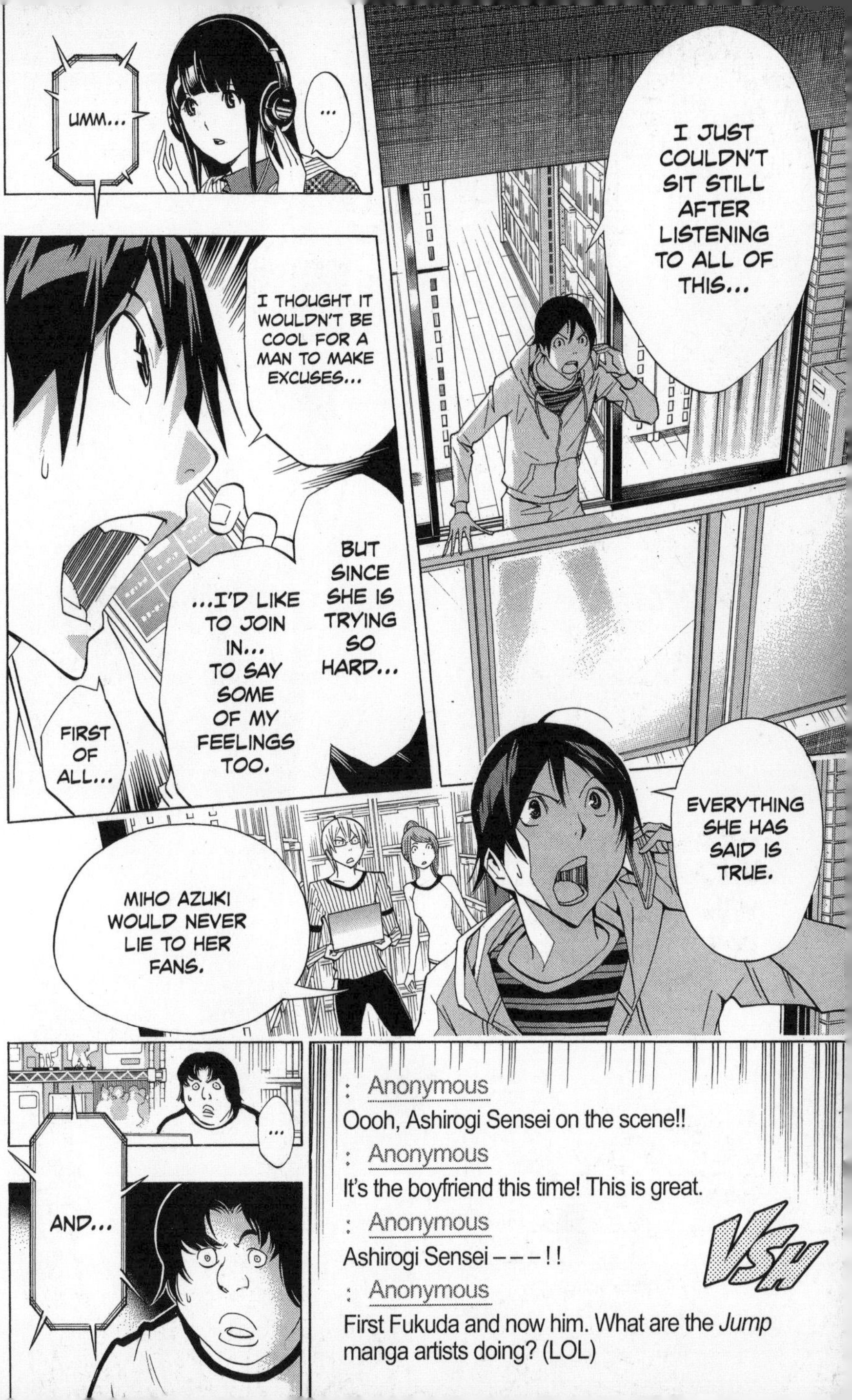
I JUST COULDN'T SIT STILL AFTER LISTENING TO ALL OF THIS...
UMM...
...
I THOUGHT IT WOULDN'T BE COOL FOR A MAN TO MAKE EXCUSES...
BUT SINCE SHE IS TRYING SO HARD...
...I'D LIKE TO JOIN IN... TO SAY SOME OF MY FEELINGS TOO.
FIRST OF ALL...
EVERYTHING SHE HAS SAID IS TRUE.
MIHO AZUKI WOULD NEVER LIE TO HER FANS.
: Anonymous
Oooh, Ashirogi Sensei on the scene!!
: Anonymous
It's the boyfriend this time! This is great.
: Anonymous
Ashirogi Sensei – – – ! !
: Anonymous
First Fukuda and now him. What are the *Jump* manga artists doing? (LOL)
VSH
...
AND...

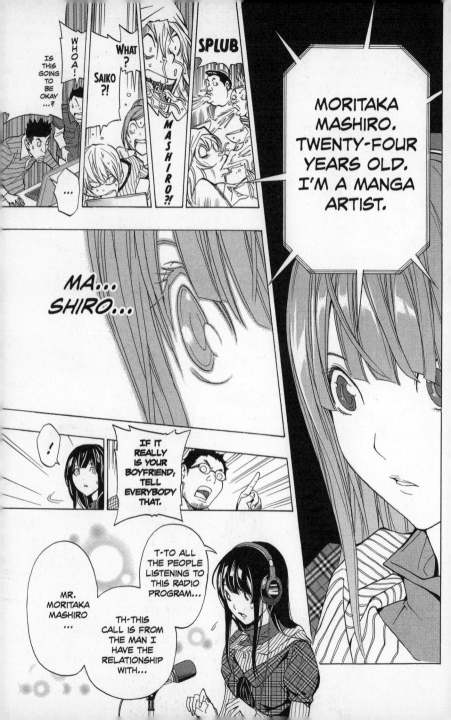

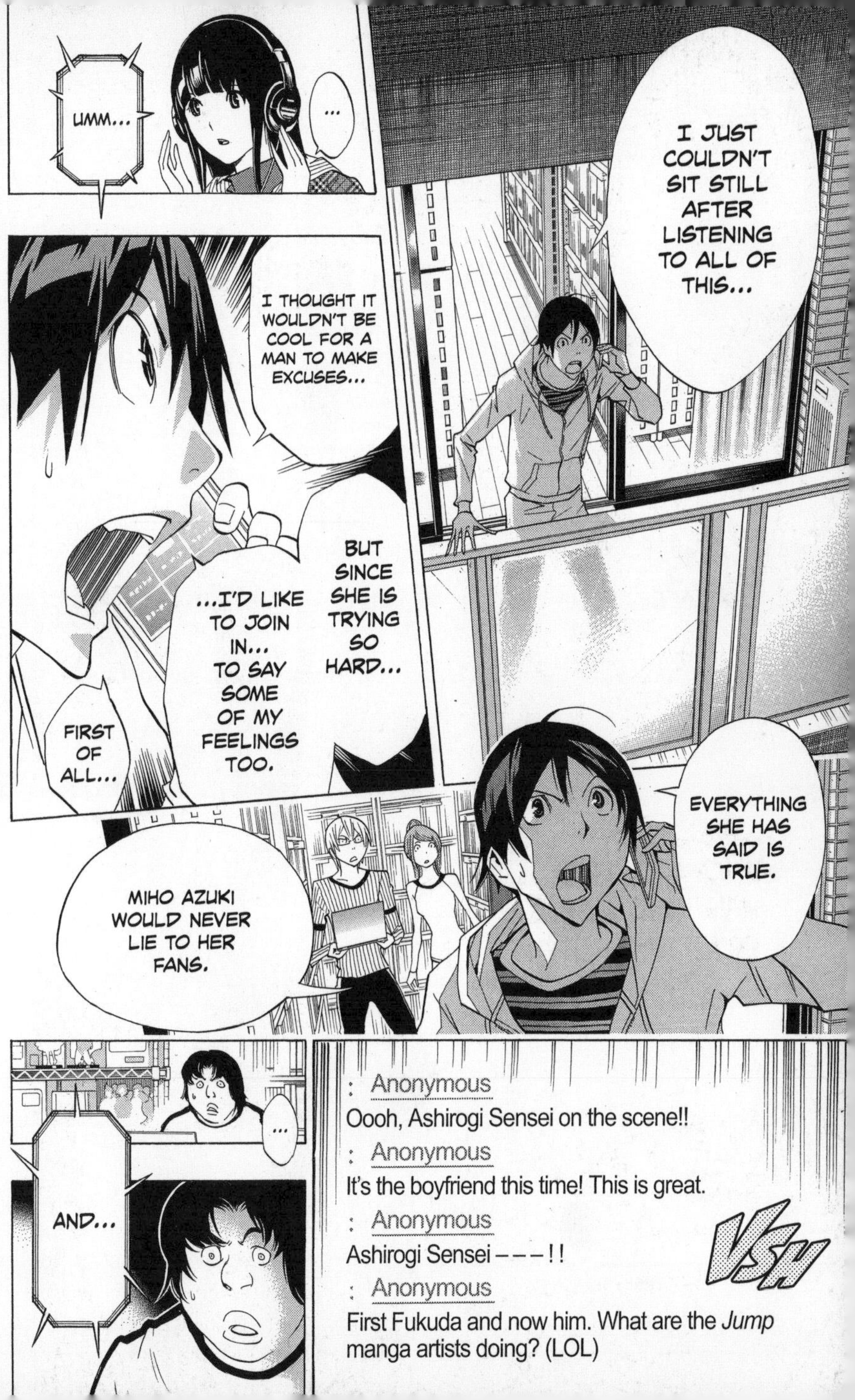
I JUST COULDN'T SIT STILL AFTER LISTENING TO ALL OF THIS...
UMM...
...
I THOUGHT IT WOULDN'T BE COOL FOR A MAN TO MAKE EXCUSES...
BUT SINCE SHE IS TRYING SO HARD...
...I'D LIKE TO JOIN IN... TO SAY SOME OF MY FEELINGS TOO.
FIRST OF ALL...
EVERYTHING SHE HAS SAID IS TRUE.
MIHO AZUKI WOULD NEVER LIE TO HER FANS.
: Anonymous
Oooh, Ashirogi Sensei on the scene!!
: Anonymous
It's the boyfriend this time! This is great.
: Anonymous
Ashirogi Sensei – – – ! !
: Anonymous
First Fukuda and now him. What are the *Jump* manga artists doing? (LOL)
VSH
...
AND...

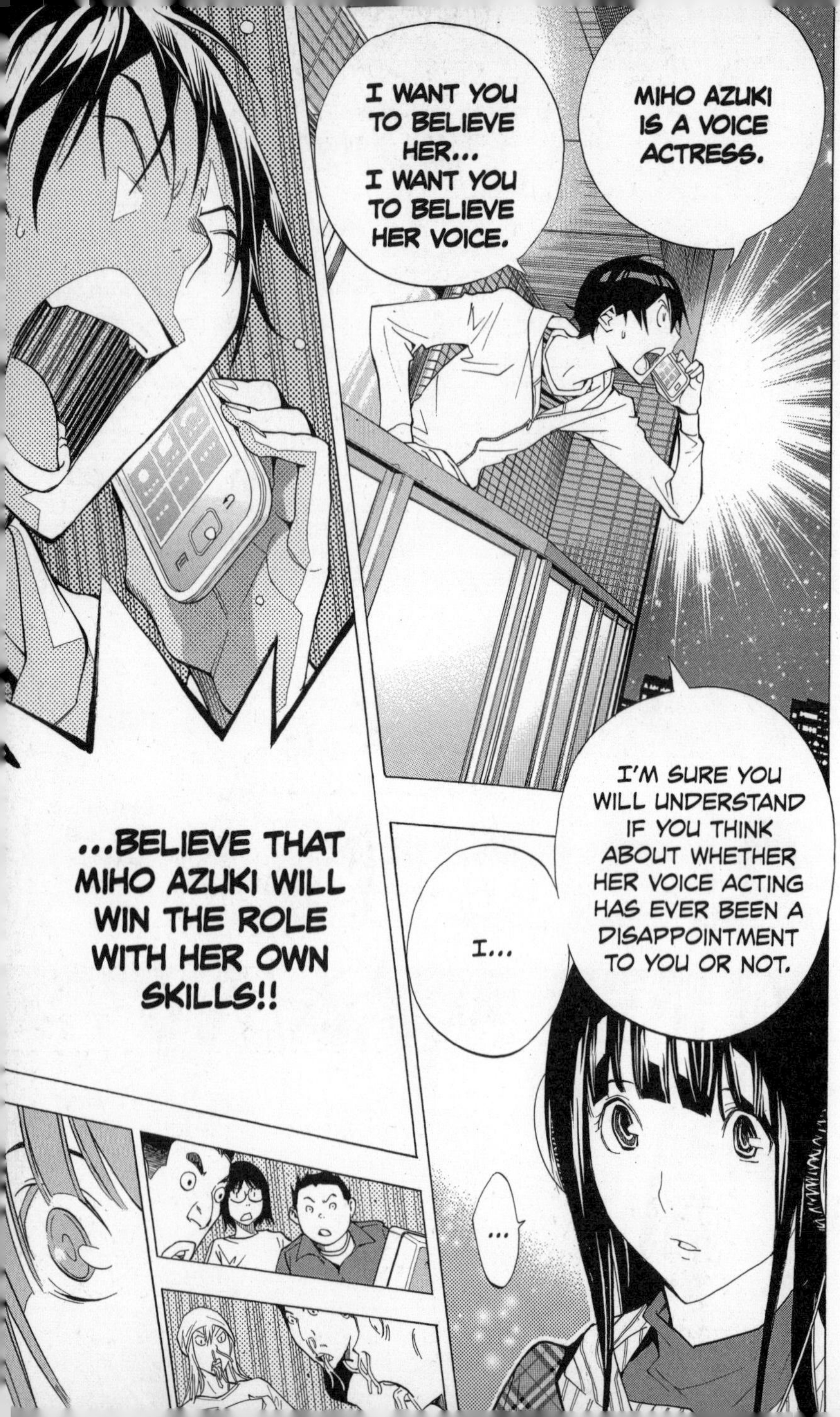
MIHO AZUKI IS A VOICE ACTRESS.
I WANT YOU TO BELIEVE HER... I WANT YOU TO BELIEVE HER VOICE.
...BELIEVE THAT MIHO AZUKI WILL WIN THE ROLE WITH HER OWN SKILLS!!
I'M SURE YOU WILL UNDERSTAND IF YOU THINK ABOUT WHETHER HER VOICE ACTING HAS EVER BEEN A DISAPPOINTMENT TO YOU OR NOT.
I...
...

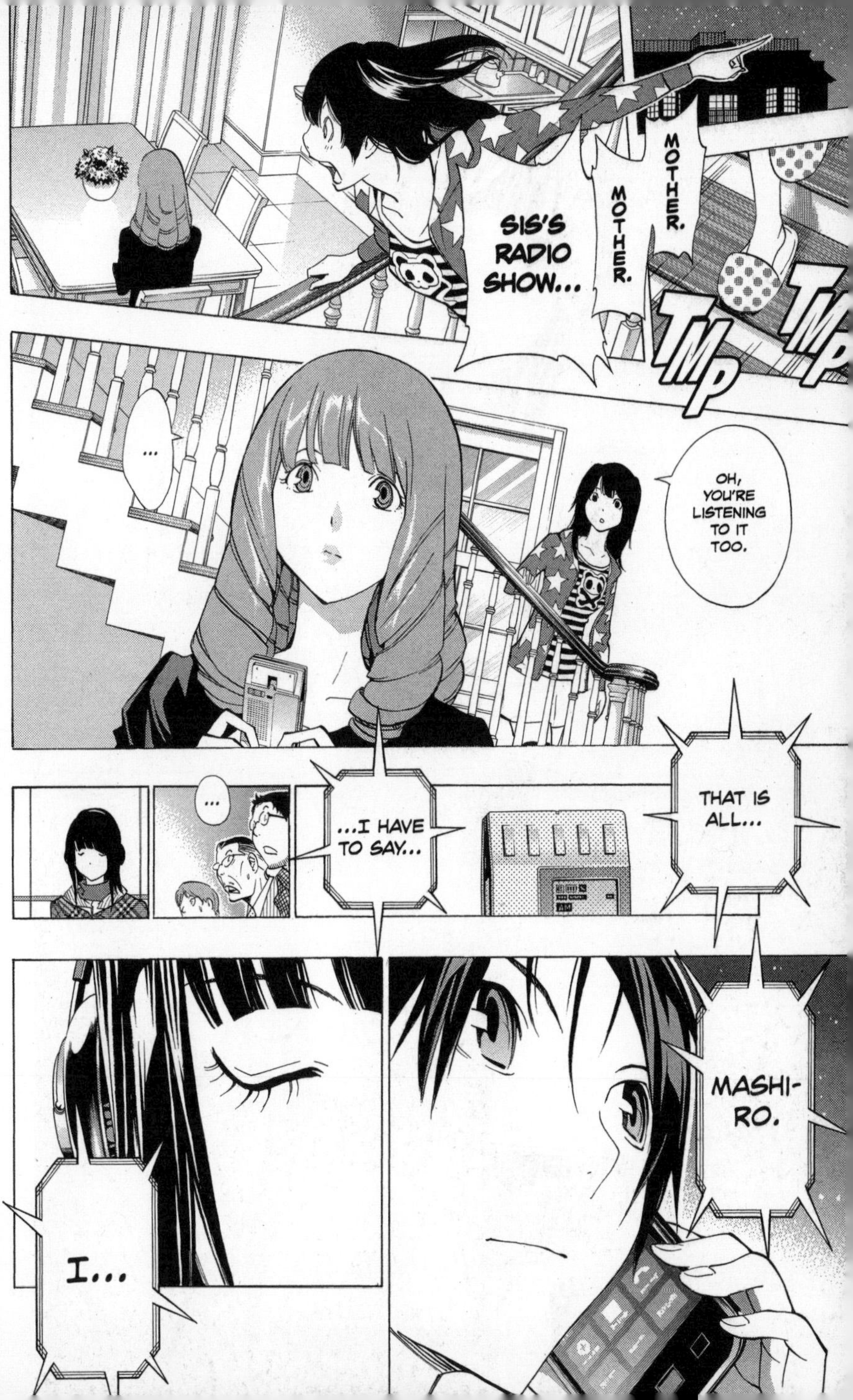
MOTHER.
MOTHER.
SIS'S RADIO SHOW...
TMP TMP
OH, YOU'RE LISTENING TO IT TOO.
...
THAT IS ALL...
...I HAVE TO SAY...
...
MASHIRO.
I...

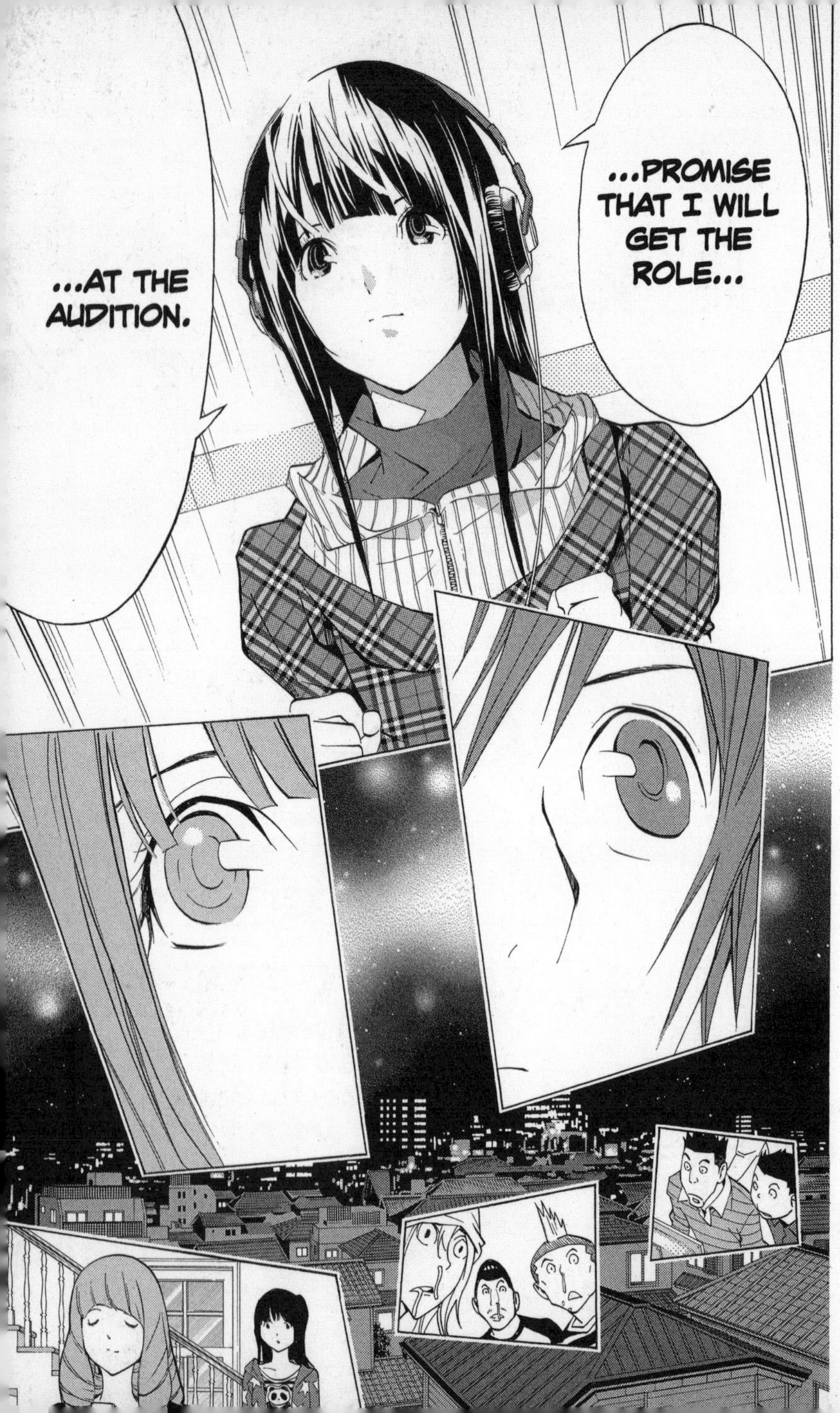
...PROMISE THAT I WILL GET THE ROLE...
...AT THE AUDITION.

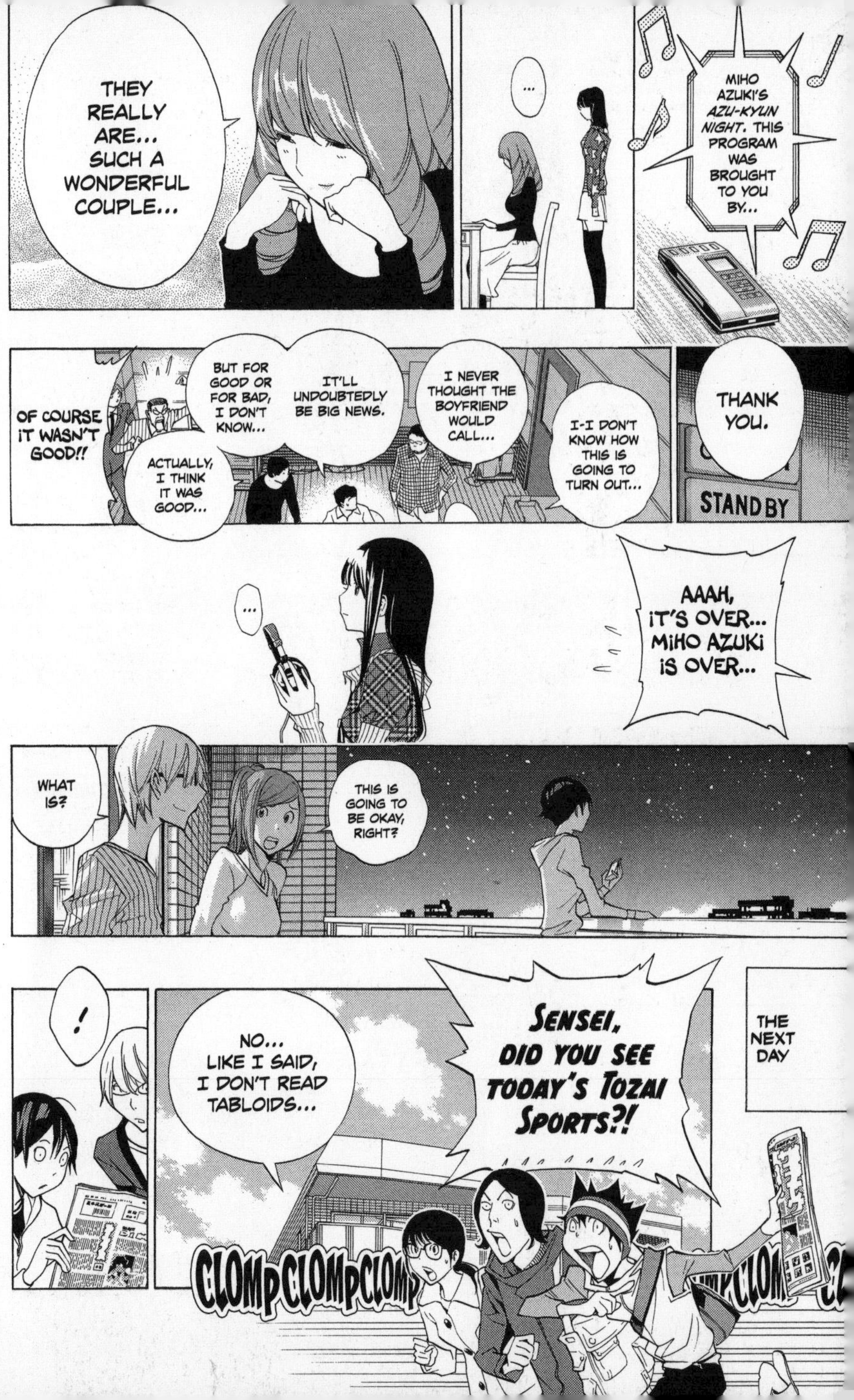
MIHO AZUKI'S *AZU-KYUN NIGHT*. THIS PROGRAM WAS BROUGHT TO YOU BY...
...
THEY REALLY ARE... SUCH A WONDERFUL COUPLE...
THANK YOU.
STANDBY
I-I DON'T KNOW HOW THIS IS GOING TO TURN OUT...
I NEVER THOUGHT THE BOYFRIEND WOULD CALL...
IT'LL UNDOUBTEDLY BE BIG NEWS.
BUT FOR GOOD OR FOR BAD, I DON'T KNOW...
ACTUALLY, I THINK IT WAS GOOD...
OF COURSE IT WASN'T GOOD!!
AAAH, IT'S OVER... MIHO AZUKI IS OVER...
...
THIS IS GOING TO BE OKAY, RIGHT?
WHAT IS?
THE NEXT DAY
SENSEI, DID YOU SEE TODAY'S TOZAI SPORTS?!
NO... LIKE I SAID, I DON'T READ TABLOIDS...
CLOMP CLOMP CLOMP
!

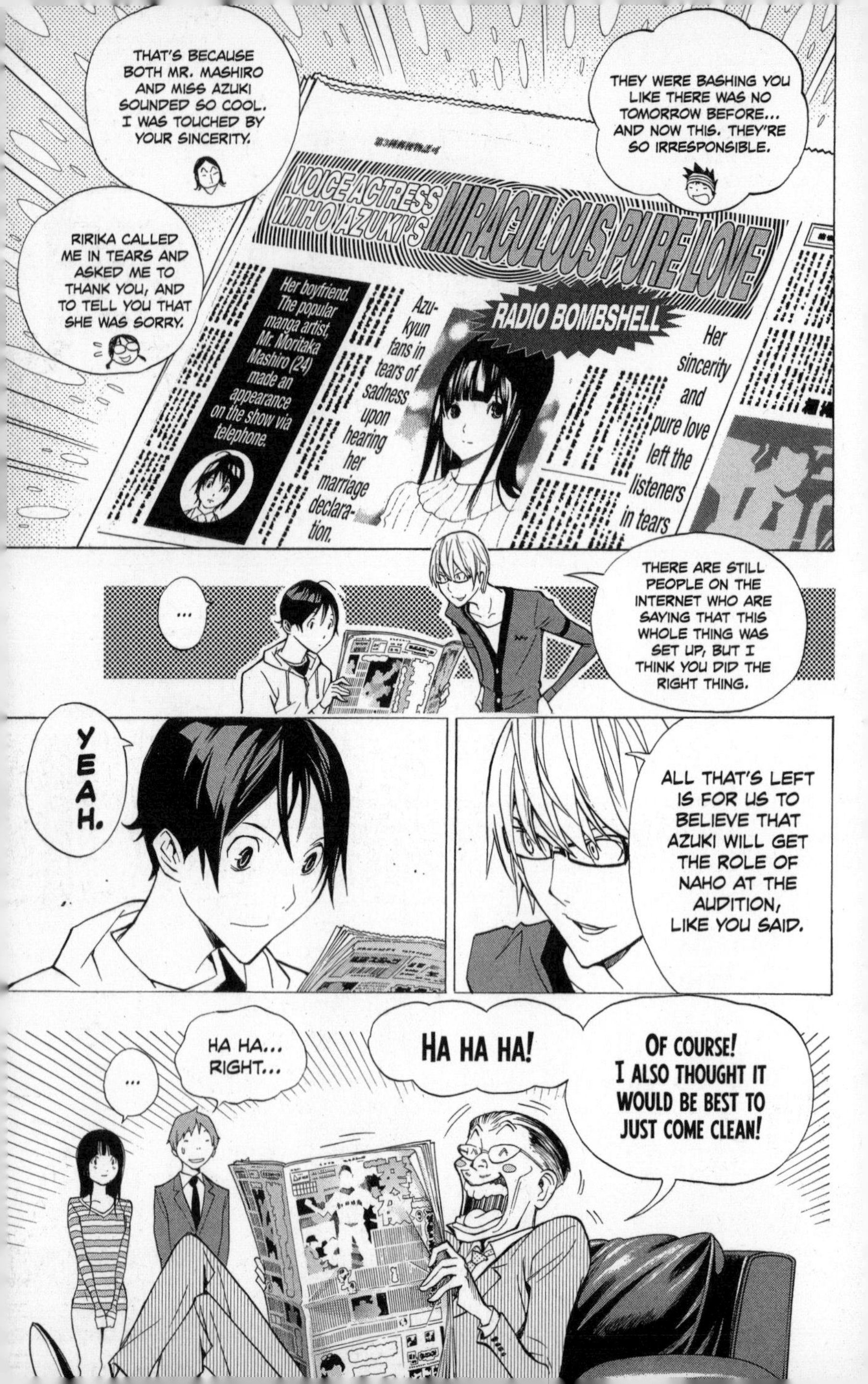
THEY WERE BASHING YOU LIKE THERE WAS NO TOMORROW BEFORE... AND NOW THIS. THEY'RE SO IRRESPONSIBLE.
THAT'S BECAUSE BOTH MR. MASHIRO AND MISS AZUKI SOUNDED SO COOL. I WAS TOUCHED BY YOUR SINCERITY.
VOICE ACTRESS MIHO AZUKI'S MIRACULOUS PURE LOVE
RADIO BOMBSHELL
Her sincerity and pure love left the listeners in tears
Azu-kyun fans in tears of sadness upon hearing her marriage declara-tion.
Her boyfriend. The popular manga artist, Mr. Moritaka Mashiro (24) made an appearance on the show via telephone.
RIRIKA CALLED ME IN TEARS AND ASKED ME TO THANK YOU, AND TO TELL YOU THAT SHE WAS SORRY.
THERE ARE STILL PEOPLE ON THE INTERNET WHO ARE SAYING THAT THIS WHOLE THING WAS SET UP, BUT I THINK YOU DID THE RIGHT THING.
...
ALL THAT'S LEFT IS FOR US TO BELIEVE THAT AZUKI WILL GET THE ROLE OF NAHO AT THE AUDITION, LIKE YOU SAID.
YEAH.
OF COURSE! I ALSO THOUGHT IT WOULD BE BEST TO JUST COME CLEAN!
HA HA HA!
HA HA... RIGHT...
...

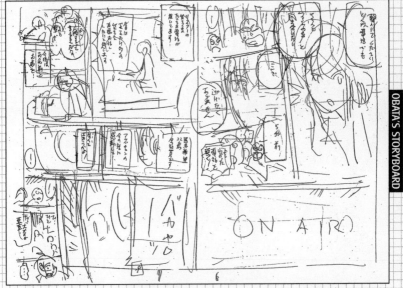

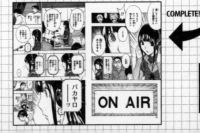

OHBA'S STORYBOARD

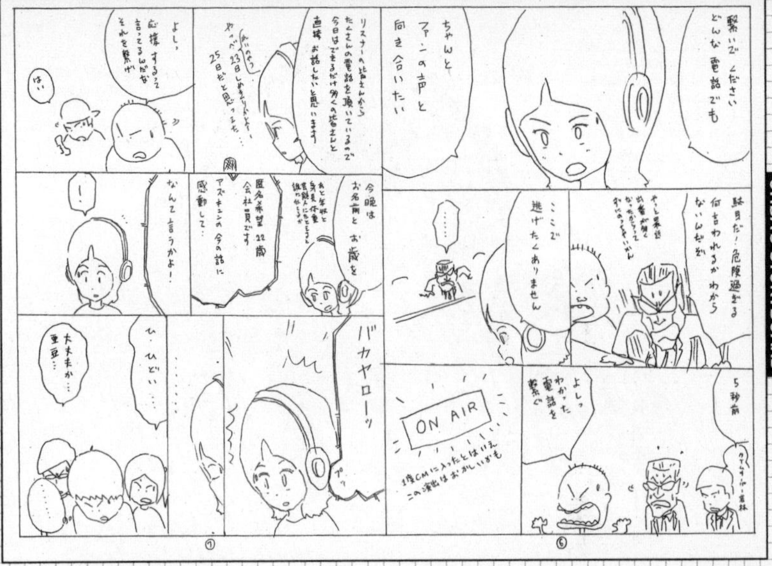

繋いでください どんな電話でも
ちゃんと ファンの声と 向き合いたい
駄目だ！危険過ぎる 何言われるか わからないんだぞ
ここで 逃げたく ありません
……
5秒前
よしっ わかった 電話を 繋ぐ
ON AIR
リスナーの皆さんから たくさんの電話を頂いているので 今日はできるだけ多くの皆さんと 直接お話ししたいと思います
よし、応援するって 言ってるんだな それを繋げ
はい
今晩は お名前と お歳を
匿名希望 22歳 会社員です アズキュンの今の話に 感動して…
なんて言うかよ！
！
バカヤローッ
プッ
……
ひ…ひどい……
大丈夫か… 亜豆…

OBATA'S STORYBOARD

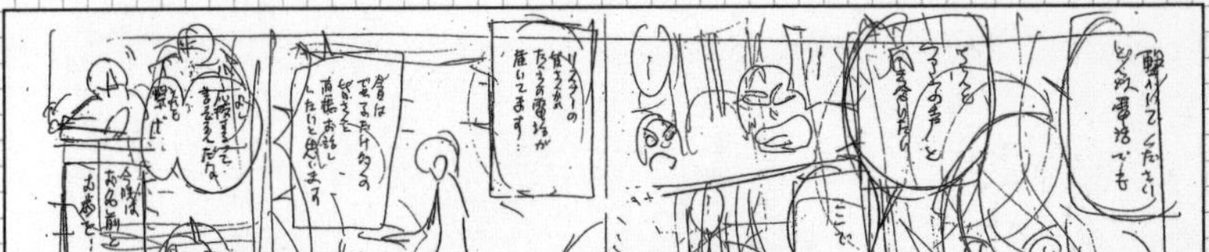

ON AIR
バカヤロ

COMPLETE!

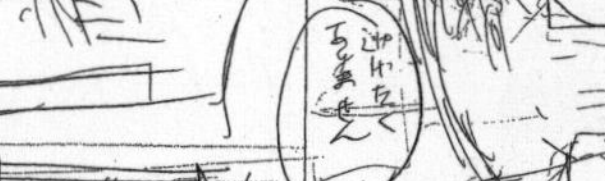

ON AIR
バカヤロ──ッ

※CREATOR STORYBOARDS AND FINISHED PAGES IN JAPANESE

BAKUMAN。 vol.20

"Until the Final Draft Is Complete"

Chapter 169, pp. 16-17

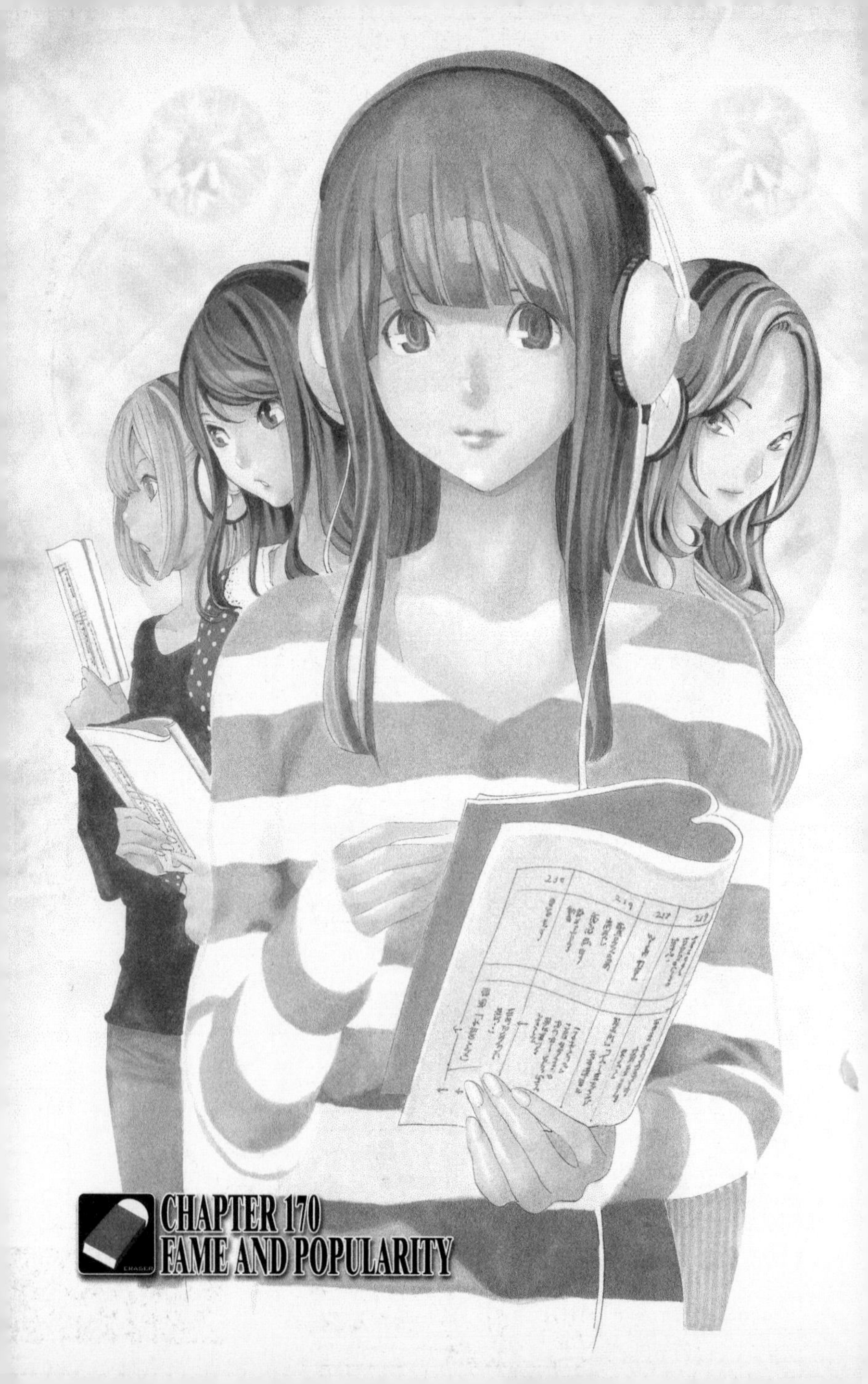
CHAPTER 170
FAME AND POPULARITY
ERASER

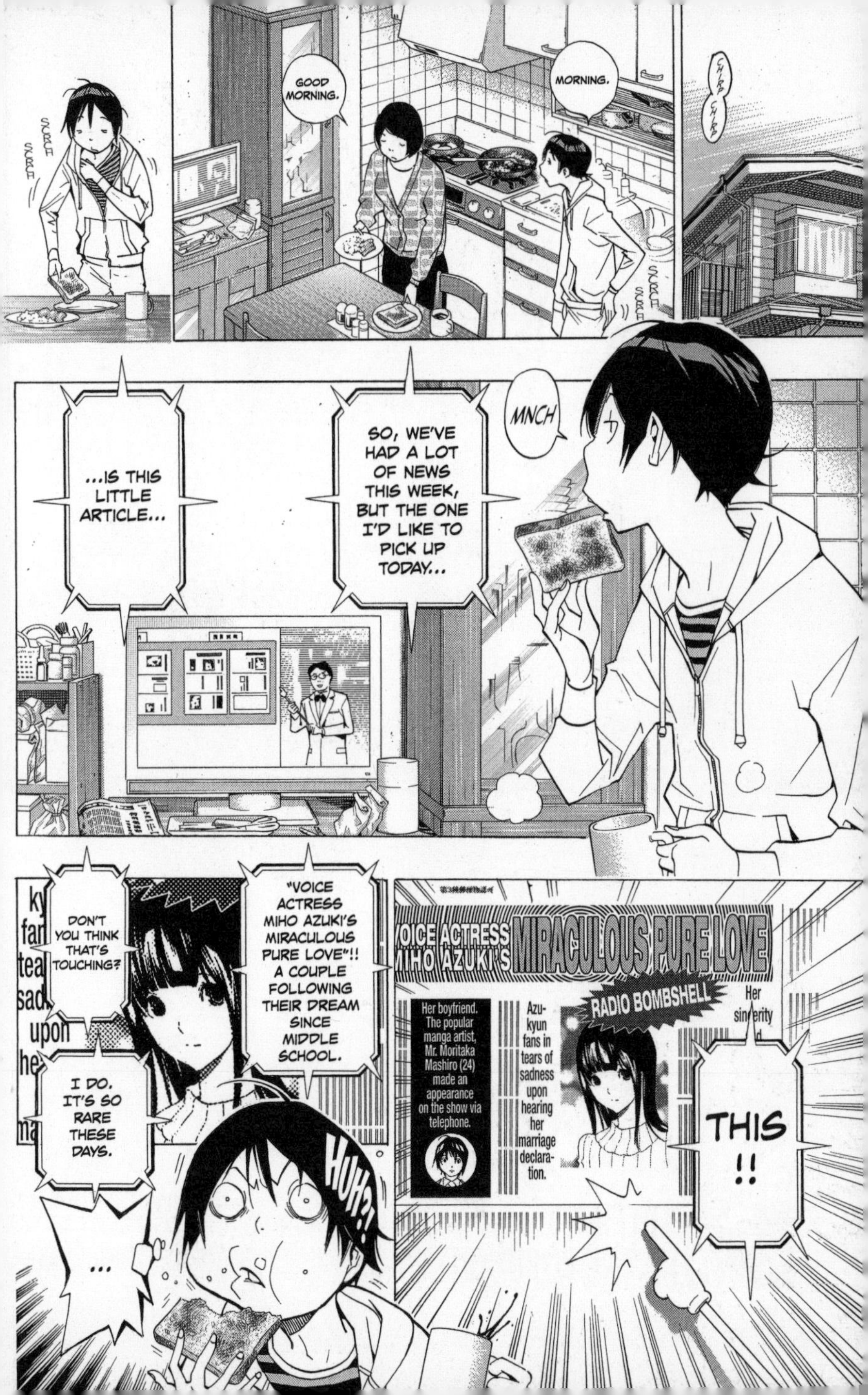
CHIRP CHIRP
MORNING.
SCRCH SCRCH
GOOD MORNING.
SCRCH SCRCH
MNCH
SO, WE'VE HAD A LOT OF NEWS THIS WEEK, BUT THE ONE I'D LIKE TO PICK UP TODAY...
...IS THIS LITTLE ARTICLE...
VOICE ACTRESS MIHO AZUKI'S MIRACULOUS PURE LOVE
RADIO BOMBSHELL
Azu-kyun fans in tears of sadness upon hearing her marriage declara-tion.
Her boyfriend. The popular manga artist, Mr. Moritaka Mashiro (24) made an appearance on the show via telephone.
THIS !!
"VOICE ACTRESS MIHO AZUKI'S MIRACULOUS PURE LOVE"!! A COUPLE FOLLOWING THEIR DREAM SINCE MIDDLE SCHOOL.
DON'T YOU THINK THAT'S TOUCHING?
I DO. IT'S SO RARE THESE DAYS.
HUH?!
...

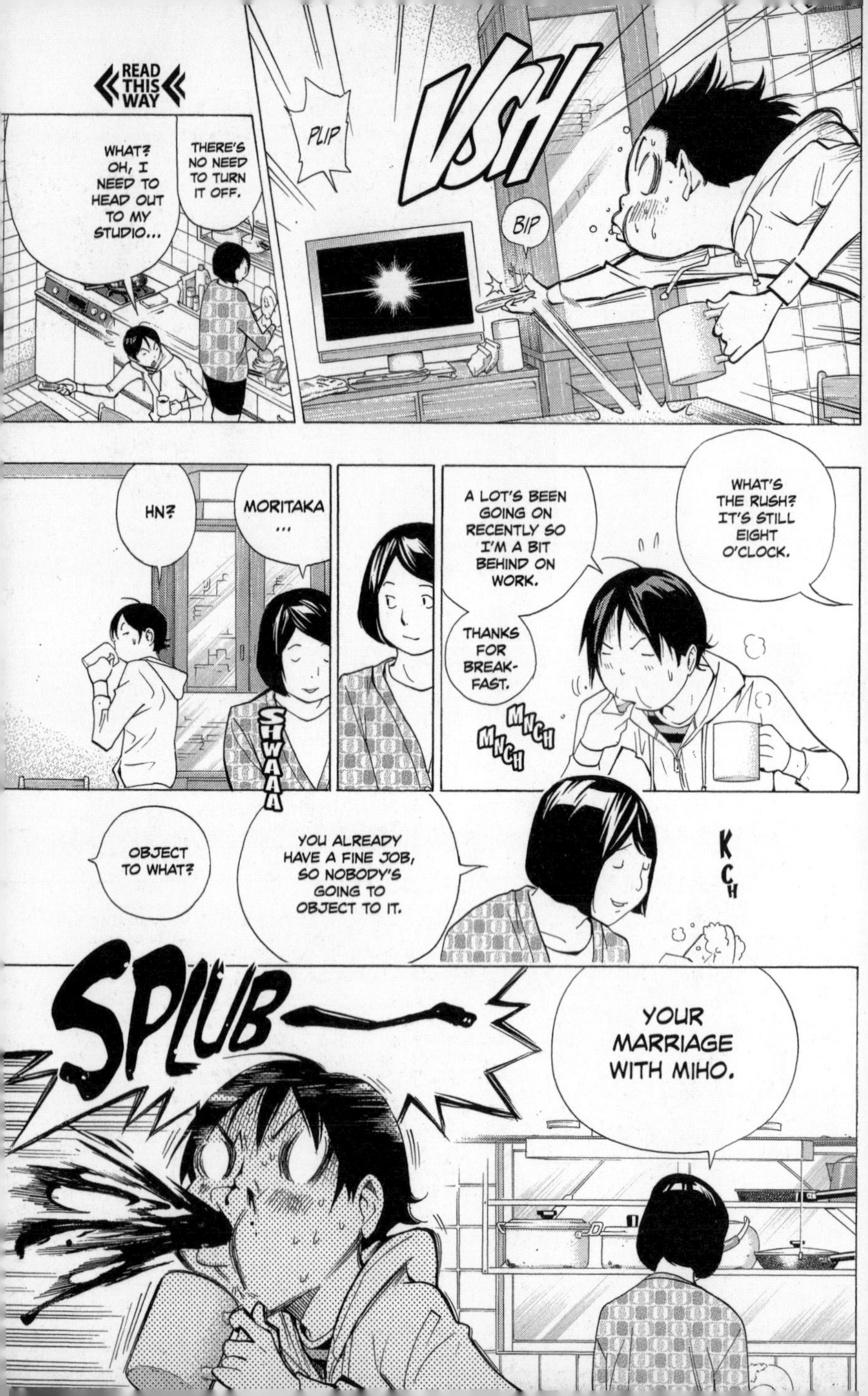
READ THIS WAY
VSH
BIP
PLIP
THERE'S NO NEED TO TURN IT OFF.
WHAT? OH, I NEED TO HEAD OUT TO MY STUDIO...
WHAT'S THE RUSH? IT'S STILL EIGHT O'CLOCK.
A LOT'S BEEN GOING ON RECENTLY SO I'M A BIT BEHIND ON WORK.
THANKS FOR BREAK-FAST.
MNCH MNCH
MORITAKA ...
SHWAAA
HN?
KCH
YOU ALREADY HAVE A FINE JOB, SO NOBODY'S GOING TO OBJECT TO IT.
OBJECT TO WHAT?
YOUR MARRIAGE WITH MIHO.
SPLUB

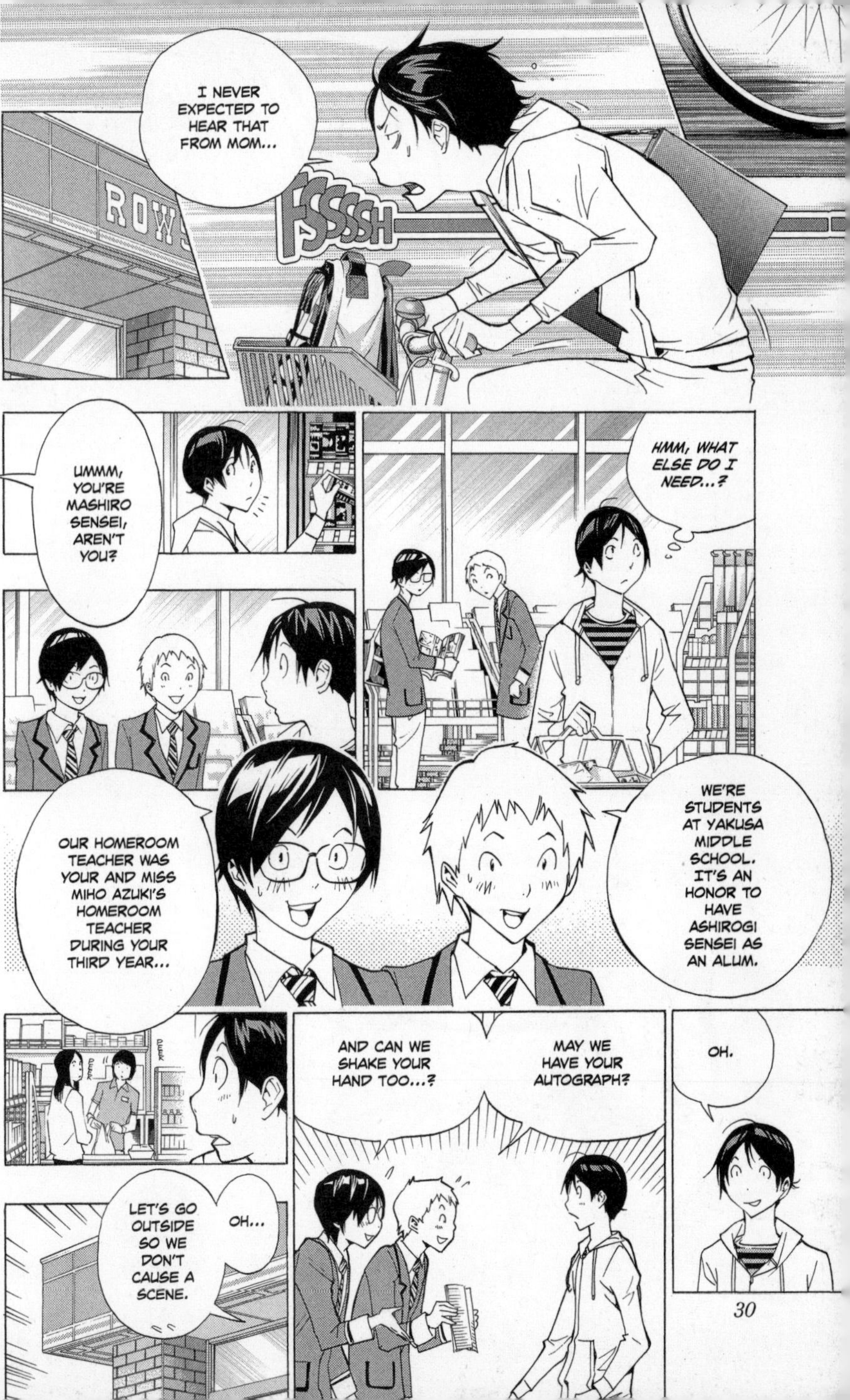
I NEVER EXPECTED TO HEAR THAT FROM MOM...
FSSSSH
HMM, WHAT ELSE DO I NEED...?
UMMM, YOU'RE MASHIRO SENSEI, AREN'T YOU?
WE'RE STUDENTS AT YAKUSA MIDDLE SCHOOL. IT'S AN HONOR TO HAVE ASHIROGI SENSEI AS AN ALUM.
OUR HOMEROOM TEACHER WAS YOUR AND MISS MIHO AZUKI'S HOMEROOM TEACHER DURING YOUR THIRD YEAR...
OH.
MAY WE HAVE YOUR AUTOGRAPH?
AND CAN WE SHAKE YOUR HAND TOO...?
PEEK
PEEK
OH...
LET'S GO OUTSIDE SO WE DON'T CAUSE A SCENE.

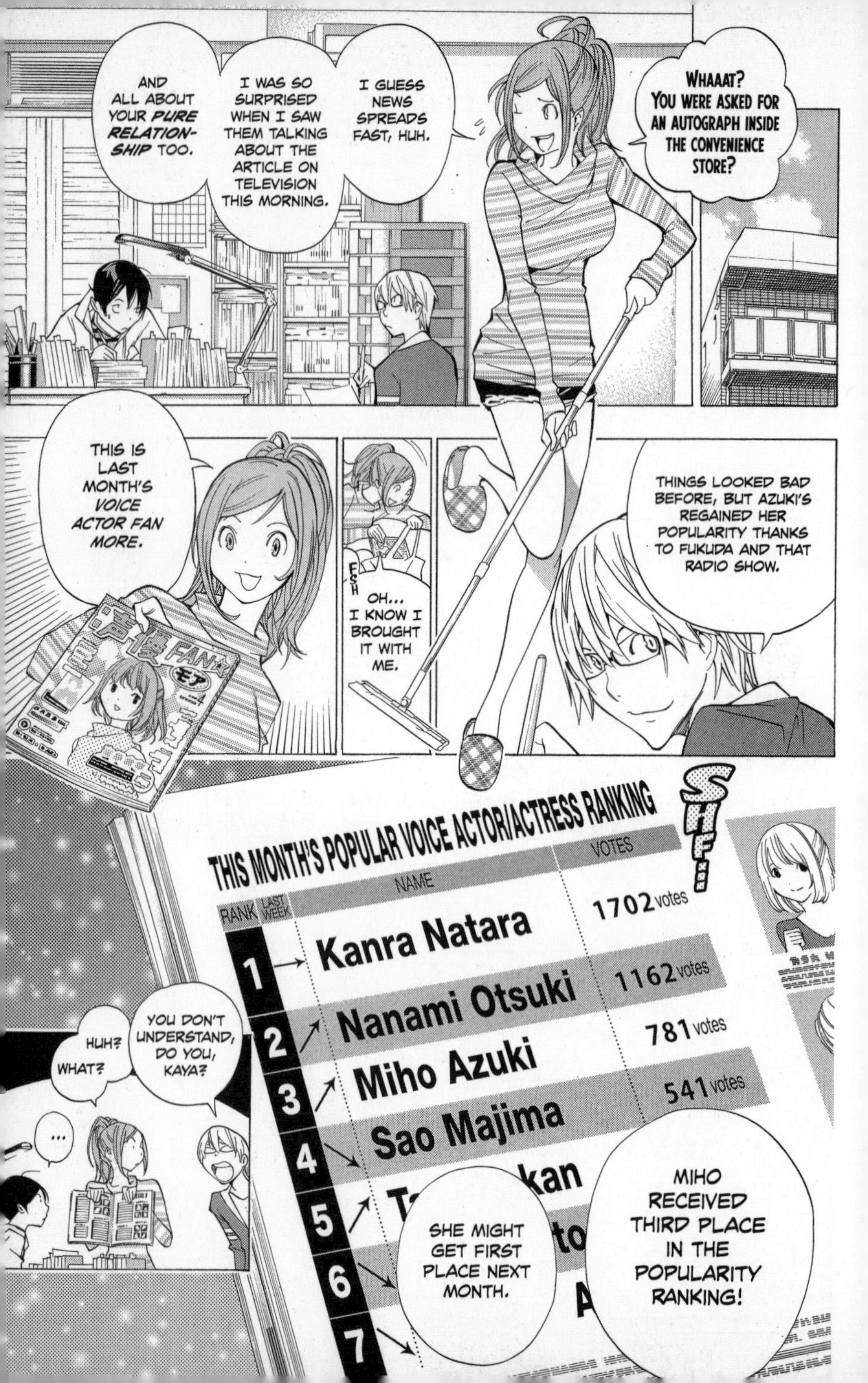

WHAAAT? YOU WERE ASKED FOR AN AUTOGRAPH INSIDE THE CONVENIENCE STORE?
I GUESS NEWS SPREADS FAST, HUH.
I WAS SO SURPRISED WHEN I SAW THEM TALKING ABOUT THE ARTICLE ON TELEVISION THIS MORNING.
AND ALL ABOUT YOUR *PURE RELATIONSHIP* TOO.
THINGS LOOKED BAD BEFORE, BUT AZUKI'S REGAINED HER POPULARITY THANKS TO FUKUDA AND THAT RADIO SHOW.
FSH
OH... I KNOW I BROUGHT IT WITH ME.
THIS IS LAST MONTH'S *VOICE ACTOR FAN MORE.*
FAN
モア
SHF..
THIS MONTH'S POPULAR VOICE ACTOR/ACTRESS RANKING
RANK
LAST WEEK
NAME
VOTES
1 Kanra Natara 1702 votes
2 Nanami Otsuki 1162 votes
3 Miho Azuki 781 votes
4 Sao Majima 541 votes
5
6
7
MIHO RECEIVED THIRD PLACE IN THE POPULARITY RANKING!
SHE MIGHT GET FIRST PLACE NEXT MONTH.
YOU DON'T UNDERSTAND, DO YOU, KAYA?
HUH? WHAT?
...

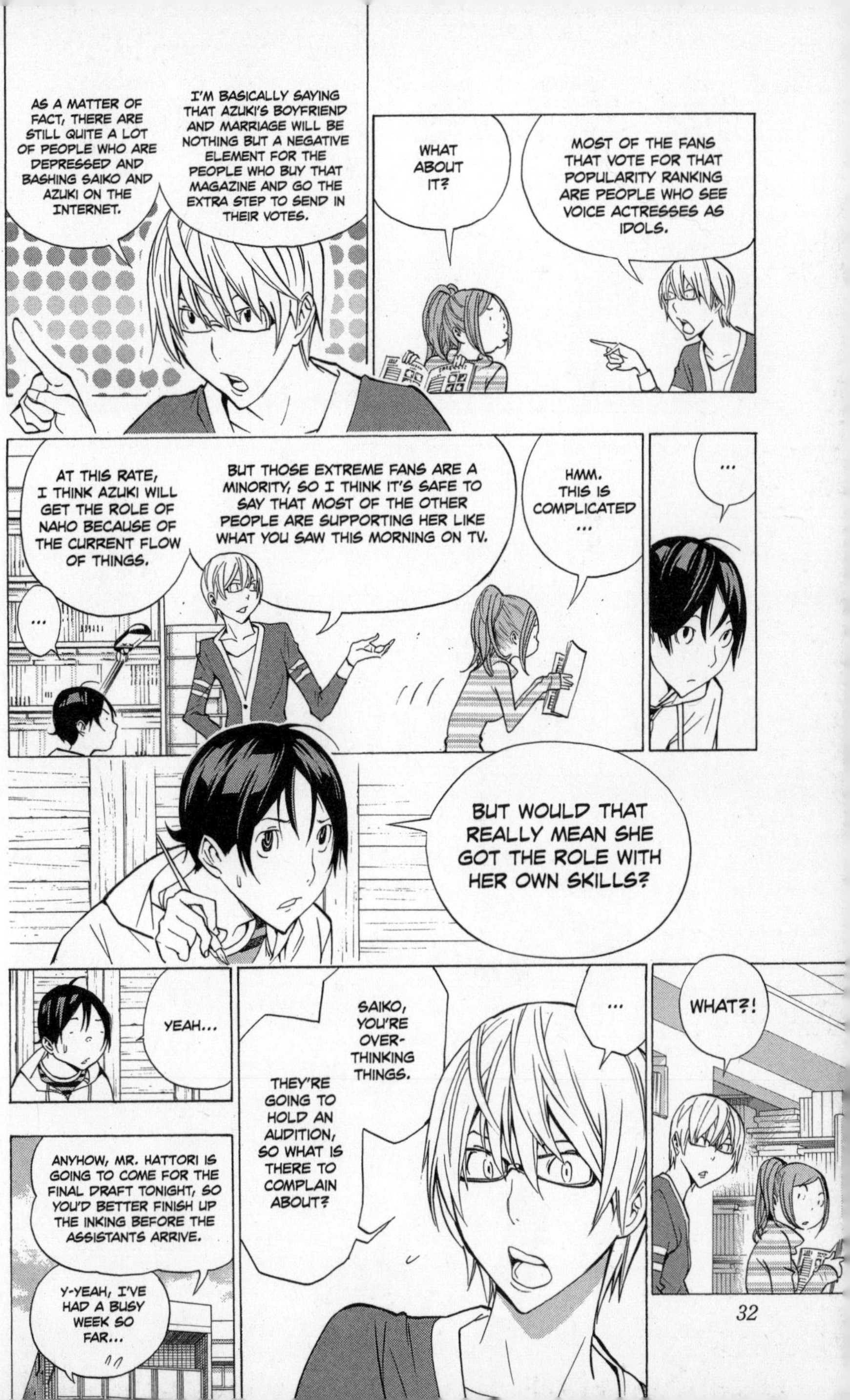

MOST OF THE FANS THAT VOTE FOR THAT POPULARITY RANKING ARE PEOPLE WHO SEE VOICE ACTRESSES AS IDOLS.
WHAT ABOUT IT?
I'M BASICALLY SAYING THAT AZUKI'S BOYFRIEND AND MARRIAGE WILL BE NOTHING BUT A NEGATIVE ELEMENT FOR THE PEOPLE WHO BUY THAT MAGAZINE AND GO THE EXTRA STEP TO SEND IN THEIR VOTES.
AS A MATTER OF FACT, THERE ARE STILL QUITE A LOT OF PEOPLE WHO ARE DEPRESSED AND BASHING SAIKO AND AZUKI ON THE INTERNET.
...
HMM. THIS IS COMPLICATED...
AT THIS RATE, I THINK AZUKI WILL GET THE ROLE OF NAHO BECAUSE OF THE CURRENT FLOW OF THINGS.
BUT THOSE EXTREME FANS ARE A MINORITY, SO I THINK IT'S SAFE TO SAY THAT MOST OF THE OTHER PEOPLE ARE SUPPORTING HER LIKE WHAT YOU SAW THIS MORNING ON TV.
...
BUT WOULD THAT REALLY MEAN SHE GOT THE ROLE WITH HER OWN SKILLS?
WHAT?!
...
SAIKO, YOU'RE OVER-THINKING THINGS.
THEY'RE GOING TO HOLD AN AUDITION, SO WHAT IS THERE TO COMPLAIN ABOUT?
YEAH...
ANYHOW, MR. HATTORI IS GOING TO COME FOR THE FINAL DRAFT TONIGHT, SO YOU'D BETTER FINISH UP THE INKING BEFORE THE ASSISTANTS ARRIVE.
Y-YEAH, I'VE HAD A BUSY WEEK SO FAR...

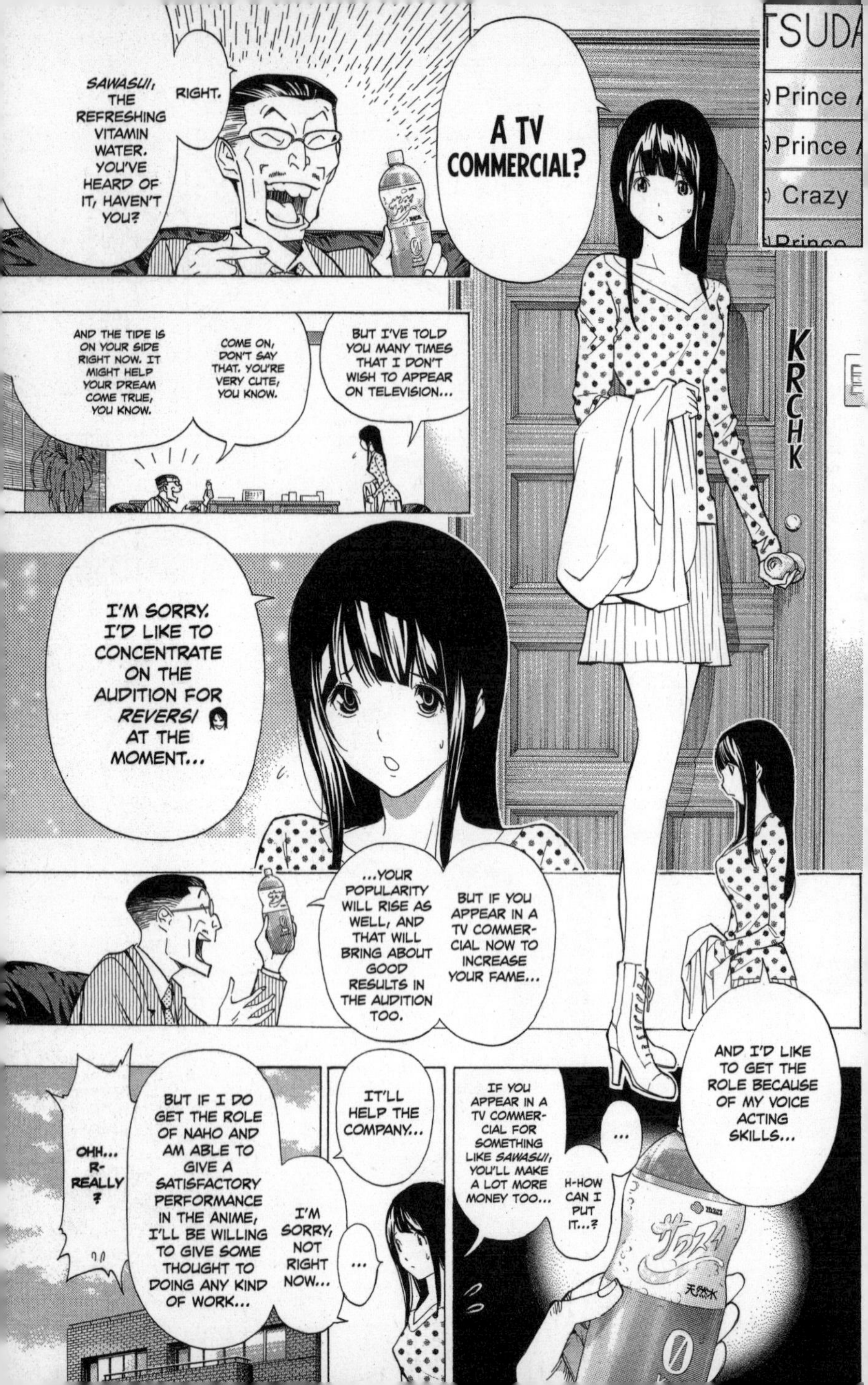
TSUDA
Prince
Prince
Crazy
KRCHK
A TV COMMERCIAL?
RIGHT.
SAWASUI, THE REFRESHING VITAMIN WATER. YOU'VE HEARD OF IT, HAVEN'T YOU?
BUT I'VE TOLD YOU MANY TIMES THAT I DON'T WISH TO APPEAR ON TELEVISION...
COME ON, DON'T SAY THAT. YOU'RE VERY CUTE, YOU KNOW.
AND THE TIDE IS ON YOUR SIDE RIGHT NOW. IT MIGHT HELP YOUR DREAM COME TRUE, YOU KNOW.
I'M SORRY. I'D LIKE TO CONCENTRATE ON THE AUDITION FOR *REVERSI* AT THE MOMENT...
BUT IF YOU APPEAR IN A TV COMMERCIAL NOW TO INCREASE YOUR FAME...
...YOUR POPULARITY WILL RISE AS WELL, AND THAT WILL BRING ABOUT GOOD RESULTS IN THE AUDITION TOO.
AND I'D LIKE TO GET THE ROLE BECAUSE OF MY VOICE ACTING SKILLS...
...
IF YOU APPEAR IN A TV COMMERCIAL FOR SOMETHING LIKE *SAWASUI*, YOU'LL MAKE A LOT MORE MONEY TOO...
H-HOW CAN I PUT IT...?
IT'LL HELP THE COMPANY...
I'M SORRY, NOT RIGHT NOW...
...
BUT IF I DO GET THE ROLE OF NAHO AND AM ABLE TO GIVE A SATISFACTORY PERFORMANCE IN THE ANIME, I'LL BE WILLING TO GIVE SOME THOUGHT TO DOING ANY KIND OF WORK...
OHH... R-REALLY?

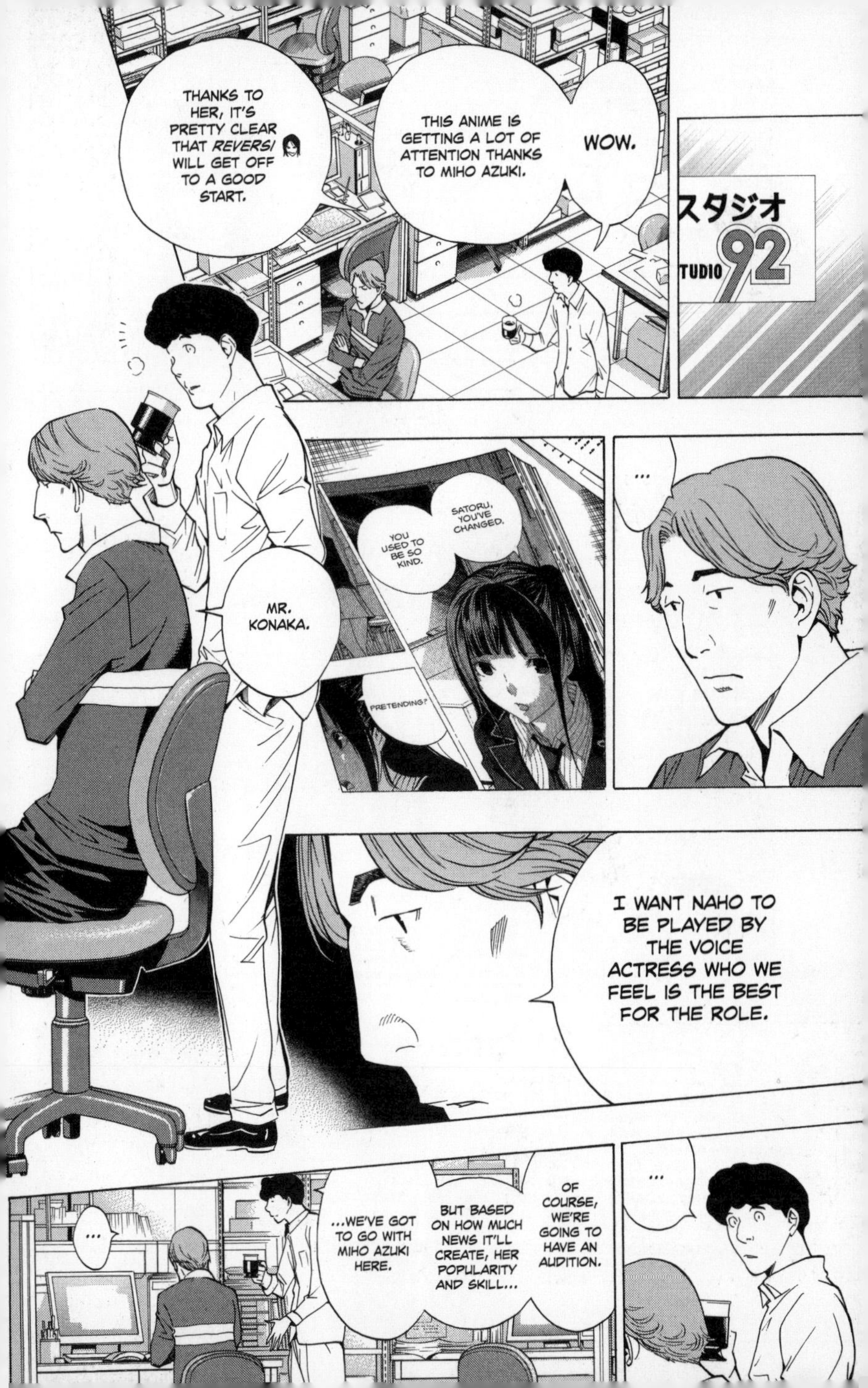

スタジオ
TUDIO 92
WOW.
THIS ANIME IS GETTING A LOT OF ATTENTION THANKS TO MIHO AZUKI.
THANKS TO HER, IT'S PRETTY CLEAR THAT *REVERSI* WILL GET OFF TO A GOOD START.
...
SATORU, YOU'VE CHANGED.
YOU USED TO BE SO KIND.
PRETENDING?
I WANT NAHO TO BE PLAYED BY THE VOICE ACTRESS WHO WE FEEL IS THE BEST FOR THE ROLE.
MR. KONAKA.
...
OF COURSE, WE'RE GOING TO HAVE AN AUDITION.
BUT BASED ON HOW MUCH NEWS IT'LL CREATE, HER POPULARITY AND SKILL...
...WE'VE GOT TO GO WITH MIHO AZUKI HERE.
...

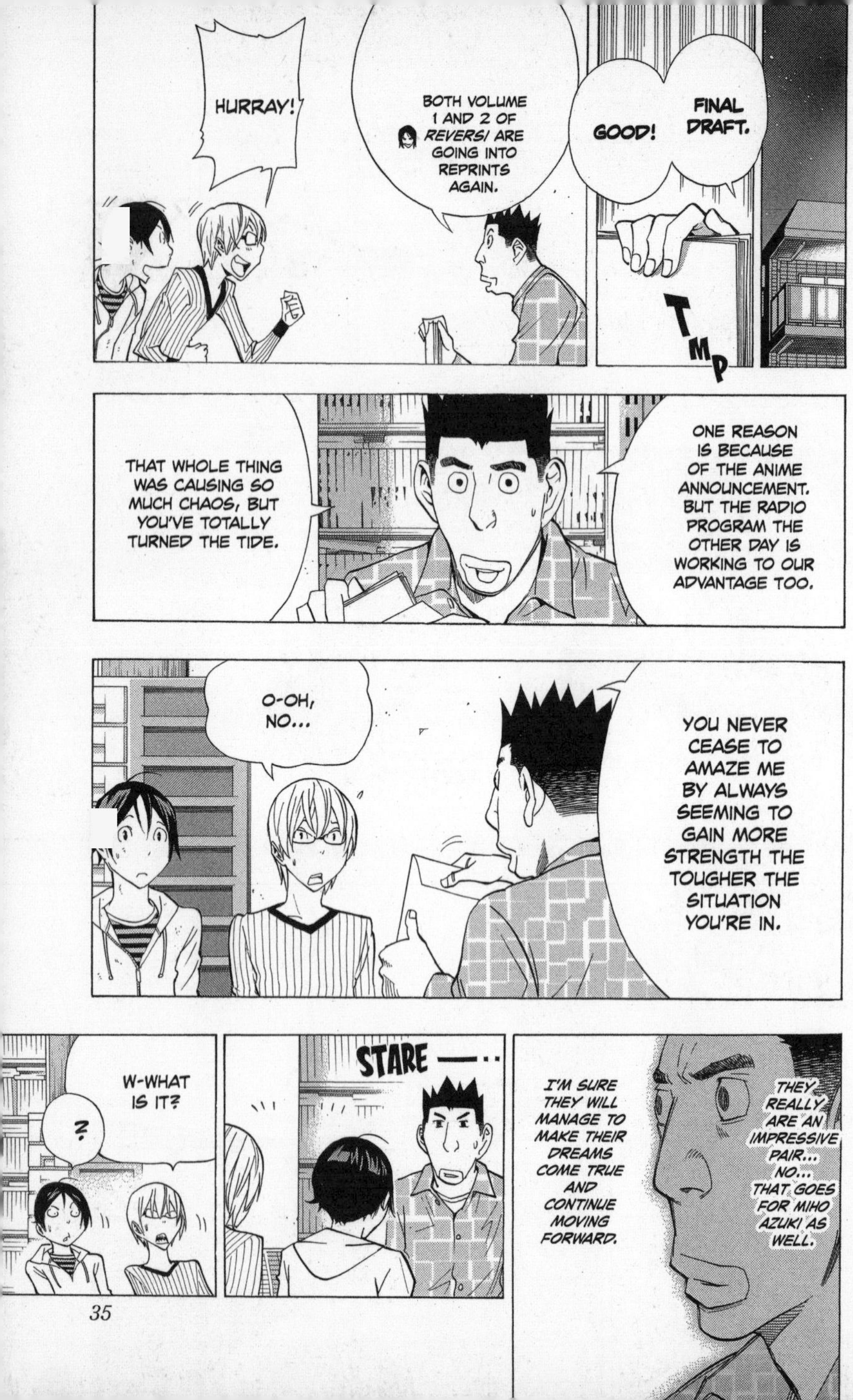
FINAL DRAFT.
GOOD!
TMP
BOTH VOLUME 1 AND 2 OF *REVERSI* ARE GOING INTO REPRINTS AGAIN.
HURRAY!
ONE REASON IS BECAUSE OF THE ANIME ANNOUNCEMENT. BUT THE RADIO PROGRAM THE OTHER DAY IS WORKING TO OUR ADVANTAGE TOO.
THAT WHOLE THING WAS CAUSING SO MUCH CHAOS, BUT YOU'VE TOTALLY TURNED THE TIDE.
YOU NEVER CEASE TO AMAZE ME BY ALWAYS SEEMING TO GAIN MORE STRENGTH THE TOUGHER THE SITUATION YOU'RE IN.
O-OH, NO...
THEY REALLY ARE AN IMPRESSIVE PAIR... NO... THAT GOES FOR MIHO AZUKI AS WELL.
I'M SURE THEY WILL MANAGE TO MAKE THEIR DREAMS COME TRUE AND CONTINUE MOVING FORWARD.
STARE —..
W-WHAT IS IT?
?

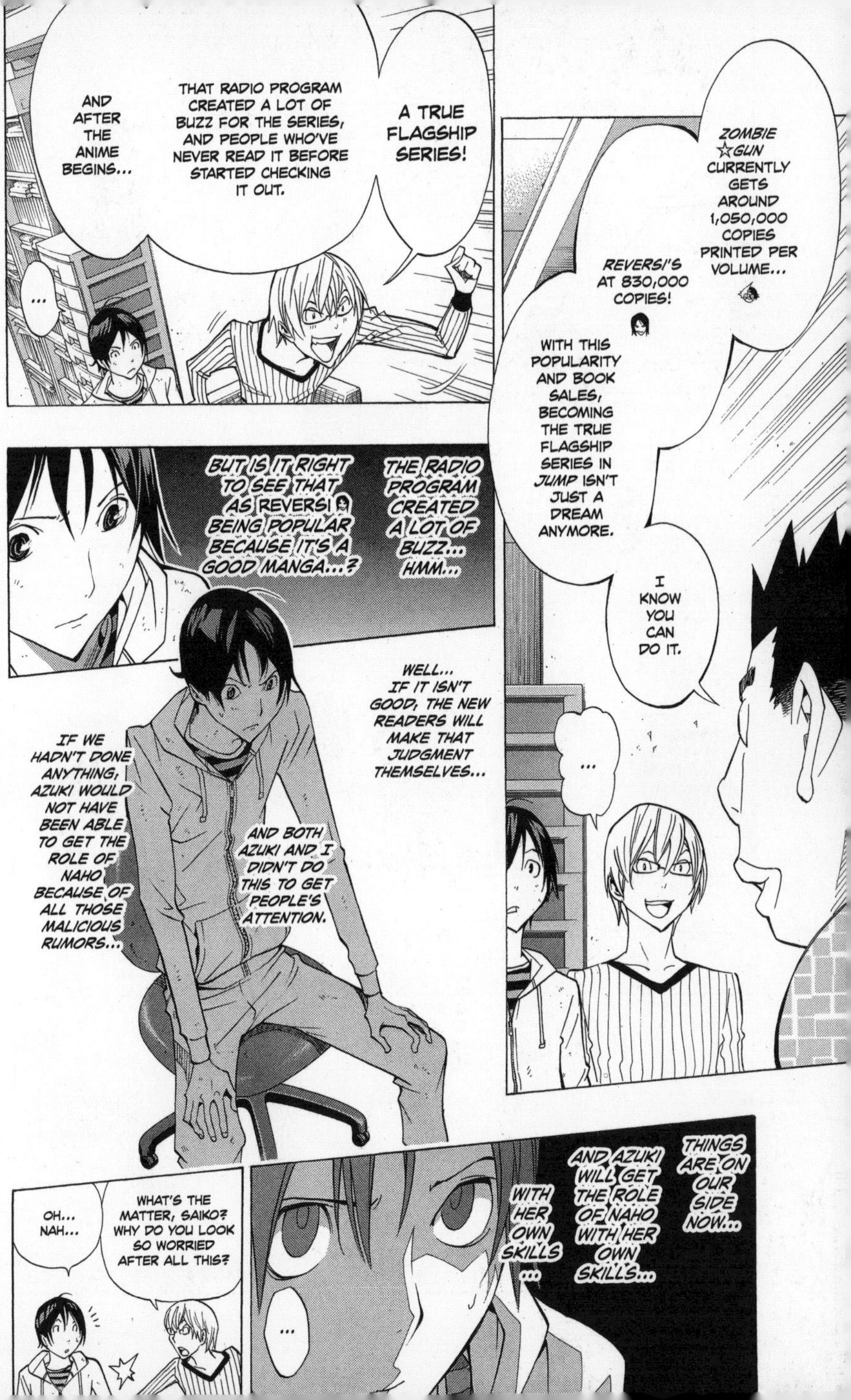
ZOMBIE ☆GUN CURRENTLY GETS AROUND 1,050,000 COPIES PRINTED PER VOLUME...
REVERSI'S AT 830,000 COPIES!
WITH THIS POPULARITY AND BOOK SALES, BECOMING THE TRUE FLAGSHIP SERIES IN JUMP ISN'T JUST A DREAM ANYMORE.
I KNOW YOU CAN DO IT.
...
A TRUE FLAGSHIP SERIES!
THAT RADIO PROGRAM CREATED A LOT OF BUZZ FOR THE SERIES, AND PEOPLE WHO'VE NEVER READ IT BEFORE STARTED CHECKING IT OUT.
AND AFTER THE ANIME BEGINS...
...
THE RADIO PROGRAM CREATED A LOT OF BUZZ... HMM...
BUT IS IT RIGHT TO SEE THAT AS REVERSI BEING POPULAR BECAUSE IT'S A GOOD MANGA...?
WELL... IF IT ISN'T GOOD, THE NEW READERS WILL MAKE THAT JUDGMENT THEMSELVES...
AND BOTH AZUKI AND I DIDN'T DO THIS TO GET PEOPLE'S ATTENTION.
IF WE HADN'T DONE ANYTHING, AZUKI WOULD NOT HAVE BEEN ABLE TO GET THE ROLE OF NAHO BECAUSE OF ALL THOSE MALICIOUS RUMORS...
THINGS ARE ON OUR SIDE NOW...
AND AZUKI WILL GET THE ROLE OF NAHO WITH HER OWN SKILLS...
WITH HER OWN SKILLS...
...
WHAT'S THE MATTER, SAIKO? WHY DO YOU LOOK SO WORRIED AFTER ALL THIS?
OH... NAH...

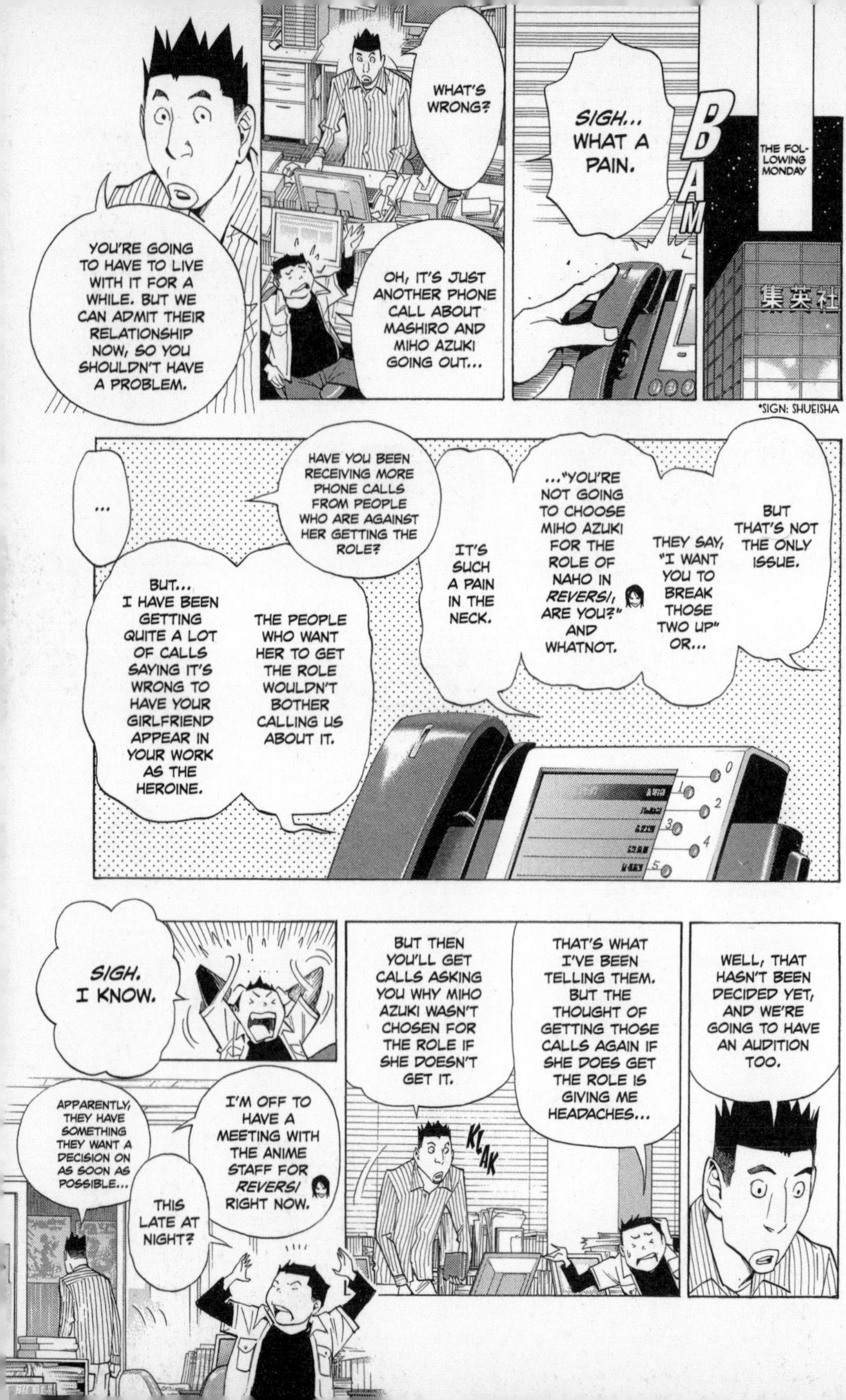
THE FOLLOWING MONDAY
集英社
BAM
SIGH... WHAT A PAIN.
WHAT'S WRONG?
OH, IT'S JUST ANOTHER PHONE CALL ABOUT MASHIRO AND MIHO AZUKI GOING OUT...
YOU'RE GOING TO HAVE TO LIVE WITH IT FOR A WHILE. BUT WE CAN ADMIT THEIR RELATIONSHIP NOW, SO YOU SHOULDN'T HAVE A PROBLEM.
*SIGN: SHUEISHA
BUT THAT'S NOT THE ONLY ISSUE.
THEY SAY, "I WANT YOU TO BREAK THOSE TWO UP" OR...
..."YOU'RE NOT GOING TO CHOOSE MIHO AZUKI FOR THE ROLE OF NAHO IN *REVERSI*, ARE YOU?" AND WHATNOT.
IT'S SUCH A PAIN IN THE NECK.
HAVE YOU BEEN RECEIVING MORE PHONE CALLS FROM PEOPLE WHO ARE AGAINST HER GETTING THE ROLE?
...
BUT... I HAVE BEEN GETTING QUITE A LOT OF CALLS SAYING IT'S WRONG TO HAVE YOUR GIRLFRIEND APPEAR IN YOUR WORK AS THE HEROINE.
THE PEOPLE WHO WANT HER TO GET THE ROLE WOULDN'T BOTHER CALLING US ABOUT IT.
WELL, THAT HASN'T BEEN DECIDED YET, AND WE'RE GOING TO HAVE AN AUDITION TOO.
THAT'S WHAT I'VE BEEN TELLING THEM. BUT THE THOUGHT OF GETTING THOSE CALLS AGAIN IF SHE DOES GET THE ROLE IS GIVING ME HEADACHES...
BUT THEN YOU'LL GET CALLS ASKING YOU WHY MIHO AZUKI WASN'T CHOSEN FOR THE ROLE IF SHE DOESN'T GET IT.
KLAK
SIGH. I KNOW.
I'M OFF TO HAVE A MEETING WITH THE ANIME STAFF FOR *REVERSI* RIGHT NOW.
THIS LATE AT NIGHT?
APPARENTLY, THEY HAVE SOMETHING THEY WANT A DECISION ON AS SOON AS POSSIBLE...

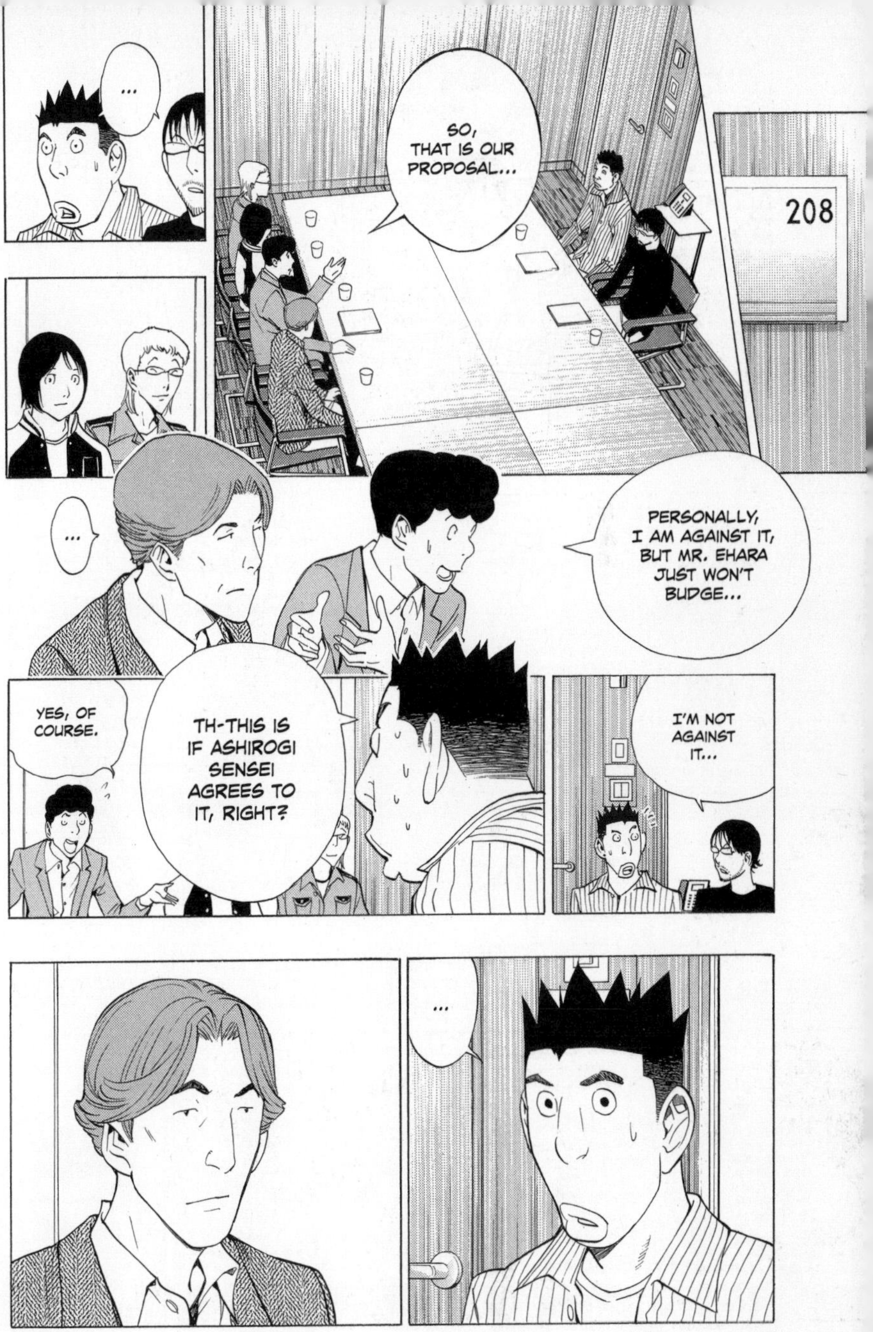
SO, THAT IS OUR PROPOSAL...
...
PERSONALLY, I AM AGAINST IT, BUT MR. EHARA JUST WON'T BUDGE...
...
I'M NOT AGAINST IT...
TH-THIS IS IF ASHIROGI SENSEI AGREES TO IT, RIGHT?
YES, OF COURSE.
...

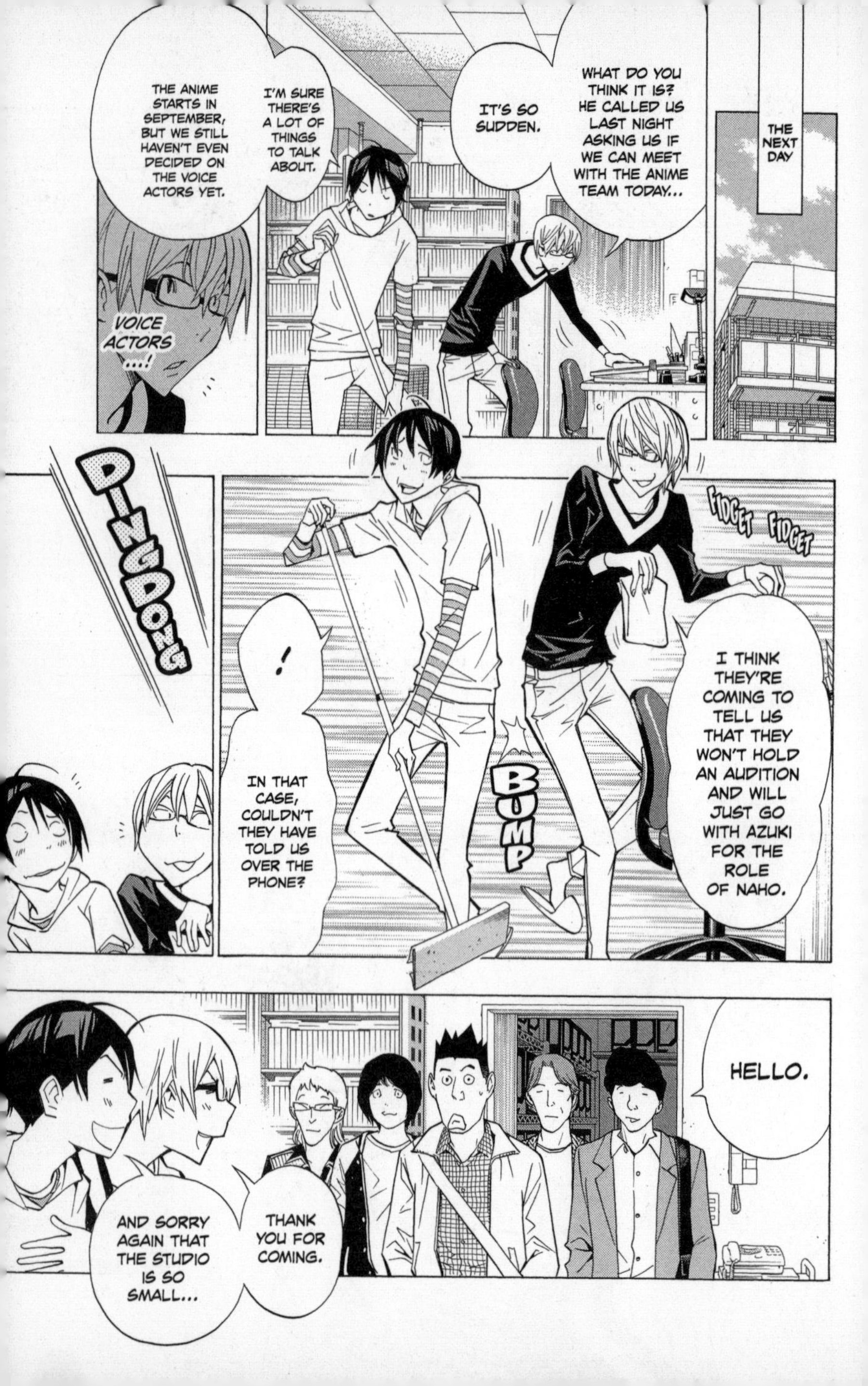
THE NEXT DAY
WHAT DO YOU THINK IT IS? HE CALLED US LAST NIGHT ASKING US IF WE CAN MEET WITH THE ANIME TEAM TODAY...
IT'S SO SUDDEN.
I'M SURE THERE'S A LOT OF THINGS TO TALK ABOUT.
THE ANIME STARTS IN SEPTEMBER, BUT WE STILL HAVEN'T EVEN DECIDED ON THE VOICE ACTORS YET.
VOICE ACTORS ...!
FIDGET FIDGET
I THINK THEY'RE COMING TO TELL US THAT THEY WON'T HOLD AN AUDITION AND WILL JUST GO WITH AZUKI FOR THE ROLE OF NAHO.
BUMP
IN THAT CASE, COULDN'T THEY HAVE TOLD US OVER THE PHONE?
!
DINGDONG
HELLO.
THANK YOU FOR COMING.
AND SORRY AGAIN THAT THE STUDIO IS SO SMALL...

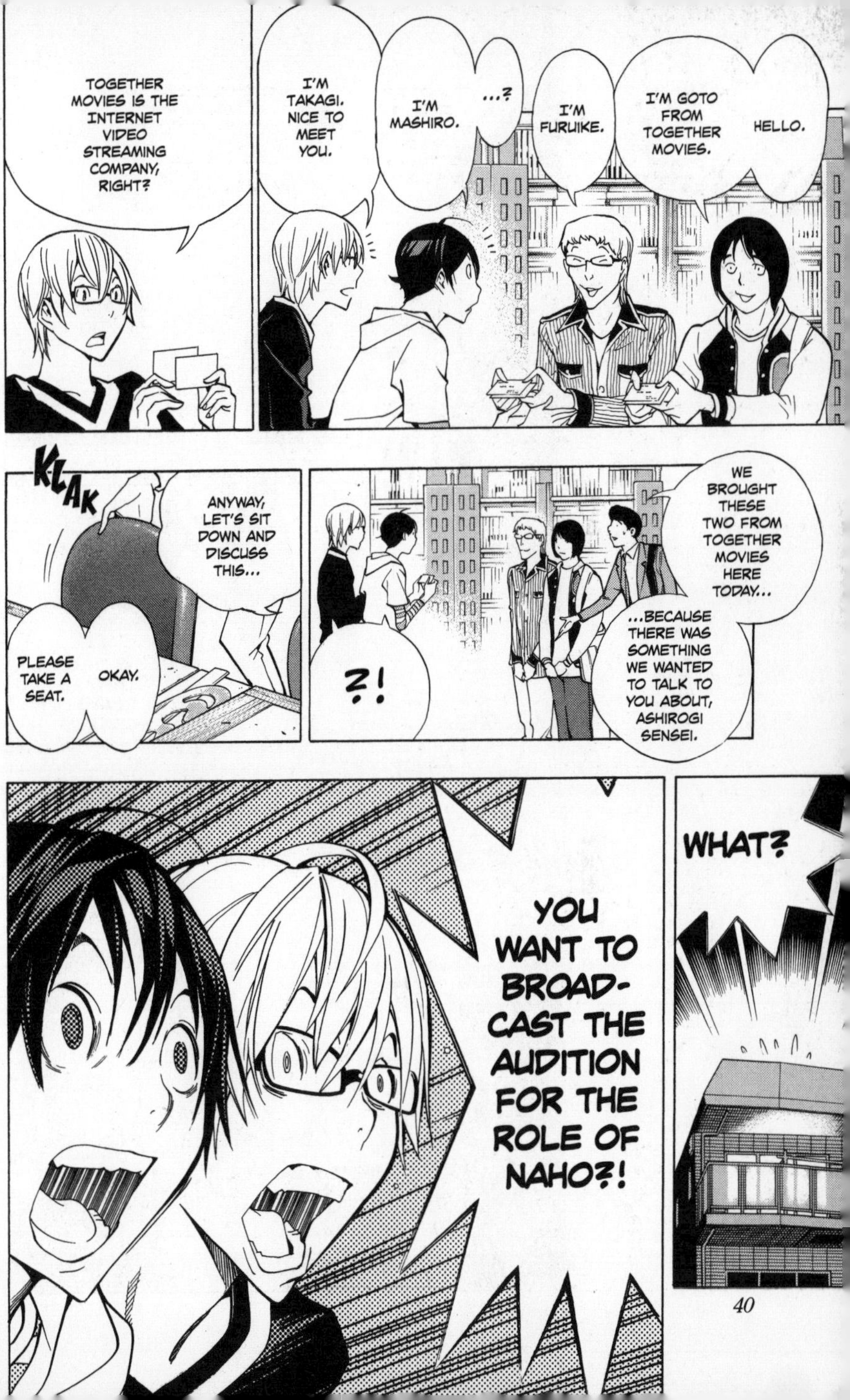
HELLO.
I'M GOTO FROM TOGETHER MOVIES.
I'M FURUIKE.
...?
I'M MASHIRO.
I'M TAKAGI. NICE TO MEET YOU.
TOGETHER MOVIES IS THE INTERNET VIDEO STREAMING COMPANY, RIGHT?
WE BROUGHT THESE TWO FROM TOGETHER MOVIES HERE TODAY...
...BECAUSE THERE WAS SOMETHING WE WANTED TO TALK TO YOU ABOUT, ASHIROGI SENSEI.
?!
K-LAK
ANYWAY, LET'S SIT DOWN AND DISCUSS THIS...
OKAY.
PLEASE TAKE A SEAT.
WHAT?
YOU WANT TO BROAD-CAST THE AUDITION FOR THE ROLE OF NAHO?!

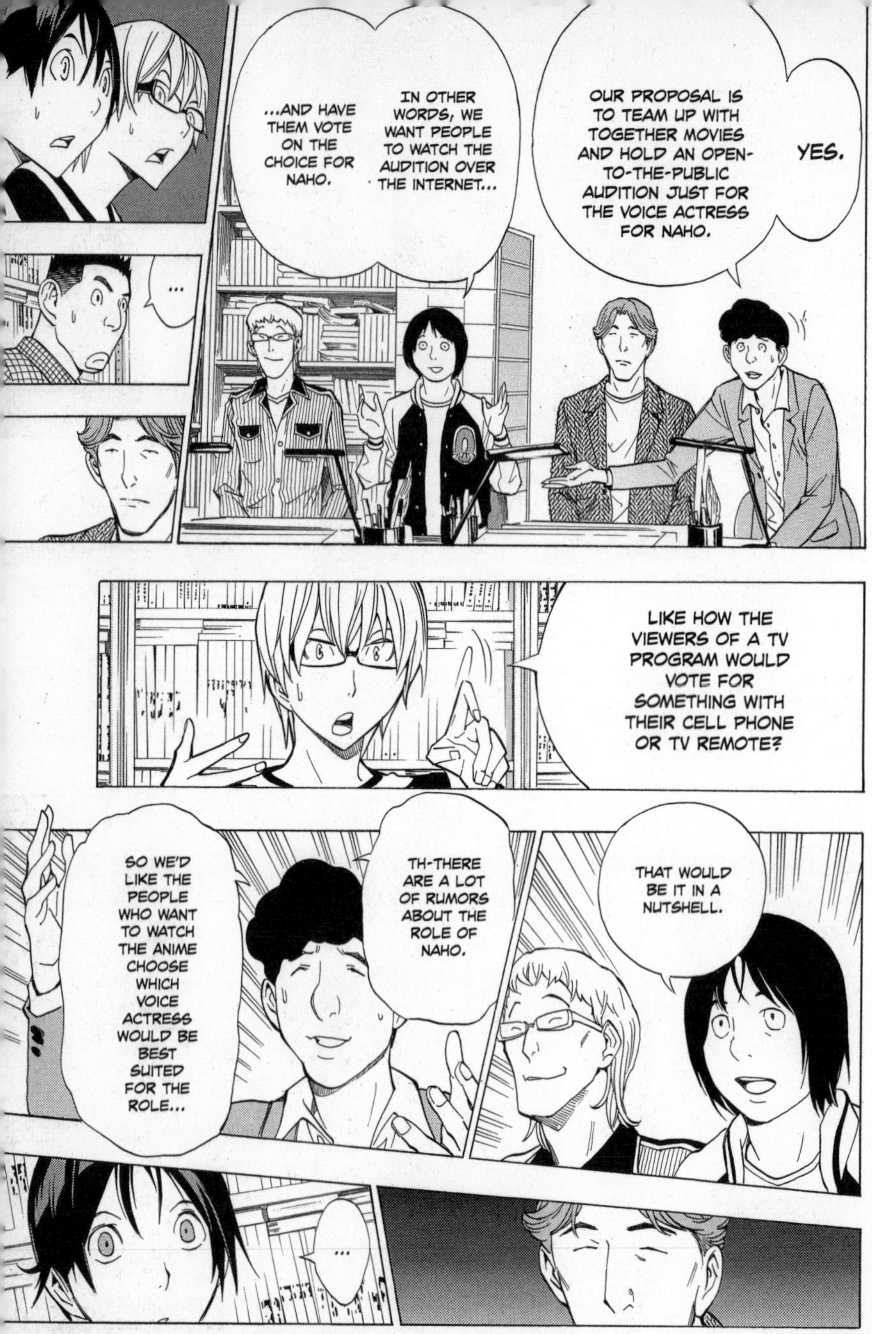
YES.
OUR PROPOSAL IS TO TEAM UP WITH TOGETHER MOVIES AND HOLD AN OPEN-TO-THE-PUBLIC AUDITION JUST FOR THE VOICE ACTRESS FOR NAHO.
IN OTHER WORDS, WE WANT PEOPLE TO WATCH THE AUDITION OVER THE INTERNET...
...AND HAVE THEM VOTE ON THE CHOICE FOR NAHO.
...
LIKE HOW THE VIEWERS OF A TV PROGRAM WOULD VOTE FOR SOMETHING WITH THEIR CELL PHONE OR TV REMOTE?
THAT WOULD BE IT IN A NUTSHELL.
TH-THERE ARE A LOT OF RUMORS ABOUT THE ROLE OF NAHO.
SO WE'D LIKE THE PEOPLE WHO WANT TO WATCH THE ANIME CHOOSE WHICH VOICE ACTRESS WOULD BE BEST SUITED FOR THE ROLE...
...

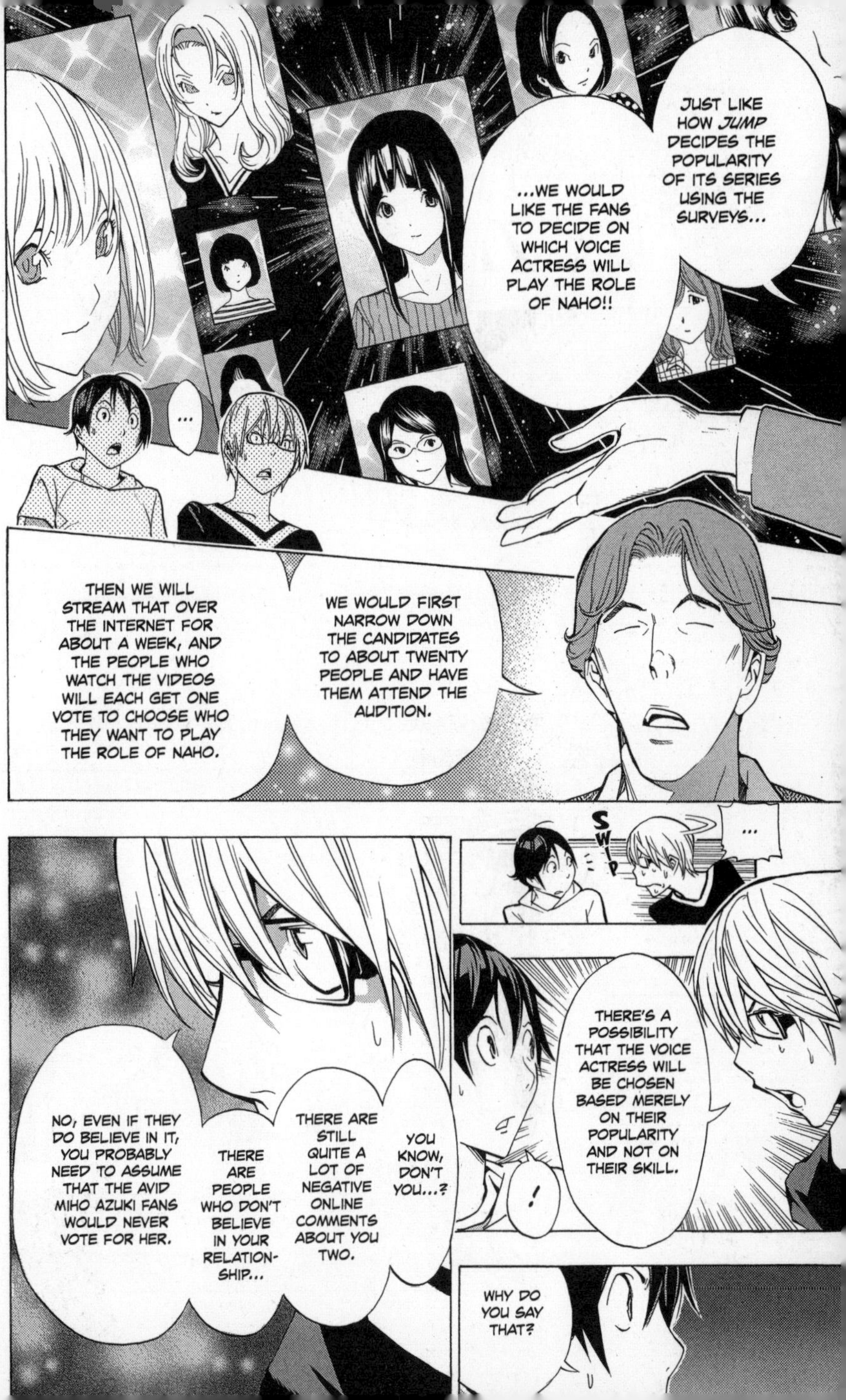
JUST LIKE HOW *JUMP* DECIDES THE POPULARITY OF ITS SERIES USING THE SURVEYS...
...WE WOULD LIKE THE FANS TO DECIDE ON WHICH VOICE ACTRESS WILL PLAY THE ROLE OF NAHO!!
...
WE WOULD FIRST NARROW DOWN THE CANDIDATES TO ABOUT TWENTY PEOPLE AND HAVE THEM ATTEND THE AUDITION.
THEN WE WILL STREAM THAT OVER THE INTERNET FOR ABOUT A WEEK, AND THE PEOPLE WHO WATCH THE VIDEOS WILL EACH GET ONE VOTE TO CHOOSE WHO THEY WANT TO PLAY THE ROLE OF NAHO.
...
SWIP
THERE'S A POSSIBILITY THAT THE VOICE ACTRESS WILL BE CHOSEN BASED MERELY ON THEIR POPULARITY AND NOT ON THEIR SKILL.
!
WHY DO YOU SAY THAT?
YOU KNOW, DON'T YOU...?
THERE ARE STILL QUITE A LOT OF NEGATIVE ONLINE COMMENTS ABOUT YOU TWO.
THERE ARE PEOPLE WHO DON'T BELIEVE IN YOUR RELATION-SHIP...
NO, EVEN IF THEY DO BELIEVE IN IT, YOU PROBABLY NEED TO ASSUME THAT THE AVID MIHO AZUKI FANS WOULD NEVER VOTE FOR HER.

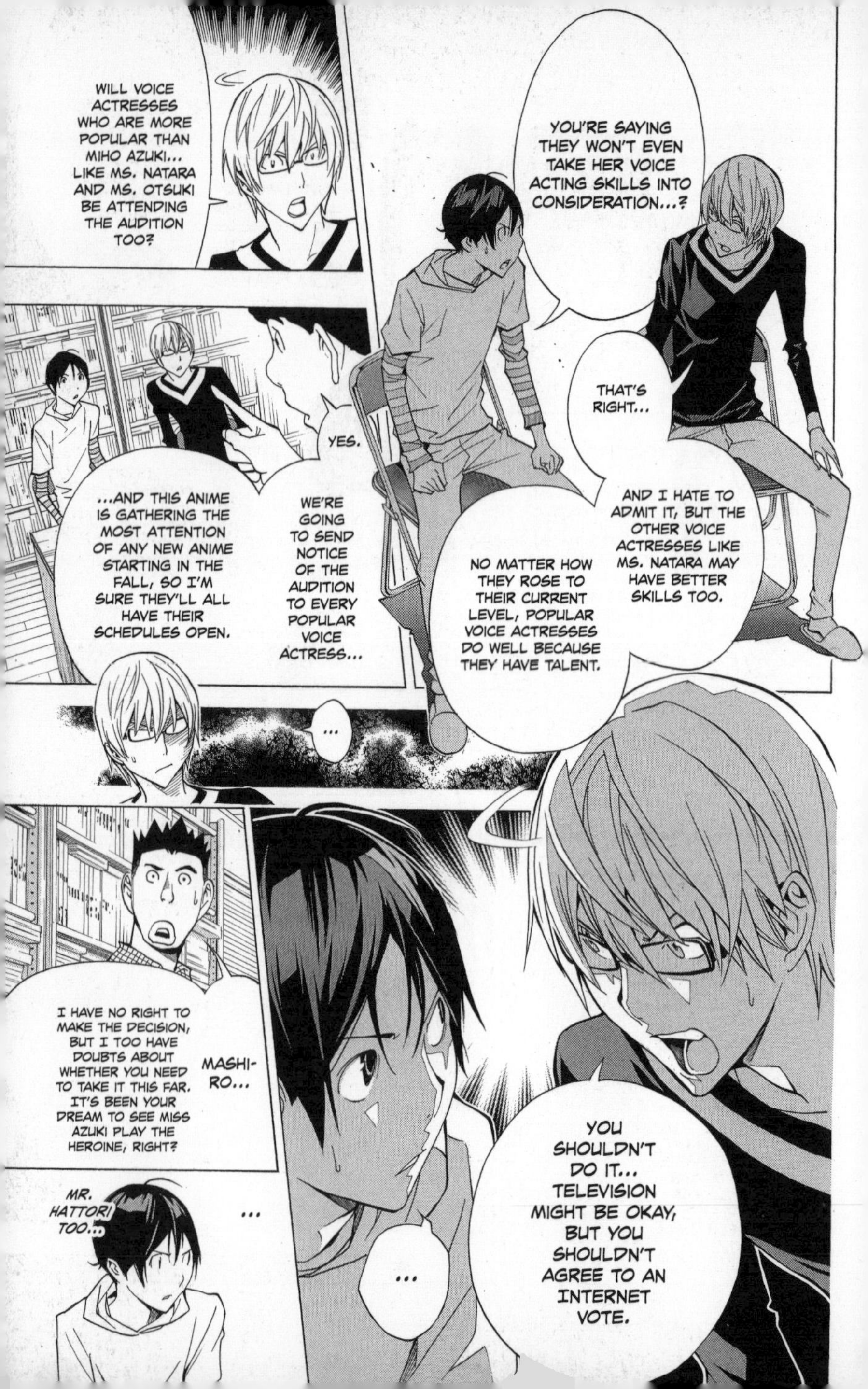
YOU'RE SAYING THEY WON'T EVEN TAKE HER VOICE ACTING SKILLS INTO CONSIDERATION...?
THAT'S RIGHT...
AND I HATE TO ADMIT IT, BUT THE OTHER VOICE ACTRESSES LIKE MS. NATARA MAY HAVE BETTER SKILLS TOO.
NO MATTER HOW THEY ROSE TO THEIR CURRENT LEVEL, POPULAR VOICE ACTRESSES DO WELL BECAUSE THEY HAVE TALENT.
WILL VOICE ACTRESSES WHO ARE MORE POPULAR THAN MIHO AZUKI... LIKE MS. NATARA AND MS. OTSUKI BE ATTENDING THE AUDITION TOO?
YES.
WE'RE GOING TO SEND NOTICE OF THE AUDITION TO EVERY POPULAR VOICE ACTRESS...
...AND THIS ANIME IS GATHERING THE MOST ATTENTION OF ANY NEW ANIME STARTING IN THE FALL, SO I'M SURE THEY'LL ALL HAVE THEIR SCHEDULES OPEN.
...
YOU SHOULDN'T DO IT... TELEVISION MIGHT BE OKAY, BUT YOU SHOULDN'T AGREE TO AN INTERNET VOTE.
...
MASHIRO...
I HAVE NO RIGHT TO MAKE THE DECISION, BUT I TOO HAVE DOUBTS ABOUT WHETHER YOU NEED TO TAKE IT THIS FAR. IT'S BEEN YOUR DREAM TO SEE MISS AZUKI PLAY THE HEROINE, RIGHT?
...
MR. HATTORI TOO...

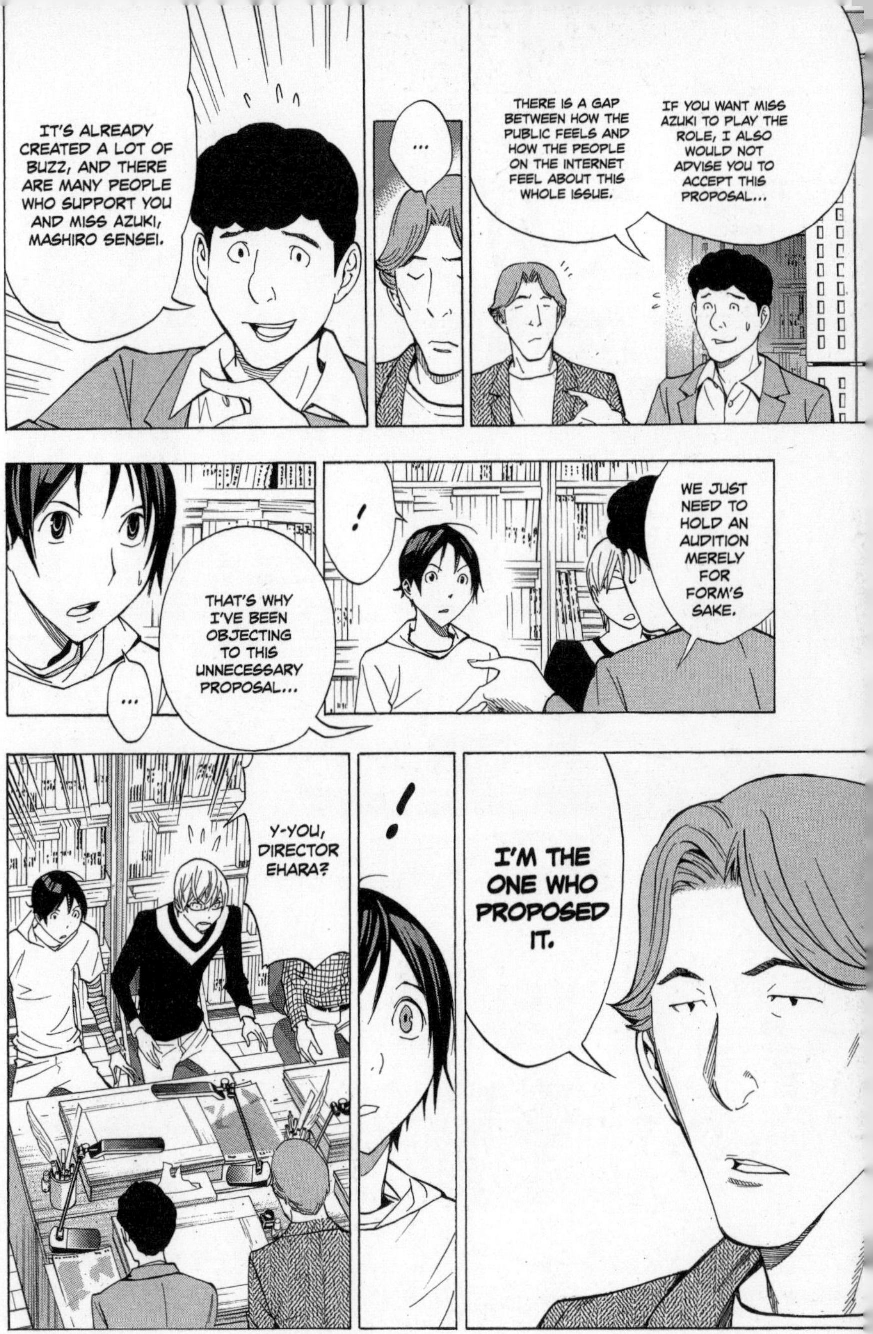
IF YOU WANT MISS AZUKI TO PLAY THE ROLE, I ALSO WOULD NOT ADVISE YOU TO ACCEPT THIS PROPOSAL...
THERE IS A GAP BETWEEN HOW THE PUBLIC FEELS AND HOW THE PEOPLE ON THE INTERNET FEEL ABOUT THIS WHOLE ISSUE.
...
IT'S ALREADY CREATED A LOT OF BUZZ, AND THERE ARE MANY PEOPLE WHO SUPPORT YOU AND MISS AZUKI, MASHIRO SENSEI.
WE JUST NEED TO HOLD AN AUDITION MERELY FOR FORM'S SAKE.
!
THAT'S WHY I'VE BEEN OBJECTING TO THIS UNNECESSARY PROPOSAL...
...
I'M THE ONE WHO PROPOSED IT.
!
Y-YOU, DIRECTOR EHARA?

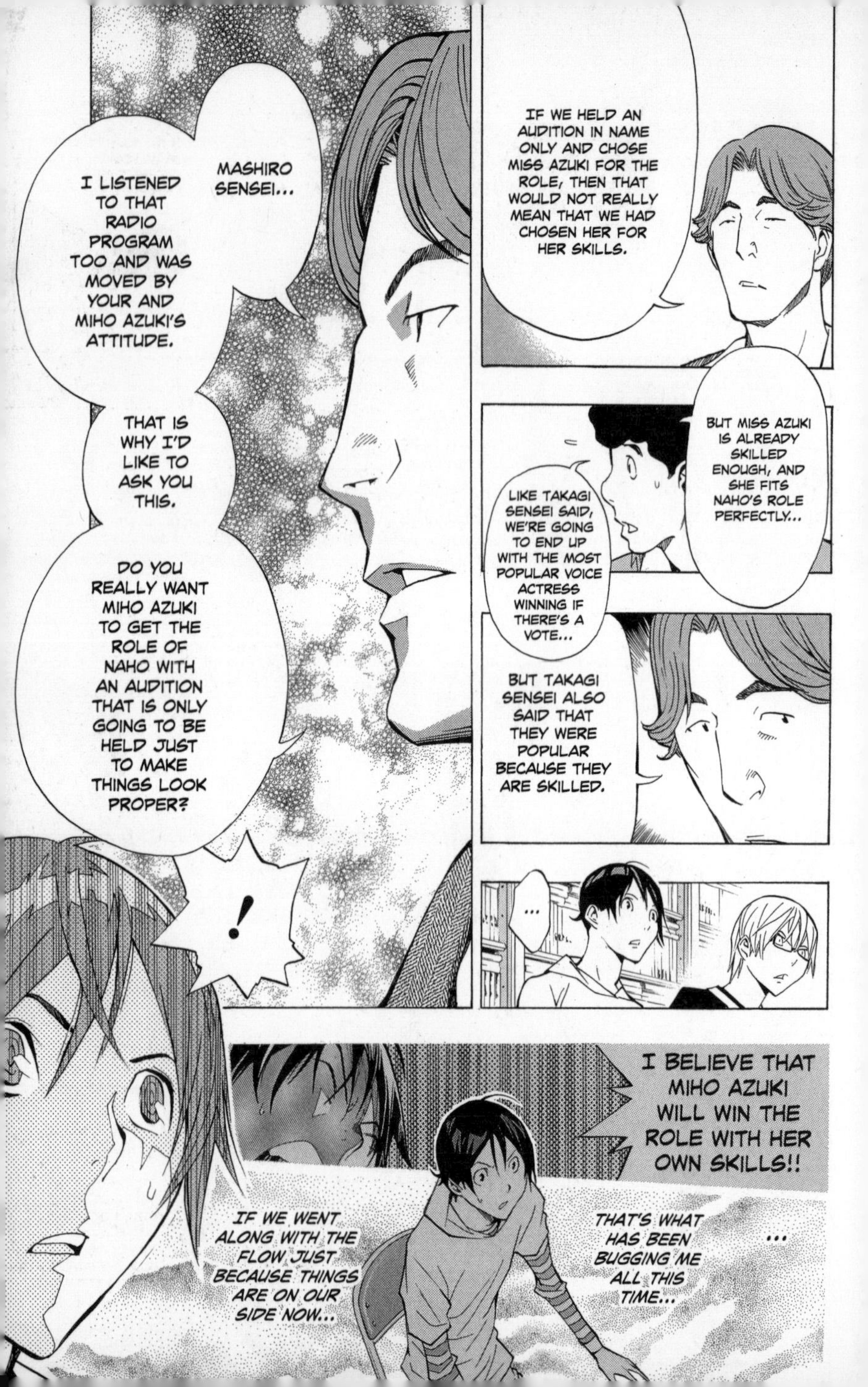
IF WE HELD AN AUDITION IN NAME ONLY AND CHOSE MISS AZUKI FOR THE ROLE, THEN THAT WOULD NOT REALLY MEAN THAT WE HAD CHOSEN HER FOR HER SKILLS.
BUT MISS AZUKI IS ALREADY SKILLED ENOUGH, AND SHE FITS NAHO'S ROLE PERFECTLY...
LIKE TAKAGI SENSEI SAID, WE'RE GOING TO END UP WITH THE MOST POPULAR VOICE ACTRESS WINNING IF THERE'S A VOTE...
BUT TAKAGI SENSEI ALSO SAID THAT THEY WERE POPULAR BECAUSE THEY ARE SKILLED.
...
MASHIRO SENSEI...
I LISTENED TO THAT RADIO PROGRAM TOO AND WAS MOVED BY YOUR AND MIHO AZUKI'S ATTITUDE.
THAT IS WHY I'D LIKE TO ASK YOU THIS.
DO YOU REALLY WANT MIHO AZUKI TO GET THE ROLE OF NAHO WITH AN AUDITION THAT IS ONLY GOING TO BE HELD JUST TO MAKE THINGS LOOK PROPER?
!
I BELIEVE THAT MIHO AZUKI WILL WIN THE ROLE WITH HER OWN SKILLS!!
...
THAT'S WHAT HAS BEEN BUGGING ME ALL THIS TIME...
IF WE WENT ALONG WITH THE FLOW JUST BECAUSE THINGS ARE ON OUR SIDE NOW...

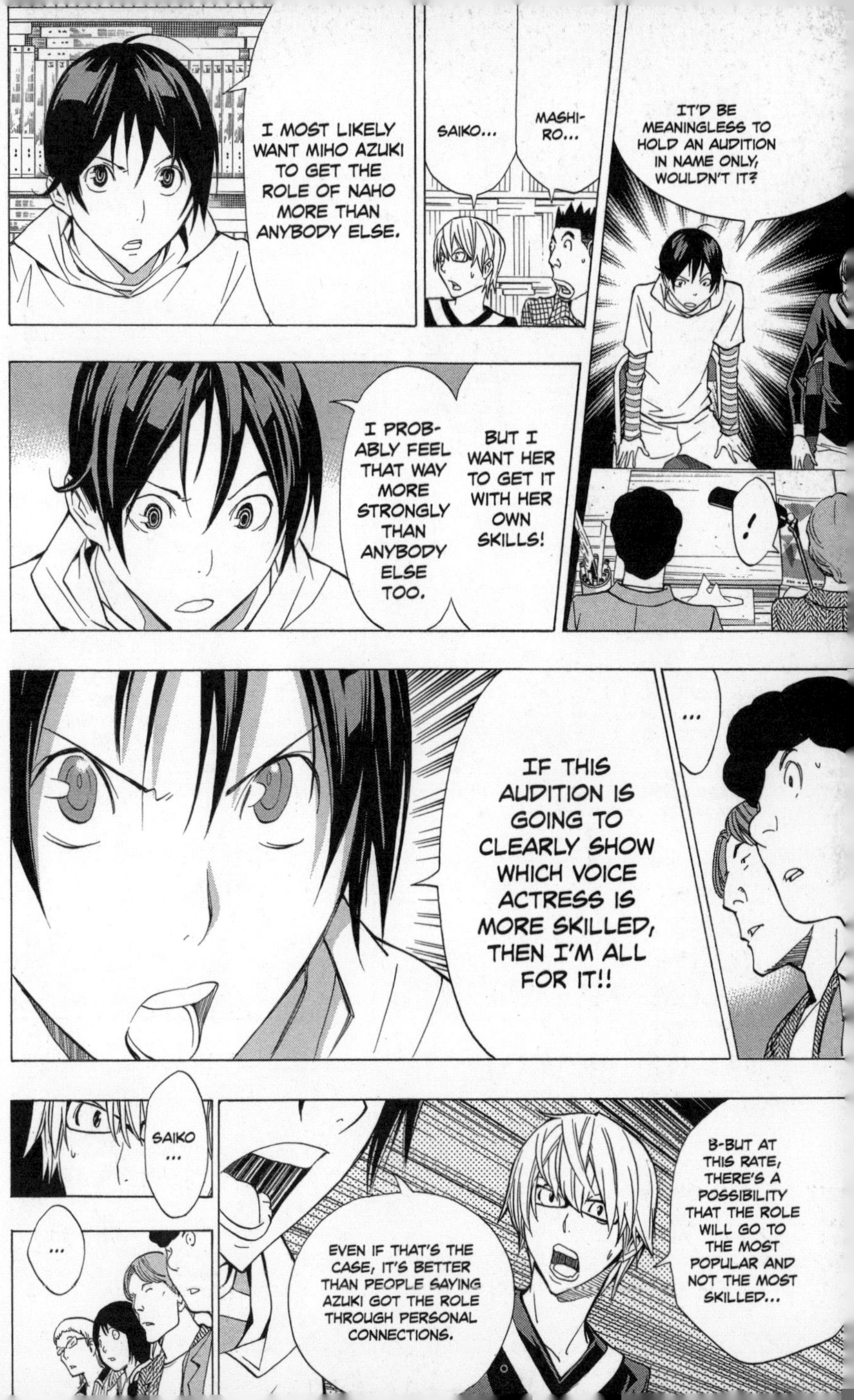
IT'D BE MEANINGLESS TO HOLD AN AUDITION IN NAME ONLY, WOULDN'T IT?
MASHIRO...
SAIKO...
I MOST LIKELY WANT MIHO AZUKI TO GET THE ROLE OF NAHO MORE THAN ANYBODY ELSE.
!
BUT I WANT HER TO GET IT WITH HER OWN SKILLS!
I PROBABLY FEEL THAT WAY MORE STRONGLY THAN ANYBODY ELSE TOO.
...
IF THIS AUDITION IS GOING TO CLEARLY SHOW WHICH VOICE ACTRESS IS MORE SKILLED, THEN I'M ALL FOR IT!!
B-BUT AT THIS RATE, THERE'S A POSSIBILITY THAT THE ROLE WILL GO TO THE MOST POPULAR AND NOT THE MOST SKILLED...
EVEN IF THAT'S THE CASE, IT'S BETTER THAN PEOPLE SAYING AZUKI GOT THE ROLE THROUGH PERSONAL CONNECTIONS.
SAIKO...
...

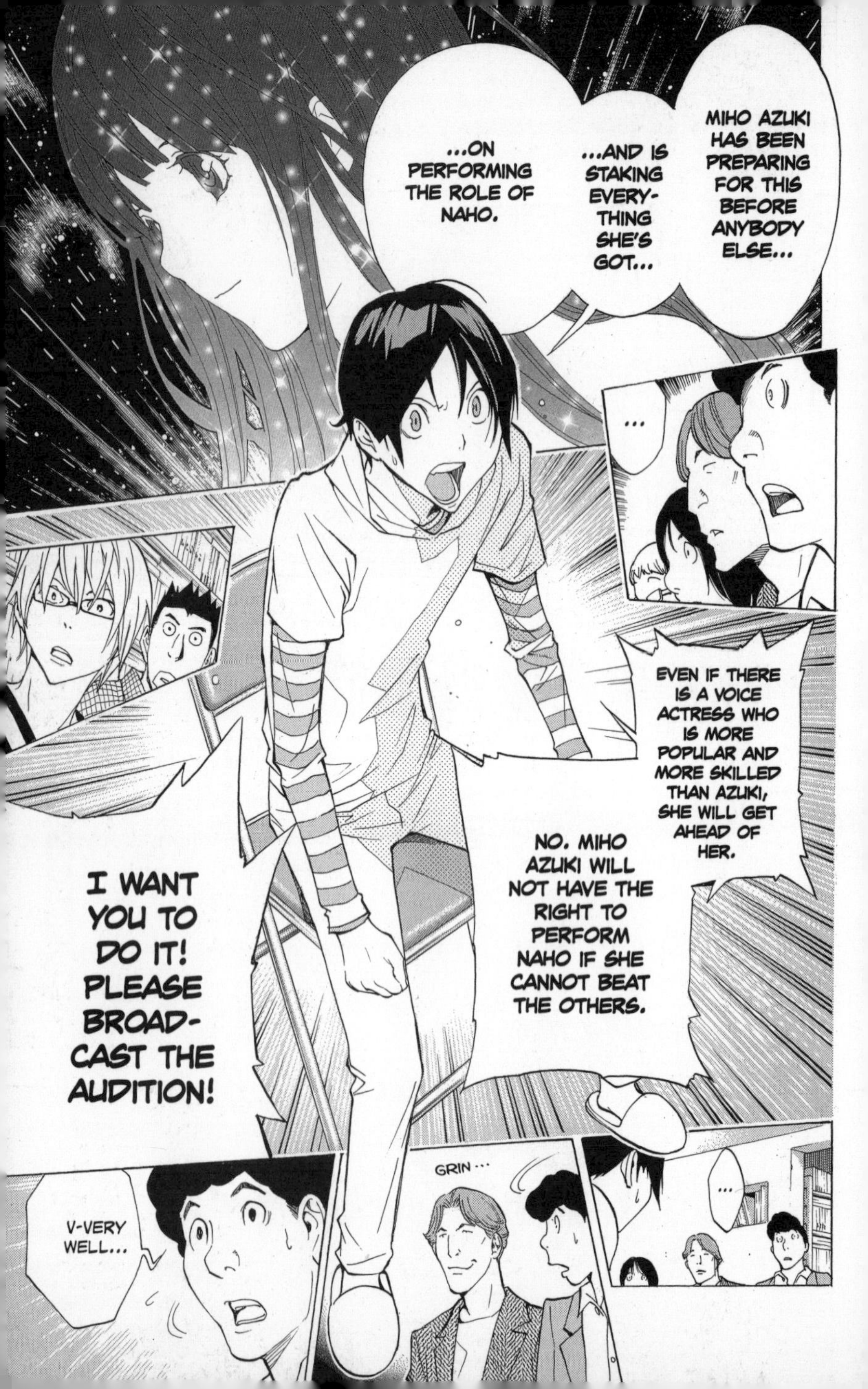
MIHO AZUKI HAS BEEN PREPARING FOR THIS BEFORE ANYBODY ELSE...
...AND IS STAKING EVERY-THING SHE'S GOT...
...ON PERFORMING THE ROLE OF NAHO.
...
EVEN IF THERE IS A VOICE ACTRESS WHO IS MORE POPULAR AND MORE SKILLED THAN AZUKI, SHE WILL GET AHEAD OF HER.
NO. MIHO AZUKI WILL NOT HAVE THE RIGHT TO PERFORM NAHO IF SHE CANNOT BEAT THE OTHERS.
I WANT YOU TO DO IT! PLEASE BROAD-CAST THE AUDITION!
...
GRIN...
V-VERY WELL...

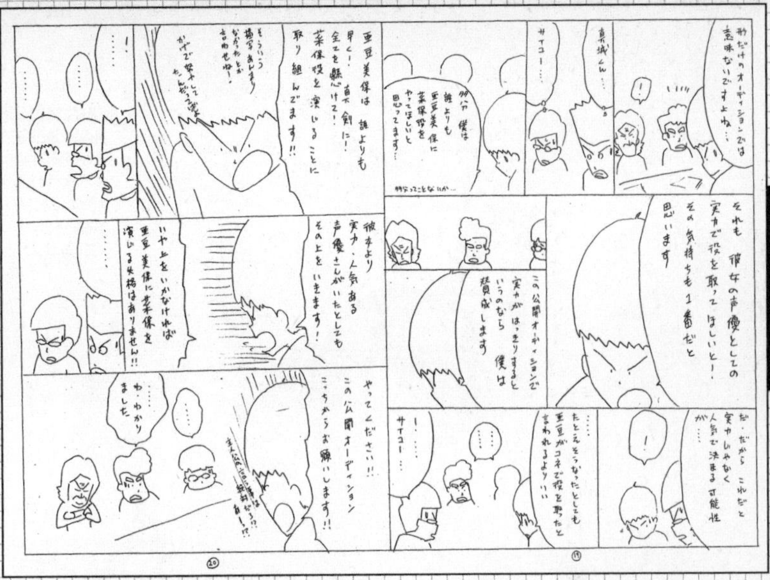
形だけのオーディションでは意味ないですよね…
!
真城くん…
サイコー…
多分僕は誰よりも亜豆美保にやってほしいと思ってます…
それも彼女の声優としての実力で役を取ってほしいと!その気持ちも1番だと思います
この公開オーディションで実力がはっきりするというのなら僕は賛成します
だ・だからこれだと実力じゃなく人気で決まる可能性が…
!
たとえそうなったとしても亜豆がコネで役を取ったと言われるよりいい
……
!……
サイコー…
19
亜豆美保は誰よりも早く!全てを懸けて!真剣に!茉保役を演じることに取り組んでます!!
!
……
……
彼女より実力・人気ある声優さんがいたとしてもその上をいきます!
……
いや上をいかなければ亜豆美保に茉保を演じる資格はありません!!
やってください!!この公開オーディションこっちからお願いします!!
……
わ・わかりました
20

OHBA'S STORYBOARD

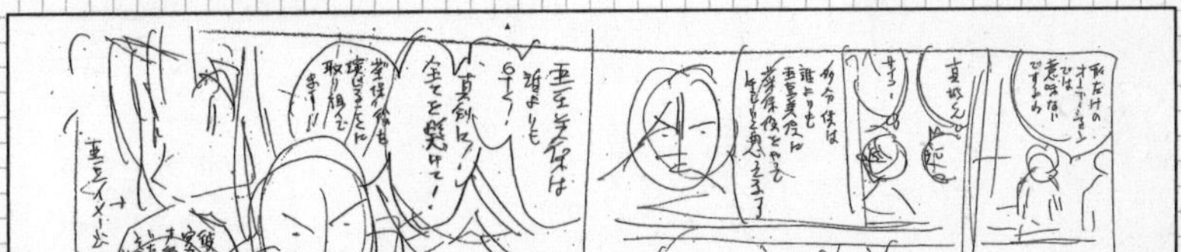

OBATA'S STORYBOARD

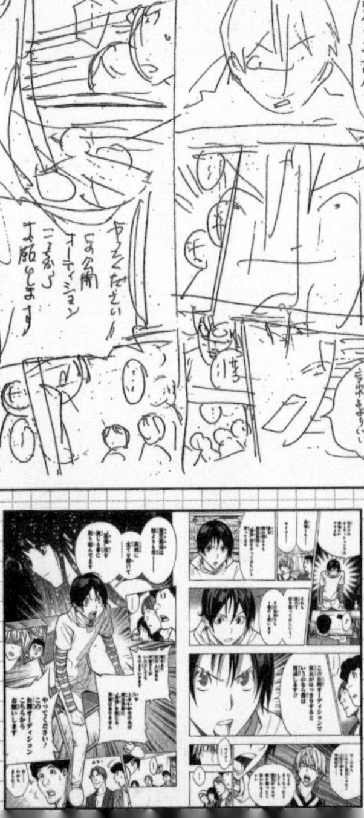

COMPLETE!

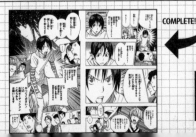

*CREATOR STORYBOARDS AND FINISHED PAGES IN JAPANESE

BAKUMAN。 vol.20

"Until the Final Draft Is Complete"

Chapter 170, pp. 50-51

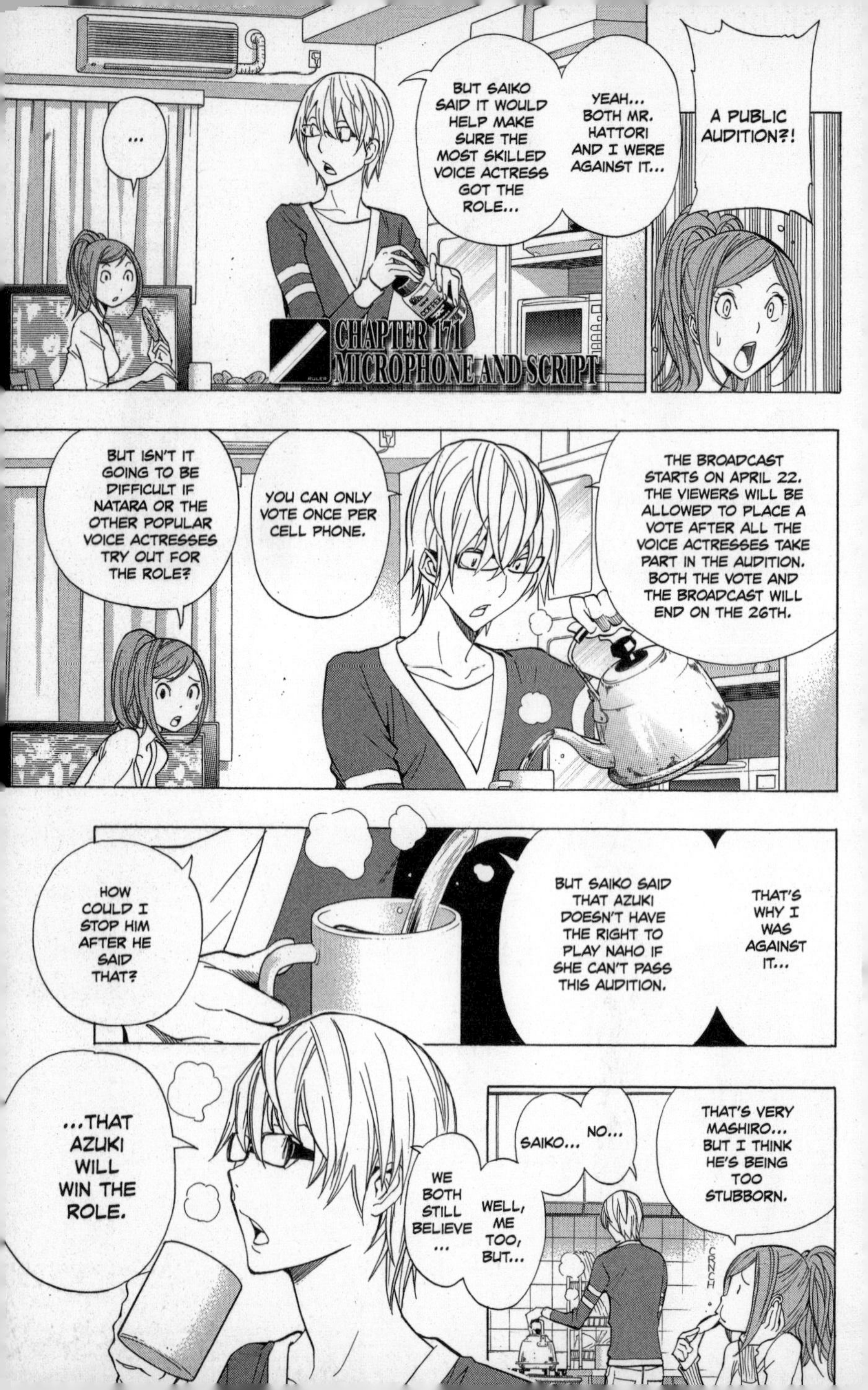
A PUBLIC AUDITION?!
YEAH... BOTH MR. HATTORI AND I WERE AGAINST IT...
BUT SAIKO SAID IT WOULD HELP MAKE SURE THE MOST SKILLED VOICE ACTRESS GOT THE ROLE...
...
CHAPTER 171
MICROPHONE AND SCRIPT
THE BROADCAST STARTS ON APRIL 22. THE VIEWERS WILL BE ALLOWED TO PLACE A VOTE AFTER ALL THE VOICE ACTRESSES TAKE PART IN THE AUDITION. BOTH THE VOTE AND THE BROADCAST WILL END ON THE 26TH.
YOU CAN ONLY VOTE ONCE PER CELL PHONE.
BUT ISN'T IT GOING TO BE DIFFICULT IF NATARA OR THE OTHER POPULAR VOICE ACTRESSES TRY OUT FOR THE ROLE?
THAT'S WHY I WAS AGAINST IT...
BUT SAIKO SAID THAT AZUKI DOESN'T HAVE THE RIGHT TO PLAY NAHO IF SHE CAN'T PASS THIS AUDITION.
HOW COULD I STOP HIM AFTER HE SAID THAT?
THAT'S VERY MASHIRO... BUT I THINK HE'S BEING TOO STUBBORN.
NO...
SAIKO...
CRNCH
WELL, ME TOO, BUT...
WE BOTH STILL BELIEVE...
...THAT AZUKI WILL WIN THE ROLE.

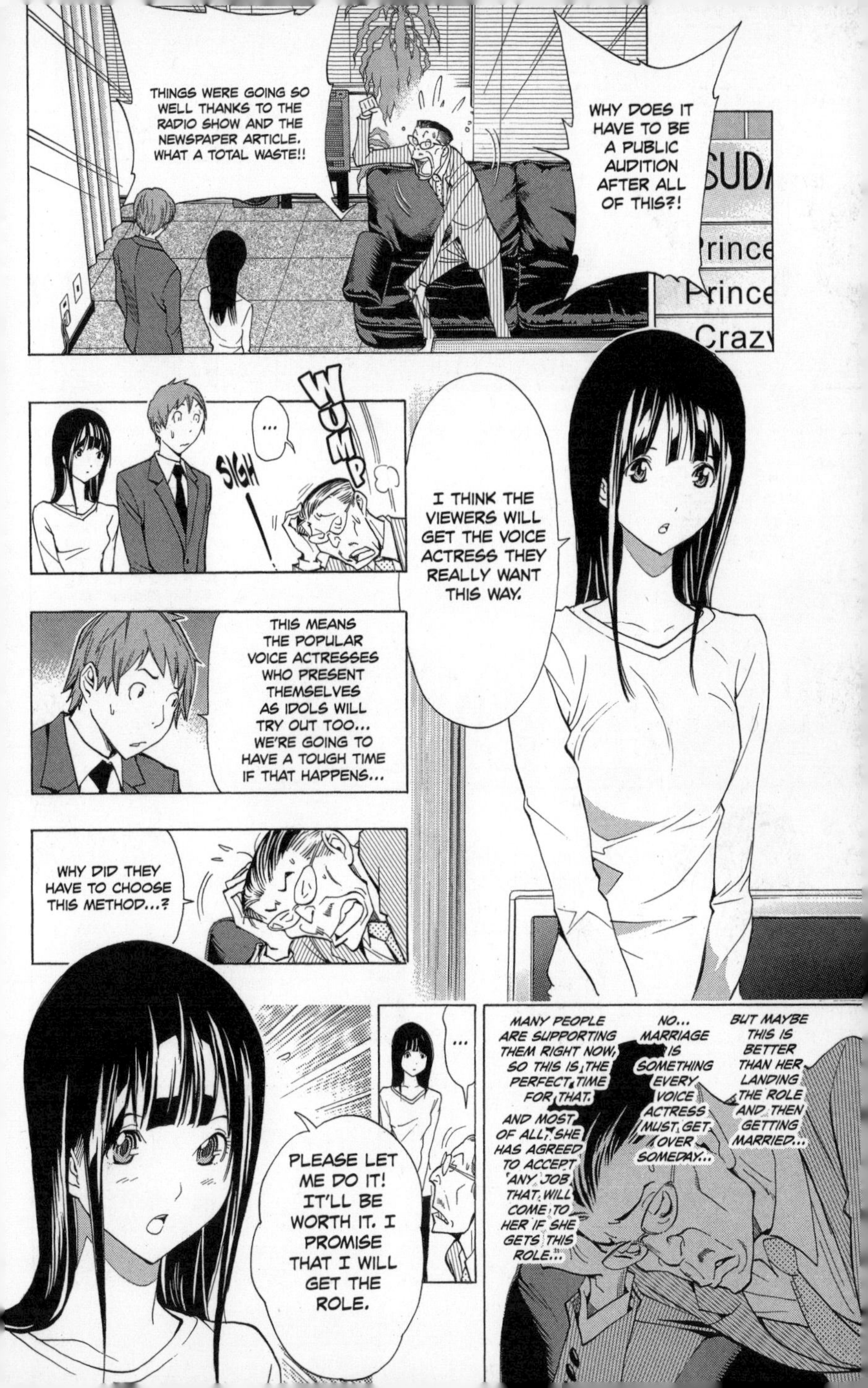
WHY DOES IT HAVE TO BE A PUBLIC AUDITION AFTER ALL OF THIS?!
THINGS WERE GOING SO WELL THANKS TO THE RADIO SHOW AND THE NEWSPAPER ARTICLE. WHAT A TOTAL WASTE!!
I THINK THE VIEWERS WILL GET THE VOICE ACTRESS THEY REALLY WANT THIS WAY.
WUMP
...
SIGH
THIS MEANS THE POPULAR VOICE ACTRESSES WHO PRESENT THEMSELVES AS IDOLS WILL TRY OUT TOO... WE'RE GOING TO HAVE A TOUGH TIME IF THAT HAPPENS...
WHY DID THEY HAVE TO CHOOSE THIS METHOD...?
BUT MAYBE THIS IS BETTER THAN HER LANDING THE ROLE AND THEN GETTING MARRIED...
NO... MARRIAGE IS SOMETHING EVERY VOICE ACTRESS MUST GET OVER SOMEDAY...
MANY PEOPLE ARE SUPPORTING THEM RIGHT NOW, SO THIS IS THE PERFECT TIME FOR THAT.
AND MOST OF ALL, SHE HAS AGREED TO ACCEPT ANY JOB THAT WILL COME TO HER IF SHE GETS THIS ROLE...
...
PLEASE LET ME DO IT! IT'LL BE WORTH IT. I PROMISE THAT I WILL GET THE ROLE.

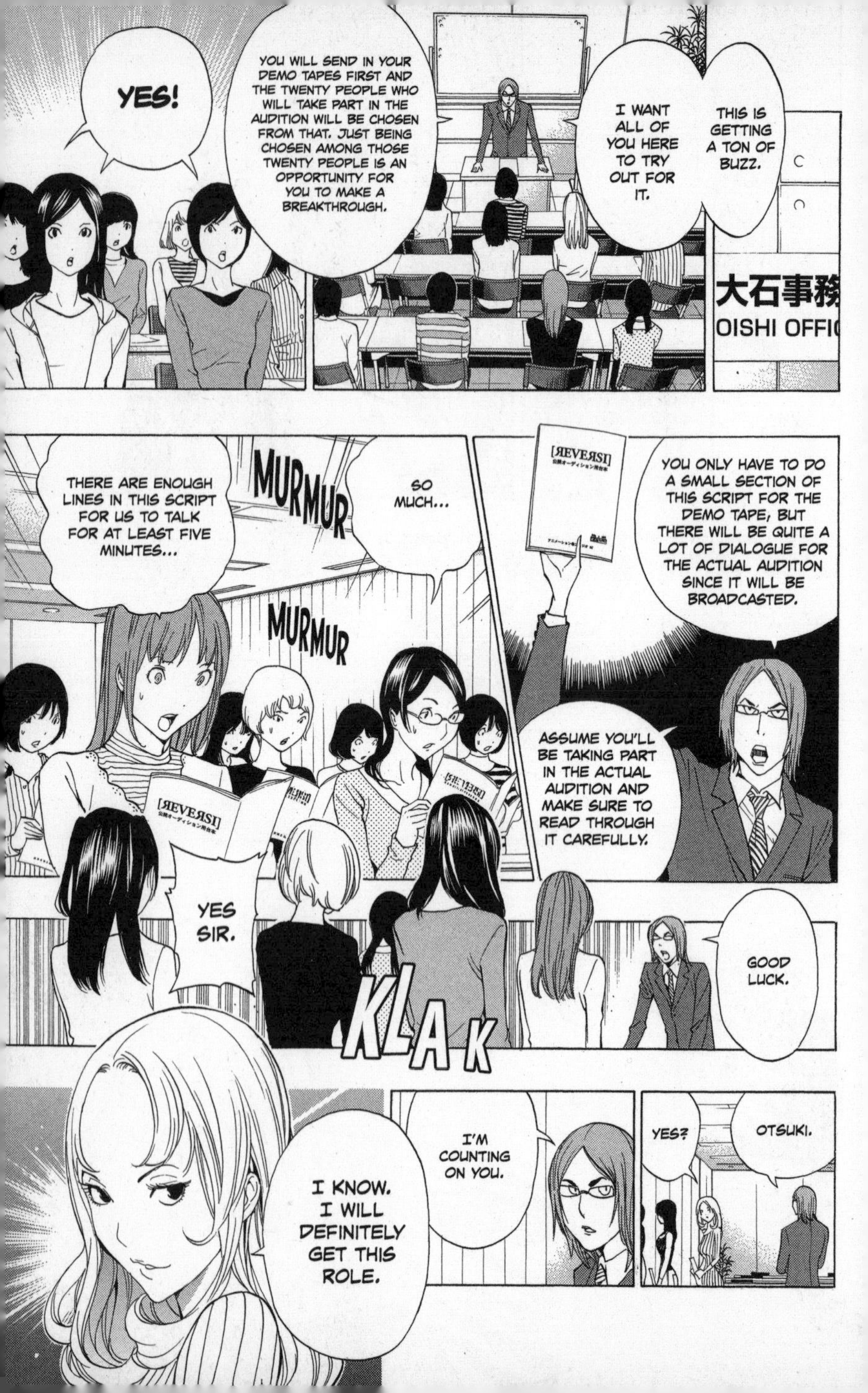
大石事務
OISHI OFFIC
THIS IS GETTING A TON OF BUZZ.
I WANT ALL OF YOU HERE TO TRY OUT FOR IT.
YOU WILL SEND IN YOUR DEMO TAPES FIRST AND THE TWENTY PEOPLE WHO WILL TAKE PART IN THE AUDITION WILL BE CHOSEN FROM THAT. JUST BEING CHOSEN AMONG THOSE TWENTY PEOPLE IS AN OPPORTUNITY FOR YOU TO MAKE A BREAKTHROUGH.
YES!
[ЯEVEЯSI]
公開オーディション用台本
YOU ONLY HAVE TO DO A SMALL SECTION OF THIS SCRIPT FOR THE DEMO TAPE, BUT THERE WILL BE QUITE A LOT OF DIALOGUE FOR THE ACTUAL AUDITION SINCE IT WILL BE BROADCASTED.
ASSUME YOU'LL BE TAKING PART IN THE ACTUAL AUDITION AND MAKE SURE TO READ THROUGH IT CAREFULLY.
MURMUR
SO MUCH...
THERE ARE ENOUGH LINES IN THIS SCRIPT FOR US TO TALK FOR AT LEAST FIVE MINUTES...
MURMUR
GOOD LUCK.
YES SIR.
KLAK
OTSUKI.
YES?
I'M COUNTING ON YOU.
I KNOW. I WILL DEFINITELY GET THIS ROLE.

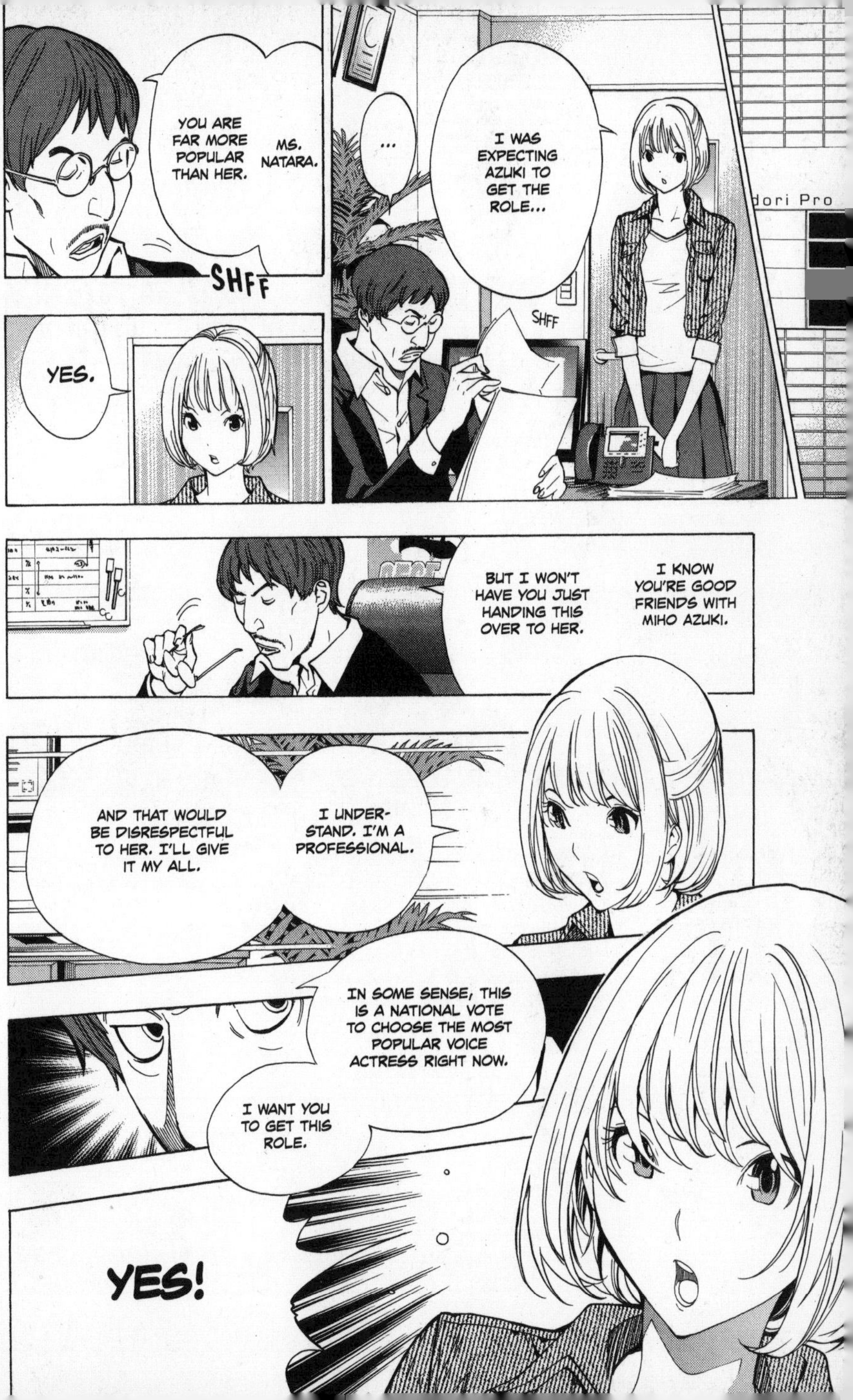
dori Pro
I WAS EXPECTING AZUKI TO GET THE ROLE...
...
SHFF
MS. NATARA.
YOU ARE FAR MORE POPULAR THAN HER.
SHFF
YES.
I KNOW YOU'RE GOOD FRIENDS WITH MIHO AZUKI.
BUT I WON'T HAVE YOU JUST HANDING THIS OVER TO HER.
I UNDER-STAND. I'M A PROFESSIONAL.
AND THAT WOULD BE DISRESPECTFUL TO HER. I'LL GIVE IT MY ALL.
IN SOME SENSE, THIS IS A NATIONAL VOTE TO CHOOSE THE MOST POPULAR VOICE ACTRESS RIGHT NOW.
I WANT YOU TO GET THIS ROLE.
YES!

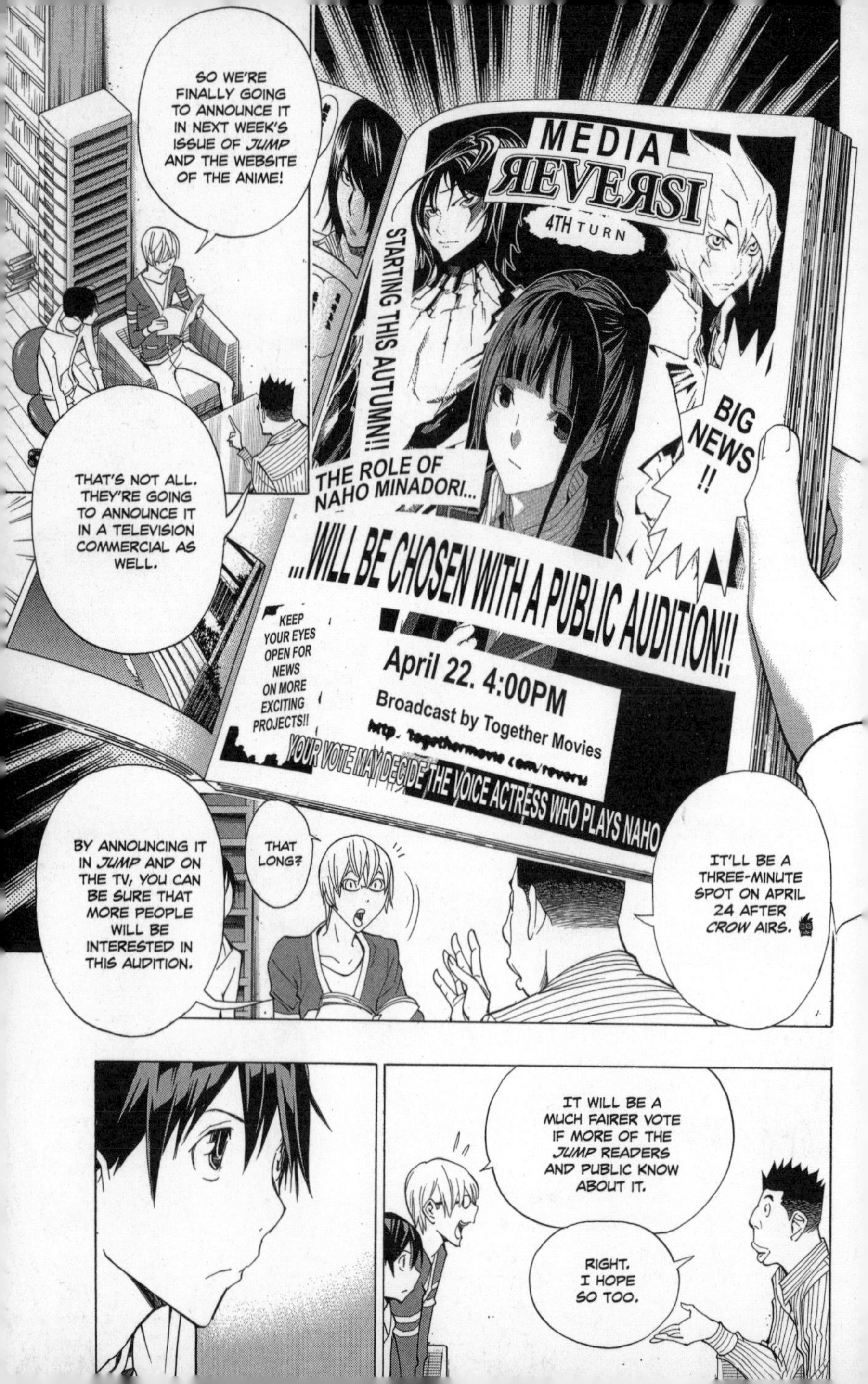
MEDIA REVERSI
4TH TURN
STARTING THIS AUTUMN!!
BIG NEWS!!
THE ROLE OF NAHO MINADORI...
...WILL BE CHOSEN WITH A PUBLIC AUDITION!!
KEEP YOUR EYES OPEN FOR NEWS ON MORE EXCITING PROJECTS!!
April 22. 4:00PM
Broadcast by Together Movies
YOUR VOTE MAY DECIDE THE VOICE ACTRESS WHO PLAYS NAHO
SO WE'RE FINALLY GOING TO ANNOUNCE IT IN NEXT WEEK'S ISSUE OF JUMP AND THE WEBSITE OF THE ANIME!
THAT'S NOT ALL. THEY'RE GOING TO ANNOUNCE IT IN A TELEVISION COMMERCIAL AS WELL.
IT'LL BE A THREE-MINUTE SPOT ON APRIL 24 AFTER CROW AIRS.
THAT LONG?
BY ANNOUNCING IT IN JUMP AND ON THE TV, YOU CAN BE SURE THAT MORE PEOPLE WILL BE INTERESTED IN THIS AUDITION.
IT WILL BE A MUCH FAIRER VOTE IF MORE OF THE JUMP READERS AND PUBLIC KNOW ABOUT IT.
RIGHT. I HOPE SO TOO.

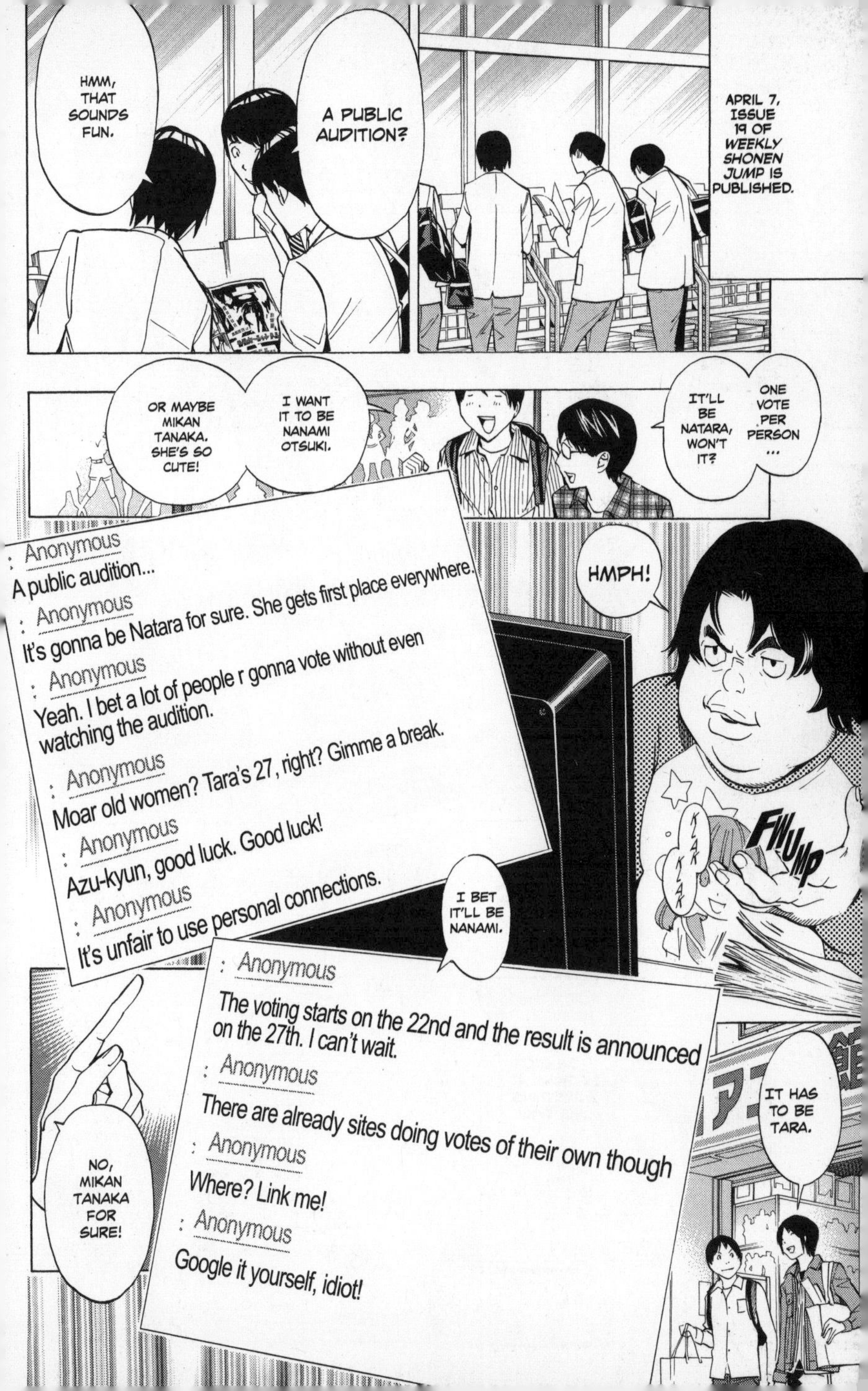
APRIL 7, ISSUE 19 OF WEEKLY SHONEN JUMP IS PUBLISHED.
A PUBLIC AUDITION?
HMM, THAT SOUNDS FUN.
ONE VOTE PER PERSON...
IT'LL BE NATARA, WON'T IT?
I WANT IT TO BE NANAMI OTSUKI.
OR MAYBE MIKAN TANAKA. SHE'S SO CUTE!
HMPH!
FWUMP
KLAK KLAK
: Anonymous
A public audition...
: Anonymous
It's gonna be Natara for sure. She gets first place everywhere.
: Anonymous
Yeah. I bet a lot of people r gonna vote without even watching the audition.
: Anonymous
Moar old women? Tara's 27, right? Gimme a break.
: Anonymous
Azu-kyun, good luck. Good luck!
: Anonymous
It's unfair to use personal connections.
I BET IT'LL BE NANAMI.
IT HAS TO BE TARA.
: Anonymous
The voting starts on the 22nd and the result is announced on the 27th. I can't wait.
: Anonymous
There are already sites doing votes of their own though
: Anonymous
Where? Link me!
: Anonymous
Google it yourself, idiot!
NO, MIKAN TANAKA FOR SURE!

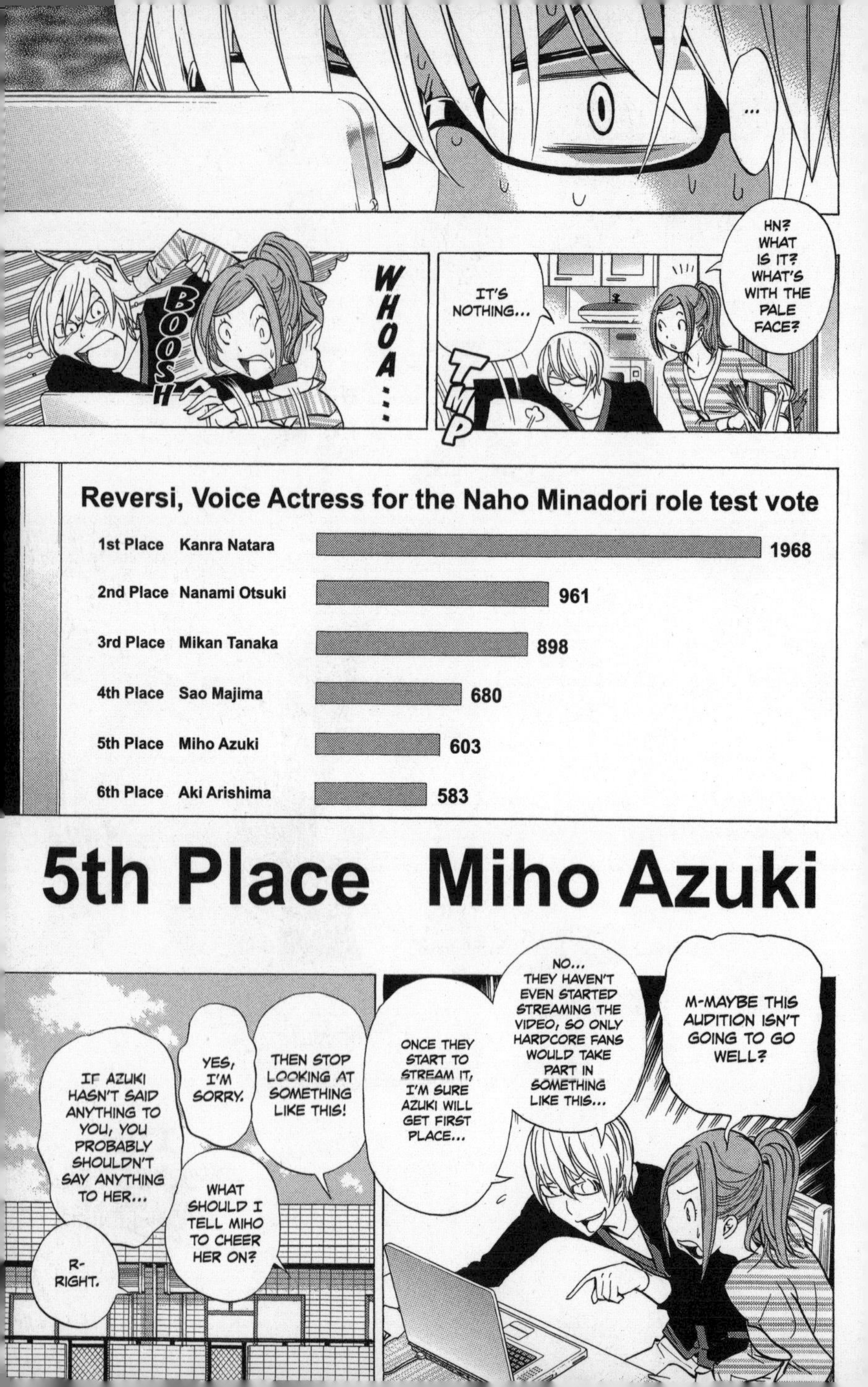
...
HN? WHAT IS IT? WHAT'S WITH THE PALE FACE?
IT'S NOTHING...
TMP
WHOA...
BOOSH
Reversi, Voice Actress for the Naho Minadori role test vote
1st Place Kanra Natara 1968
2nd Place Nanami Otsuki 961
3rd Place Mikan Tanaka 898
4th Place Sao Majima 680
5th Place Miho Azuki 603
6th Place Aki Arishima 583
5th Place Miho Azuki
M-MAYBE THIS AUDITION ISN'T GOING TO GO WELL?
NO... THEY HAVEN'T EVEN STARTED STREAMING THE VIDEO, SO ONLY HARDCORE FANS WOULD TAKE PART IN SOMETHING LIKE THIS...
ONCE THEY START TO STREAM IT, I'M SURE AZUKI WILL GET FIRST PLACE...
THEN STOP LOOKING AT SOMETHING LIKE THIS!
YES, I'M SORRY.
IF AZUKI HASN'T SAID ANYTHING TO YOU, YOU PROBABLY SHOULDN'T SAY ANYTHING TO HER...
WHAT SHOULD I TELL MIHO TO CHEER HER ON?
R-RIGHT.

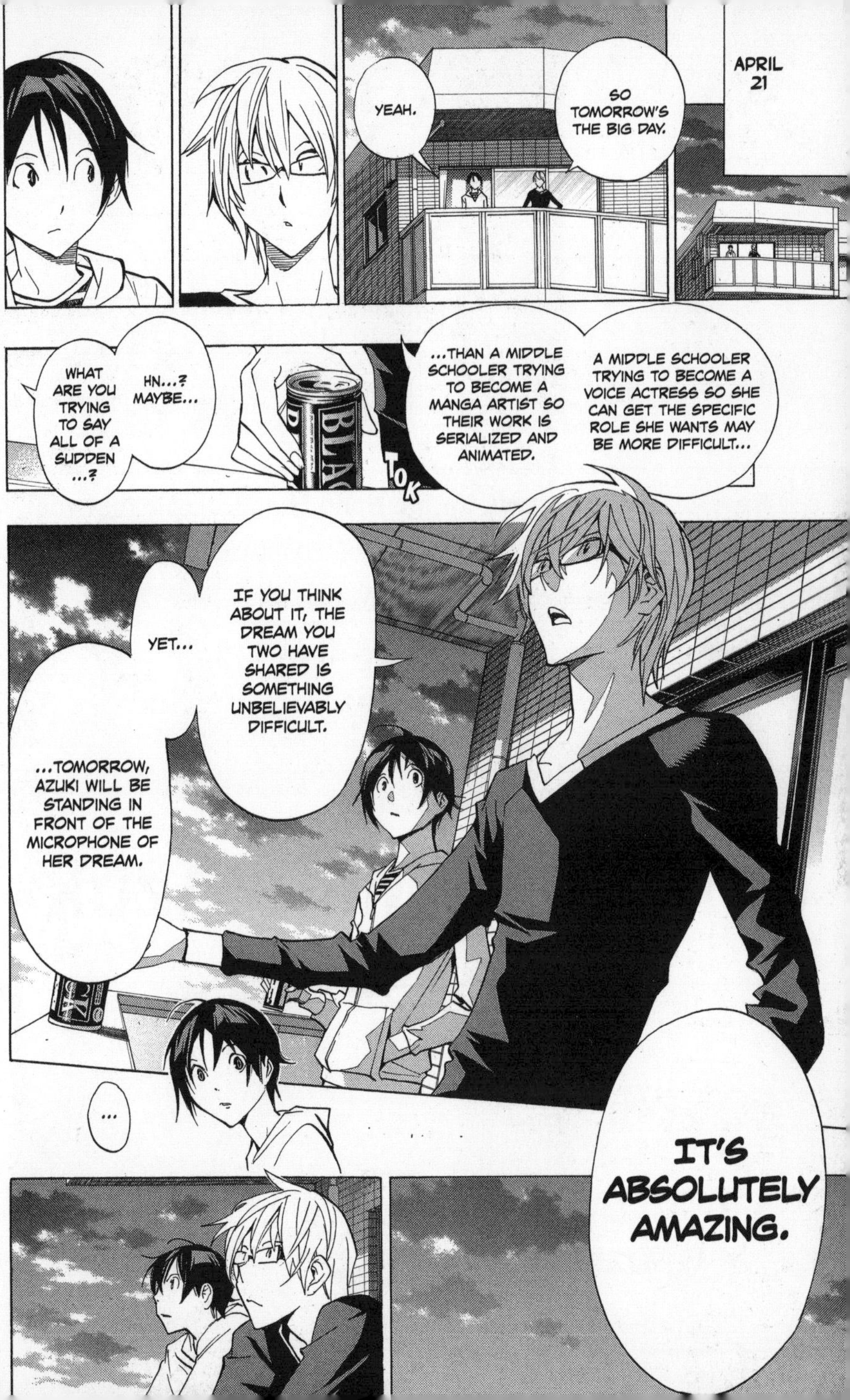
APRIL 21
SO TOMORROW'S THE BIG DAY.
YEAH.
A MIDDLE SCHOOLER TRYING TO BECOME A VOICE ACTRESS SO SHE CAN GET THE SPECIFIC ROLE SHE WANTS MAY BE MORE DIFFICULT...
...THAN A MIDDLE SCHOOLER TRYING TO BECOME A MANGA ARTIST SO THEIR WORK IS SERIALIZED AND ANIMATED.
TOK
HN...? MAYBE...
WHAT ARE YOU TRYING TO SAY ALL OF A SUDDEN...?
IF YOU THINK ABOUT IT, THE DREAM YOU TWO HAVE SHARED IS SOMETHING UNBELIEVABLY DIFFICULT.
YET...
...TOMORROW, AZUKI WILL BE STANDING IN FRONT OF THE MICROPHONE OF HER DREAM.
...
IT'S ABSOLUTELY AMAZING.

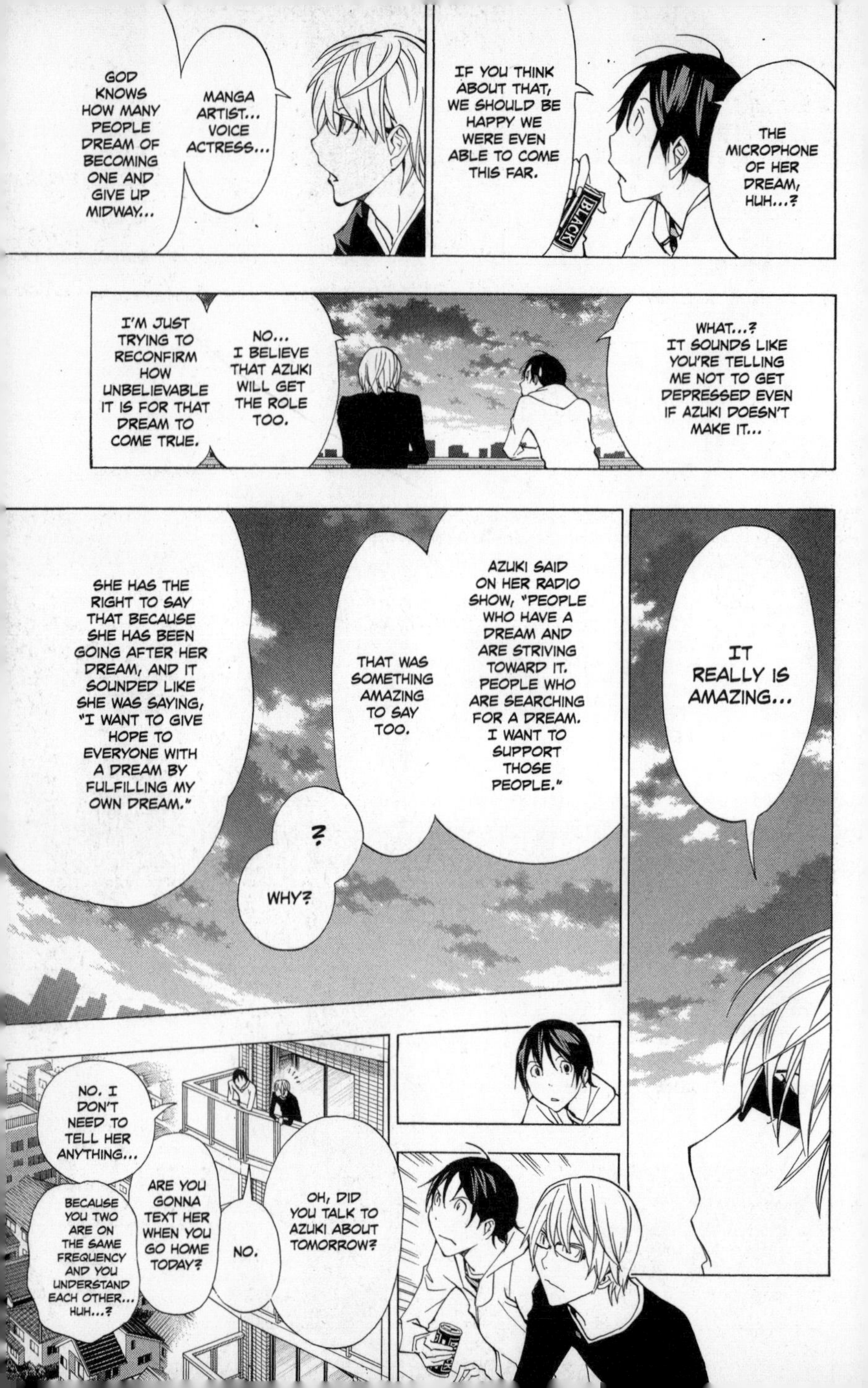
THE MICROPHONE OF HER DREAM, HUH...?
IF YOU THINK ABOUT THAT, WE SHOULD BE HAPPY WE WERE EVEN ABLE TO COME THIS FAR.
BLACK
MANGA ARTIST... VOICE ACTRESS...
GOD KNOWS HOW MANY PEOPLE DREAM OF BECOMING ONE AND GIVE UP MIDWAY...
WHAT...? IT SOUNDS LIKE YOU'RE TELLING ME NOT TO GET DEPRESSED EVEN IF AZUKI DOESN'T MAKE IT...
NO... I BELIEVE THAT AZUKI WILL GET THE ROLE TOO.
I'M JUST TRYING TO RECONFIRM HOW UNBELIEVABLE IT IS FOR THAT DREAM TO COME TRUE.
IT REALLY IS AMAZING...
AZUKI SAID ON HER RADIO SHOW, "PEOPLE WHO HAVE A DREAM AND ARE STRIVING TOWARD IT. PEOPLE WHO ARE SEARCHING FOR A DREAM. I WANT TO SUPPORT THOSE PEOPLE."
THAT WAS SOMETHING AMAZING TO SAY TOO.
SHE HAS THE RIGHT TO SAY THAT BECAUSE SHE HAS BEEN GOING AFTER HER DREAM, AND IT SOUNDED LIKE SHE WAS SAYING, "I WANT TO GIVE HOPE TO EVERYONE WITH A DREAM BY FULFILLING MY OWN DREAM."
?
WHY?
OH, DID YOU TALK TO AZUKI ABOUT TOMORROW?
NO.
ARE YOU GONNA TEXT HER WHEN YOU GO HOME TODAY?
NO. I DON'T NEED TO TELL HER ANYTHING...
BECAUSE YOU TWO ARE ON THE SAME FREQUENCY AND YOU UNDERSTAND EACH OTHER... HUH...?

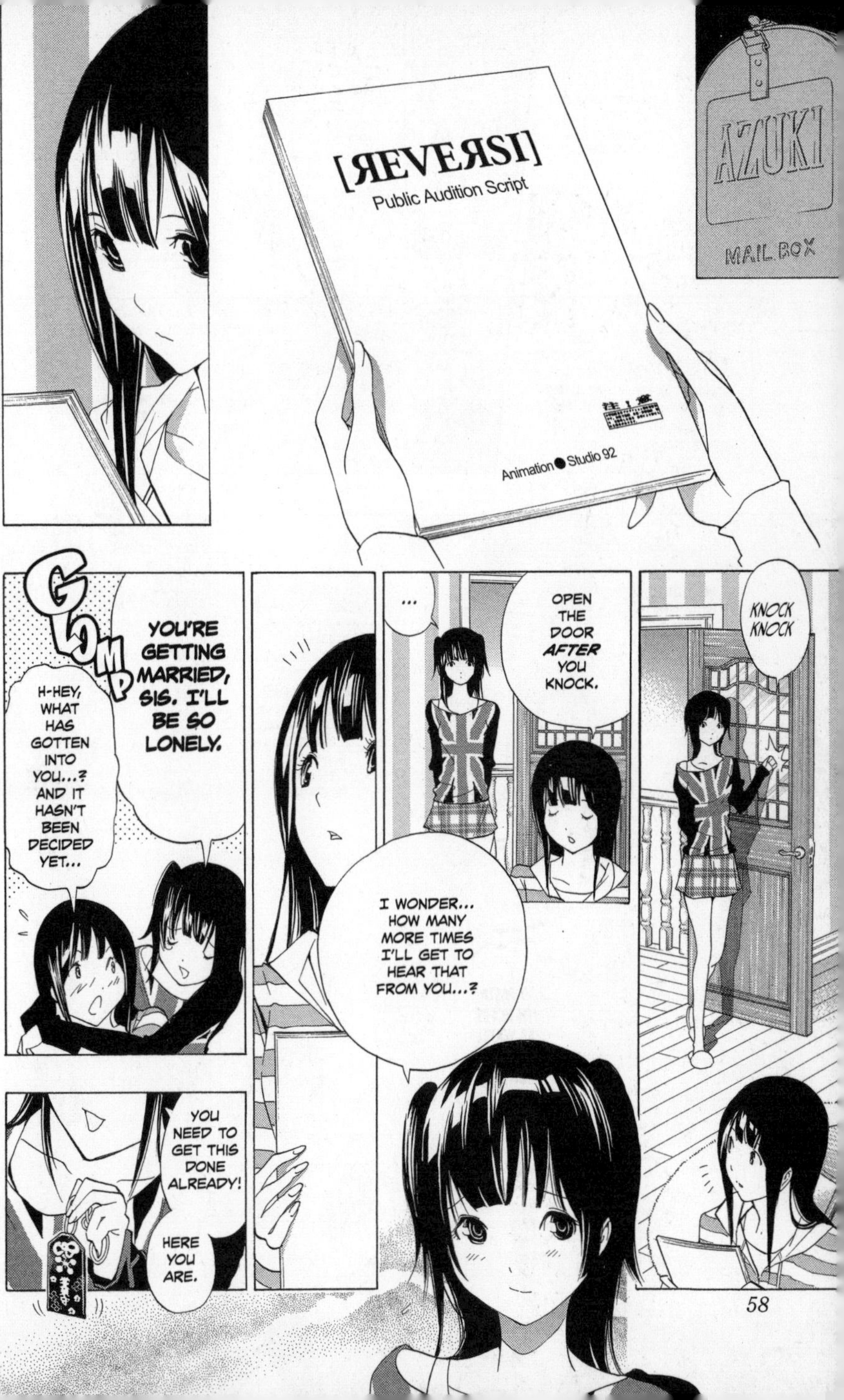

AZUKI
MAIL.BOX
[ЯEVEЯSI]
Public Audition Script
Animation Studio 92
KNOCK KNOCK
OPEN THE DOOR *AFTER* YOU KNOCK.
...
GLOMP
YOU'RE GETTING MARRIED, SIS. I'LL BE SO LONELY.
H-HEY, WHAT HAS GOTTEN INTO YOU...? AND IT HASN'T BEEN DECIDED YET...
I WONDER... HOW MANY MORE TIMES I'LL GET TO HEAR THAT FROM YOU...?
YOU NEED TO GET THIS DONE ALREADY!
HERE YOU ARE.

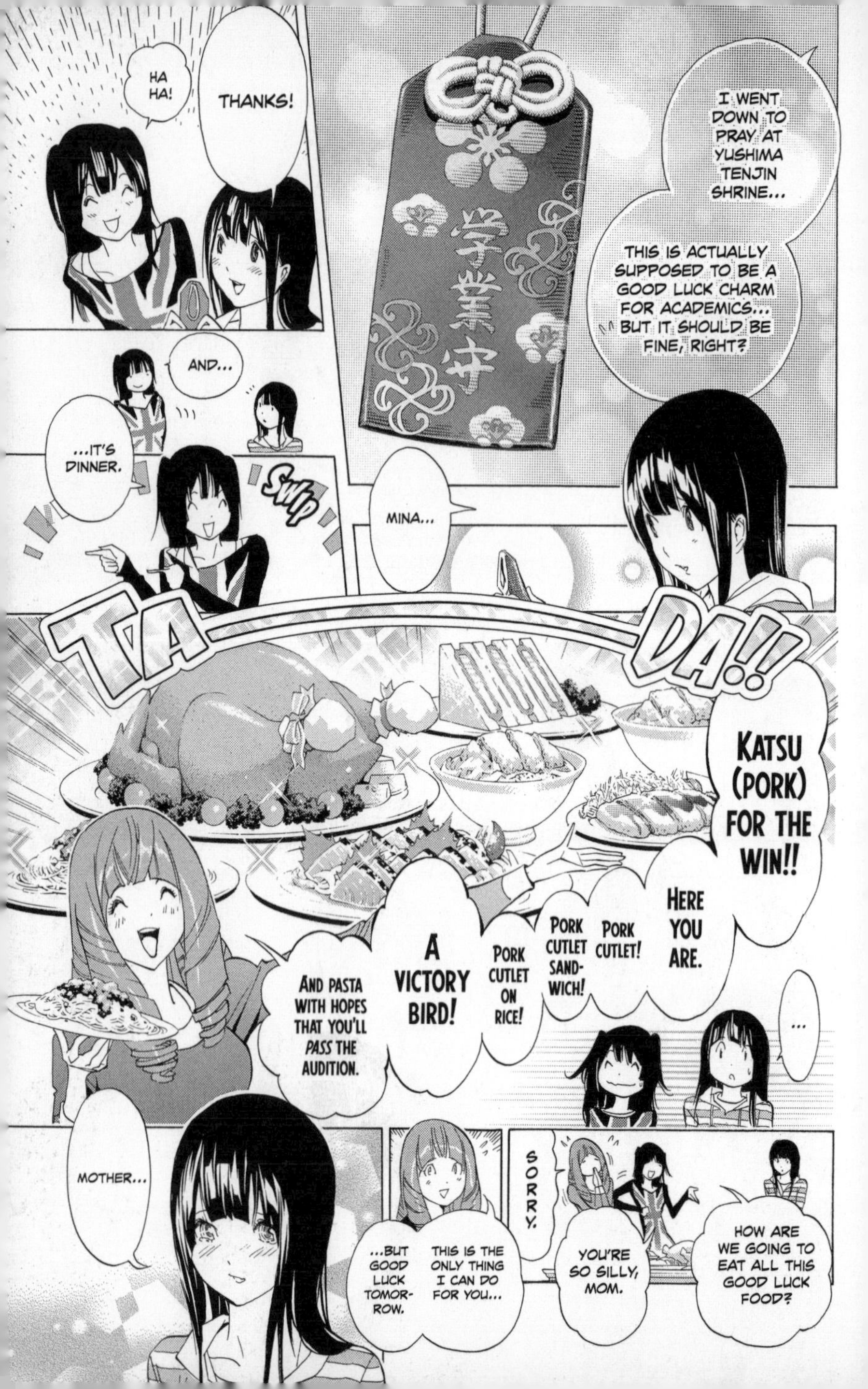

I WENT DOWN TO PRAY AT YUSHIMA TENJIN SHRINE...
THIS IS ACTUALLY SUPPOSED TO BE A GOOD LUCK CHARM FOR ACADEMICS... BUT IT SHOULD BE FINE, RIGHT?
学業守
THANKS!
HA HA!
AND...
...IT'S DINNER.
SWIP
MINA...
TA DA!!
KATSU (PORK) FOR THE WIN!!
HERE YOU ARE.
PORK CUTLET!
PORK CUTLET SANDWICH!
PORK CUTLET ON RICE!
A VICTORY BIRD!
AND PASTA WITH HOPES THAT YOU'LL *PASS* THE AUDITION.
...
HOW ARE WE GOING TO EAT ALL THIS GOOD LUCK FOOD?
YOU'RE SO SILLY, MOM.
SORRY.
THIS IS THE ONLY THING I CAN DO FOR YOU...
...BUT GOOD LUCK TOMORROW.
MOTHER...

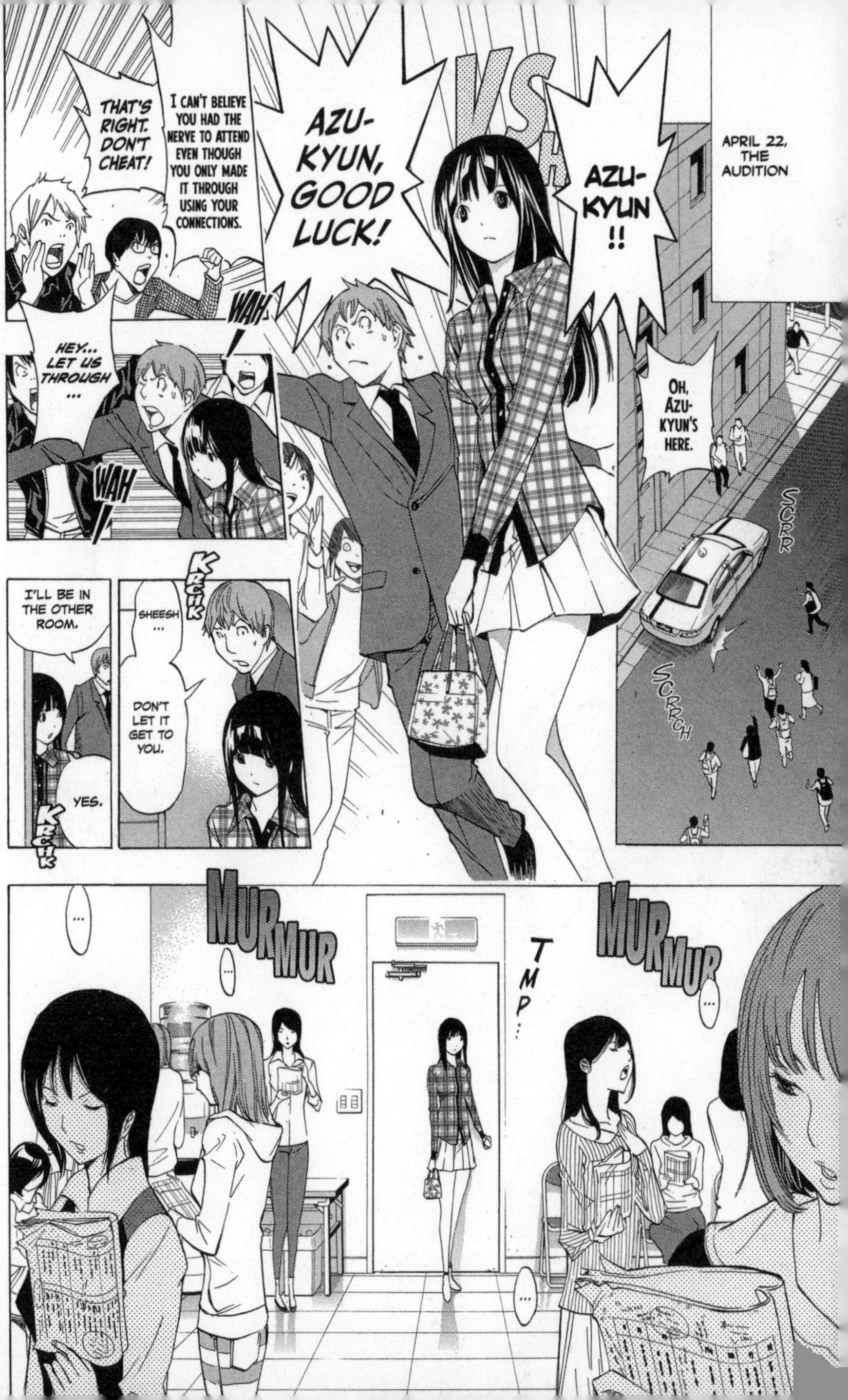

APRIL 22, THE AUDITION
OH, AZU-KYUN'S HERE.
SCRR
SCRRCH
VSH
AZU-KYUN!!
AZU-KYUN, GOOD LUCK!
I CAN'T BELIEVE YOU HAD THE NERVE TO ATTEND EVEN THOUGH YOU ONLY MADE IT THROUGH USING YOUR CONNECTIONS.
THAT'S RIGHT. DON'T CHEAT!
WAH!
HEY... LET US THROUGH...
WAH!
KRCHK
SHEESH...
DON'T LET IT GET TO YOU.
I'LL BE IN THE OTHER ROOM.
YES.
KRCHK
MURMUR
...
TMP...
MURMUR
...
...
...

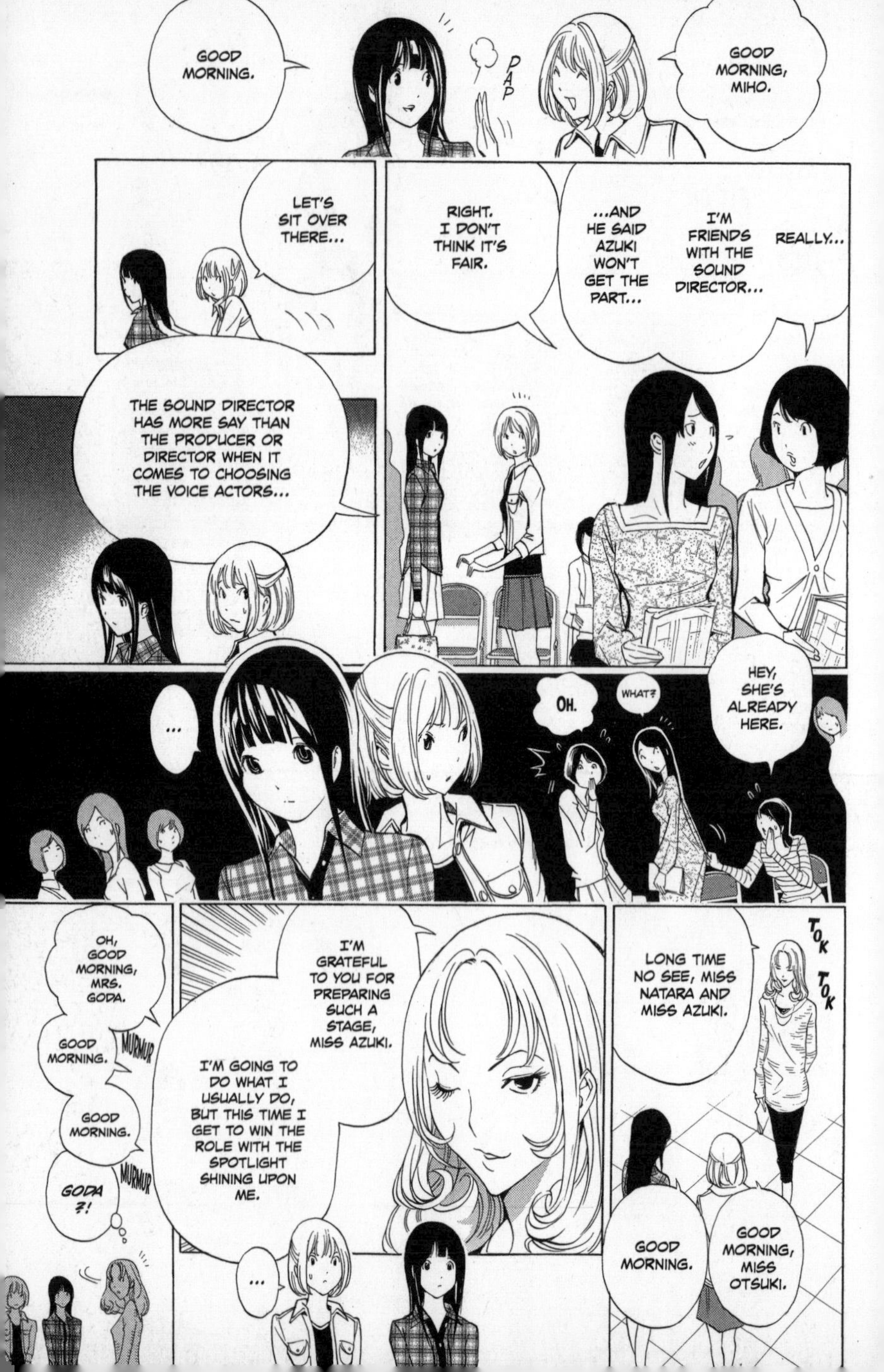
GOOD MORNING, MIHO.
PAP
GOOD MORNING.
REALLY...
I'M FRIENDS WITH THE SOUND DIRECTOR...
...AND HE SAID AZUKI WON'T GET THE PART...
RIGHT. I DON'T THINK IT'S FAIR.
LET'S SIT OVER THERE...
THE SOUND DIRECTOR HAS MORE SAY THAN THE PRODUCER OR DIRECTOR WHEN IT COMES TO CHOOSING THE VOICE ACTORS...
HEY, SHE'S ALREADY HERE.
WHAT?
OH.
...
TOK TOK
LONG TIME NO SEE, MISS NATARA AND MISS AZUKI.
GOOD MORNING, MISS OTSUKI.
GOOD MORNING.
I'M GRATEFUL TO YOU FOR PREPARING SUCH A STAGE, MISS AZUKI.
I'M GOING TO DO WHAT I USUALLY DO, BUT THIS TIME I GET TO WIN THE ROLE WITH THE SPOTLIGHT SHINING UPON ME.
...
OH, GOOD MORNING, MRS. GODA.
GOOD MORNING.
MURMUR
GOOD MORNING.
MURMUR
GODA?!

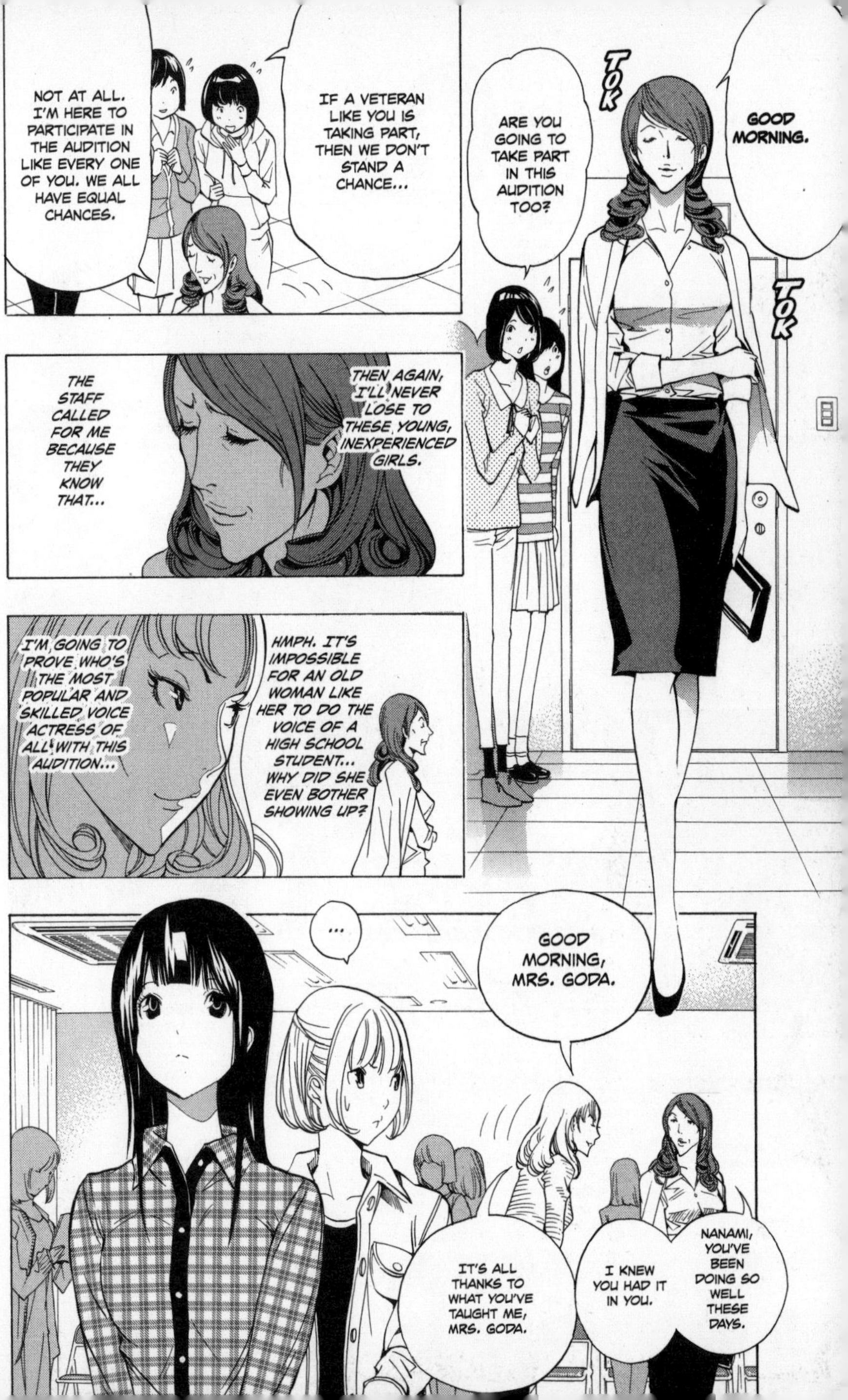
GOOD MORNING.
TOK
ARE YOU GOING TO TAKE PART IN THIS AUDITION TOO?
TOK
IF A VETERAN LIKE YOU IS TAKING PART, THEN WE DON'T STAND A CHANCE...
NOT AT ALL. I'M HERE TO PARTICIPATE IN THE AUDITION LIKE EVERY ONE OF YOU. WE ALL HAVE EQUAL CHANCES.
THEN AGAIN, I'LL NEVER LOSE TO THESE YOUNG, INEXPERIENCED GIRLS.
THE STAFF CALLED FOR ME BECAUSE THEY KNOW THAT...
HMPH. IT'S IMPOSSIBLE FOR AN OLD WOMAN LIKE HER TO DO THE VOICE OF A HIGH SCHOOL STUDENT... WHY DID SHE EVEN BOTHER SHOWING UP?
I'M GOING TO PROVE WHO'S THE MOST POPULAR AND SKILLED VOICE ACTRESS OF ALL WITH THIS AUDITION...
GOOD MORNING, MRS. GODA.
...
NANAMI, YOU'VE BEEN DOING SO WELL THESE DAYS.
I KNEW YOU HAD IT IN YOU.
IT'S ALL THANKS TO WHAT YOU'VE TAUGHT ME, MRS. GODA.

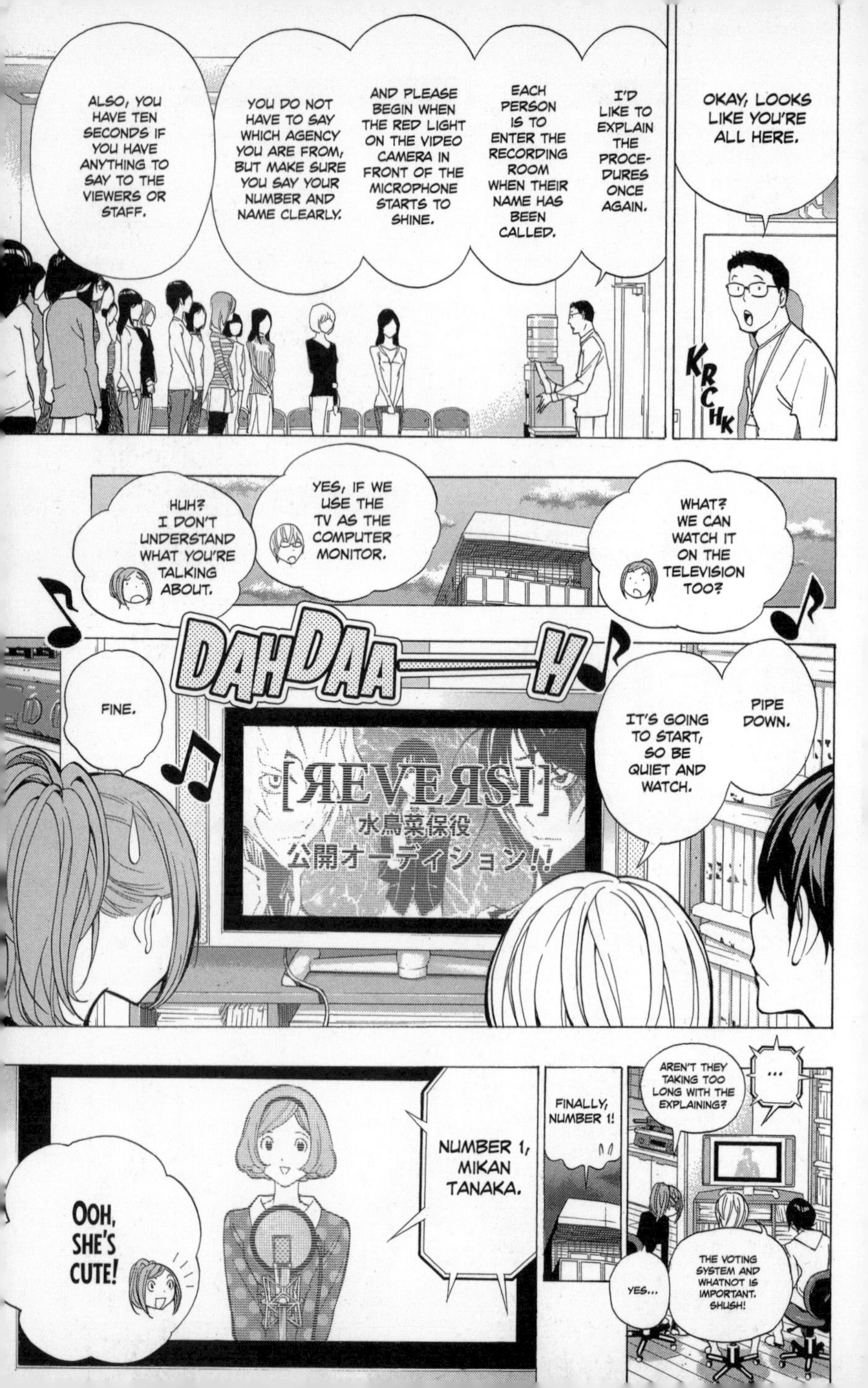
OKAY, LOOKS LIKE YOU'RE ALL HERE.
KRCHK
I'D LIKE TO EXPLAIN THE PROCEDURES ONCE AGAIN.
EACH PERSON IS TO ENTER THE RECORDING ROOM WHEN THEIR NAME HAS BEEN CALLED.
AND PLEASE BEGIN WHEN THE RED LIGHT ON THE VIDEO CAMERA IN FRONT OF THE MICROPHONE STARTS TO SHINE.
YOU DO NOT HAVE TO SAY WHICH AGENCY YOU ARE FROM, BUT MAKE SURE YOU SAY YOUR NUMBER AND NAME CLEARLY.
ALSO, YOU HAVE TEN SECONDS IF YOU HAVE ANYTHING TO SAY TO THE VIEWERS OR STAFF.
WHAT? WE CAN WATCH IT ON THE TELEVISION TOO?
YES, IF WE USE THE TV AS THE COMPUTER MONITOR.
HUH? I DON'T UNDERSTAND WHAT YOU'RE TALKING ABOUT.
DAHDAA—H
PIPE DOWN.
IT'S GOING TO START, SO BE QUIET AND WATCH.
[REVERSI]
水鳥菜保役
公開オーディション!!
FINE.
...
AREN'T THEY TAKING TOO LONG WITH THE EXPLAINING?
THE VOTING SYSTEM AND WHATNOT IS IMPORTANT. SHUSH!
YES...
FINALLY, NUMBER 1!
NUMBER 1, MIKAN TANAKA.
OOH, SHE'S CUTE!

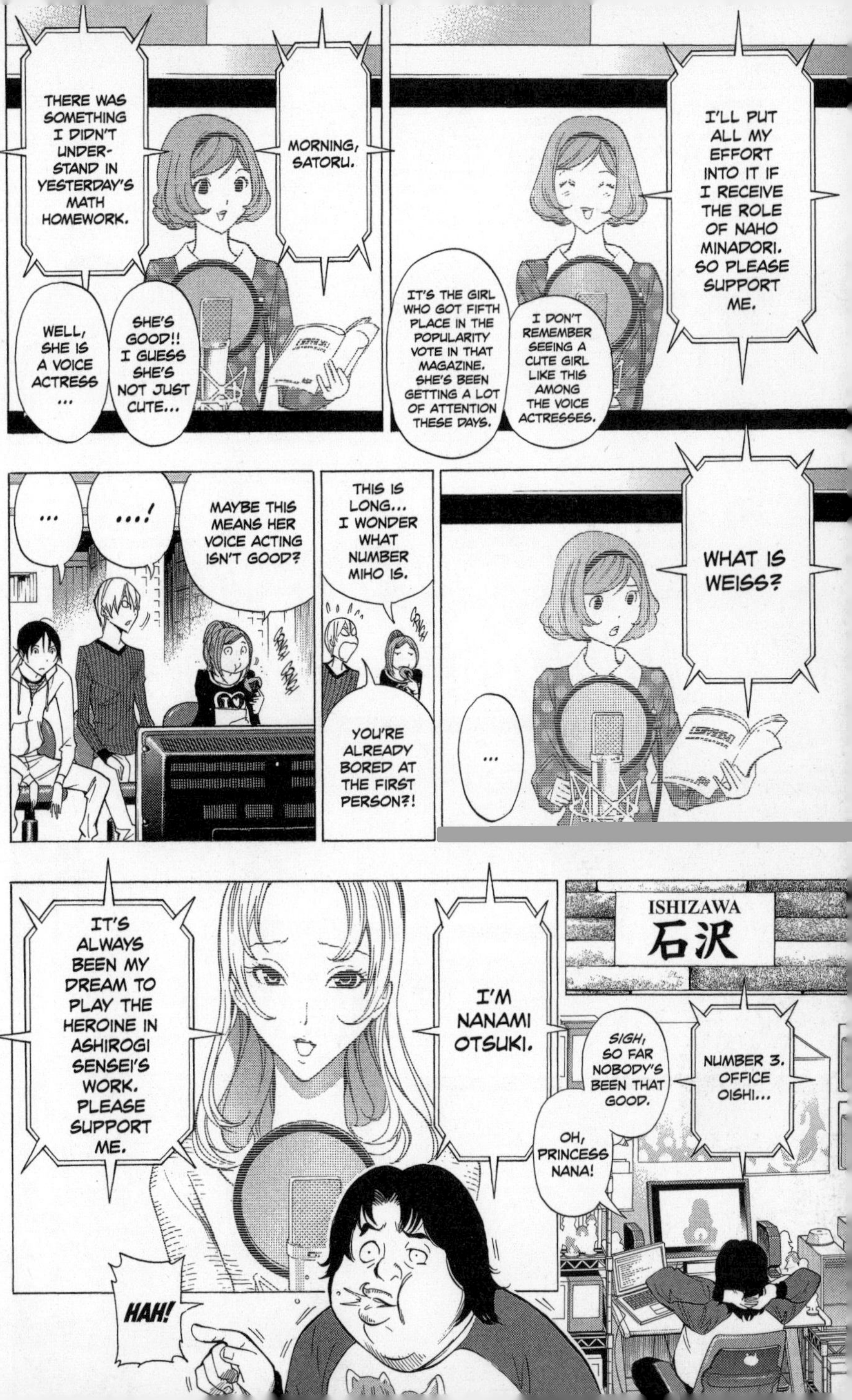
I'LL PUT ALL MY EFFORT INTO IT IF I RECEIVE THE ROLE OF NAHO MINADORI. SO PLEASE SUPPORT ME.
I DON'T REMEMBER SEEING A CUTE GIRL LIKE THIS AMONG THE VOICE ACTRESSES.
IT'S THE GIRL WHO GOT FIFTH PLACE IN THE POPULARITY VOTE IN THAT MAGAZINE. SHE'S BEEN GETTING A LOT OF ATTENTION THESE DAYS.
MORNING, SATORU.
THERE WAS SOMETHING I DIDN'T UNDER-STAND IN YESTERDAY'S MATH HOMEWORK.
SHE'S GOOD!! I GUESS SHE'S NOT JUST CUTE...
WELL, SHE IS A VOICE ACTRESS ...
WHAT IS WEISS?
...
THIS IS LONG... I WONDER WHAT NUMBER MIHO IS.
YOU'RE ALREADY BORED AT THE FIRST PERSON?!
MAYBE THIS MEANS HER VOICE ACTING ISN'T GOOD?
...!
...
ISHIZAWA
石沢
NUMBER 3. OFFICE OISHI...
SIGH, SO FAR NOBODY'S BEEN THAT GOOD.
OH, PRINCESS NANA!
I'M NANAMI OTSUKI.
IT'S ALWAYS BEEN MY DREAM TO PLAY THE HEROINE IN ASHIROGI SENSEI'S WORK. PLEASE SUPPORT ME.
HAH!

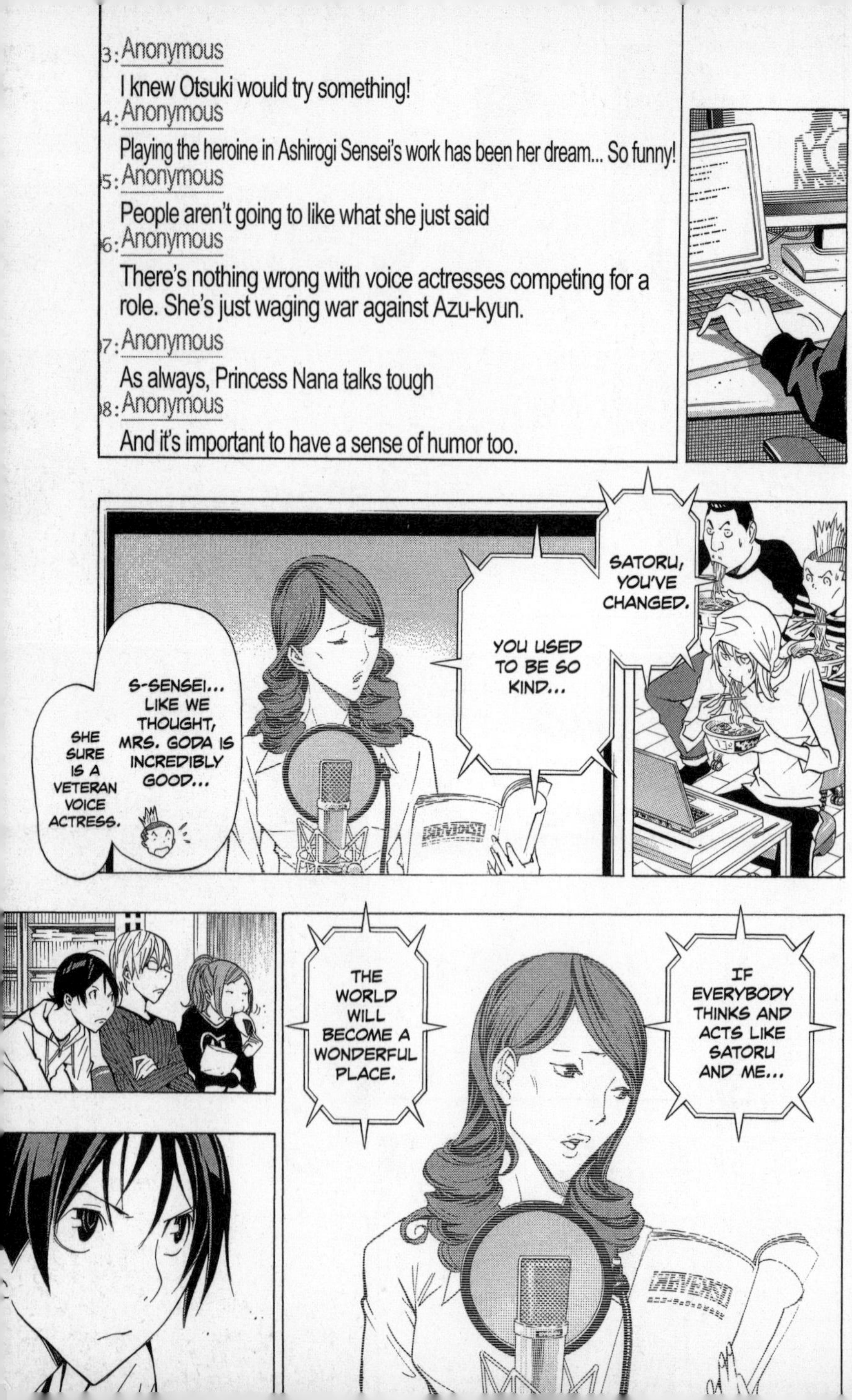
3: Anonymous
I knew Otsuki would try something!
4: Anonymous
Playing the heroine in Ashirogi Sensei's work has been her dream... So funny!
5: Anonymous
People aren't going to like what she just said
6: Anonymous
There's nothing wrong with voice actresses competing for a role. She's just waging war against Azu-kyun.
7: Anonymous
As always, Princess Nana talks tough
8: Anonymous
And it's important to have a sense of humor too.
SATORU, YOU'VE CHANGED.
YOU USED TO BE SO KIND...
S-SENSEI... LIKE WE THOUGHT, MRS. GODA IS INCREDIBLY GOOD...
SHE SURE IS A VETERAN VOICE ACTRESS.
IF EVERYBODY THINKS AND ACTS LIKE SATORU AND ME...
THE WORLD WILL BECOME A WONDERFUL PLACE.

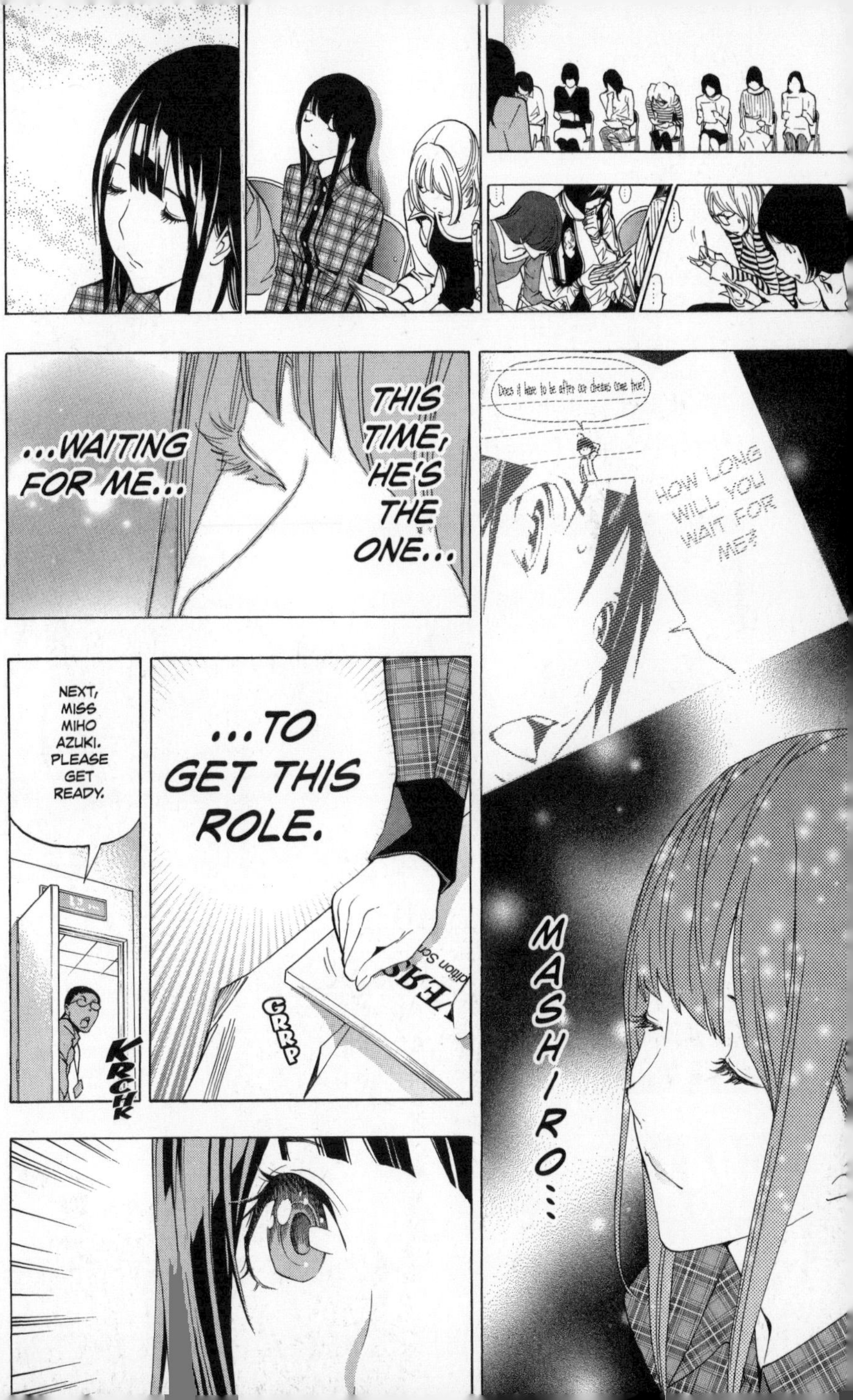
Does it have to be after our dreams come true?
HOW LONG WILL YOU WAIT FOR ME?
MASHIRO...
THIS TIME, HE'S THE ONE...
...WAITING FOR ME...
...TO GET THIS ROLE.
GRRP
NEXT, MISS MIHO AZUKI. PLEASE GET READY.
KRCHK

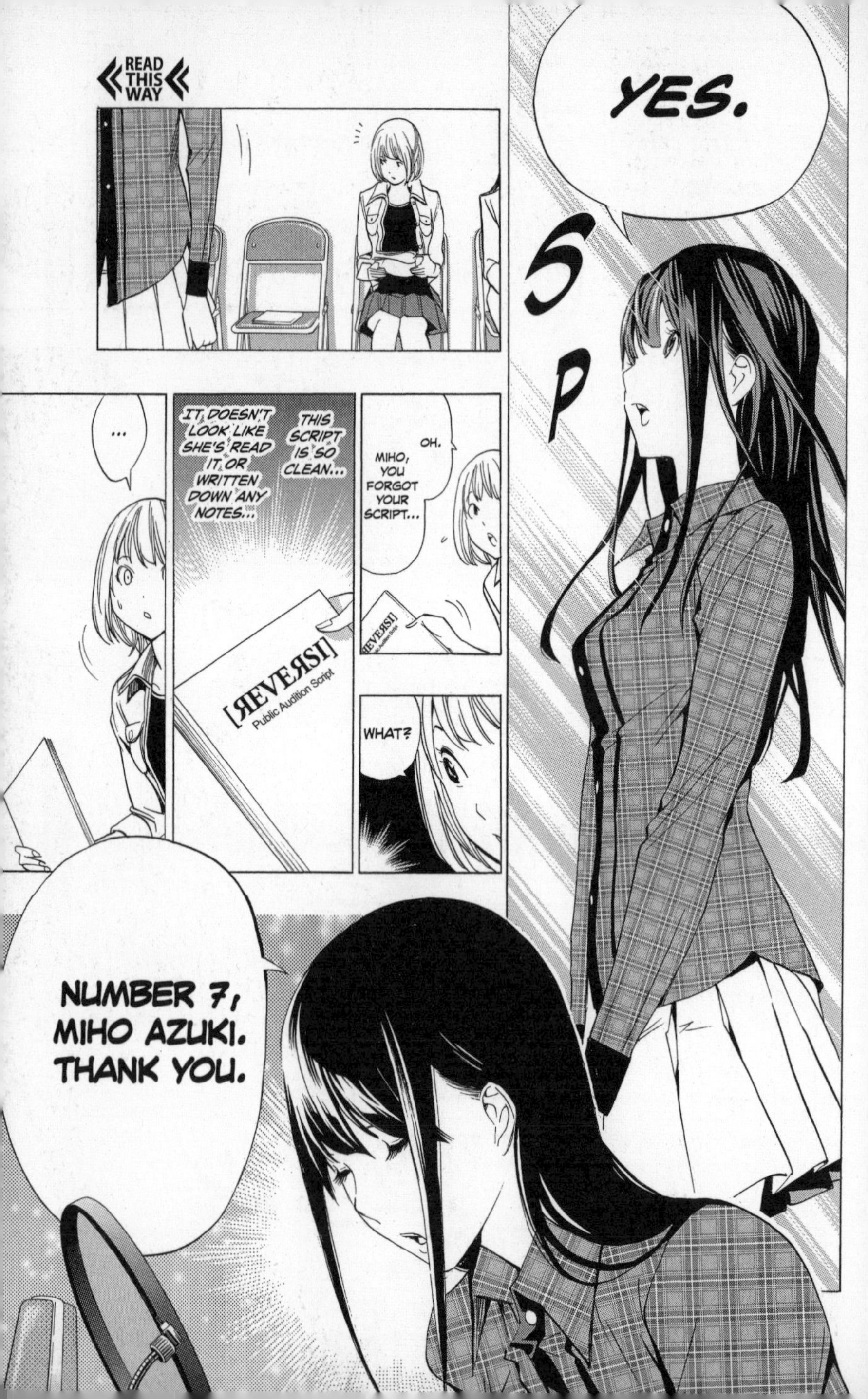
READ THIS WAY
YES.
SP
OH.
MIHO, YOU FORGOT YOUR SCRIPT...
WHAT?
THIS SCRIPT IS SO CLEAN...
IT DOESN'T LOOK LIKE SHE'S READ IT OR WRITTEN DOWN ANY NOTES...
[ЯEVEЯSI]
Public Audition Script
...
NUMBER 7, MIHO AZUKI. THANK YOU.

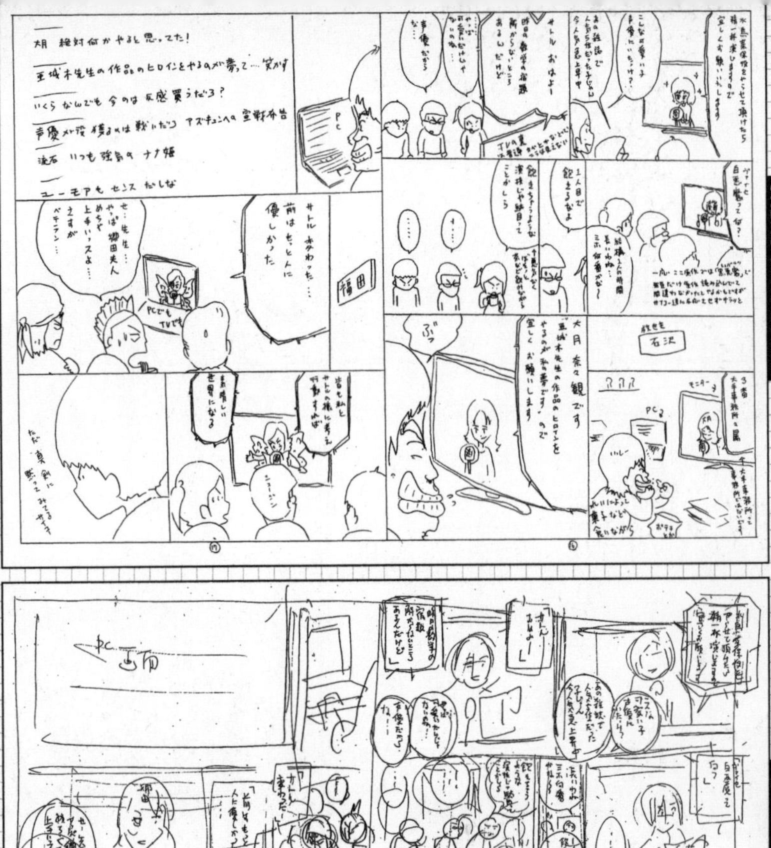
大月 絶対何かやると思ってた!
亜城木先生の作品のヒロインをやるのが夢って…笑かす
いくらなんでも 今のは反感買うだろ?
声優が役選ぶのは戦いだろ アズキュンへの宣戦布告
流石 いつも強気の ナナ姫
ユーモアもセンスだしな

OHBA'S STORYBOARD

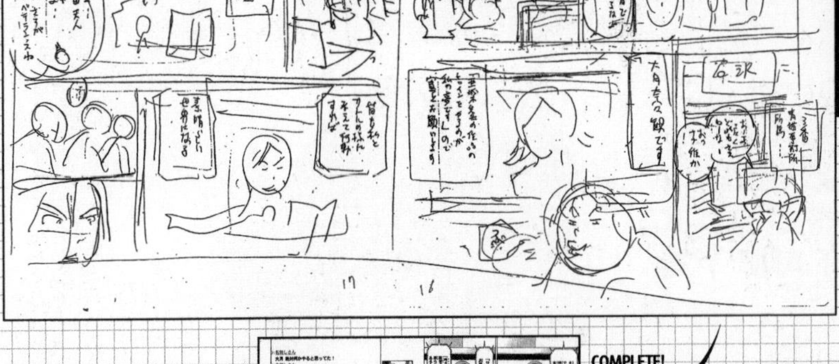

OBATA'S STORYBOARD

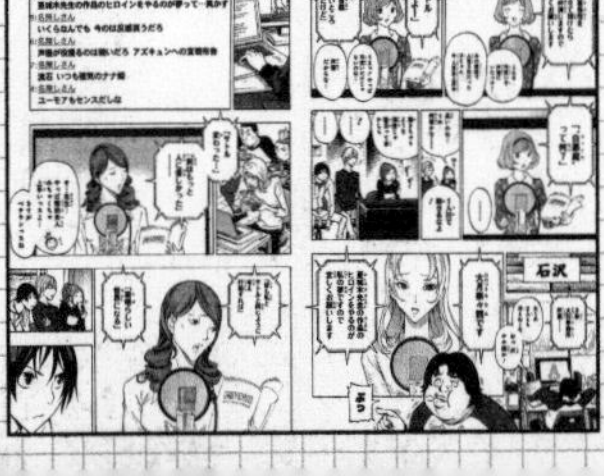

COMPLETE!

*CREATOR STORYBOARDS AND FINISHED PAGES IN JAPANESE

BAKUMAN。 vol.20

"Until the Final Draft Is Complete"

Chapter 171, pp. 68-69

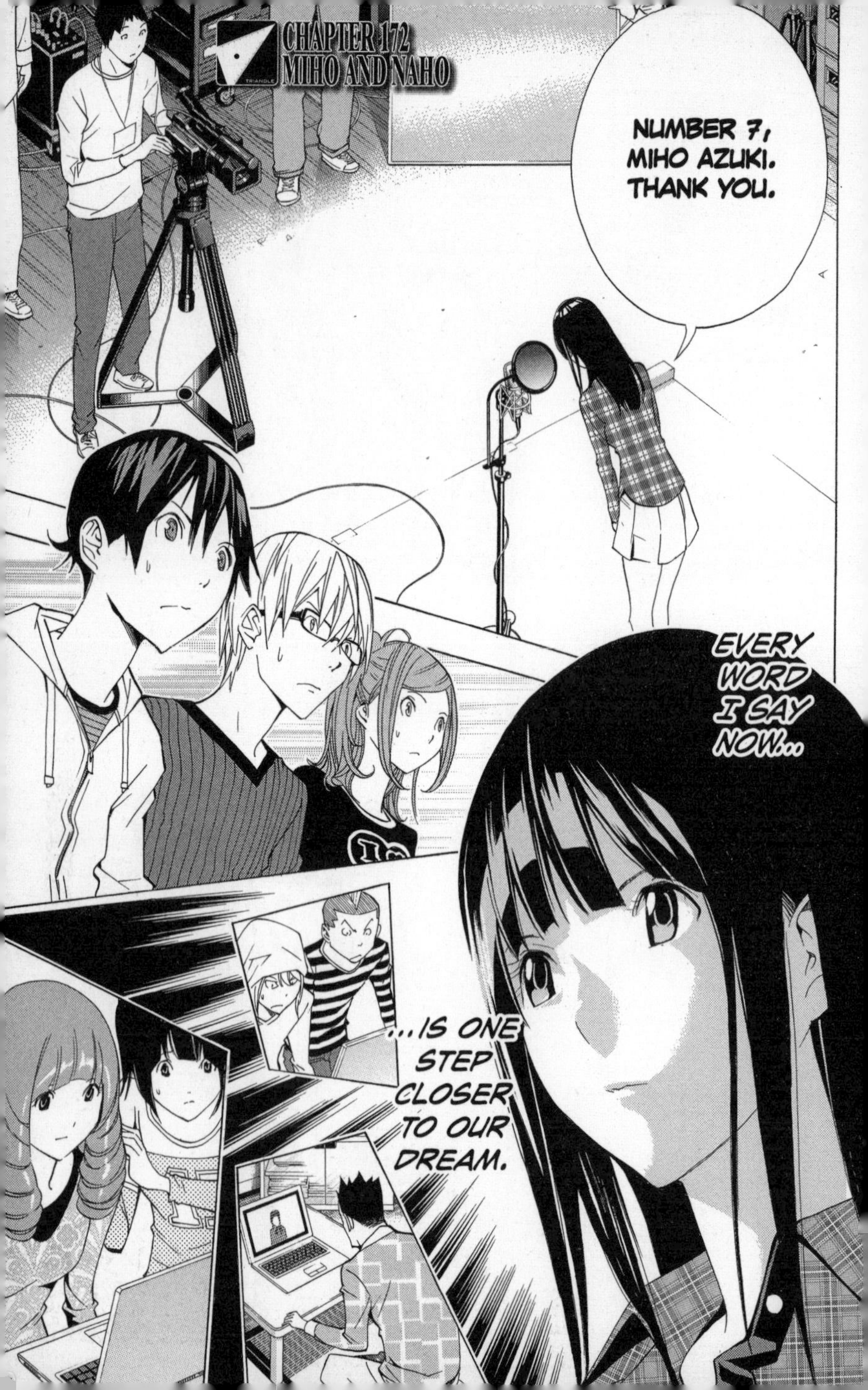
CHAPTER 172
MIHO AND NAHO
TRIANGLE
NUMBER 7, MIHO AZUKI. THANK YOU.
EVERY WORD I SAY NOW...
...IS ONE STEP CLOSER TO OUR DREAM.

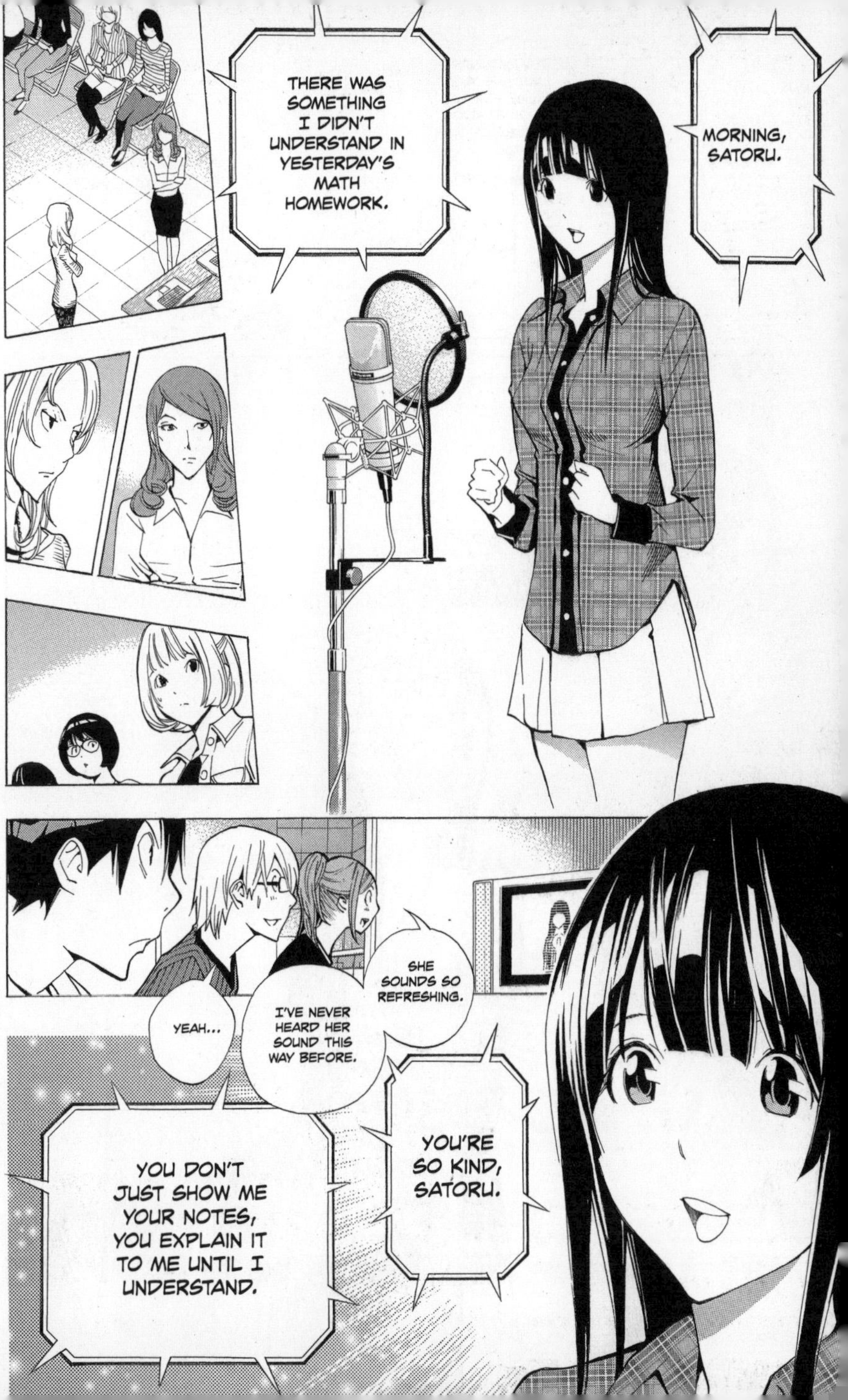
MORNING, SATORU.
THERE WAS SOMETHING I DIDN'T UNDERSTAND IN YESTERDAY'S MATH HOMEWORK.
SHE SOUNDS SO REFRESHING.
I'VE NEVER HEARD HER SOUND THIS WAY BEFORE.
YEAH...
YOU'RE SO KIND, SATORU.
YOU DON'T JUST SHOW ME YOUR NOTES, YOU EXPLAIN IT TO ME UNTIL I UNDERSTAND.

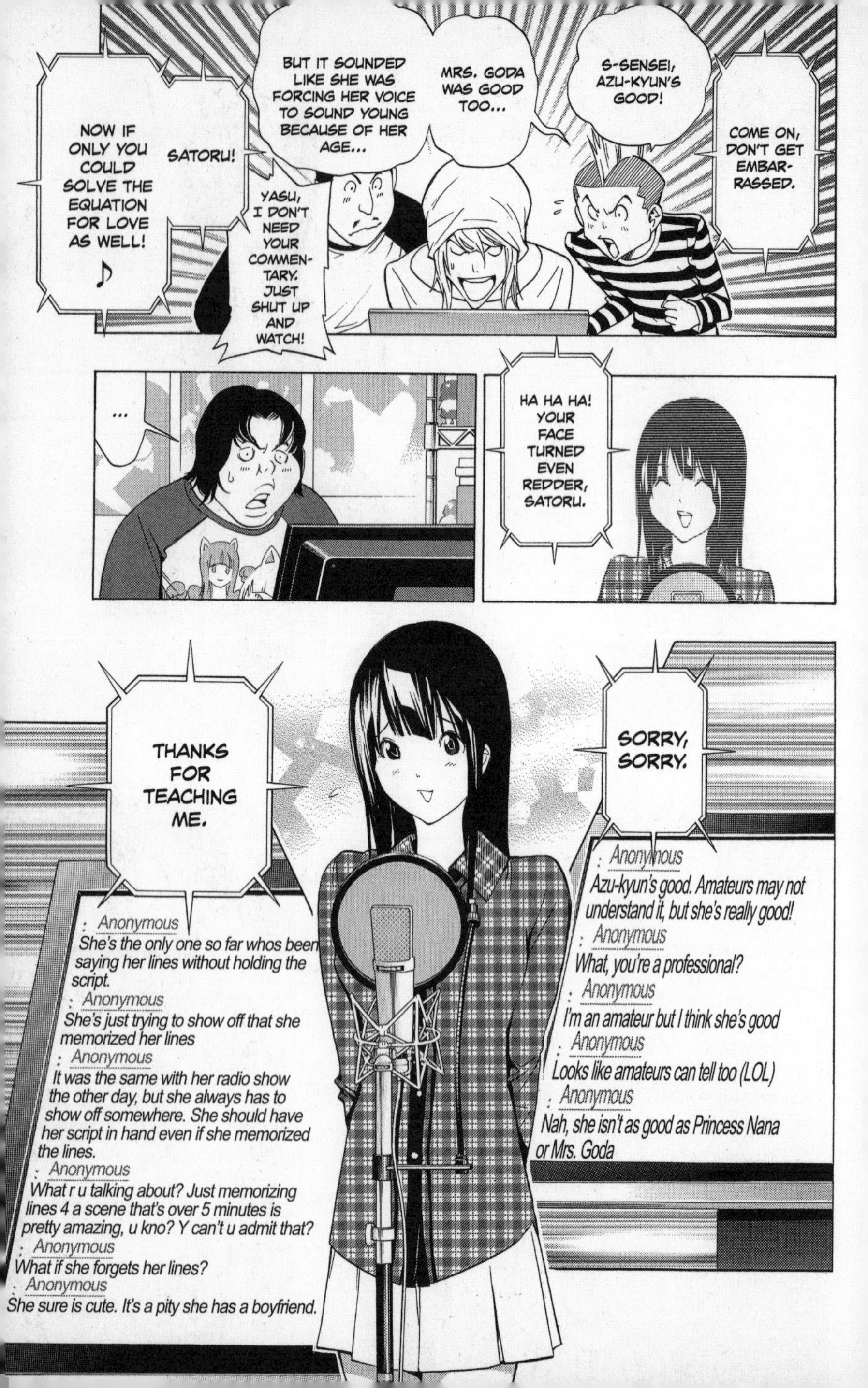
COME ON, DON'T GET EMBARRASSED.
S-SENSEI, AZU-KYUN'S GOOD!
MRS. GODA WAS GOOD TOO...
BUT IT SOUNDED LIKE SHE WAS FORCING HER VOICE TO SOUND YOUNG BECAUSE OF HER AGE...
YASU, I DON'T NEED YOUR COMMENTARY. JUST SHUT UP AND WATCH!
SATORU!
NOW IF ONLY YOU COULD SOLVE THE EQUATION FOR LOVE AS WELL! ♪
HA HA HA! YOUR FACE TURNED EVEN REDDER, SATORU.
...
SORRY, SORRY.
THANKS FOR TEACHING ME.
: Anonymous
Azu-kyun's good. Amateurs may not understand it, but she's really good!
: Anonymous
What, you're a professional?
: Anonymous
I'm an amateur but I think she's good
: Anonymous
Looks like amateurs can tell too (LOL)
: Anonymous
Nah, she isn't as good as Princess Nana or Mrs. Goda
: Anonymous
She's the only one so far whos been saying her lines without holding the script.
: Anonymous
She's just trying to show off that she memorized her lines
: Anonymous
It was the same with her radio show the other day, but she always has to show off somewhere. She should have her script in hand even if she memorized the lines.
: Anonymous
What r u talking about? Just memorizing lines 4 a scene that's over 5 minutes is pretty amazing, u kno? Y can't u admit that?
: Anonymous
What if she forgets her lines?
: Anonymous
She sure is cute. It's a pity she has a boyfriend.

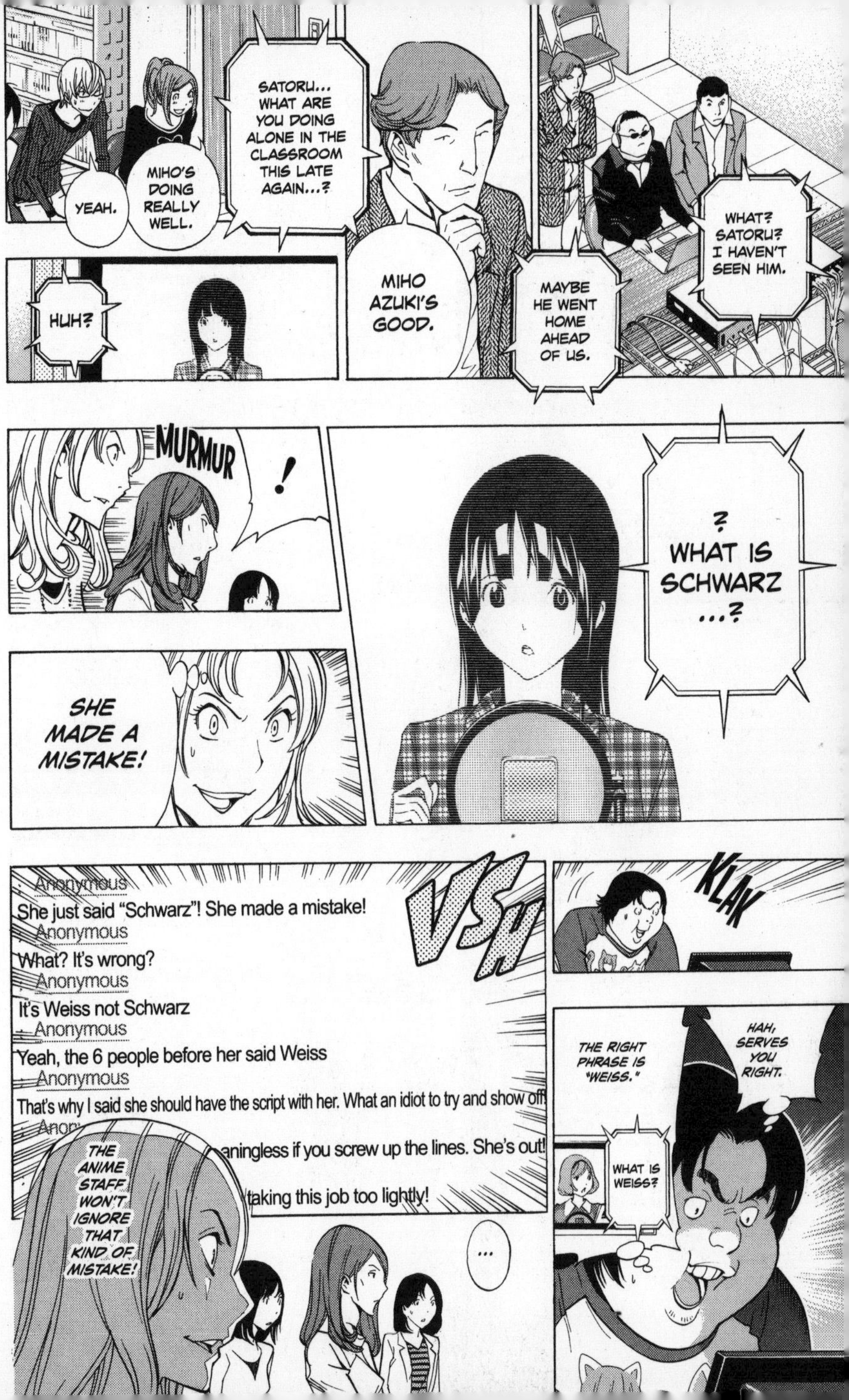

WHAT? SATORU? I HAVEN'T SEEN HIM.
MAYBE HE WENT HOME AHEAD OF US.
SATORU... WHAT ARE YOU DOING ALONE IN THE CLASSROOM THIS LATE AGAIN...?
MIHO AZUKI'S GOOD.
MIHO'S DOING REALLY WELL.
YEAH.
HUH?
? WHAT IS SCHWARZ ...?
MURMUR
!
SHE MADE A MISTAKE!
KLAK
HAH, SERVES YOU RIGHT.
THE RIGHT PHRASE IS "WEISS."
WHAT IS WEISS?
VSH
Anonymous
She just said "Schwarz"! She made a mistake!
Anonymous
What? It's wrong?
Anonymous
It's Weiss not Schwarz
Anonymous
Yeah, the 6 people before her said Weiss
Anonymous
That's why I said she should have the script with her. What an idiot to try and show off!
aningless if you screw up the lines. She's out!
taking this job too lightly!
THE ANIME STAFF WON'T IGNORE THAT KIND OF MISTAKE!
...

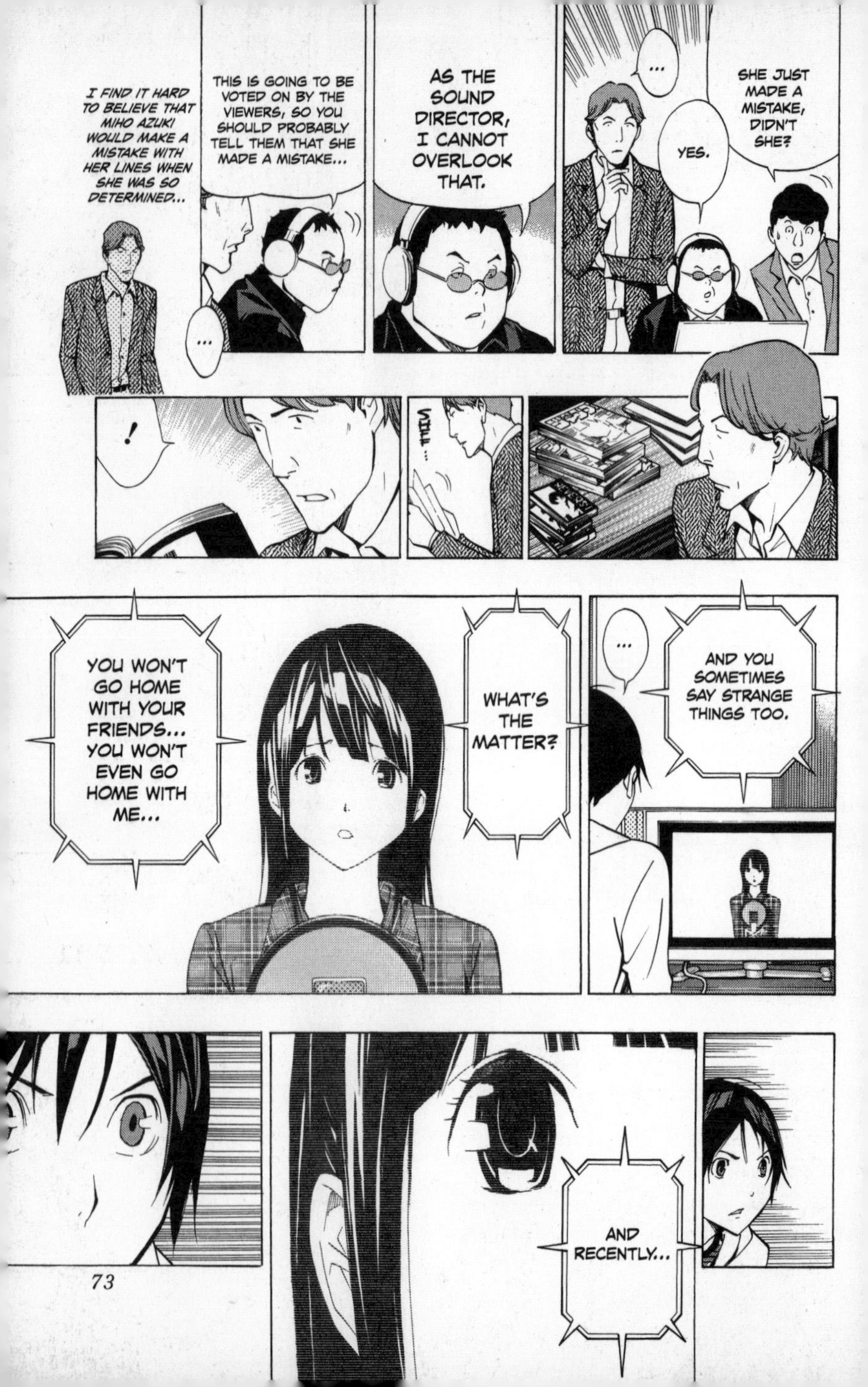
...
SHE JUST MADE A MISTAKE, DIDN'T SHE?
YES.
AS THE SOUND DIRECTOR, I CANNOT OVERLOOK THAT.
THIS IS GOING TO BE VOTED ON BY THE VIEWERS, SO YOU SHOULD PROBABLY TELL THEM THAT SHE MADE A MISTAKE...
...
I FIND IT HARD TO BELIEVE THAT MIHO AZUKI WOULD MAKE A MISTAKE WITH HER LINES WHEN SHE WAS SO DETERMINED...
!
...
AND YOU SOMETIMES SAY STRANGE THINGS TOO.
WHAT'S THE MATTER?
YOU WON'T GO HOME WITH YOUR FRIENDS... YOU WON'T EVEN GO HOME WITH ME...
AND RECENTLY...

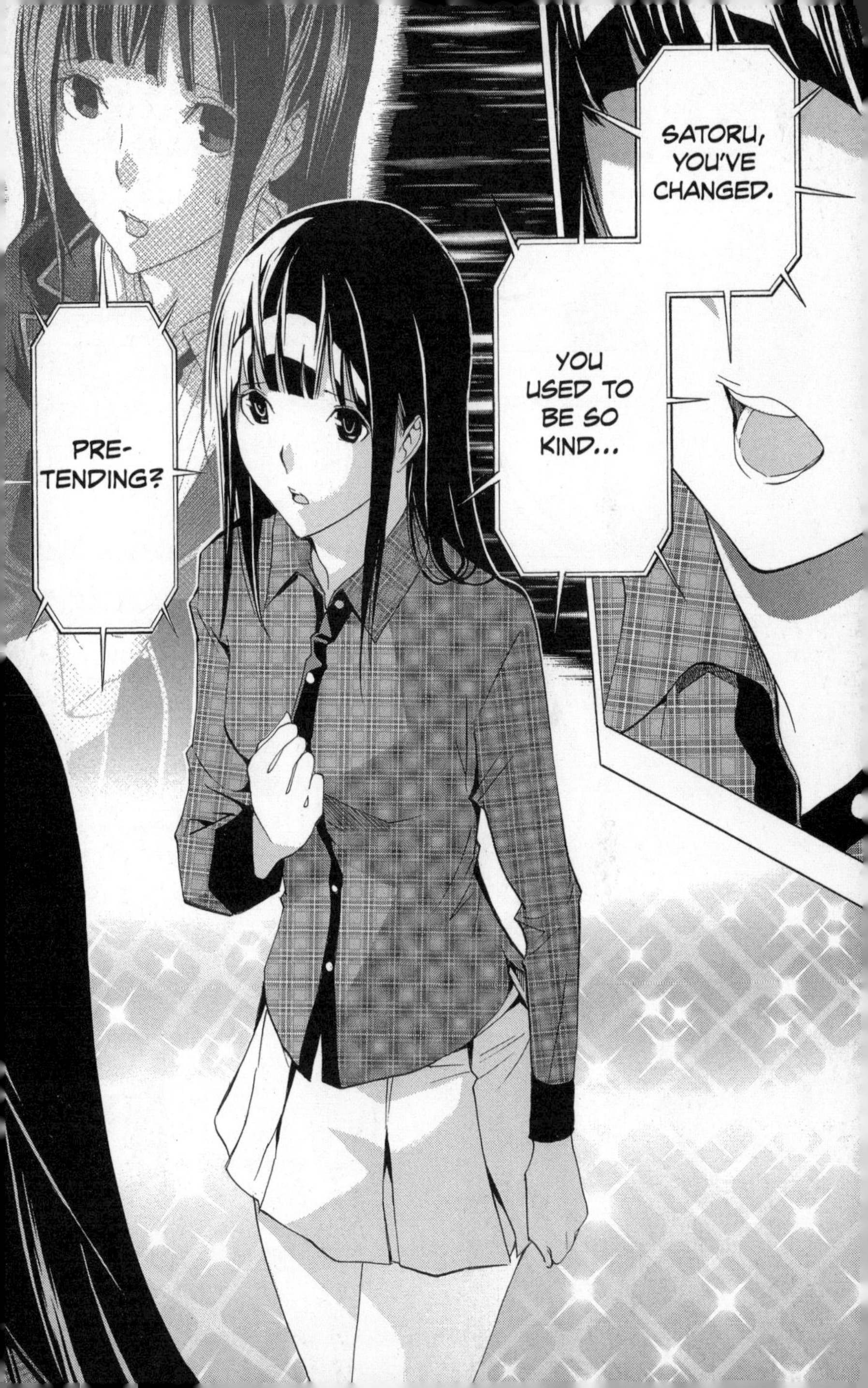
SATORU, YOU'VE CHANGED.
YOU USED TO BE SO KIND...
PRE-TENDING?

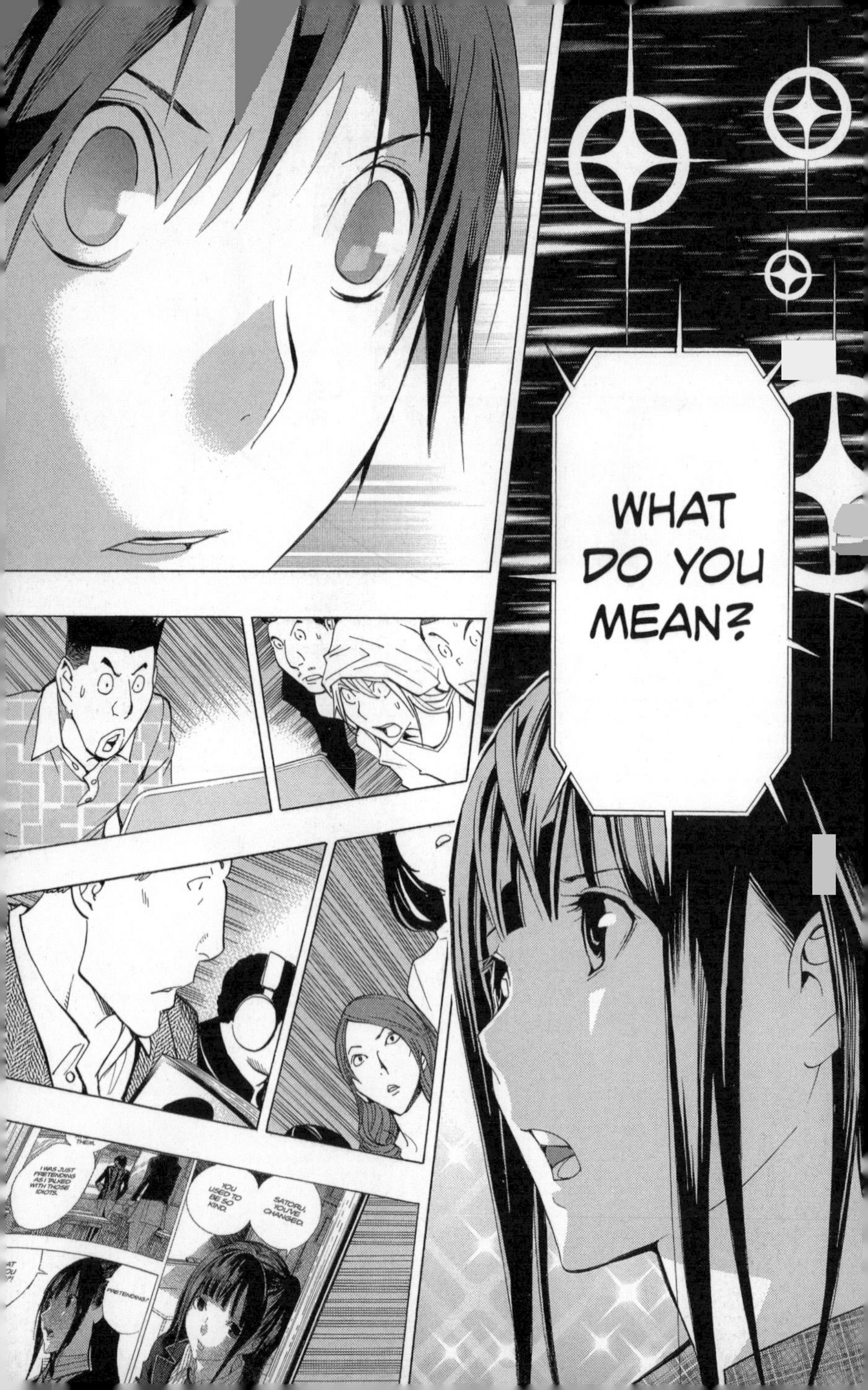
WHAT DO YOU MEAN?
SATORU, YOU'VE CHANGED.
YOU USED TO BE SO KIND.
I WAS JUST PRETENDING AS I TALKED WITH THOSE IDIOTS.
PRETENDING?!

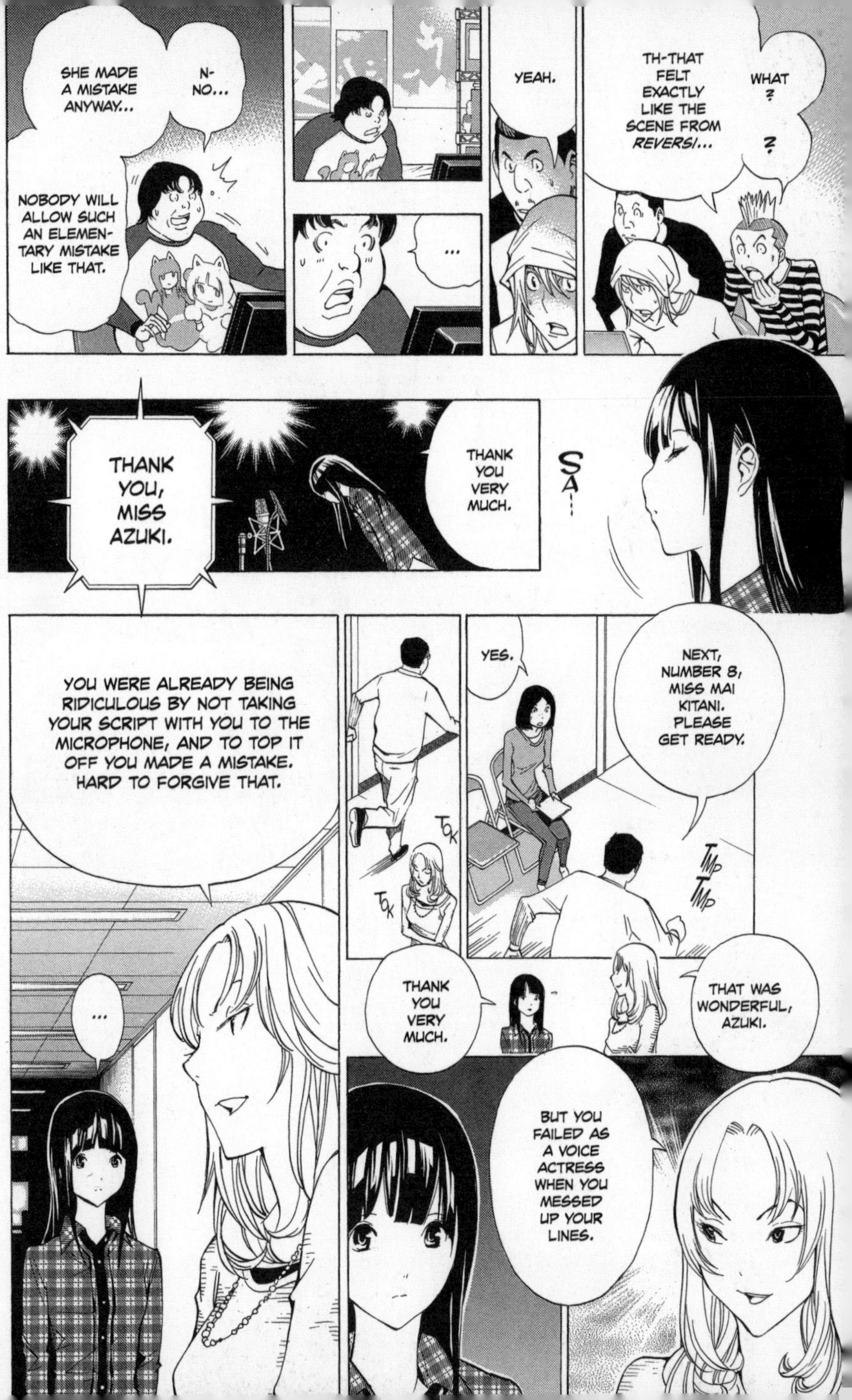
WHAT??
TH-THAT FELT EXACTLY LIKE THE SCENE FROM *REVERSI*...
YEAH.
...
N-NO...
SHE MADE A MISTAKE ANYWAY...
NOBODY WILL ALLOW SUCH AN ELEMENTARY MISTAKE LIKE THAT.
SA...
THANK YOU VERY MUCH.
THANK YOU, MISS AZUKI.
NEXT, NUMBER 8, MISS MAI KITANI. PLEASE GET READY.
YES.
TMP TMP
TOK
TOK
THAT WAS WONDERFUL, AZUKI.
THANK YOU VERY MUCH.
BUT YOU FAILED AS A VOICE ACTRESS WHEN YOU MESSED UP YOUR LINES.
YOU WERE ALREADY BEING RIDICULOUS BY NOT TAKING YOUR SCRIPT WITH YOU TO THE MICROPHONE, AND TO TOP IT OFF YOU MADE A MISTAKE. HARD TO FORGIVE THAT.
...

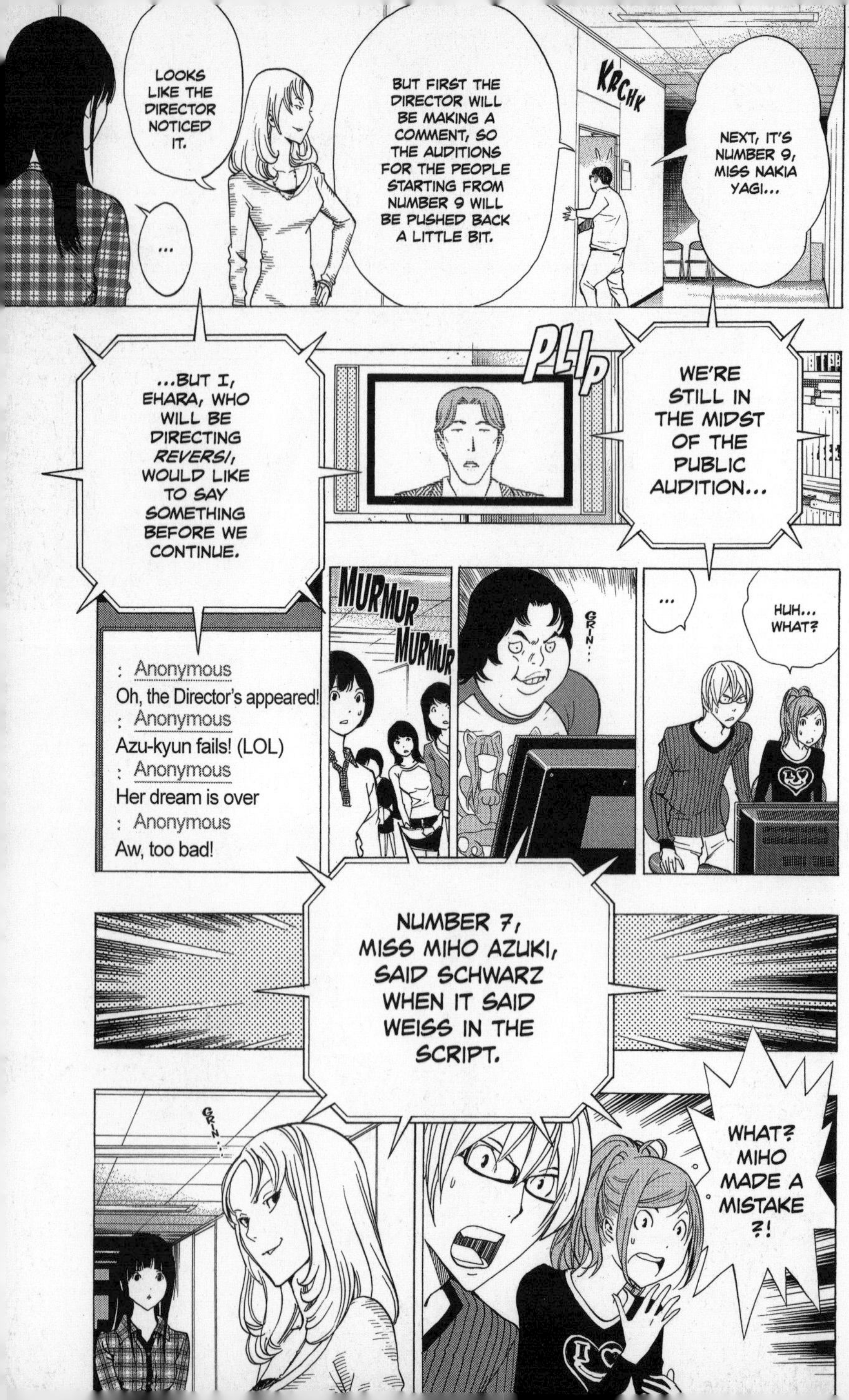
NEXT, IT'S NUMBER 9, MISS NAKIA YAGI...
KRCHK
BUT FIRST THE DIRECTOR WILL BE MAKING A COMMENT, SO THE AUDITIONS FOR THE PEOPLE STARTING FROM NUMBER 9 WILL BE PUSHED BACK A LITTLE BIT.
LOOKS LIKE THE DIRECTOR NOTICED IT.
...
PLIP
WE'RE STILL IN THE MIDST OF THE PUBLIC AUDITION...
...BUT I, EHARA, WHO WILL BE DIRECTING *REVERSI*, WOULD LIKE TO SAY SOMETHING BEFORE WE CONTINUE.
HUH... WHAT?
...
GRIN...
MURMUR
MURMUR
: Anonymous
Oh, the Director's appeared!
: Anonymous
Azu-kyun fails! (LOL)
: Anonymous
Her dream is over
: Anonymous
Aw, too bad!
NUMBER 7, MISS MIHO AZUKI, SAID SCHWARZ WHEN IT SAID WEISS IN THE SCRIPT.
WHAT? MIHO MADE A MISTAKE?!
GRIN...

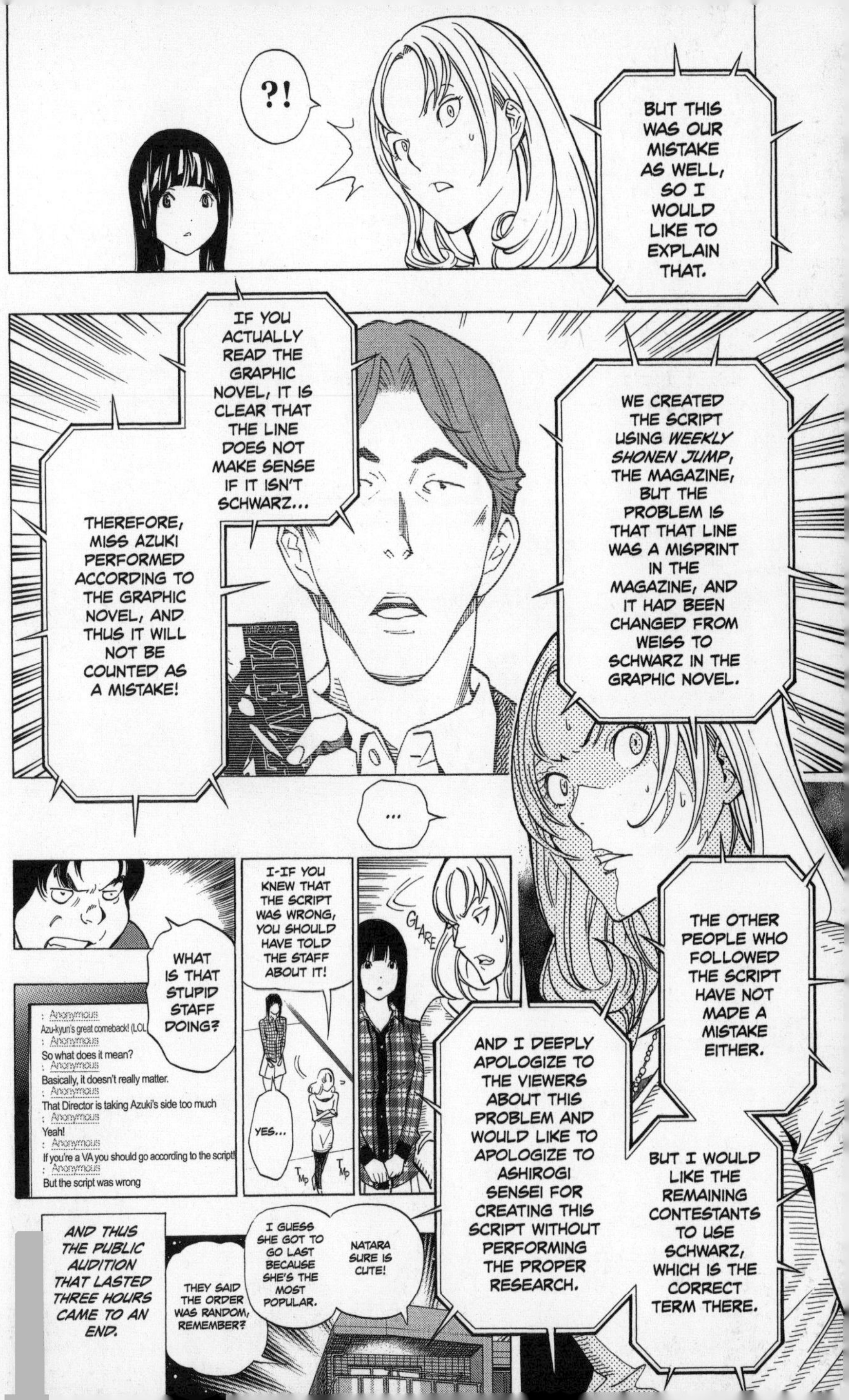
BUT THIS WAS OUR MISTAKE AS WELL, SO I WOULD LIKE TO EXPLAIN THAT.
?!
WE CREATED THE SCRIPT USING *WEEKLY SHONEN JUMP*, THE MAGAZINE, BUT THE PROBLEM IS THAT THAT LINE WAS A MISPRINT IN THE MAGAZINE, AND IT HAD BEEN CHANGED FROM WEISS TO SCHWARZ IN THE GRAPHIC NOVEL.
IF YOU ACTUALLY READ THE GRAPHIC NOVEL, IT IS CLEAR THAT THE LINE DOES NOT MAKE SENSE IF IT ISN'T SCHWARZ...
JUMP COMICS
THEREFORE, MISS AZUKI PERFORMED ACCORDING TO THE GRAPHIC NOVEL, AND THUS IT WILL NOT BE COUNTED AS A MISTAKE!
...
THE OTHER PEOPLE WHO FOLLOWED THE SCRIPT HAVE NOT MADE A MISTAKE EITHER.
BUT I WOULD LIKE THE REMAINING CONTESTANTS TO USE SCHWARZ, WHICH IS THE CORRECT TERM THERE.
AND I DEEPLY APOLOGIZE TO THE VIEWERS ABOUT THIS PROBLEM AND WOULD LIKE TO APOLOGIZE TO ASHIROGI SENSEI FOR CREATING THIS SCRIPT WITHOUT PERFORMING THE PROPER RESEARCH.
GLARE
I-IF YOU KNEW THAT THE SCRIPT WAS WRONG, YOU SHOULD HAVE TOLD THE STAFF ABOUT IT!
YES...
TMP TMP
WHAT IS THAT STUPID STAFF DOING?
: Anonymous
Azu-kyun's great comeback! (LOL
: Anonymous
So what does it mean?
: Anonymous
Basically, it doesn't really matter.
: Anonymous
That Director is taking Azuki's side too much
: Anonymous
Yeah!
: Anonymous
If you're a VA you should go according to the script!
: Anonymous
But the script was wrong
NATARA SURE IS CUTE!
I GUESS SHE GOT TO GO LAST BECAUSE SHE'S THE MOST POPULAR.
THEY SAID THE ORDER WAS RANDOM, REMEMBER?
AND THUS THE PUBLIC AUDITION THAT LASTED THREE HOURS CAME TO AN END.

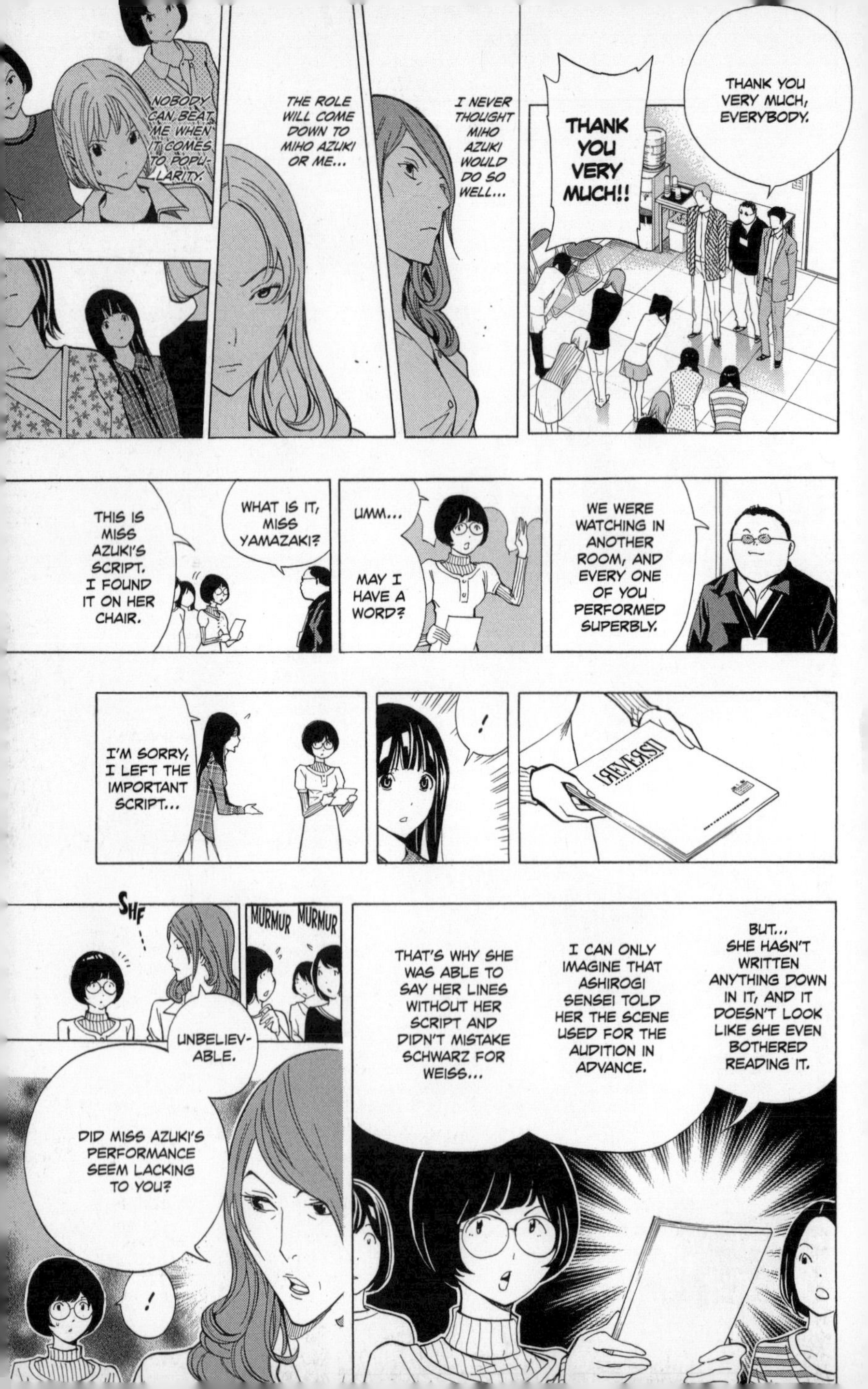
THANK YOU VERY MUCH, EVERYBODY.
THANK YOU VERY MUCH!!
I NEVER THOUGHT MIHO AZUKI WOULD DO SO WELL...
THE ROLE WILL COME DOWN TO MIHO AZUKI OR ME...
NOBODY CAN BEAT ME WHEN IT COMES TO POPULARITY.
WE WERE WATCHING IN ANOTHER ROOM, AND EVERY ONE OF YOU PERFORMED SUPERBLY.
UMM...
MAY I HAVE A WORD?
WHAT IS IT, MISS YAMAZAKI?
THIS IS MISS AZUKI'S SCRIPT. I FOUND IT ON HER CHAIR.
REVERSI
!
I'M SORRY, I LEFT THE IMPORTANT SCRIPT...
BUT... SHE HASN'T WRITTEN ANYTHING DOWN IN IT, AND IT DOESN'T LOOK LIKE SHE EVEN BOTHERED READING IT.
I CAN ONLY IMAGINE THAT ASHIROGI SENSEI TOLD HER THE SCENE USED FOR THE AUDITION IN ADVANCE.
THAT'S WHY SHE WAS ABLE TO SAY HER LINES WITHOUT HER SCRIPT AND DIDN'T MISTAKE SCHWARZ FOR WEISS...
MURMUR MURMUR
SHF
UNBELIEVABLE.
DID MISS AZUKI'S PERFORMANCE SEEM LACKING TO YOU?
!

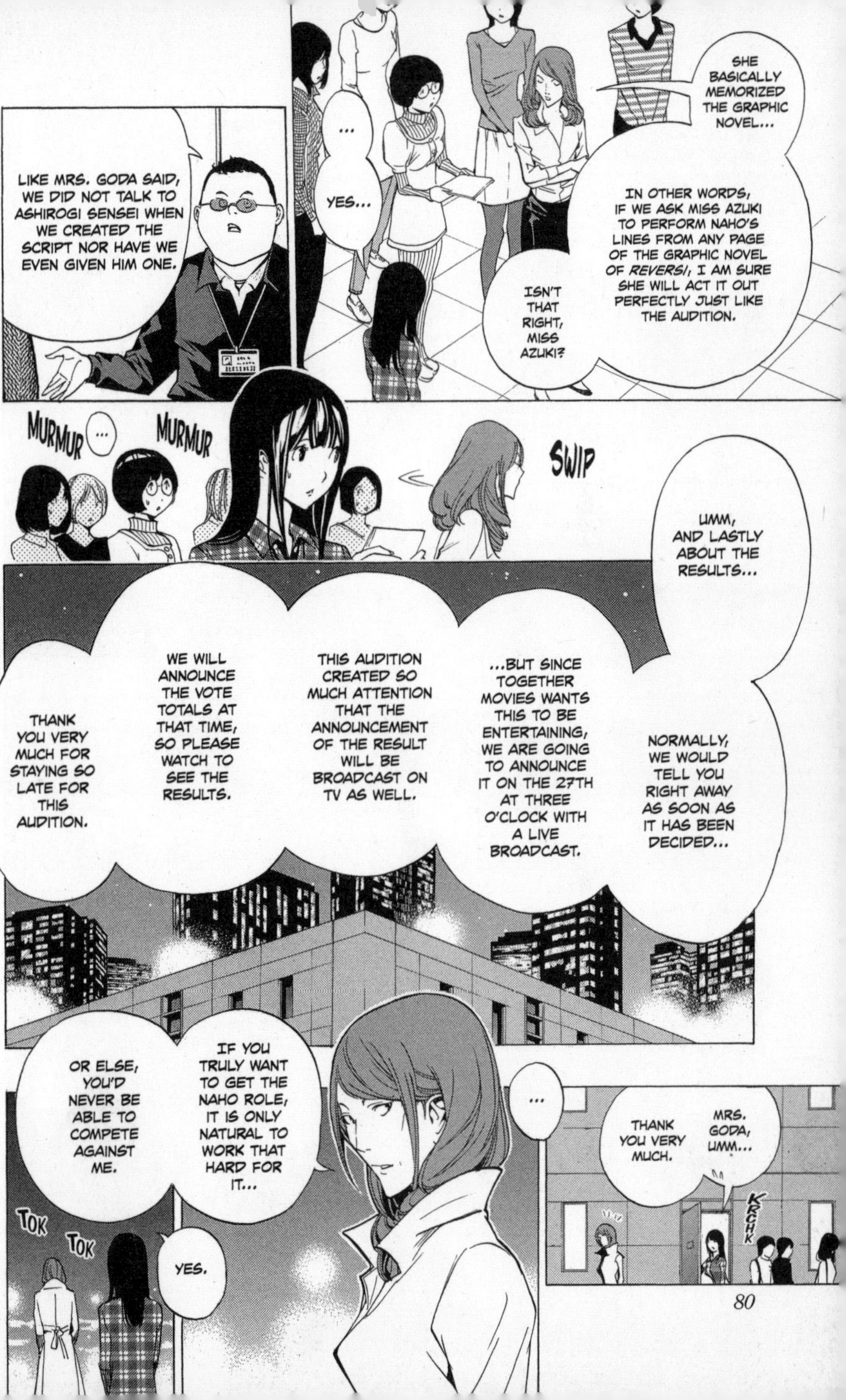
SHE BASICALLY MEMORIZED THE GRAPHIC NOVEL...
IN OTHER WORDS, IF WE ASK MISS AZUKI TO PERFORM NAHO'S LINES FROM ANY PAGE OF THE GRAPHIC NOVEL OF *REVERSI*, I AM SURE SHE WILL ACT IT OUT PERFECTLY JUST LIKE THE AUDITION.
ISN'T THAT RIGHT, MISS AZUKI?
...
YES...
LIKE MRS. GODA SAID, WE DID NOT TALK TO ASHIROGI SENSEI WHEN WE CREATED THE SCRIPT NOR HAVE WE EVEN GIVEN HIM ONE.
UMM, AND LASTLY ABOUT THE RESULTS...
SWIP
MURMUR
...
MURMUR
NORMALLY, WE WOULD TELL YOU RIGHT AWAY AS SOON AS IT HAS BEEN DECIDED...
...BUT SINCE TOGETHER MOVIES WANTS THIS TO BE ENTERTAINING, WE ARE GOING TO ANNOUNCE IT ON THE 27TH AT THREE O'CLOCK WITH A LIVE BROADCAST.
THIS AUDITION CREATED SO MUCH ATTENTION THAT THE ANNOUNCEMENT OF THE RESULT WILL BE BROADCAST ON TV AS WELL.
WE WILL ANNOUNCE THE VOTE TOTALS AT THAT TIME, SO PLEASE WATCH TO SEE THE RESULTS.
THANK YOU VERY MUCH FOR STAYING SO LATE FOR THIS AUDITION.
MRS. GODA, UMM...
KRCHK
THANK YOU VERY MUCH.
...
IF YOU TRULY WANT TO GET THE NAHO ROLE, IT IS ONLY NATURAL TO WORK THAT HARD FOR IT...
OR ELSE, YOU'D NEVER BE ABLE TO COMPETE AGAINST ME.
TOK
TOK
YES.

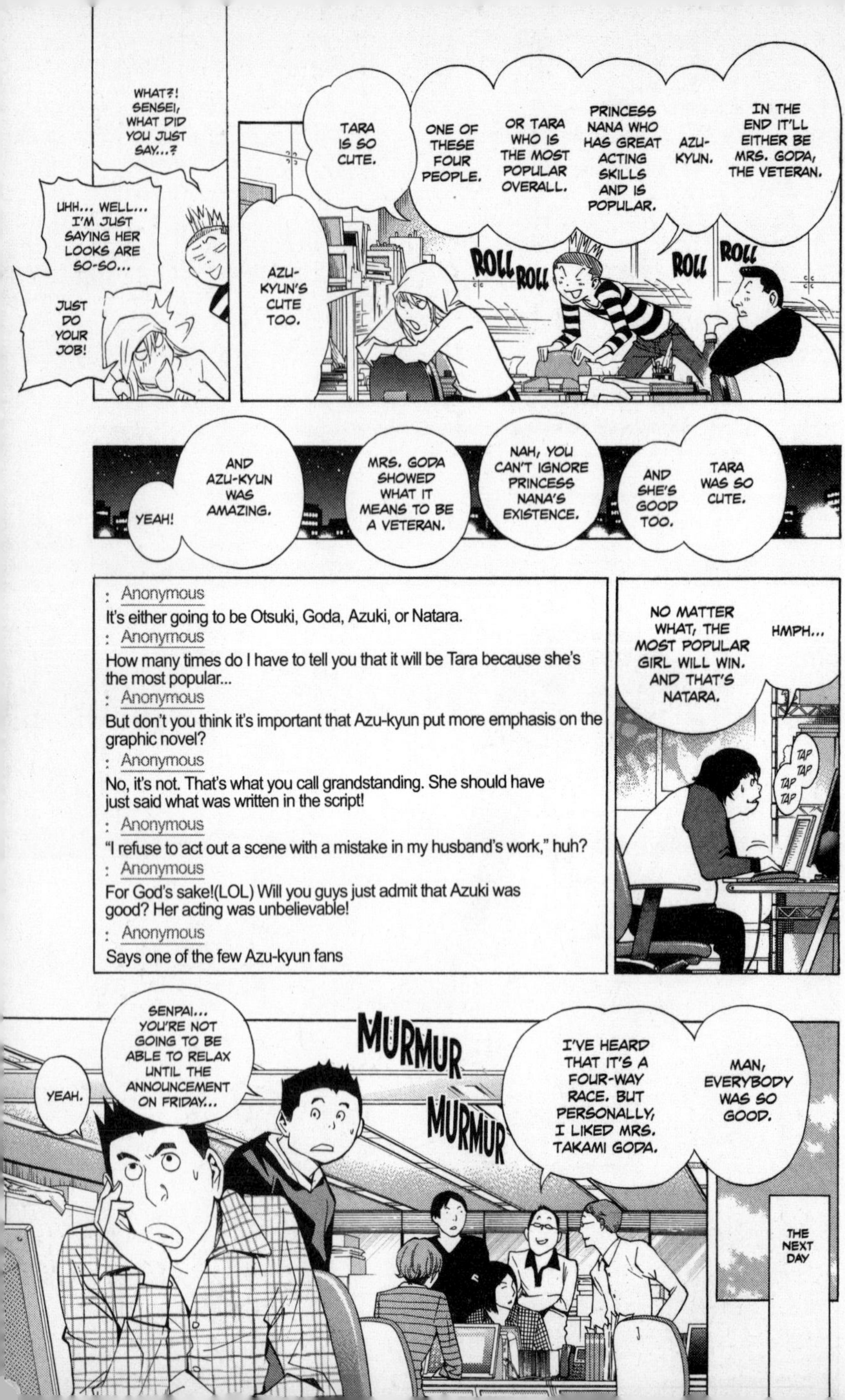
IN THE END IT'LL EITHER BE MRS. GODA, THE VETERAN.
AZU-KYUN.
PRINCESS NANA WHO HAS GREAT ACTING SKILLS AND IS POPULAR.
OR TARA WHO IS THE MOST POPULAR OVERALL.
ONE OF THESE FOUR PEOPLE.
TARA IS SO CUTE.
ROLL
ROLL
ROLL
ROLL
AZU-KYUN'S CUTE TOO.
WHAT?! SENSEI, WHAT DID YOU JUST SAY...?
UHH... WELL... I'M JUST SAYING HER LOOKS ARE SO-SO...
JUST DO YOUR JOB!
TARA WAS SO CUTE.
AND SHE'S GOOD TOO.
NAH, YOU CAN'T IGNORE PRINCESS NANA'S EXISTENCE.
MRS. GODA SHOWED WHAT IT MEANS TO BE A VETERAN.
AND AZU-KYUN WAS AMAZING.
YEAH!
HMPH...
NO MATTER WHAT, THE MOST POPULAR GIRL WILL WIN. AND THAT'S NATARA.
TAP TAP
TAP TAP
: Anonymous
It's either going to be Otsuki, Goda, Azuki, or Natara.
: Anonymous
How many times do I have to tell you that it will be Tara because she's the most popular...
: Anonymous
But don't you think it's important that Azu-kyun put more emphasis on the graphic novel?
: Anonymous
No, it's not. That's what you call grandstanding. She should have just said what was written in the script!
: Anonymous
"I refuse to act out a scene with a mistake in my husband's work," huh?
: Anonymous
For God's sake!(LOL) Will you guys just admit that Azuki was good? Her acting was unbelievable!
: Anonymous
Says one of the few Azu-kyun fans
THE NEXT DAY
MAN, EVERYBODY WAS SO GOOD.
I'VE HEARD THAT IT'S A FOUR-WAY RACE. BUT PERSONALLY, I LIKED MRS. TAKAMI GODA.
MURMUR
MURMUR
SENPAI... YOU'RE NOT GOING TO BE ABLE TO RELAX UNTIL THE ANNOUNCEMENT ON FRIDAY...
YEAH.

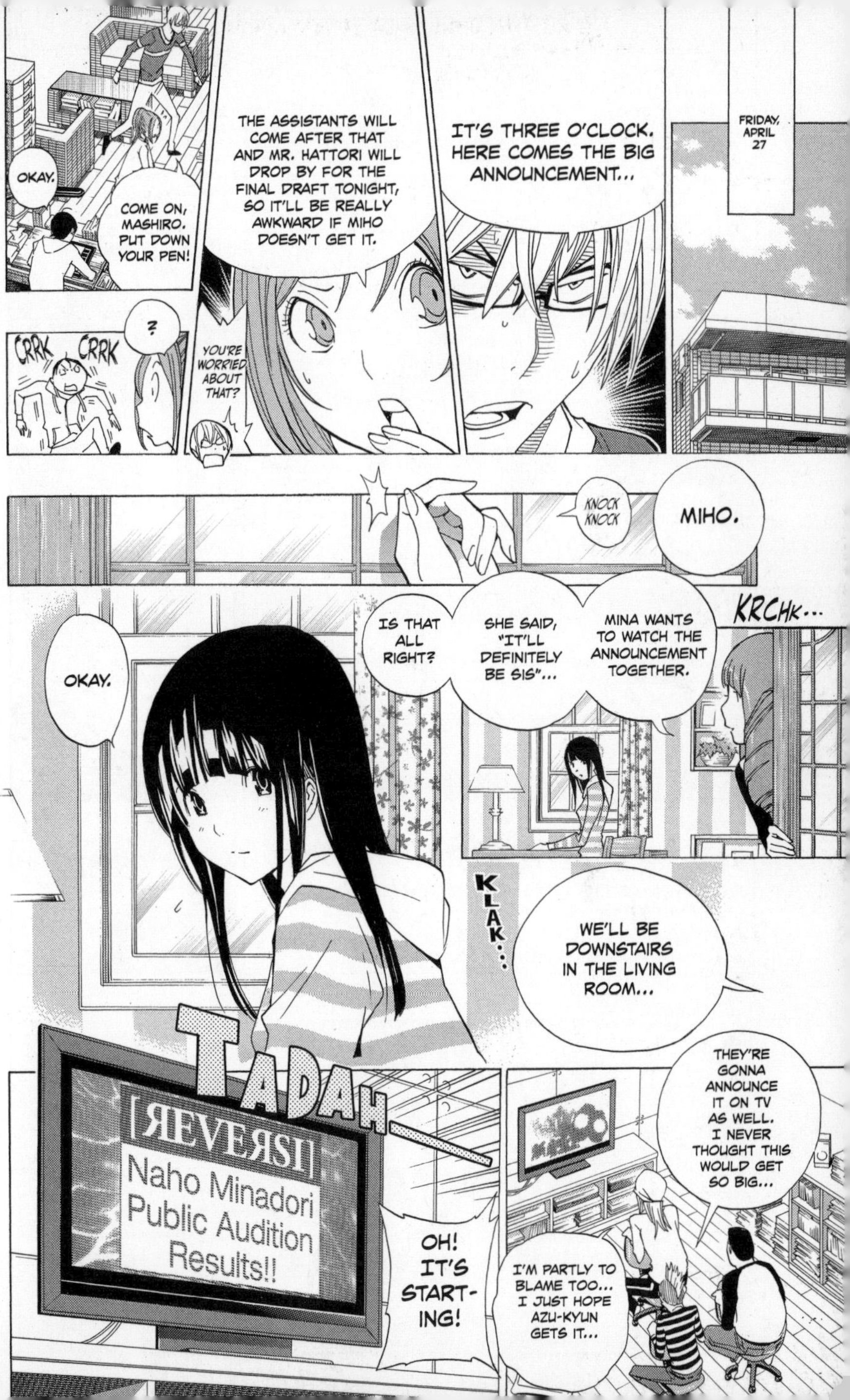
FRIDAY, APRIL 27
IT'S THREE O'CLOCK. HERE COMES THE BIG ANNOUNCEMENT...
THE ASSISTANTS WILL COME AFTER THAT AND MR. HATTORI WILL DROP BY FOR THE FINAL DRAFT TONIGHT, SO IT'LL BE REALLY AWKWARD IF MIHO DOESN'T GET IT.
YOU'RE WORRIED ABOUT THAT?
COME ON, MASHIRO. PUT DOWN YOUR PEN!
OKAY.
?
CRRK CRRK
KNOCK KNOCK
MIHO.
KRCHK...
MINA WANTS TO WATCH THE ANNOUNCEMENT TOGETHER.
SHE SAID, "IT'LL DEFINITELY BE SIS"...
IS THAT ALL RIGHT?
KLAK...
WE'LL BE DOWNSTAIRS IN THE LIVING ROOM...
OKAY.
THEY'RE GONNA ANNOUNCE IT ON TV AS WELL. I NEVER THOUGHT THIS WOULD GET SO BIG...
I'M PARTLY TO BLAME TOO... I JUST HOPE AZU-KYUN GETS IT...
OH! IT'S START-ING!
TADAH
[REVERSI]
Naho Minadori Public Audition Results!!

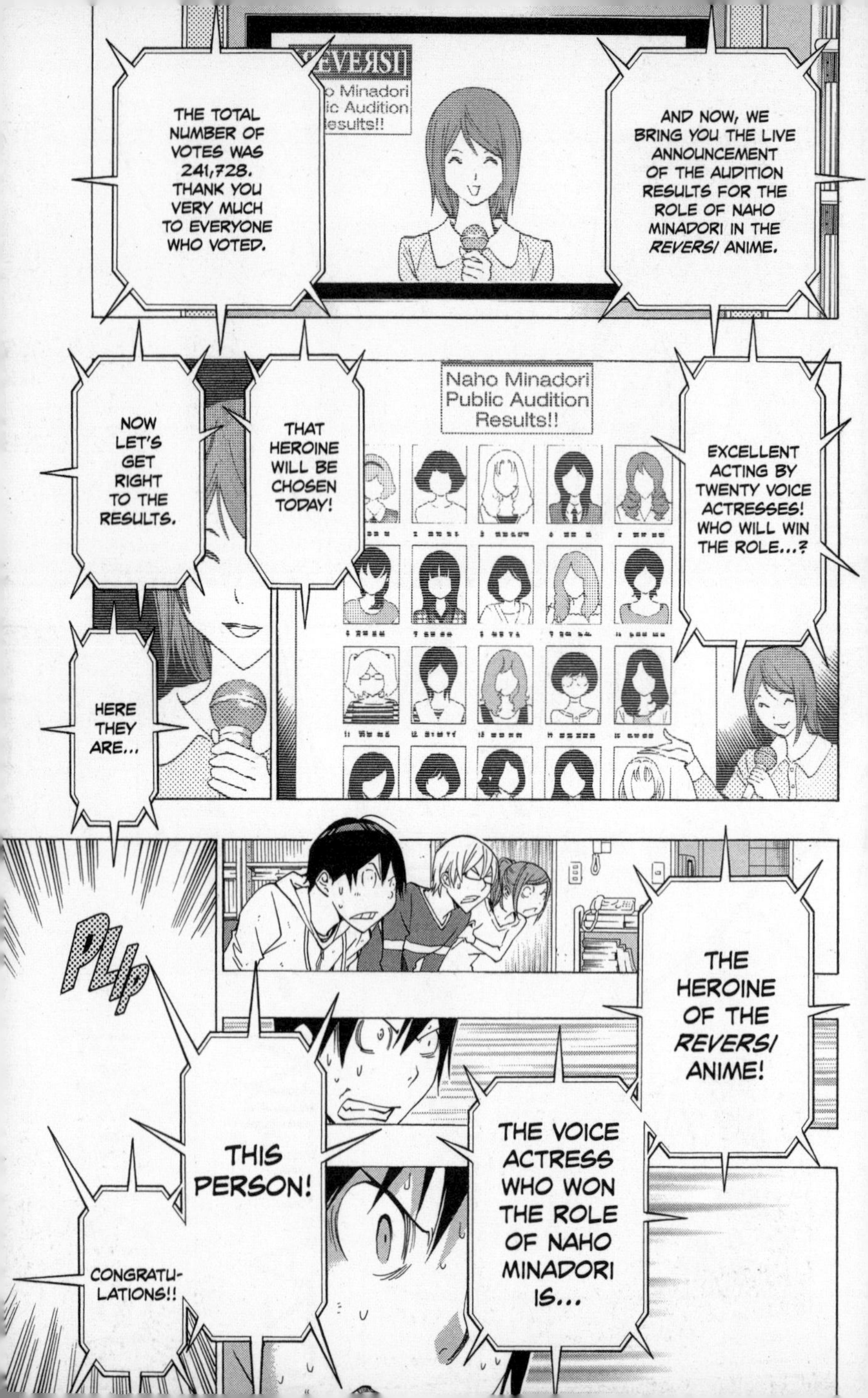
REVERSI
AND NOW, WE BRING YOU THE LIVE ANNOUNCEMENT OF THE AUDITION RESULTS FOR THE ROLE OF NAHO MINADORI IN THE *REVERSI* ANIME.
THE TOTAL NUMBER OF VOTES WAS 241,728. THANK YOU VERY MUCH TO EVERYONE WHO VOTED.
EXCELLENT ACTING BY TWENTY VOICE ACTRESSES! WHO WILL WIN THE ROLE...?
Naho Minadori Public Audition Results!!
THAT HEROINE WILL BE CHOSEN TODAY!
NOW LET'S GET RIGHT TO THE RESULTS.
HERE THEY ARE...
THE HEROINE OF THE *REVERSI* ANIME!
PLIP
THE VOICE ACTRESS WHO WON THE ROLE OF NAHO MINADORI IS...
THIS PERSON!
CONGRATULATIONS!!

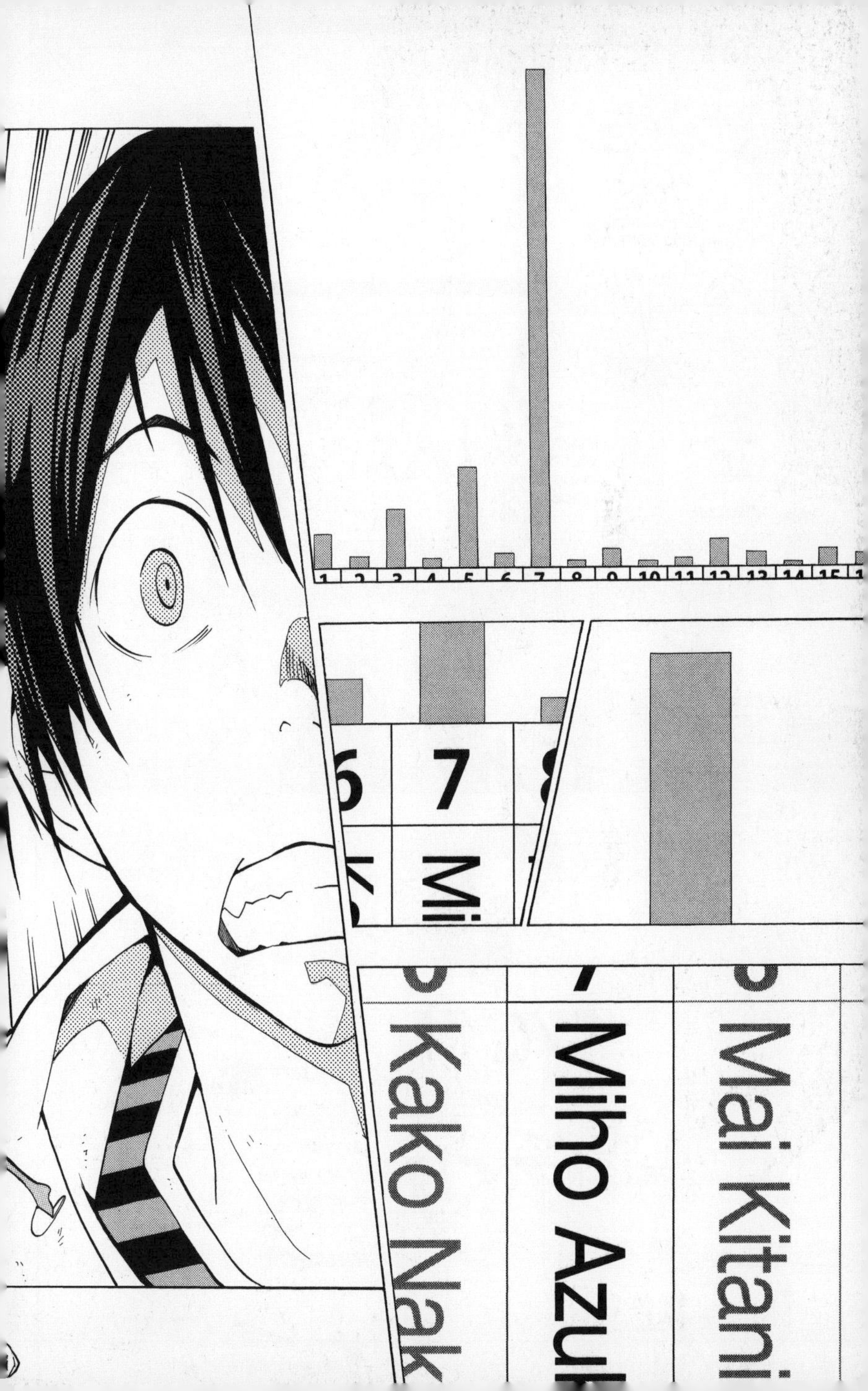
Mai Kitani
7
Miho
Kako

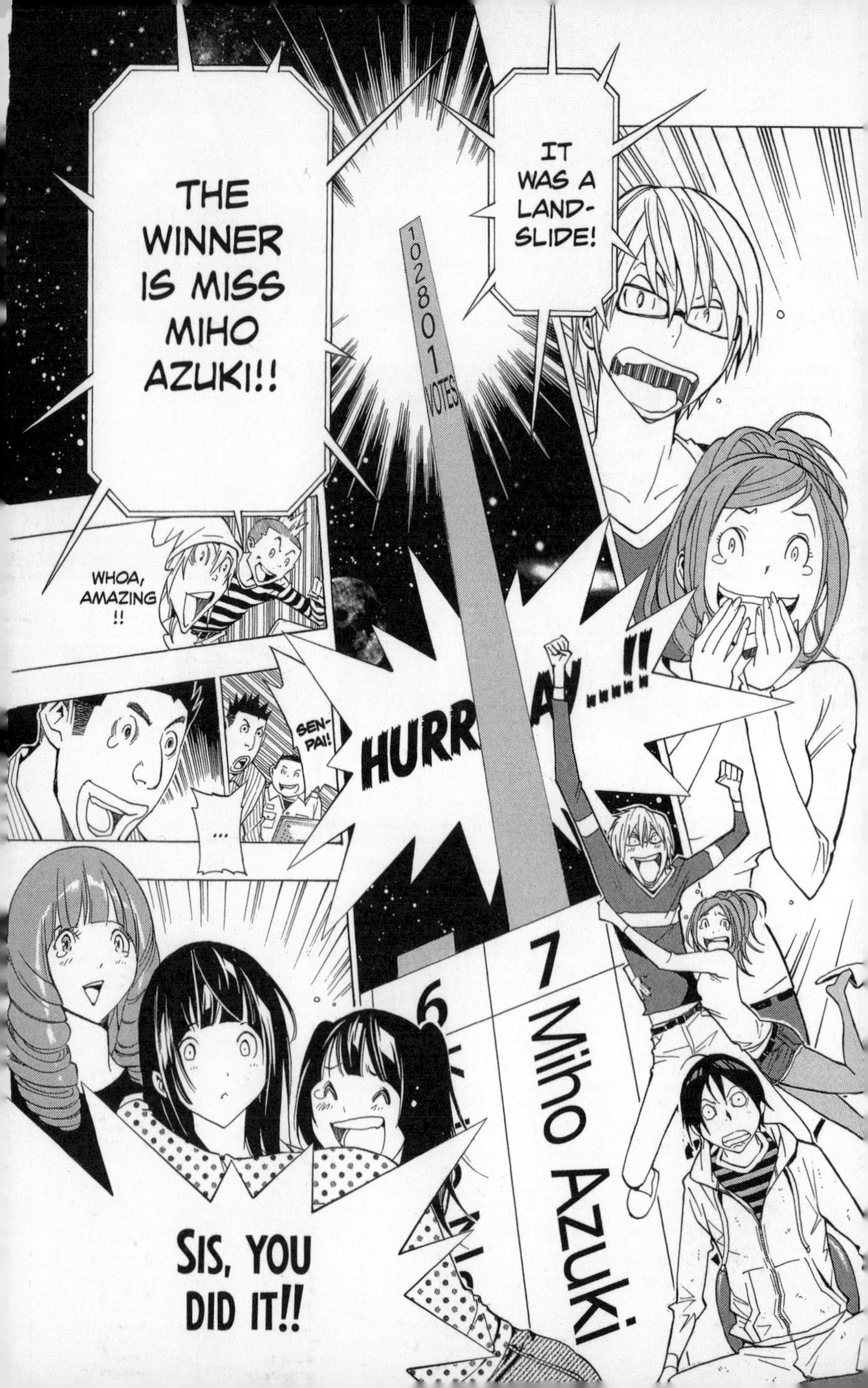
IT WAS A LANDSLIDE!
THE WINNER IS MISS MIHO AZUKI!!
102801 VOTES
WHOA, AMAZING!!
SEN-PAI!
...
HURRAY...!!
7 Miho Azuki
SIS, YOU DID IT!!

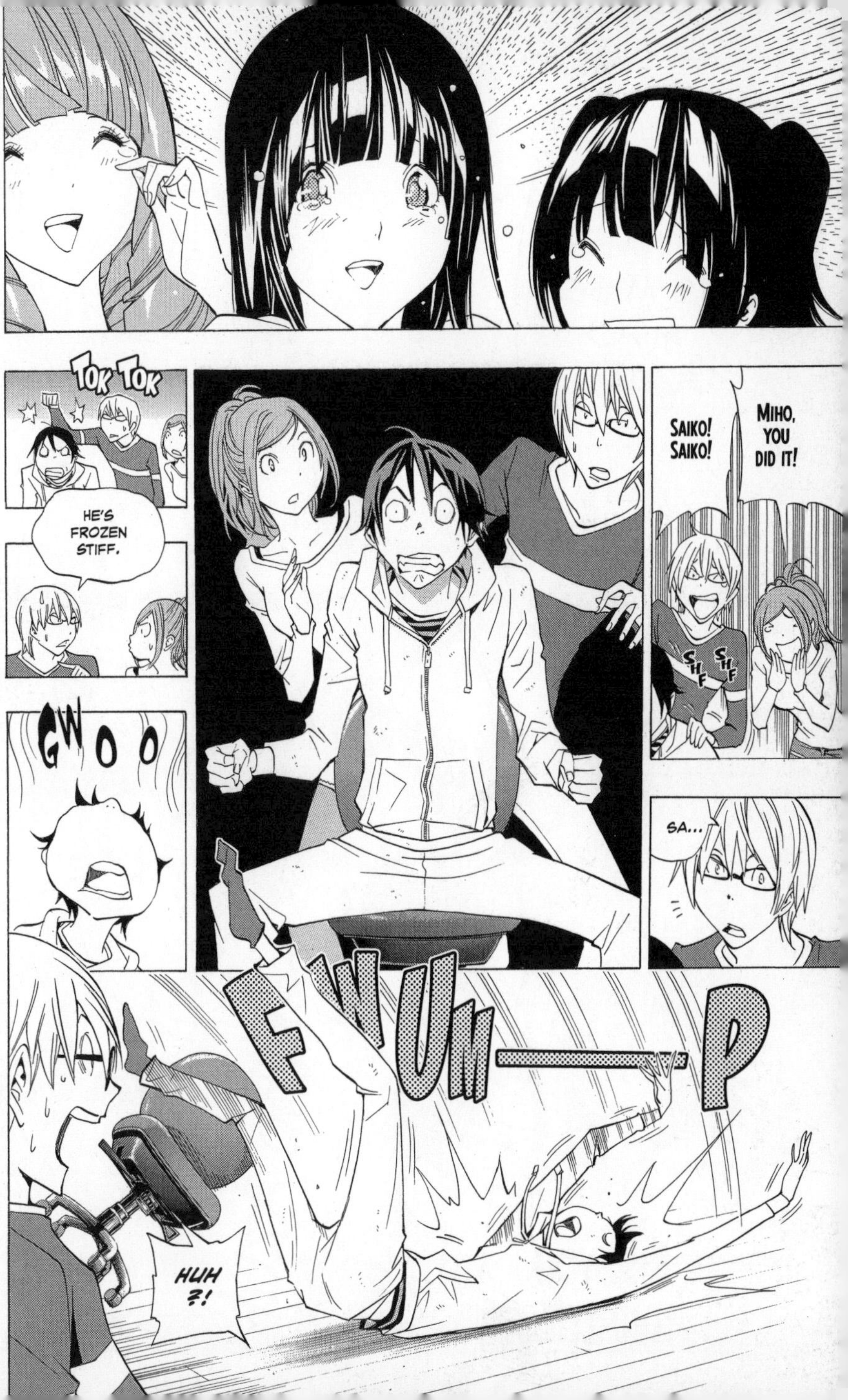
MIHO, YOU DID IT!
SAIKO! SAIKO!
SHF SHF
SHF
SA...
TOK TOK
HE'S FROZEN STIFF.
GWOO
FWUM—P
HUH?!

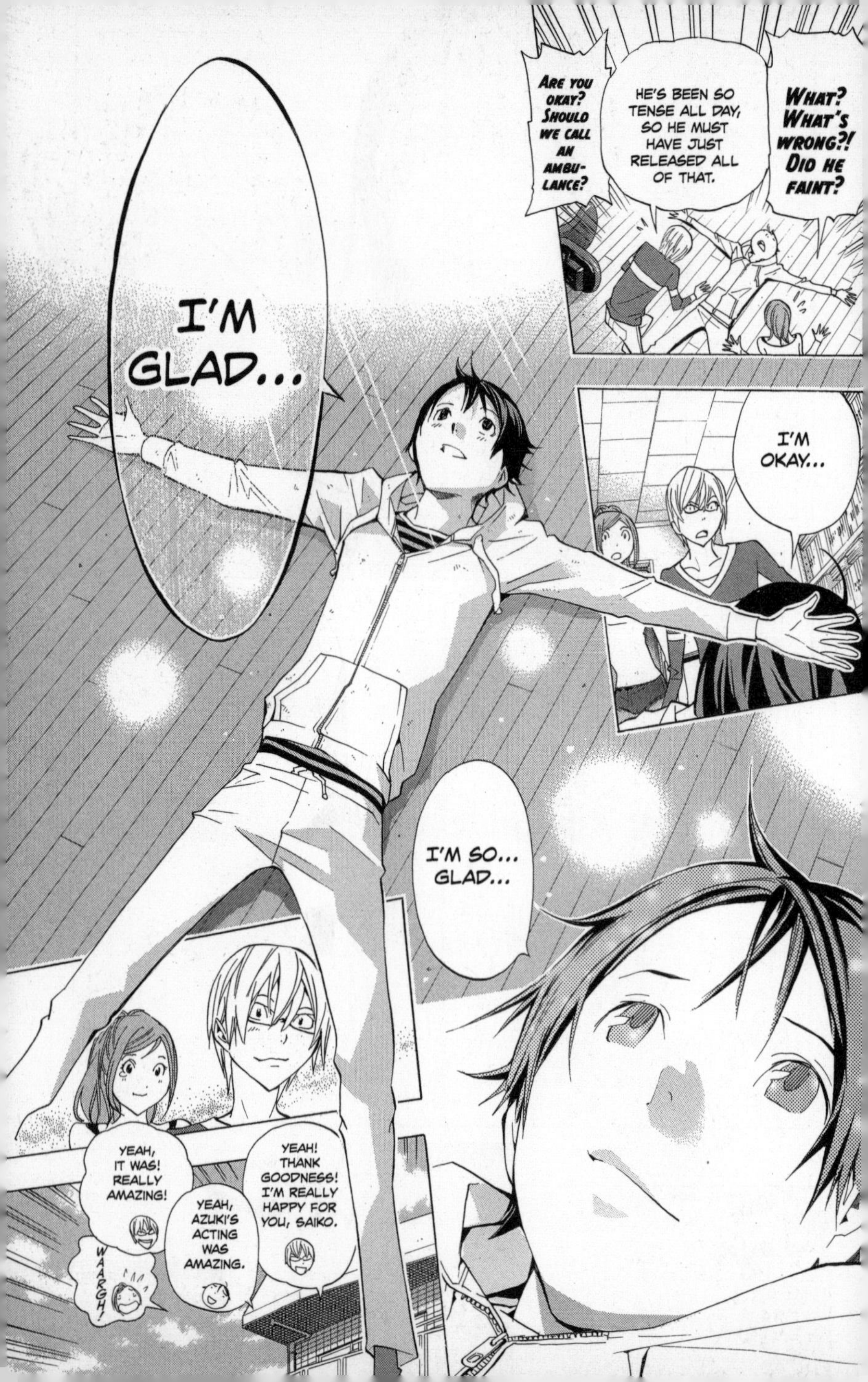
WHAT? WHAT'S WRONG?! DID HE FAINT?
HE'S BEEN SO TENSE ALL DAY, SO HE MUST HAVE JUST RELEASED ALL OF THAT.
ARE YOU OKAY? SHOULD WE CALL AN AMBU-LANCE?
I'M OKAY...
I'M GLAD...
I'M SO... GLAD...
YEAH! THANK GOODNESS! I'M REALLY HAPPY FOR YOU, SAIKO.
YEAH, AZUKI'S ACTING WAS AMAZING.
YEAH, IT WAS! REALLY AMAZING!
WAARGH!

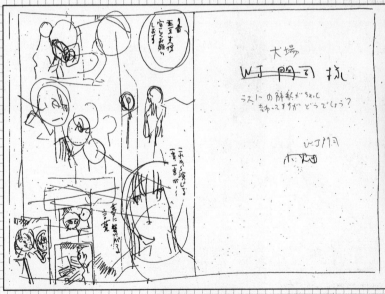

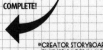

OHBA'S STORYBOARD

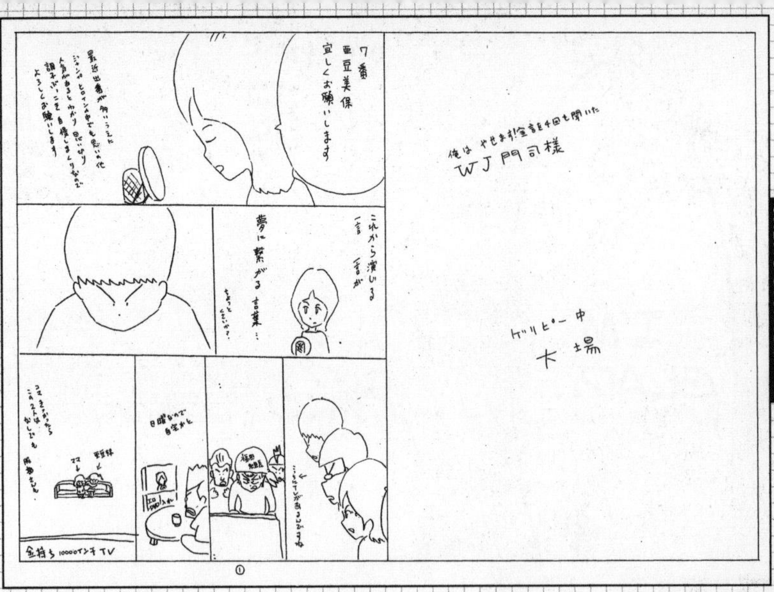

大場
7番
亜豆美保
宜しくお願いします
これから演じる一言一言が
夢に繋がる言葉…
金持ち 10000インチ TV

OBATA'S STORYBOARD

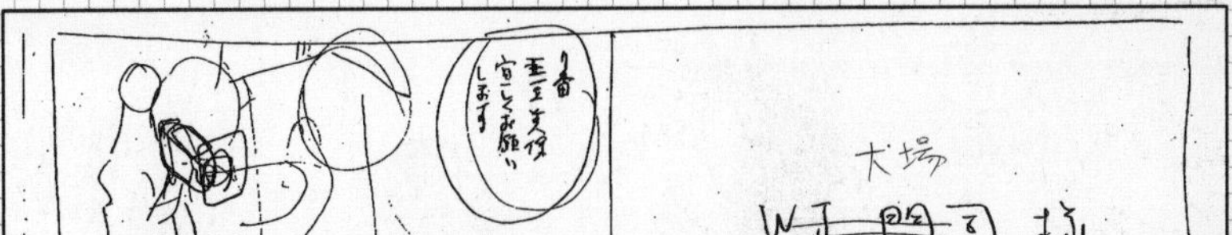

大場
WJ門司様
ラストの解釈がちょっと変わってますがどうでしょう?
WJ門司
小畑
7番
亜豆美保
宜しくお願いします
これから演じる一言一言が…!
夢に繋がる言葉

COMPLETE!

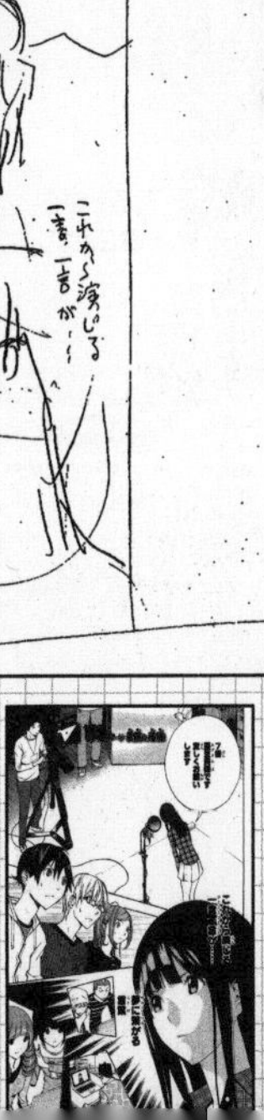

※CREATOR STORYBOARDS AND FINISHED PAGES IN JAPANESE

BAKUMAN。 vol.20

"Until the Final Draft Is Complete"

Chapter 172, p. 73

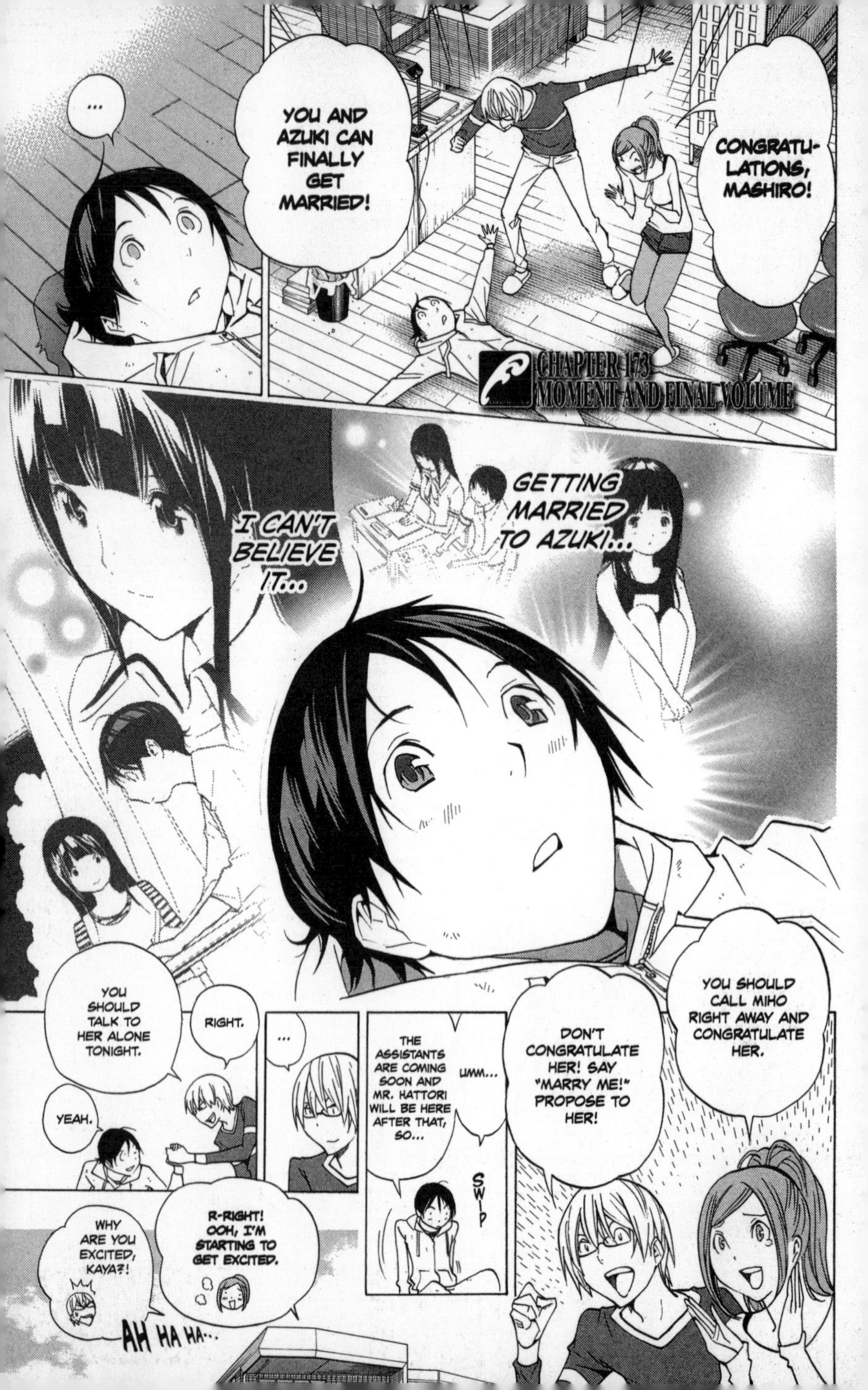
CONGRATULATIONS, MASHIRO!
YOU AND AZUKI CAN FINALLY GET MARRIED!
CHAPTER 173 MOMENT AND FINAL VOLUME
...
GETTING MARRIED TO AZUKI...
I CAN'T BELIEVE IT...
YOU SHOULD CALL MIHO RIGHT AWAY AND CONGRATULATE HER.
DON'T CONGRATULATE HER! SAY "MARRY ME!" PROPOSE TO HER!
UMM...
THE ASSISTANTS ARE COMING SOON AND MR. HATTORI WILL BE HERE AFTER THAT, SO...
SWIP
...
YOU SHOULD TALK TO HER ALONE TONIGHT.
RIGHT.
YEAH.
R-RIGHT! OOH, I'M STARTING TO GET EXCITED.
WHY ARE YOU EXCITED, KAYA?!
AH HA HA...

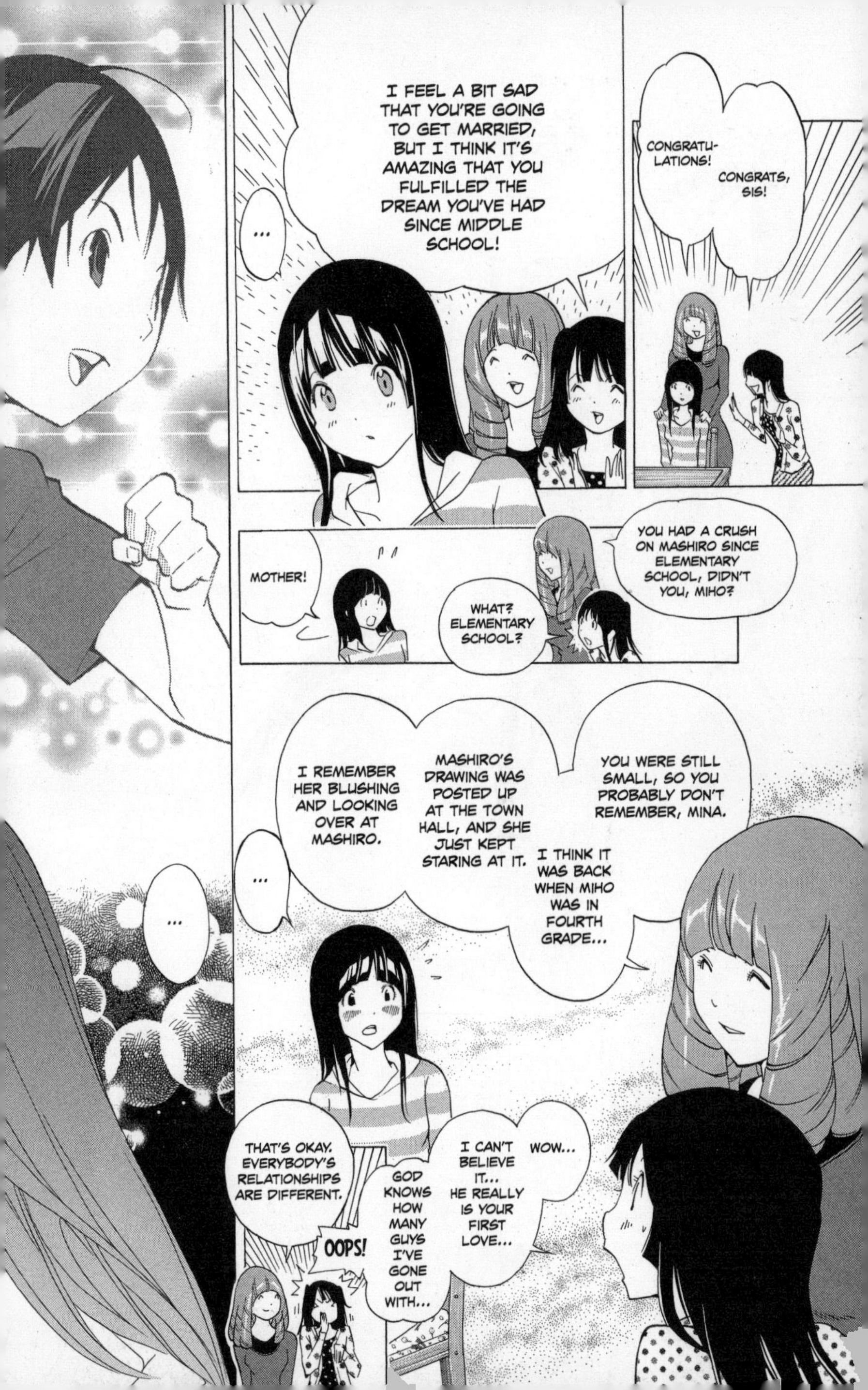
CONGRATULATIONS!
CONGRATS, SIS!
I FEEL A BIT SAD THAT YOU'RE GOING TO GET MARRIED, BUT I THINK IT'S AMAZING THAT YOU FULFILLED THE DREAM YOU'VE HAD SINCE MIDDLE SCHOOL!
...
YOU HAD A CRUSH ON MASHIRO SINCE ELEMENTARY SCHOOL, DIDN'T YOU, MIHO?
WHAT? ELEMENTARY SCHOOL?
MOTHER!
YOU WERE STILL SMALL, SO YOU PROBABLY DON'T REMEMBER, MINA.
I THINK IT WAS BACK WHEN MIHO WAS IN FOURTH GRADE...
MASHIRO'S DRAWING WAS POSTED UP AT THE TOWN HALL, AND SHE JUST KEPT STARING AT IT.
I REMEMBER HER BLUSHING AND LOOKING OVER AT MASHIRO.
...
WOW...
I CAN'T BELIEVE IT... HE REALLY IS YOUR FIRST LOVE...
GOD KNOWS HOW MANY GUYS I'VE GONE OUT WITH...
OOPS!
THAT'S OKAY. EVERYBODY'S RELATIONSHIPS ARE DIFFERENT.
...

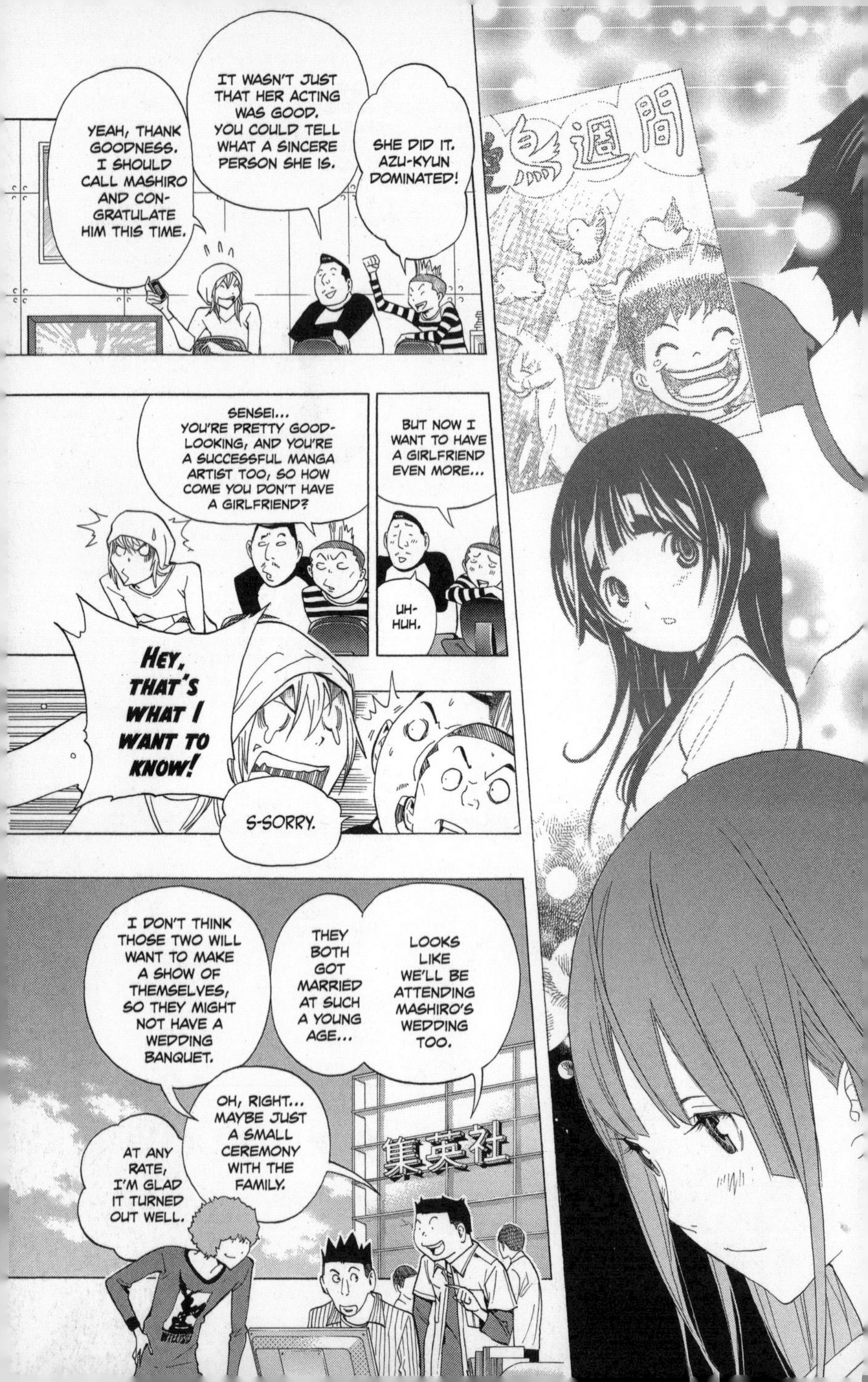
SHE DID IT. AZU-KYUN DOMINATED!
IT WASN'T JUST THAT HER ACTING WAS GOOD. YOU COULD TELL WHAT A SINCERE PERSON SHE IS.
YEAH, THANK GOODNESS. I SHOULD CALL MASHIRO AND CONGRATULATE HIM THIS TIME.
BUT NOW I WANT TO HAVE A GIRLFRIEND EVEN MORE...
UH-HUH.
SENSEI... YOU'RE PRETTY GOOD-LOOKING, AND YOU'RE A SUCCESSFUL MANGA ARTIST TOO, SO HOW COME YOU DON'T HAVE A GIRLFRIEND?
HEY, THAT'S WHAT I WANT TO KNOW!
S-SORRY.
LOOKS LIKE WE'LL BE ATTENDING MASHIRO'S WEDDING TOO.
THEY BOTH GOT MARRIED AT SUCH A YOUNG AGE...
I DON'T THINK THOSE TWO WILL WANT TO MAKE A SHOW OF THEMSELVES, SO THEY MIGHT NOT HAVE A WEDDING BANQUET.
OH, RIGHT... MAYBE JUST A SMALL CEREMONY WITH THE FAMILY.
集英社
AT ANY RATE, I'M GLAD IT TURNED OUT WELL.

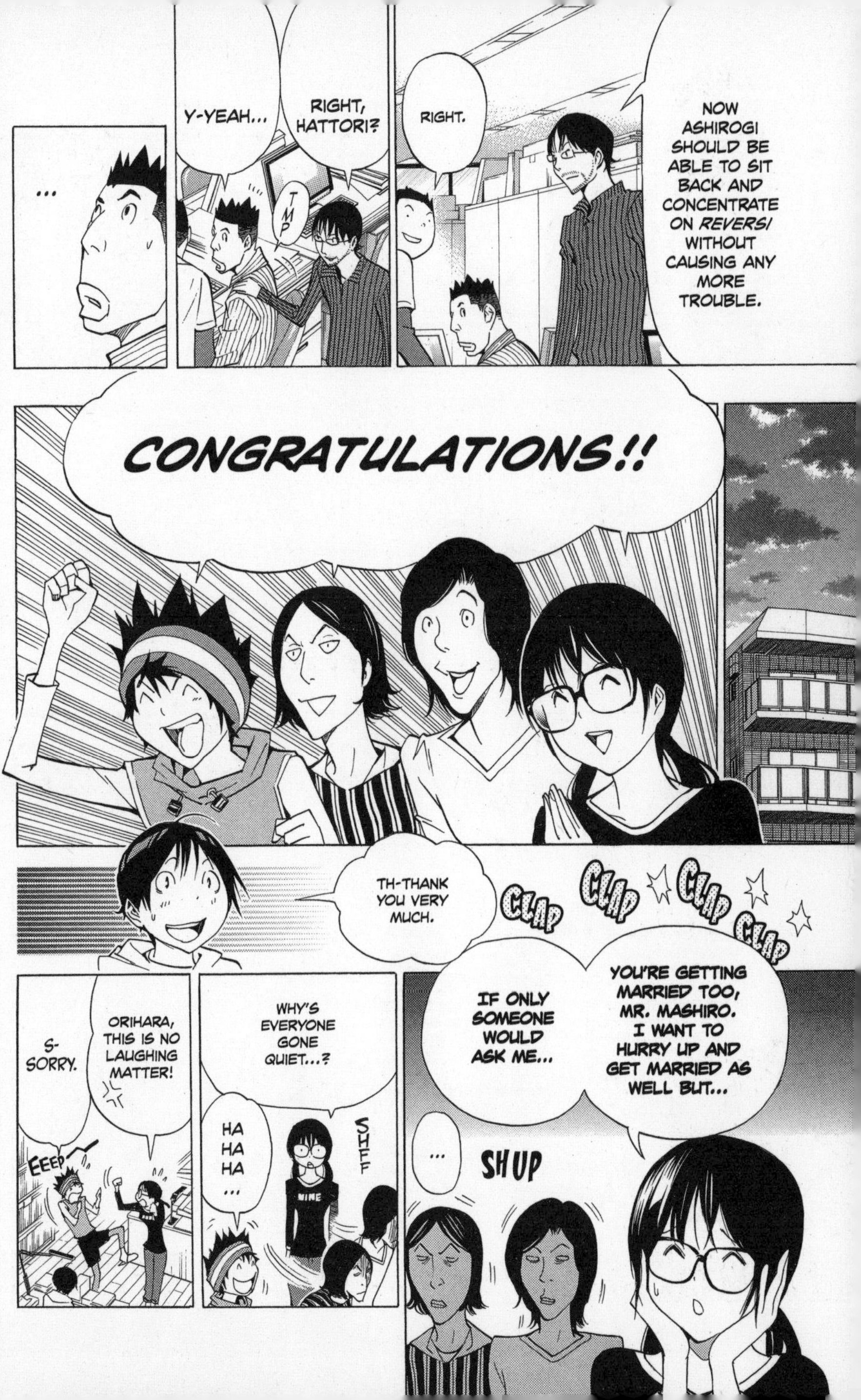
NOW ASHIROGI SHOULD BE ABLE TO SIT BACK AND CONCENTRATE ON *REVERSI* WITHOUT CAUSING ANY MORE TROUBLE.
RIGHT.
RIGHT, HATTORI?
TMP
Y-YEAH...
...
CONGRATULATIONS!!
TH-THANK YOU VERY MUCH.
CLAP
CLAP
CLAP
CLAP
YOU'RE GETTING MARRIED TOO, MR. MASHIRO. I WANT TO HURRY UP AND GET MARRIED AS WELL BUT...
IF ONLY SOMEONE WOULD ASK ME...
SHUP
...
WHY'S EVERYONE GONE QUIET...?
SHFF
HA HA HA...
ORIHARA, THIS IS NO LAUGHING MATTER!
S-SORRY.
EEEP

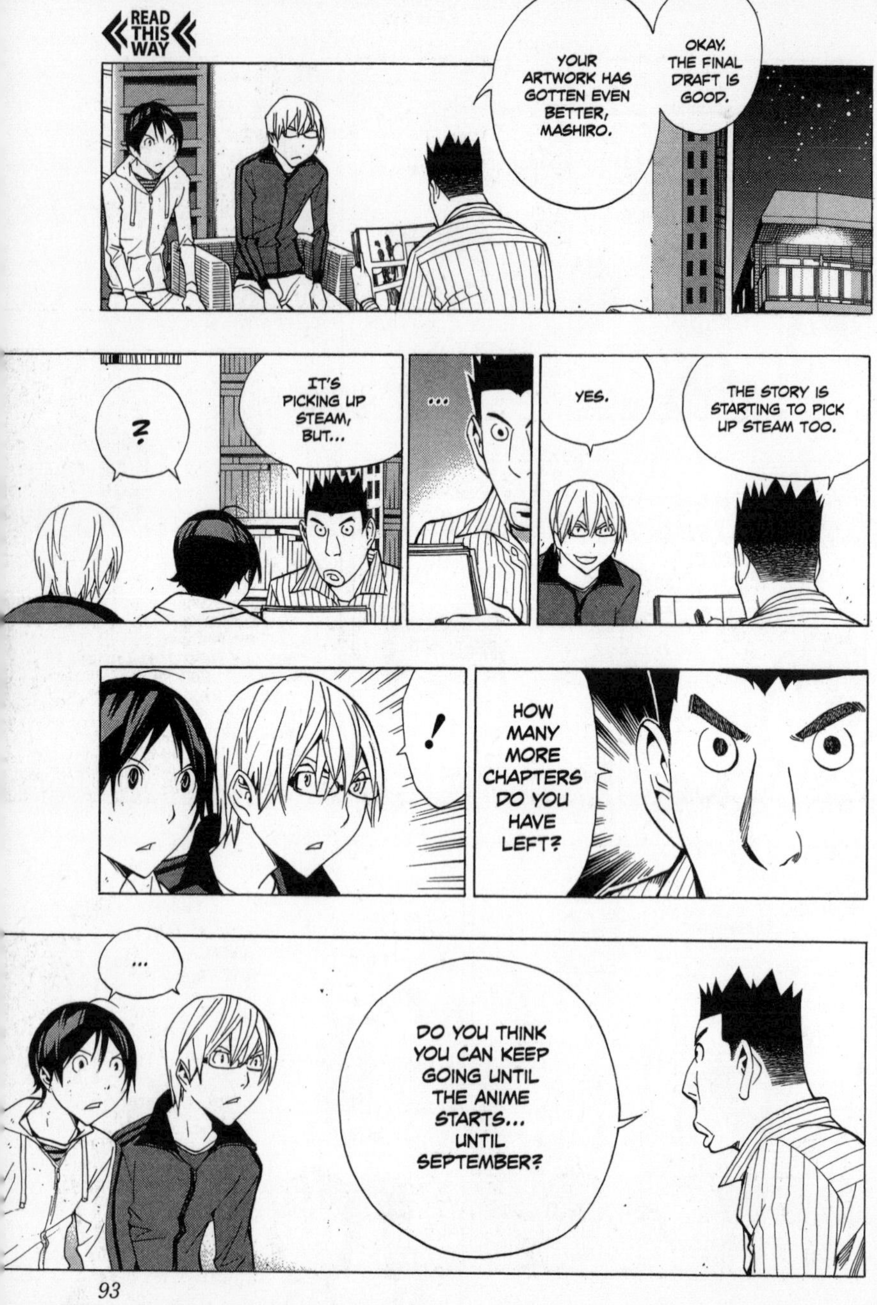
READ THIS WAY
OKAY. THE FINAL DRAFT IS GOOD.
YOUR ARTWORK HAS GOTTEN EVEN BETTER, MASHIRO.
THE STORY IS STARTING TO PICK UP STEAM TOO.
YES.
...
IT'S PICKING UP STEAM, BUT...
?
HOW MANY MORE CHAPTERS DO YOU HAVE LEFT?
!
DO YOU THINK YOU CAN KEEP GOING UNTIL THE ANIME STARTS... UNTIL SEPTEMBER?
...

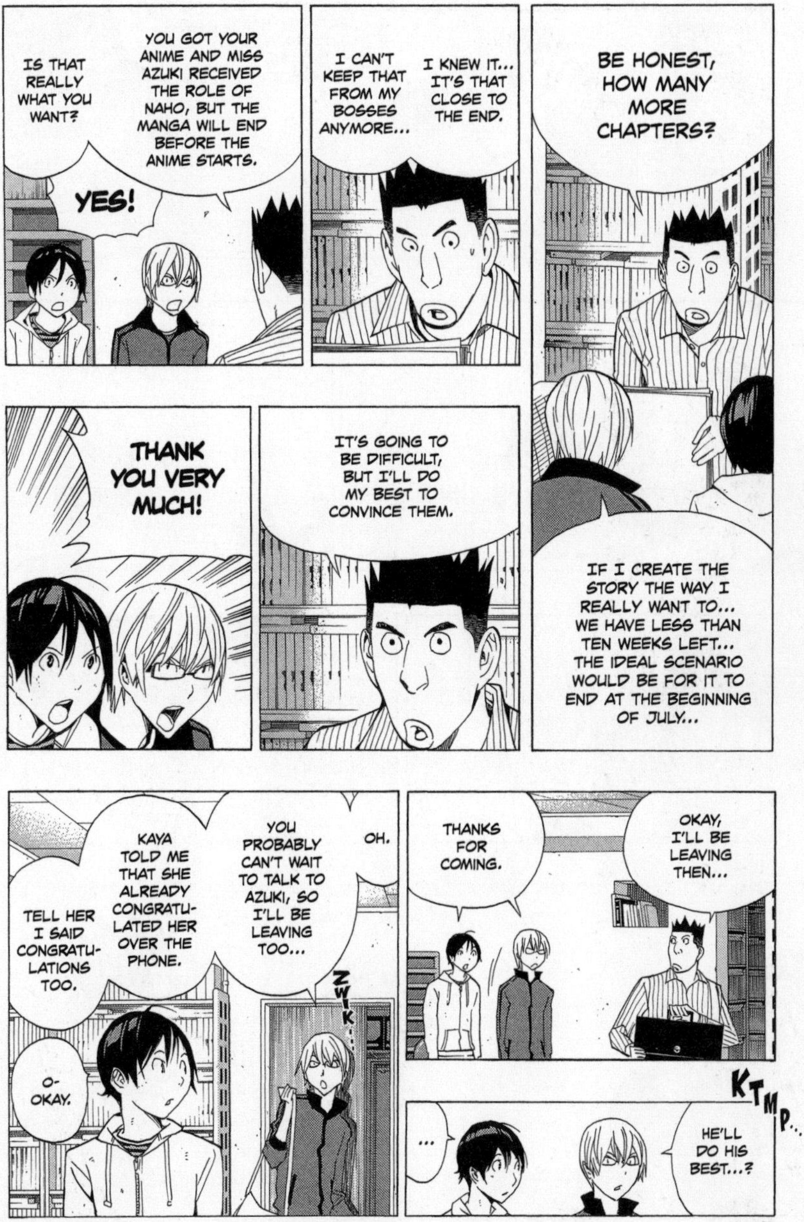
BE HONEST, HOW MANY MORE CHAPTERS?
IF I CREATE THE STORY THE WAY I REALLY WANT TO... WE HAVE LESS THAN TEN WEEKS LEFT... THE IDEAL SCENARIO WOULD BE FOR IT TO END AT THE BEGINNING OF JULY...
I KNEW IT... IT'S THAT CLOSE TO THE END.
I CAN'T KEEP THAT FROM MY BOSSES ANYMORE...
YOU GOT YOUR ANIME AND MISS AZUKI RECEIVED THE ROLE OF NAHO, BUT THE MANGA WILL END BEFORE THE ANIME STARTS.
IS THAT REALLY WHAT YOU WANT?
YES!
IT'S GOING TO BE DIFFICULT, BUT I'LL DO MY BEST TO CONVINCE THEM.
THANK YOU VERY MUCH!
OKAY, I'LL BE LEAVING THEN...
THANKS FOR COMING.
KTMP...
HE'LL DO HIS BEST...?
...
OH.
YOU PROBABLY CAN'T WAIT TO TALK TO AZUKI, SO I'LL BE LEAVING TOO...
KAYA TOLD ME THAT SHE ALREADY CONGRATULATED HER OVER THE PHONE.
TELL HER I SAID CONGRATULATIONS TOO.
ZWIK...
O-OKAY.

READ THIS WAY

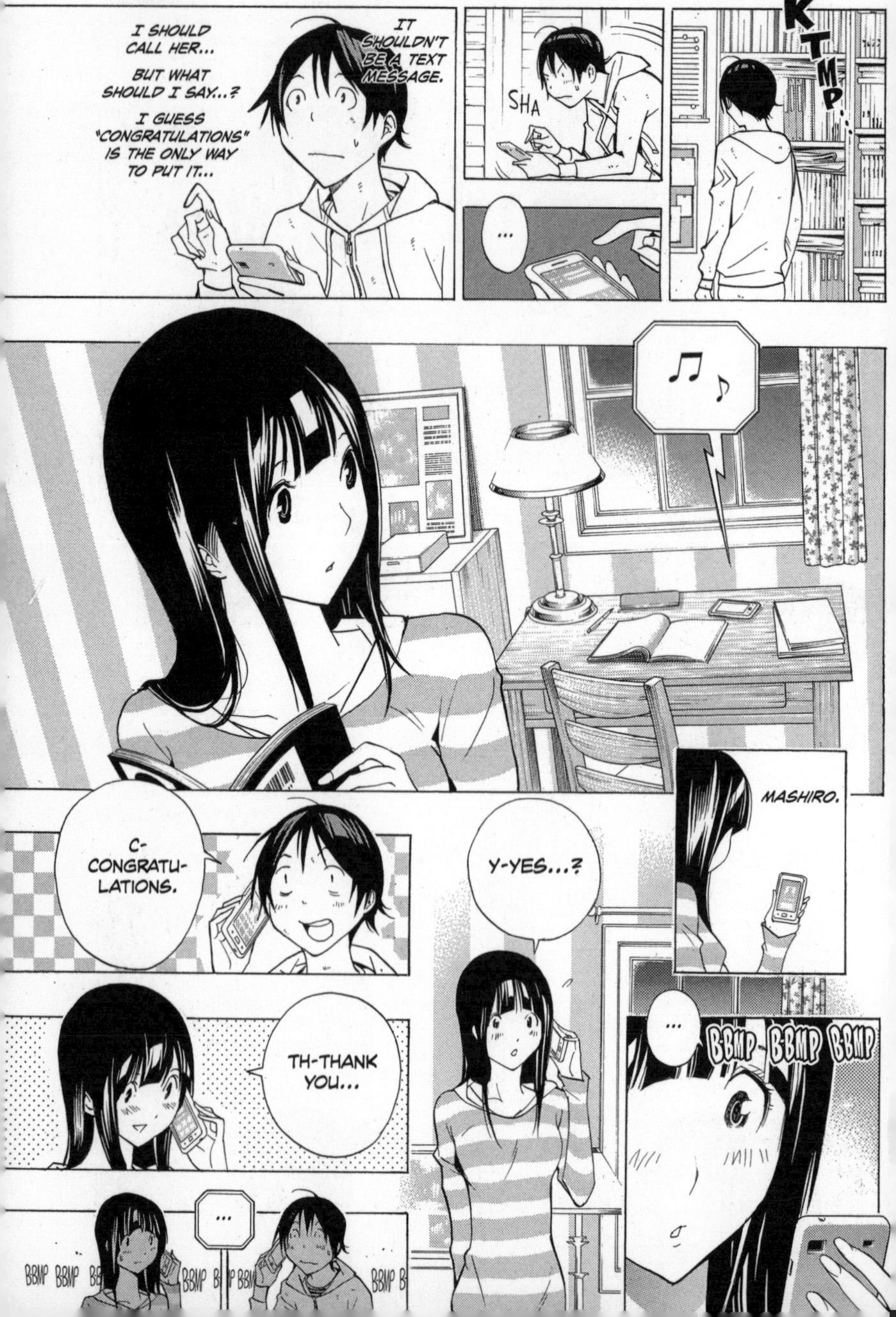
K-TMP...
SHA
...
IT SHOULDN'T BE A TEXT MESSAGE.
I SHOULD CALL HER...
BUT WHAT SHOULD I SAY...?
I GUESS "CONGRATULATIONS" IS THE ONLY WAY TO PUT IT...
♫ ♪
MASHIRO.
Y-YES...?
C-CONGRATU-LATIONS.
...
B-BMP B-BMP BBMP
TH-THANK YOU...
...
BBMP BBMP BBMP BBMP BBMP BBMP

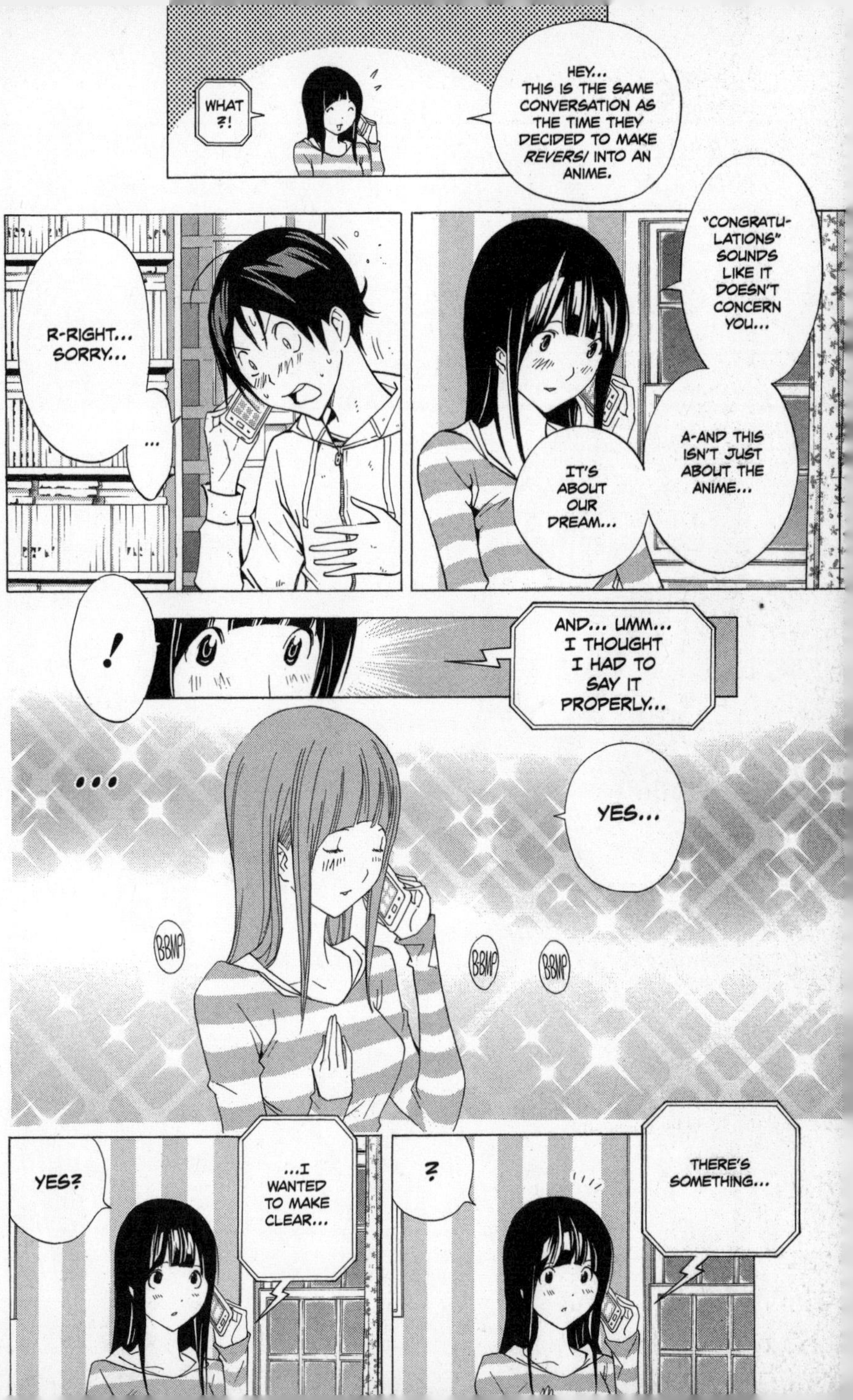
HEY... THIS IS THE SAME CONVERSATION AS THE TIME THEY DECIDED TO MAKE *REVERSI* INTO AN ANIME.
WHAT?!
"CONGRATULATIONS" SOUNDS LIKE IT DOESN'T CONCERN YOU...
A-AND THIS ISN'T JUST ABOUT THE ANIME...
IT'S ABOUT OUR DREAM...
R-RIGHT... SORRY...
...
AND... UMM... I THOUGHT I HAD TO SAY IT PROPERLY...
!
YES...
BBMP
BBMP
BBMP
...
THERE'S SOMETHING...
?
...I WANTED TO MAKE CLEAR...
YES?

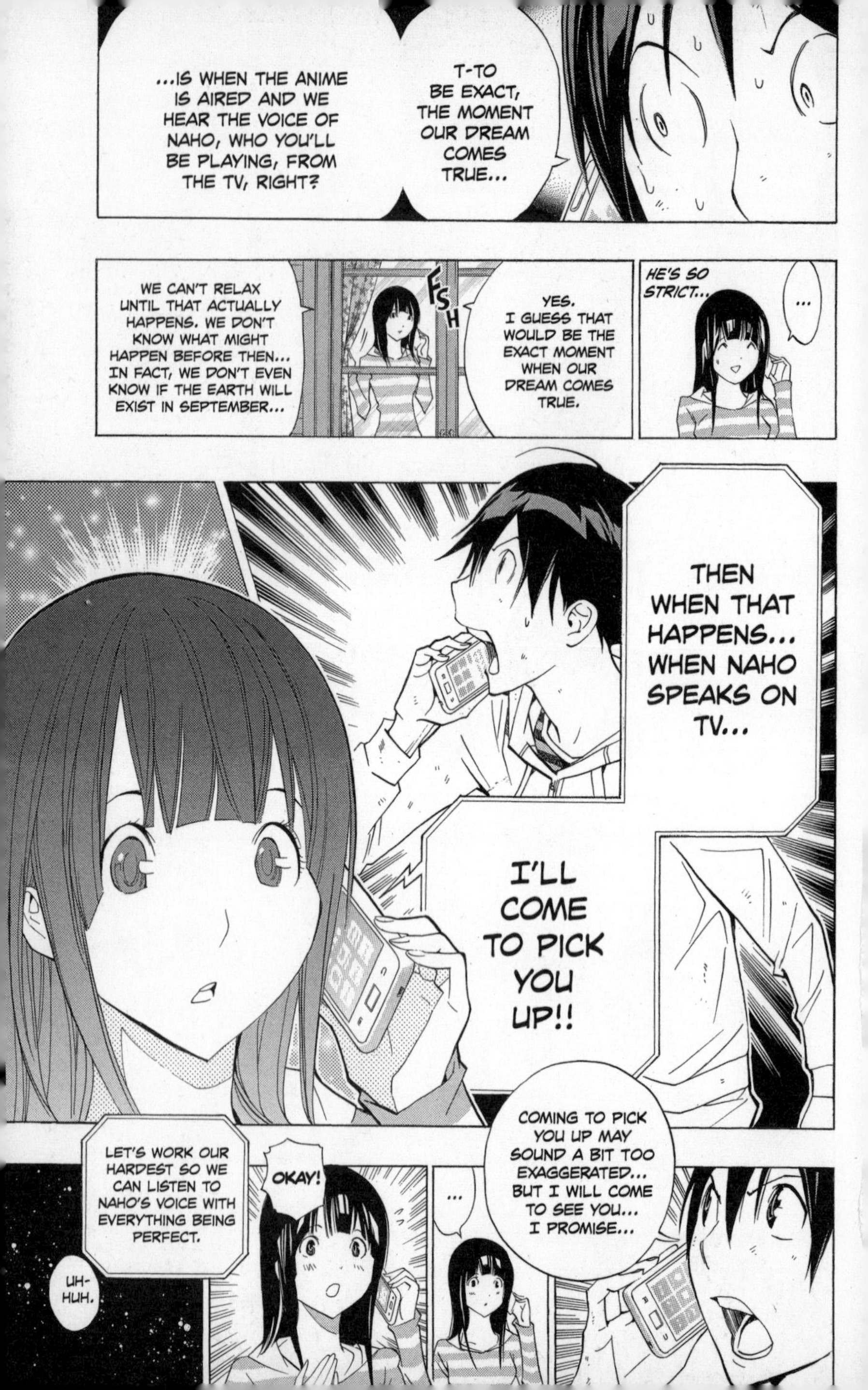
T-TO BE EXACT, THE MOMENT OUR DREAM COMES TRUE...
...IS WHEN THE ANIME IS AIRED AND WE HEAR THE VOICE OF NAHO, WHO YOU'LL BE PLAYING, FROM THE TV, RIGHT?
...
HE'S SO STRICT...
YES. I GUESS THAT WOULD BE THE EXACT MOMENT WHEN OUR DREAM COMES TRUE.
FSH
WE CAN'T RELAX UNTIL THAT ACTUALLY HAPPENS. WE DON'T KNOW WHAT MIGHT HAPPEN BEFORE THEN... IN FACT, WE DON'T EVEN KNOW IF THE EARTH WILL EXIST IN SEPTEMBER...
THEN WHEN THAT HAPPENS... WHEN NAHO SPEAKS ON TV...
I'LL COME TO PICK YOU UP!!
COMING TO PICK YOU UP MAY SOUND A BIT TOO EXAGGERATED... BUT I WILL COME TO SEE YOU... I PROMISE...
...
LET'S WORK OUR HARDEST SO WE CAN LISTEN TO NAHO'S VOICE WITH EVERYTHING BEING PERFECT.
OKAY!
UH-HUH.

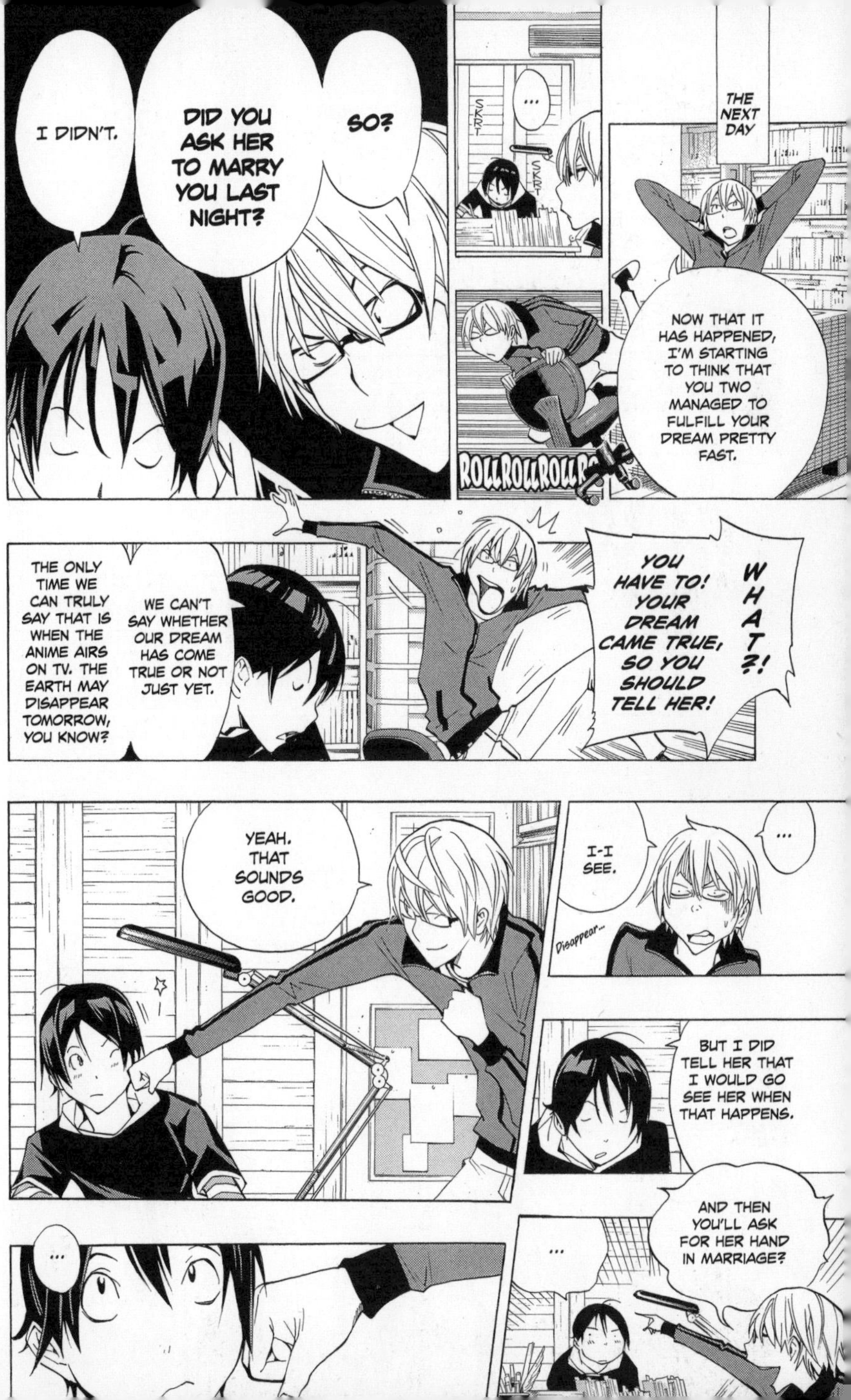
THE NEXT DAY
NOW THAT IT HAS HAPPENED, I'M STARTING TO THINK THAT YOU TWO MANAGED TO FULFILL YOUR DREAM PRETTY FAST.
...
SKRT
SKRT
ROLLROLLROLLRO
SO?
DID YOU ASK HER TO MARRY YOU LAST NIGHT?
I DIDN'T.
WHAT?!
YOU HAVE TO! YOUR DREAM CAME TRUE, SO YOU SHOULD TELL HER!
WE CAN'T SAY WHETHER OUR DREAM HAS COME TRUE OR NOT JUST YET.
THE ONLY TIME WE CAN TRULY SAY THAT IS WHEN THE ANIME AIRS ON TV. THE EARTH MAY DISAPPEAR TOMORROW, YOU KNOW?
...
I-I SEE.
Disappear...
BUT I DID TELL HER THAT I WOULD GO SEE HER WHEN THAT HAPPENS.
AND THEN YOU'LL ASK FOR HER HAND IN MARRIAGE?
...
YEAH. THAT SOUNDS GOOD.
...

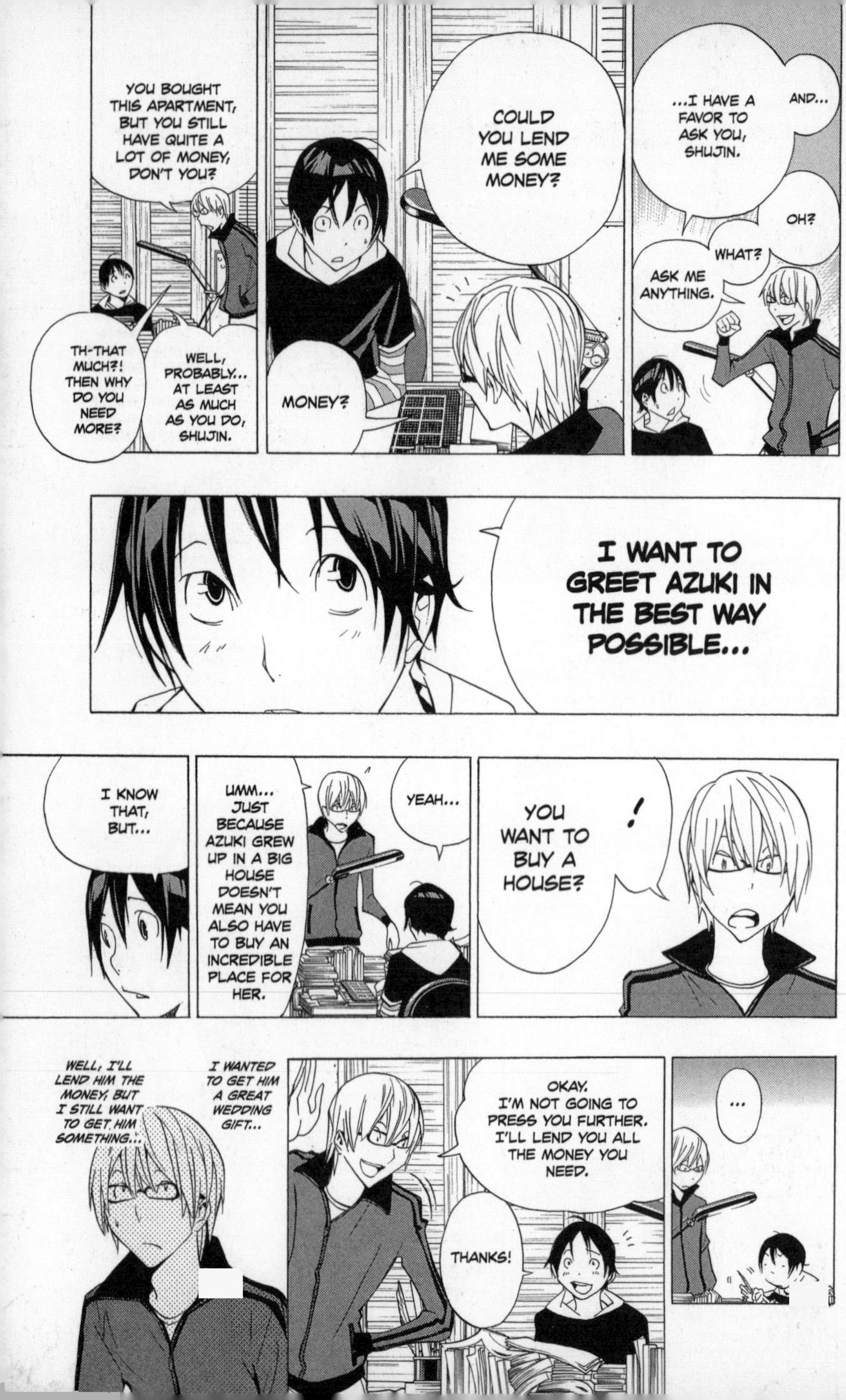

AND...
...I HAVE A FAVOR TO ASK YOU, SHUJIN.
OH?
WHAT?
ASK ME ANYTHING.
COULD YOU LEND ME SOME MONEY?
MONEY?
YOU BOUGHT THIS APARTMENT, BUT YOU STILL HAVE QUITE A LOT OF MONEY, DON'T YOU?
WELL, PROBABLY... AT LEAST AS MUCH AS YOU DO, SHUJIN.
TH-THAT MUCH?! THEN WHY DO YOU NEED MORE?
I WANT TO GREET AZUKI IN THE BEST WAY POSSIBLE...
!
YOU WANT TO BUY A HOUSE?
YEAH...
UMM... JUST BECAUSE AZUKI GREW UP IN A BIG HOUSE DOESN'T MEAN YOU ALSO HAVE TO BUY AN INCREDIBLE PLACE FOR HER.
I KNOW THAT, BUT...
...
OKAY. I'M NOT GOING TO PRESS YOU FURTHER. I'LL LEND YOU ALL THE MONEY YOU NEED.
THANKS!
I WANTED TO GET HIM A GREAT WEDDING GIFT...
WELL, I'LL LEND HIM THE MONEY, BUT I STILL WANT TO GET HIM SOMETHING...

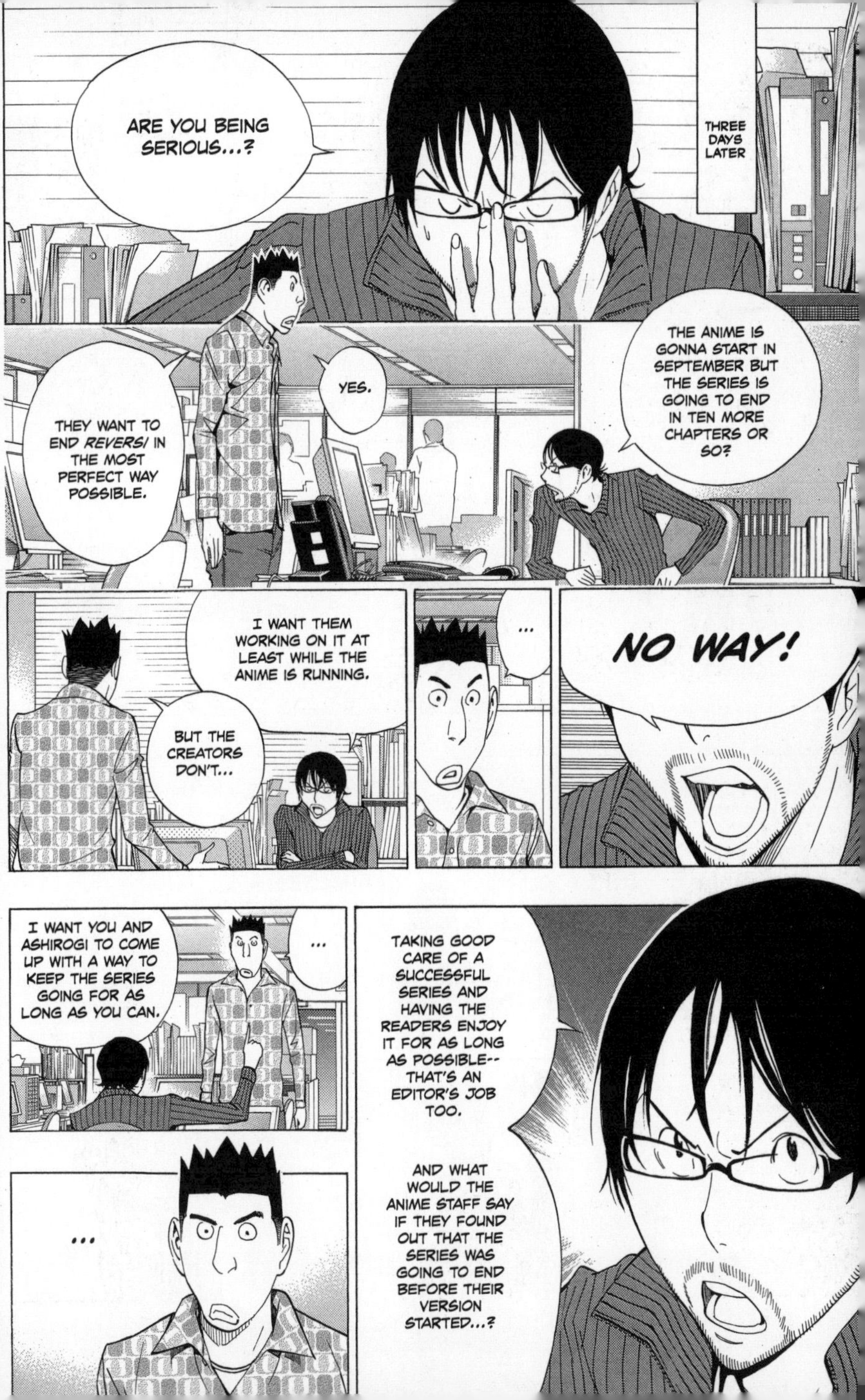
THREE DAYS LATER
ARE YOU BEING SERIOUS...?
THE ANIME IS GONNA START IN SEPTEMBER BUT THE SERIES IS GOING TO END IN TEN MORE CHAPTERS OR SO?
YES.
THEY WANT TO END *REVERSI* IN THE MOST PERFECT WAY POSSIBLE.
NO WAY!
...
I WANT THEM WORKING ON IT AT LEAST WHILE THE ANIME IS RUNNING.
BUT THE CREATORS DON'T...
TAKING GOOD CARE OF A SUCCESSFUL SERIES AND HAVING THE READERS ENJOY IT FOR AS LONG AS POSSIBLE-- THAT'S AN EDITOR'S JOB TOO.
AND WHAT WOULD THE ANIME STAFF SAY IF THEY FOUND OUT THAT THE SERIES WAS GOING TO END BEFORE THEIR VERSION STARTED...?
...
I WANT YOU AND ASHIROGI TO COME UP WITH A WAY TO KEEP THE SERIES GOING FOR AS LONG AS YOU CAN.
...

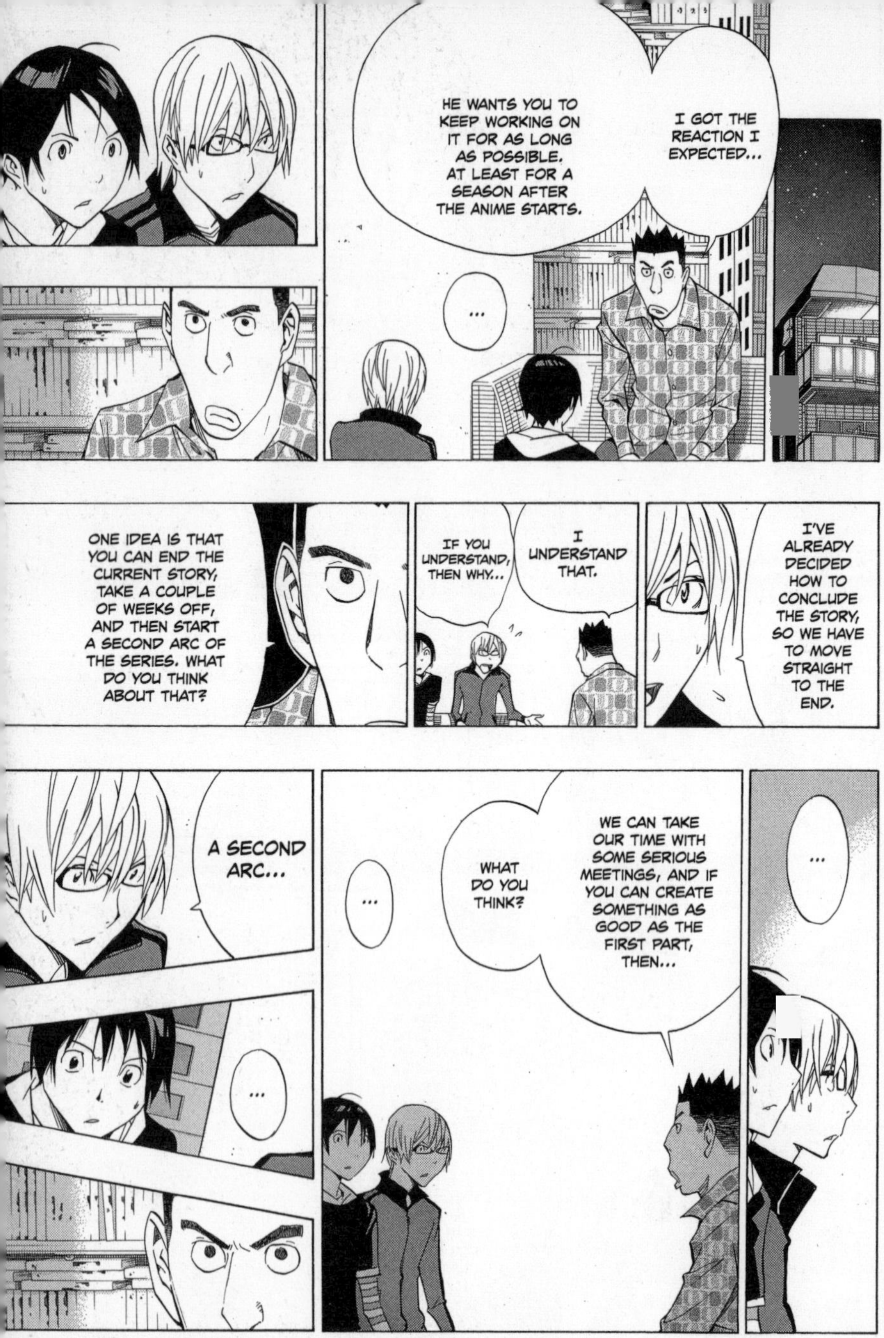
I GOT THE REACTION I EXPECTED...
HE WANTS YOU TO KEEP WORKING ON IT FOR AS LONG AS POSSIBLE. AT LEAST FOR A SEASON AFTER THE ANIME STARTS.
...
I'VE ALREADY DECIDED HOW TO CONCLUDE THE STORY, SO WE HAVE TO MOVE STRAIGHT TO THE END.
I UNDERSTAND THAT.
IF YOU UNDERSTAND, THEN WHY...
ONE IDEA IS THAT YOU CAN END THE CURRENT STORY, TAKE A COUPLE OF WEEKS OFF, AND THEN START A SECOND ARC OF THE SERIES. WHAT DO YOU THINK ABOUT THAT?
...
WE CAN TAKE OUR TIME WITH SOME SERIOUS MEETINGS, AND IF YOU CAN CREATE SOMETHING AS GOOD AS THE FIRST PART, THEN...
WHAT DO YOU THINK?
...
A SECOND ARC...
...

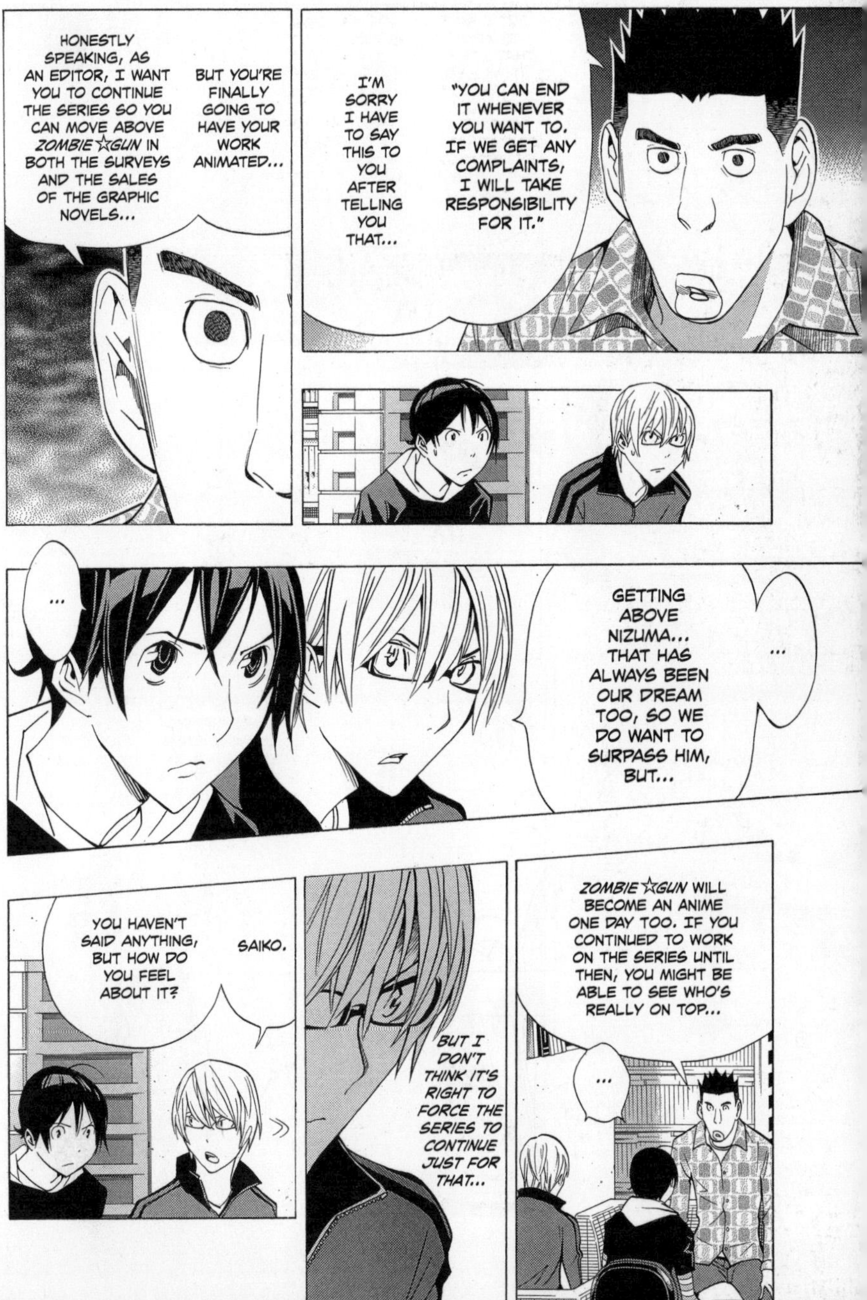
"YOU CAN END IT WHENEVER YOU WANT TO. IF WE GET ANY COMPLAINTS, I WILL TAKE RESPONSIBILITY FOR IT."
I'M SORRY I HAVE TO SAY THIS TO YOU AFTER TELLING YOU THAT...
BUT YOU'RE FINALLY GOING TO HAVE YOUR WORK ANIMATED...
HONESTLY SPEAKING, AS AN EDITOR, I WANT YOU TO CONTINUE THE SERIES SO YOU CAN MOVE ABOVE *ZOMBIE☆GUN* IN BOTH THE SURVEYS AND THE SALES OF THE GRAPHIC NOVELS...
...
GETTING ABOVE NIZUMA... THAT HAS ALWAYS BEEN OUR DREAM TOO, SO WE DO WANT TO SURPASS HIM, BUT...
...
ZOMBIE☆GUN WILL BECOME AN ANIME ONE DAY TOO. IF YOU CONTINUED TO WORK ON THE SERIES UNTIL THEN, YOU MIGHT BE ABLE TO SEE WHO'S REALLY ON TOP...
...
BUT I DON'T THINK IT'S RIGHT TO FORCE THE SERIES TO CONTINUE JUST FOR THAT...
SAIKO.
YOU HAVEN'T SAID ANYTHING, BUT HOW DO YOU FEEL ABOUT IT?

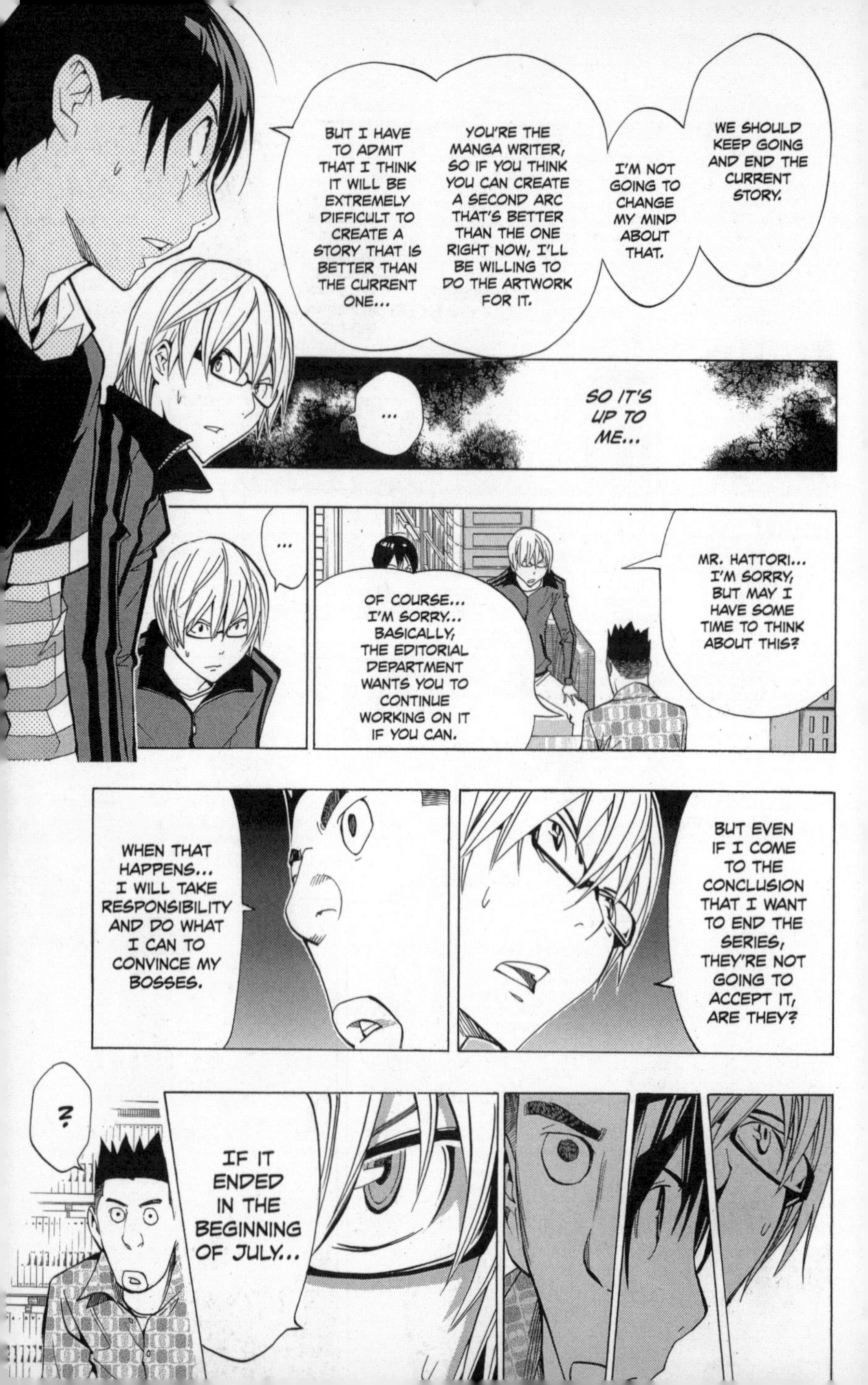
WE SHOULD KEEP GOING AND END THE CURRENT STORY.
I'M NOT GOING TO CHANGE MY MIND ABOUT THAT.
YOU'RE THE MANGA WRITER, SO IF YOU THINK YOU CAN CREATE A SECOND ARC THAT'S BETTER THAN THE ONE RIGHT NOW, I'LL BE WILLING TO DO THE ARTWORK FOR IT.
BUT I HAVE TO ADMIT THAT I THINK IT WILL BE EXTREMELY DIFFICULT TO CREATE A STORY THAT IS BETTER THAN THE CURRENT ONE...
SO IT'S UP TO ME...
...
MR. HATTORI... I'M SORRY, BUT MAY I HAVE SOME TIME TO THINK ABOUT THIS?
OF COURSE... I'M SORRY... BASICALLY, THE EDITORIAL DEPARTMENT WANTS YOU TO CONTINUE WORKING ON IT IF YOU CAN.
...
BUT EVEN IF I COME TO THE CONCLUSION THAT I WANT TO END THE SERIES, THEY'RE NOT GOING TO ACCEPT IT, ARE THEY?
WHEN THAT HAPPENS... I WILL TAKE RESPONSIBILITY AND DO WHAT I CAN TO CONVINCE MY BOSSES.
IF IT ENDED IN THE BEGINNING OF JULY...
?

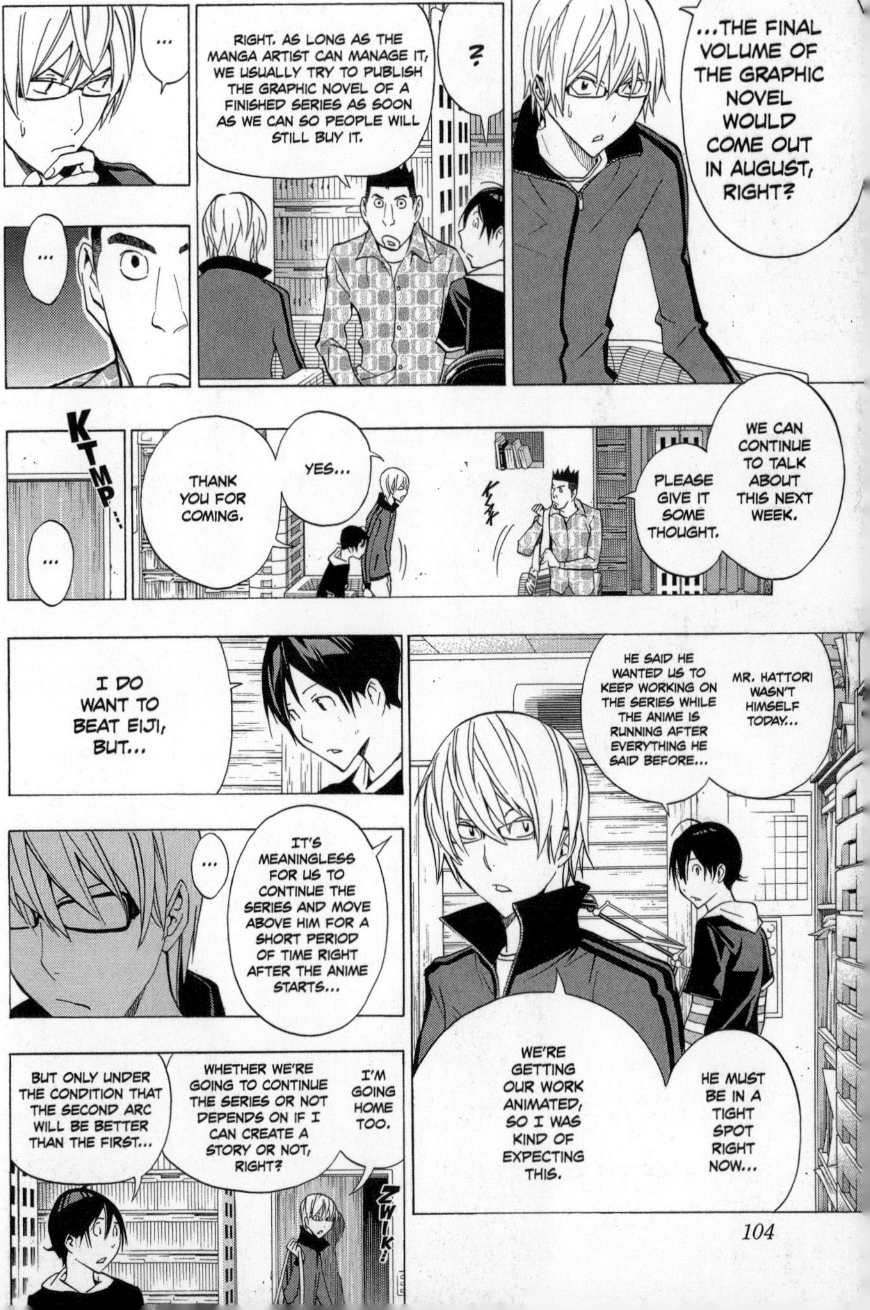
...THE FINAL VOLUME OF THE GRAPHIC NOVEL WOULD COME OUT IN AUGUST, RIGHT?
?
RIGHT. AS LONG AS THE MANGA ARTIST CAN MANAGE IT, WE USUALLY TRY TO PUBLISH THE GRAPHIC NOVEL OF A FINISHED SERIES AS SOON AS WE CAN SO PEOPLE WILL STILL BUY IT.
...
...
WE CAN CONTINUE TO TALK ABOUT THIS NEXT WEEK.
PLEASE GIVE IT SOME THOUGHT.
YES...
THANK YOU FOR COMING.
KTMP...
...
MR. HATTORI WASN'T HIMSELF TODAY...
HE SAID HE WANTED US TO KEEP WORKING ON THE SERIES WHILE THE ANIME IS RUNNING AFTER EVERYTHING HE SAID BEFORE...
HE MUST BE IN A TIGHT SPOT RIGHT NOW...
WE'RE GETTING OUR WORK ANIMATED, SO I WAS KIND OF EXPECTING THIS.
I DO WANT TO BEAT EIJI, BUT...
IT'S MEANINGLESS FOR US TO CONTINUE THE SERIES AND MOVE ABOVE HIM FOR A SHORT PERIOD OF TIME RIGHT AFTER THE ANIME STARTS...
...
I'M GOING HOME TOO.
ZWIK!
WHETHER WE'RE GOING TO CONTINUE THE SERIES OR NOT DEPENDS ON IF I CAN CREATE A STORY OR NOT, RIGHT?
BUT ONLY UNDER THE CONDITION THAT THE SECOND ARC WILL BE BETTER THAN THE FIRST...

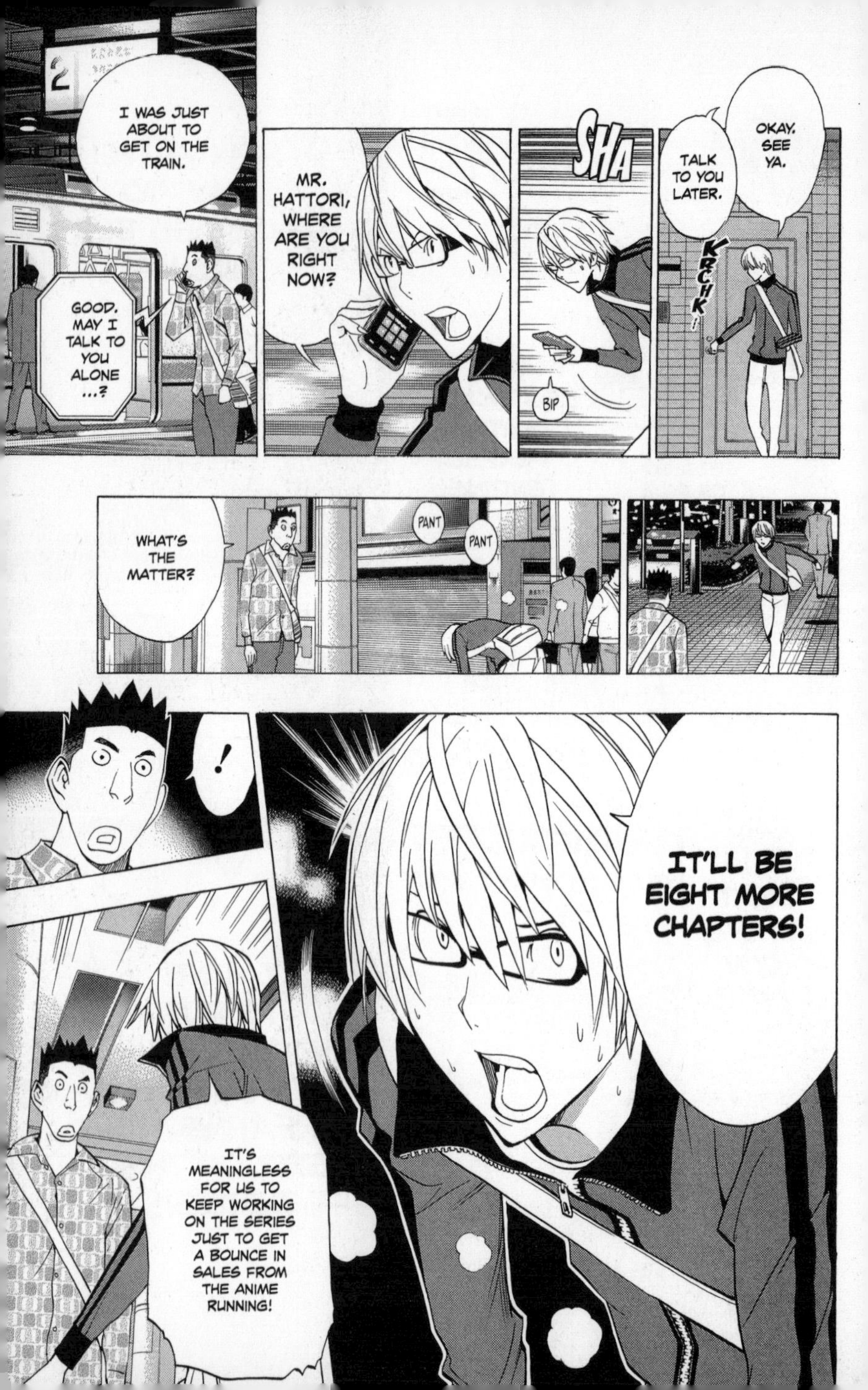
OKAY. SEE YA.
TALK TO YOU LATER.
KRCHK!
SHA
BIP
MR. HATTORI, WHERE ARE YOU RIGHT NOW?
I WAS JUST ABOUT TO GET ON THE TRAIN.
GOOD. MAY I TALK TO YOU ALONE ...?
PANT
PANT
WHAT'S THE MATTER?
IT'LL BE EIGHT MORE CHAPTERS!
!
IT'S MEANINGLESS FOR US TO KEEP WORKING ON THE SERIES JUST TO GET A BOUNCE IN SALES FROM THE ANIME RUNNING!

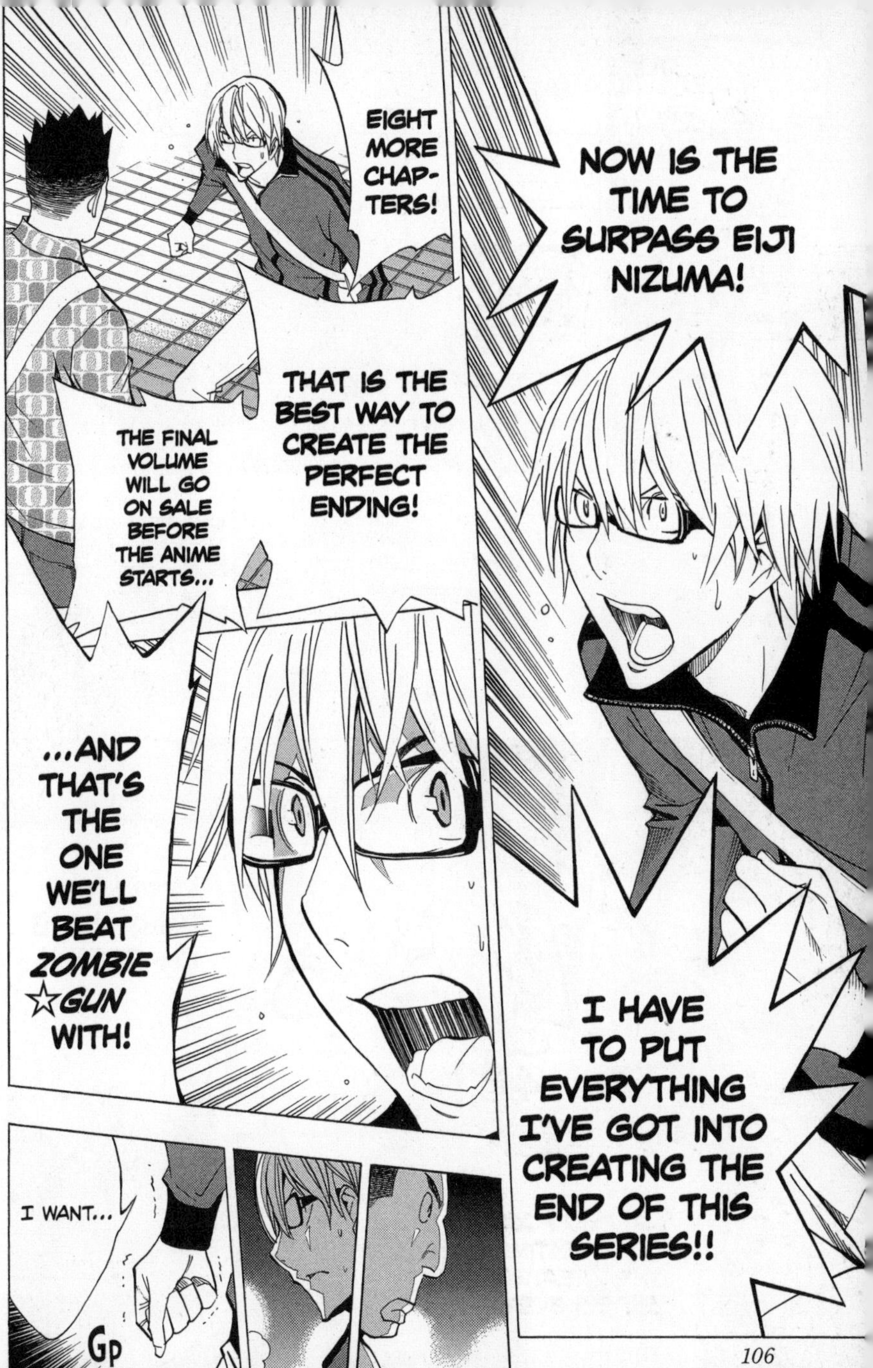
NOW IS THE TIME TO SURPASS EIJI NIZUMA!
I HAVE TO PUT EVERYTHING I'VE GOT INTO CREATING THE END OF THIS SERIES!!
EIGHT MORE CHAP-TERS!
THAT IS THE BEST WAY TO CREATE THE PERFECT ENDING!
THE FINAL VOLUME WILL GO ON SALE BEFORE THE ANIME STARTS...
...AND THAT'S THE ONE WE'LL BEAT *ZOMBIE☆GUN* WITH!
I WANT...
Gp

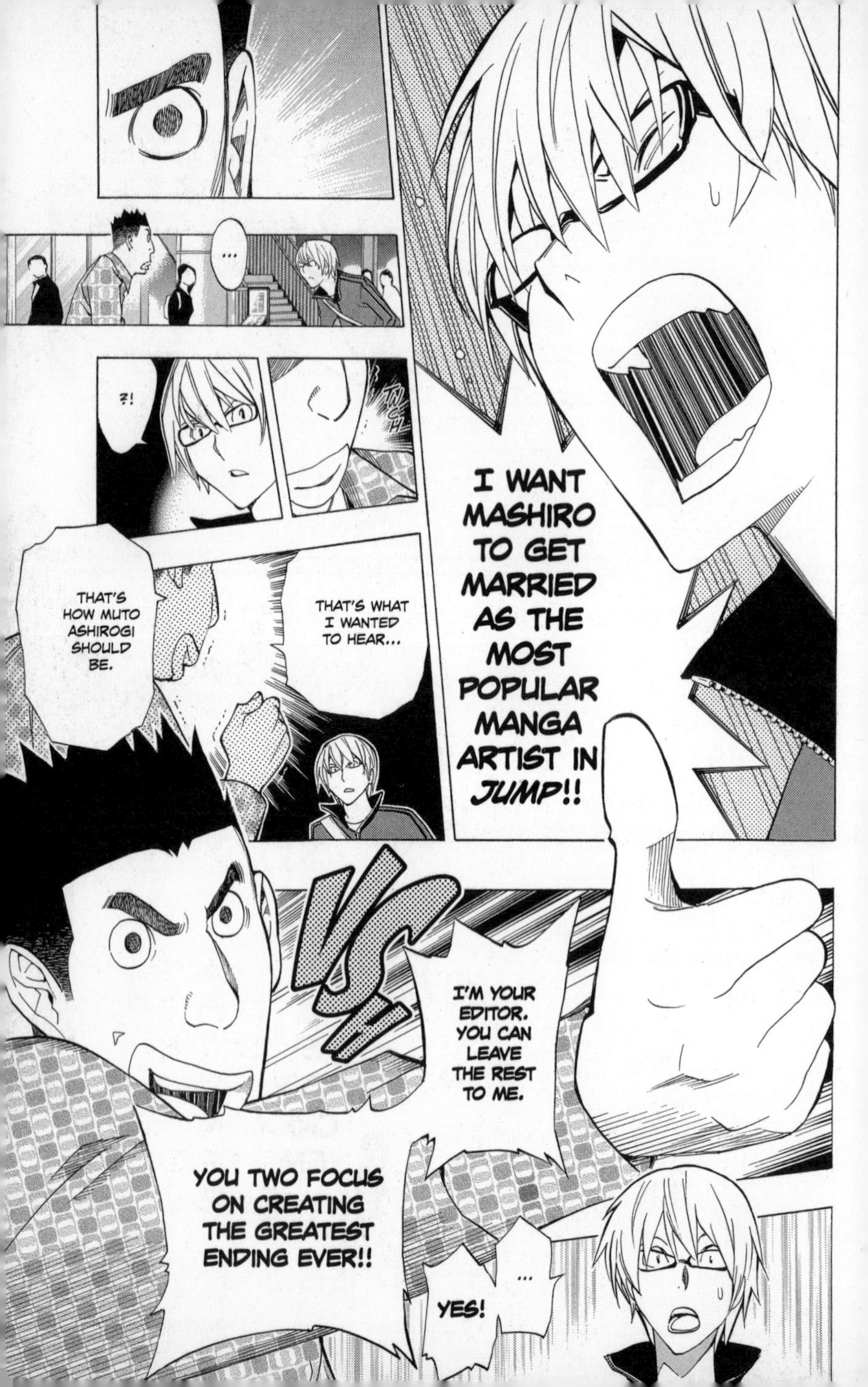
I WANT MASHIRO TO GET MARRIED AS THE MOST POPULAR MANGA ARTIST IN *JUMP*!!
...
?!
THAT'S WHAT I WANTED TO HEAR...
THAT'S HOW MUTO ASHIROGI SHOULD BE.
I'M YOUR EDITOR. YOU CAN LEAVE THE REST TO ME.
YOU TWO FOCUS ON CREATING THE GREATEST ENDING EVER!!
...
YES!

OHBA'S STORYBOARD

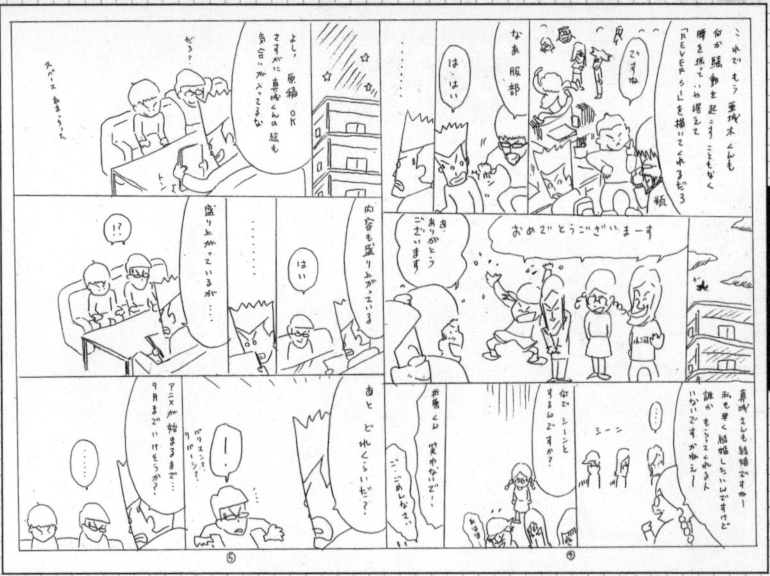

これでもう亜城木くんも
何か騒動を起こすこともなく
腰を据えて「REVERSI」を描いてくれるだろ
ですね
なあ服部
は…はい
……
おめでとうございまーす
あ、ありがとうございます
真城さんも結婚ですかー
私も早く結婚したいんですけど
誰かもらってくれる人いないですかねえ〜
……
シーン
何でシーンとするんですか?
あはは
折原くん 笑わないで…
ご…ごめんなさい
よし、原稿OK
さすがに真城くんの絵も気合いが入ってるな
だろ?
内容も盛り上がっている
はい
……
盛り上がっているが……
!?
あとどれくらいだ?
!
アニメが始まるまで…
9月までいけそうか?
……

OBATA'S STORYBOARD

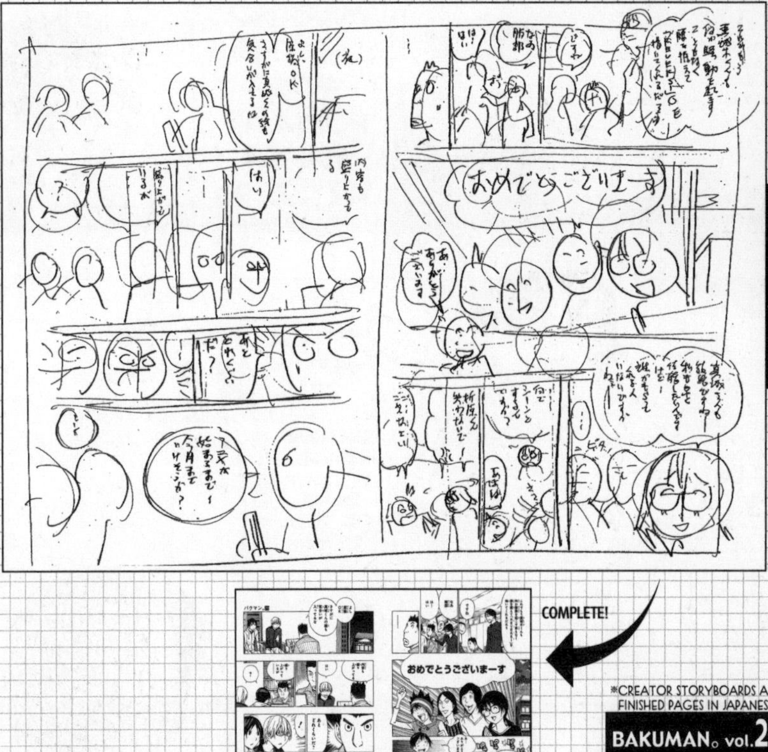

おめでとうございまーす

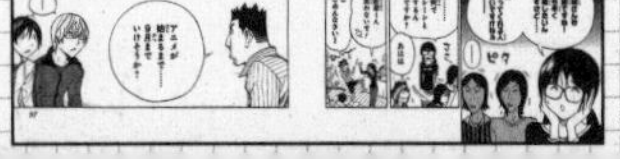

おめでとうございまーす

COMPLETE!

*CREATOR STORYBOARDS AND FINISHED PAGES IN JAPANESE

BAKUMAN。 vol.20

"Until the Final Draft Is Complete"

Chapter 173, pp. 96-97

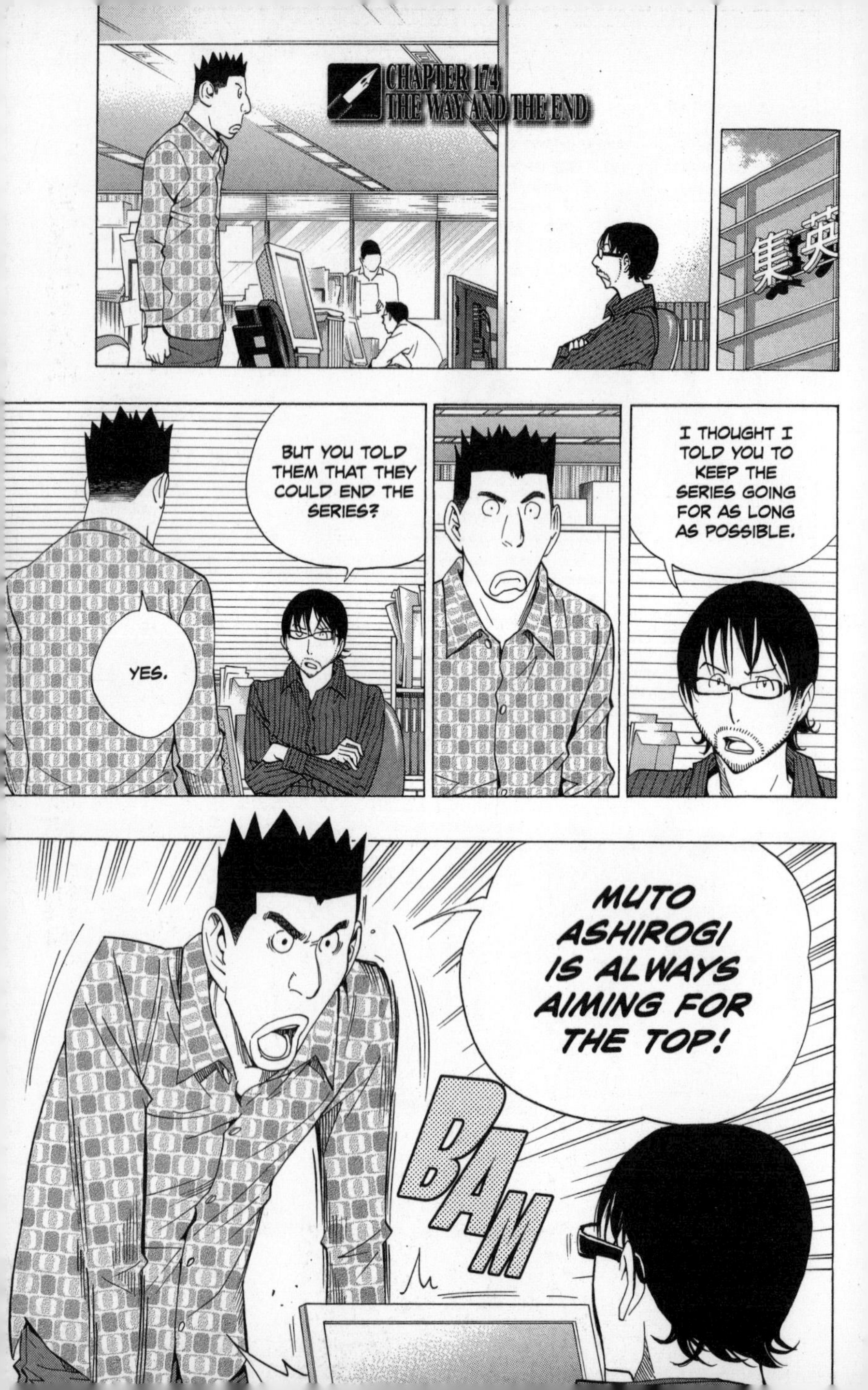

集英
CHAPTER 174
THE WAY AND THE END
I THOUGHT I TOLD YOU TO KEEP THE SERIES GOING FOR AS LONG AS POSSIBLE.
BUT YOU TOLD THEM THAT THEY COULD END THE SERIES?
YES.
MUTO ASHIROGI IS ALWAYS AIMING FOR THE TOP!
BAM

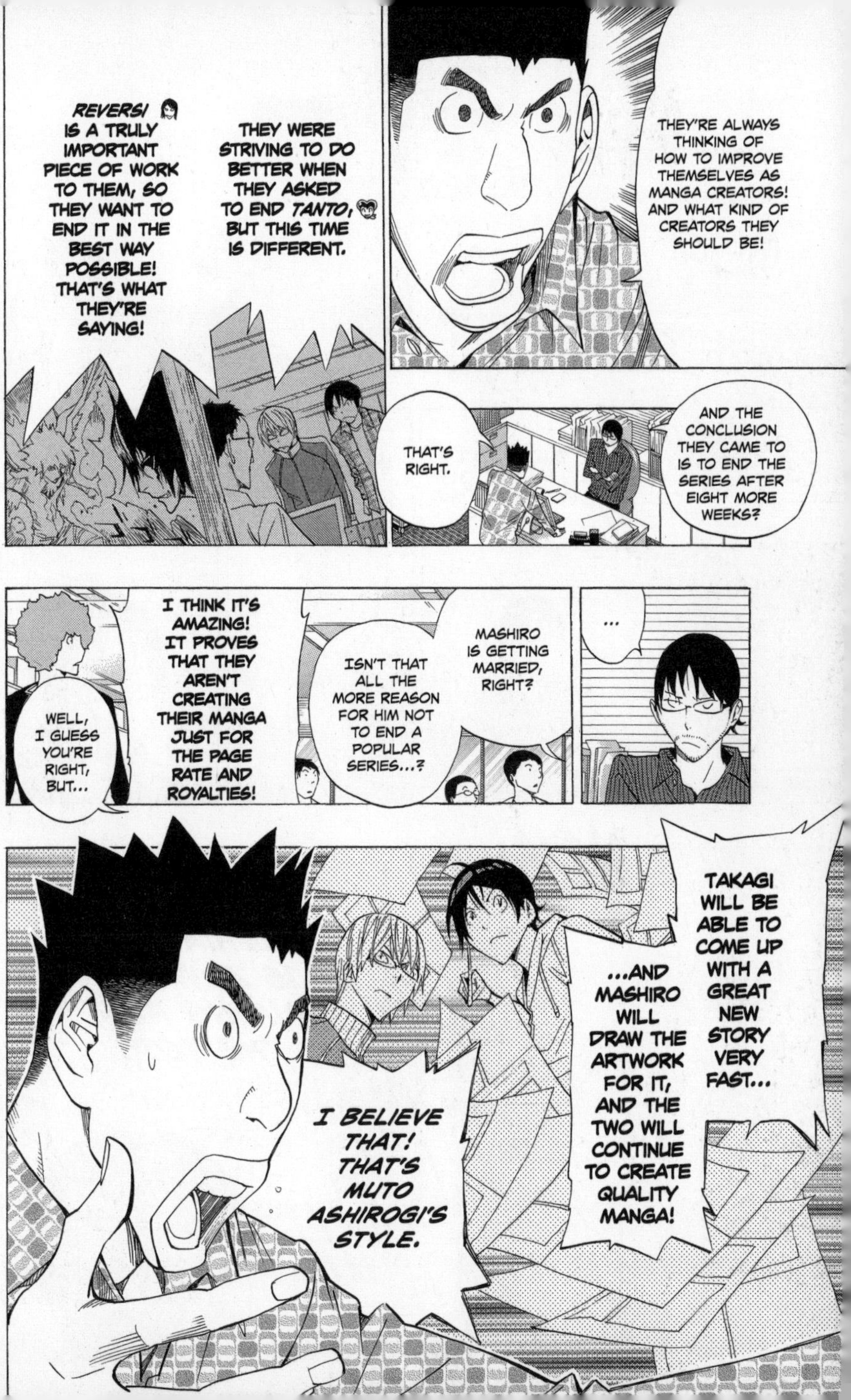
THEY'RE ALWAYS THINKING OF HOW TO IMPROVE THEMSELVES AS MANGA CREATORS! AND WHAT KIND OF CREATORS THEY SHOULD BE!
AND THE CONCLUSION THEY CAME TO IS TO END THE SERIES AFTER EIGHT MORE WEEKS?
THAT'S RIGHT.
THEY WERE STRIVING TO DO BETTER WHEN THEY ASKED TO END *TANTO*, BUT THIS TIME IS DIFFERENT.
REVERSI IS A TRULY IMPORTANT PIECE OF WORK TO THEM, SO THEY WANT TO END IT IN THE BEST WAY POSSIBLE! THAT'S WHAT THEY'RE SAYING!
...
MASHIRO IS GETTING MARRIED, RIGHT?
ISN'T THAT ALL THE MORE REASON FOR HIM NOT TO END A POPULAR SERIES...?
I THINK IT'S AMAZING! IT PROVES THAT THEY AREN'T CREATING THEIR MANGA JUST FOR THE PAGE RATE AND ROYALTIES!
WELL, I GUESS YOU'RE RIGHT, BUT...
TAKAGI WILL BE ABLE TO COME UP WITH A GREAT NEW STORY VERY FAST...
...AND MASHIRO WILL DRAW THE ARTWORK FOR IT, AND THE TWO WILL CONTINUE TO CREATE QUALITY MANGA!
I BELIEVE THAT! THAT'S MUTO ASHIROGI'S STYLE.

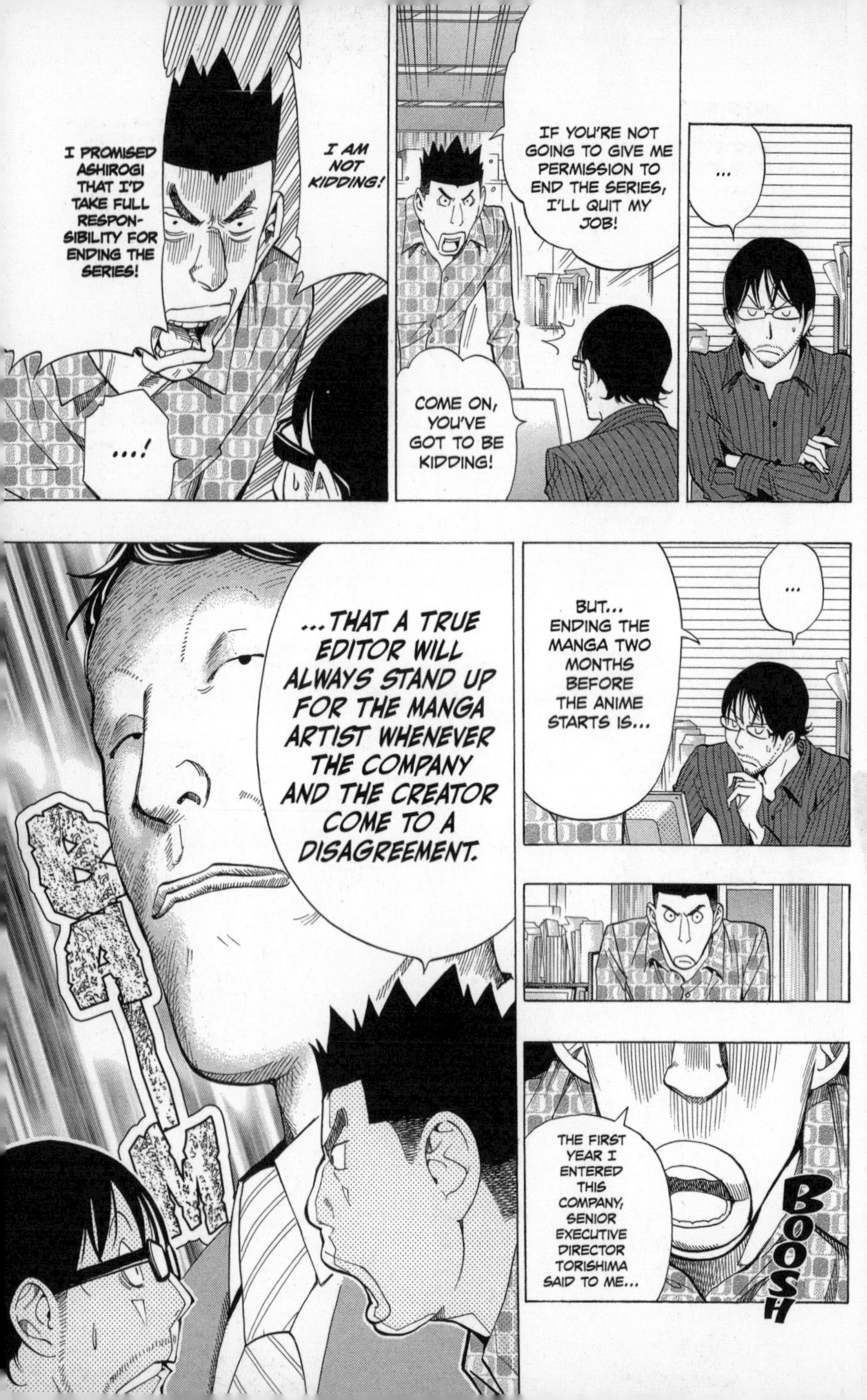
...
IF YOU'RE NOT GOING TO GIVE ME PERMISSION TO END THE SERIES, I'LL QUIT MY JOB!
COME ON, YOU'VE GOT TO BE KIDDING!
I AM NOT KIDDING!
I PROMISED ASHIROGI THAT I'D TAKE FULL RESPON-SIBILITY FOR ENDING THE SERIES!
...!
...
BUT... ENDING THE MANGA TWO MONTHS BEFORE THE ANIME STARTS IS...
THE FIRST YEAR I ENTERED THIS COMPANY, SENIOR EXECUTIVE DIRECTOR TORISHIMA SAID TO ME...
BOOSH
...THAT A TRUE EDITOR WILL ALWAYS STAND UP FOR THE MANGA ARTIST WHENEVER THE COMPANY AND THE CREATOR COME TO A DISAGREEMENT.

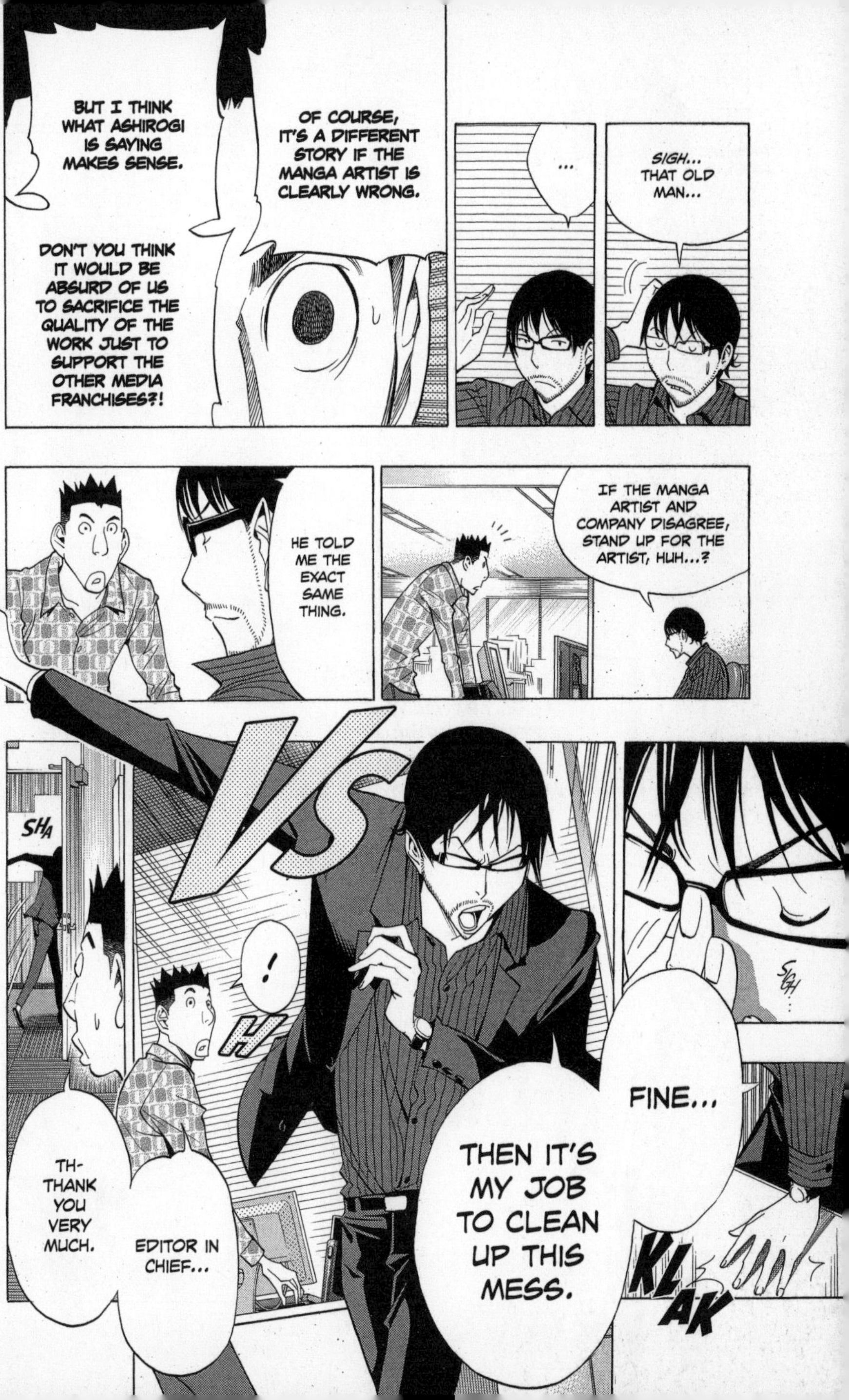
SIGH... THAT OLD MAN...
...
OF COURSE, IT'S A DIFFERENT STORY IF THE MANGA ARTIST IS CLEARLY WRONG.
BUT I THINK WHAT ASHIROGI IS SAYING MAKES SENSE.
DON'T YOU THINK IT WOULD BE ABSURD OF US TO SACRIFICE THE QUALITY OF THE WORK JUST TO SUPPORT THE OTHER MEDIA FRANCHISES?!
IF THE MANGA ARTIST AND COMPANY DISAGREE, STAND UP FOR THE ARTIST, HUH...?
HE TOLD ME THE EXACT SAME THING.
SIGH...
KLAK
FINE...
THEN IT'S MY JOB TO CLEAN UP THIS MESS.
!
H
VS
SHA
EDITOR IN CHIEF...
TH-THANK YOU VERY MUCH.

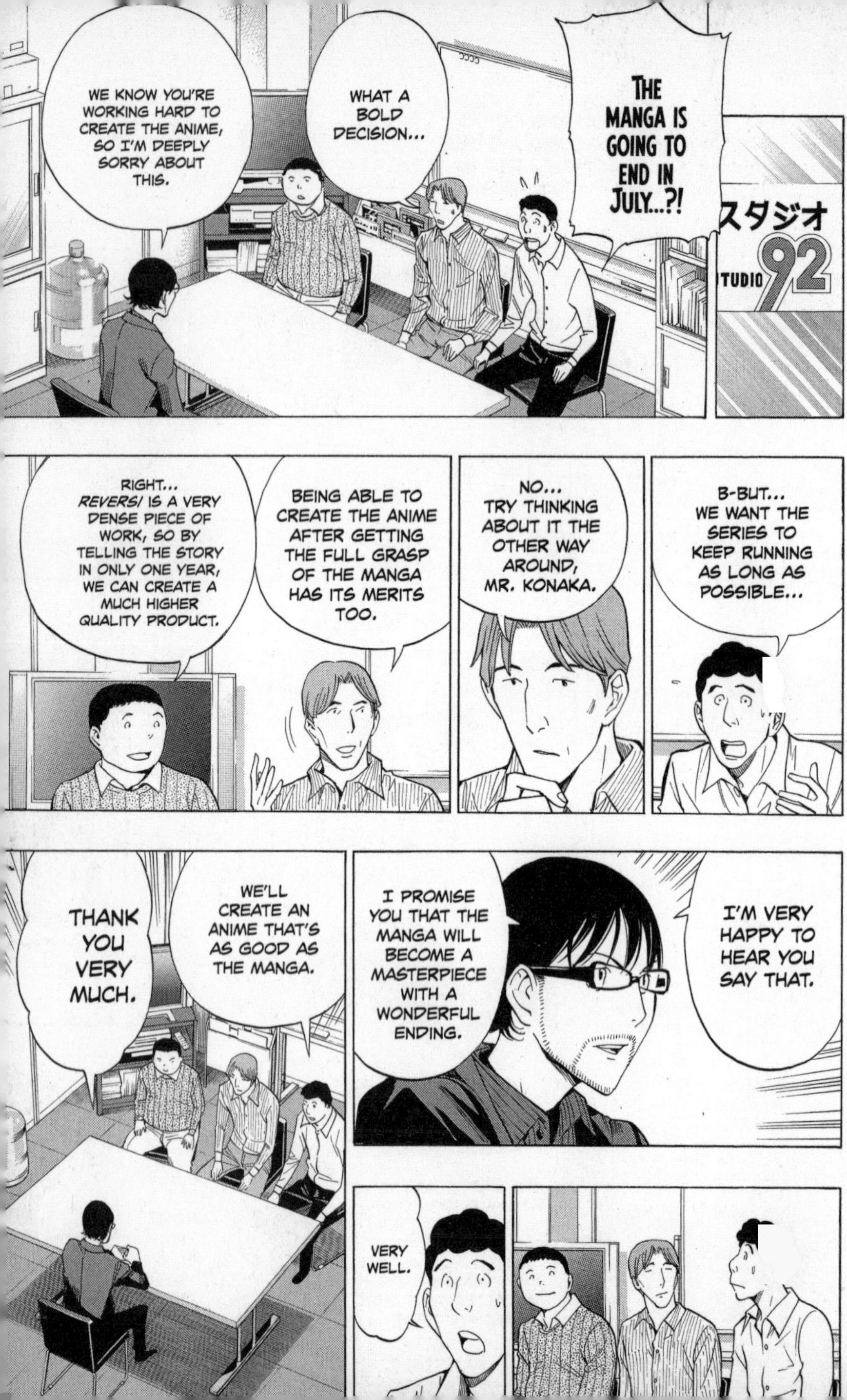
スタジオ
TUDIO 92
THE MANGA IS GOING TO END IN JULY...?!
WHAT A BOLD DECISION...
WE KNOW YOU'RE WORKING HARD TO CREATE THE ANIME, SO I'M DEEPLY SORRY ABOUT THIS.
B-BUT... WE WANT THE SERIES TO KEEP RUNNING AS LONG AS POSSIBLE...
NO... TRY THINKING ABOUT IT THE OTHER WAY AROUND, MR. KONAKA.
BEING ABLE TO CREATE THE ANIME AFTER GETTING THE FULL GRASP OF THE MANGA HAS ITS MERITS TOO.
RIGHT... *REVERSI* IS A VERY DENSE PIECE OF WORK, SO BY TELLING THE STORY IN ONLY ONE YEAR, WE CAN CREATE A MUCH HIGHER QUALITY PRODUCT.
I'M VERY HAPPY TO HEAR YOU SAY THAT.
I PROMISE YOU THAT THE MANGA WILL BECOME A MASTERPIECE WITH A WONDERFUL ENDING.
VERY WELL.
WE'LL CREATE AN ANIME THAT'S AS GOOD AS THE MANGA.
THANK YOU VERY MUCH.

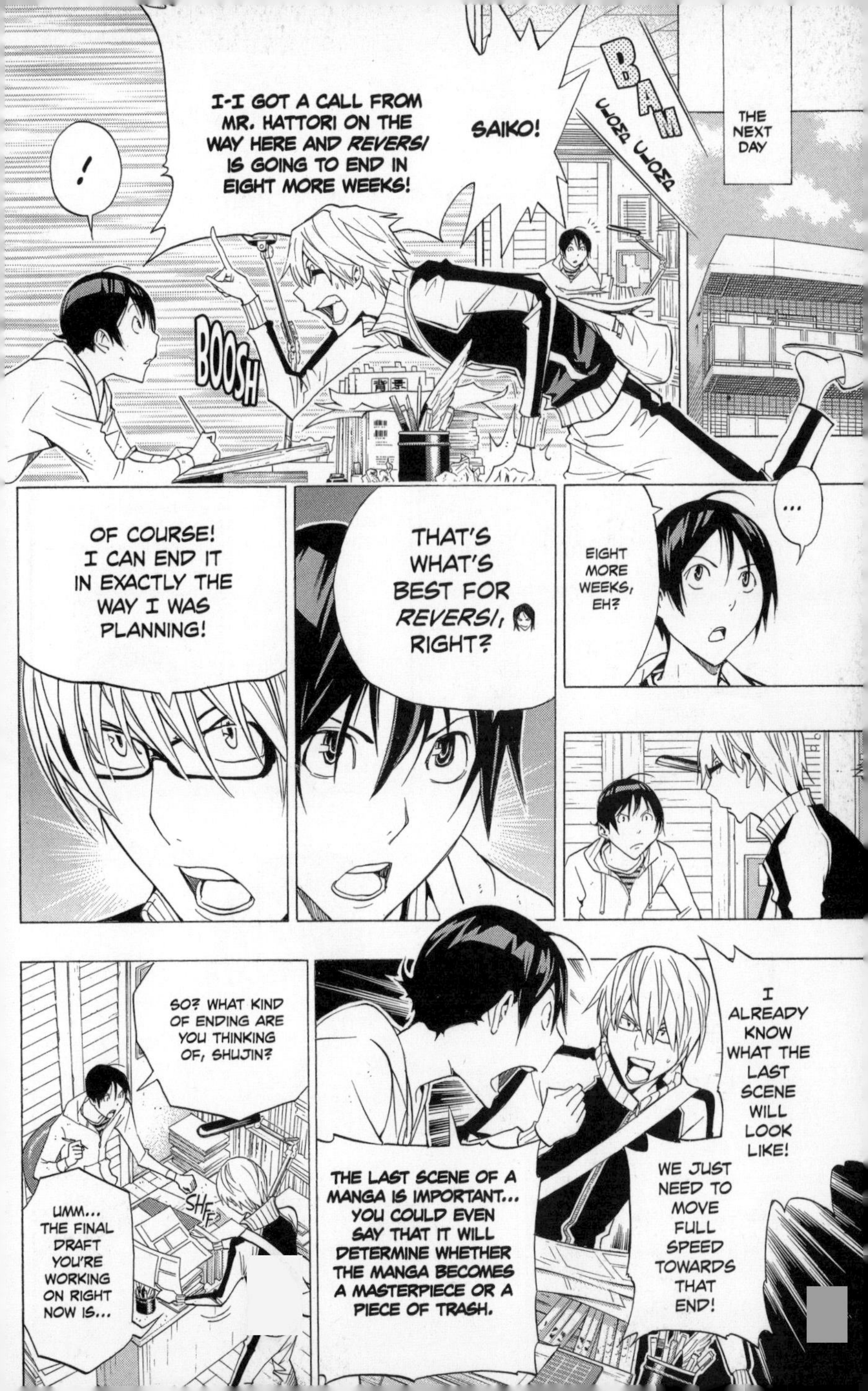
THE NEXT DAY
BAM
CLOMP CLOMP
SAIKO!
I-I GOT A CALL FROM MR. HATTORI ON THE WAY HERE AND *REVERSI* IS GOING TO END IN EIGHT MORE WEEKS!
BOOSH
!
...
EIGHT MORE WEEKS, EH?
THAT'S WHAT'S BEST FOR *REVERSI*, RIGHT?
OF COURSE! I CAN END IT IN EXACTLY THE WAY I WAS PLANNING!
I ALREADY KNOW WHAT THE LAST SCENE WILL LOOK LIKE!
WE JUST NEED TO MOVE FULL SPEED TOWARDS THAT END!
THE LAST SCENE OF A MANGA IS IMPORTANT... YOU COULD EVEN SAY THAT IT WILL DETERMINE WHETHER THE MANGA BECOMES A MASTERPIECE OR A PIECE OF TRASH.
SO? WHAT KIND OF ENDING ARE YOU THINKING OF, SHUJIN?
SHFF
UMM... THE FINAL DRAFT YOU'RE WORKING ON RIGHT NOW IS...

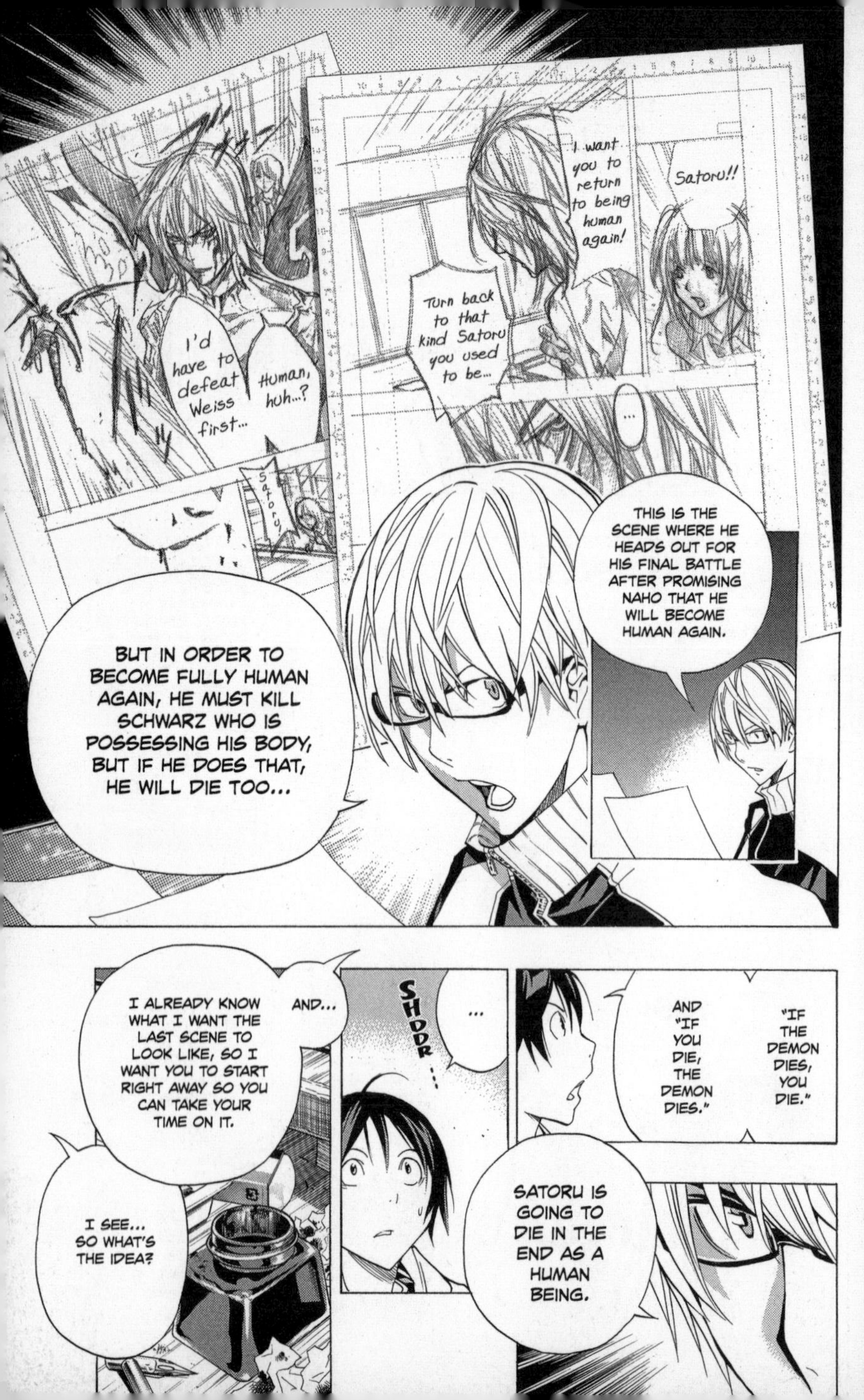
Satoru!!
I want you to return to being human again!
Turn back to that kind Satoru you used to be...
...
Human, huh...?
I'd have to defeat Weiss first...
Satoru!
THIS IS THE SCENE WHERE HE HEADS OUT FOR HIS FINAL BATTLE AFTER PROMISING NAHO THAT HE WILL BECOME HUMAN AGAIN.
BUT IN ORDER TO BECOME FULLY HUMAN AGAIN, HE MUST KILL SCHWARZ WHO IS POSSESSING HIS BODY, BUT IF HE DOES THAT, HE WILL DIE TOO...
"IF THE DEMON DIES, YOU DIE."
AND "IF YOU DIE, THE DEMON DIES."
...
SHDDR...
AND...
I ALREADY KNOW WHAT I WANT THE LAST SCENE TO LOOK LIKE, SO I WANT YOU TO START RIGHT AWAY SO YOU CAN TAKE YOUR TIME ON IT.
SATORU IS GOING TO DIE IN THE END AS A HUMAN BEING.
I SEE... SO WHAT'S THE IDEA?

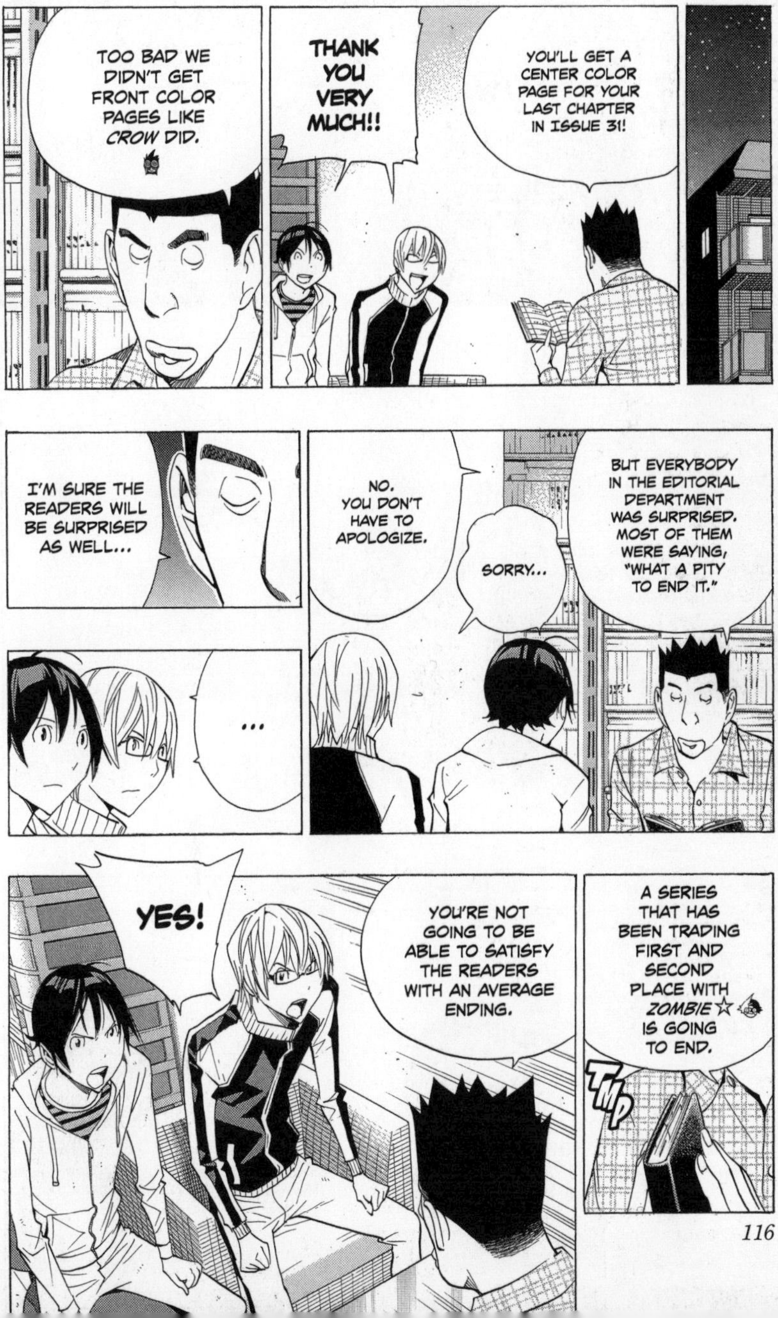
YOU'LL GET A CENTER COLOR PAGE FOR YOUR LAST CHAPTER IN ISSUE 31!
THANK YOU VERY MUCH!!
TOO BAD WE DIDN'T GET FRONT COLOR PAGES LIKE *CROW* DID.
BUT EVERYBODY IN THE EDITORIAL DEPARTMENT WAS SURPRISED. MOST OF THEM WERE SAYING, "WHAT A PITY TO END IT."
SORRY...
NO. YOU DON'T HAVE TO APOLOGIZE.
I'M SURE THE READERS WILL BE SURPRISED AS WELL...
...
A SERIES THAT HAS BEEN TRADING FIRST AND SECOND PLACE WITH *ZOMBIE*☆ IS GOING TO END.
TMP
YOU'RE NOT GOING TO BE ABLE TO SATISFY THE READERS WITH AN AVERAGE ENDING.
YES!

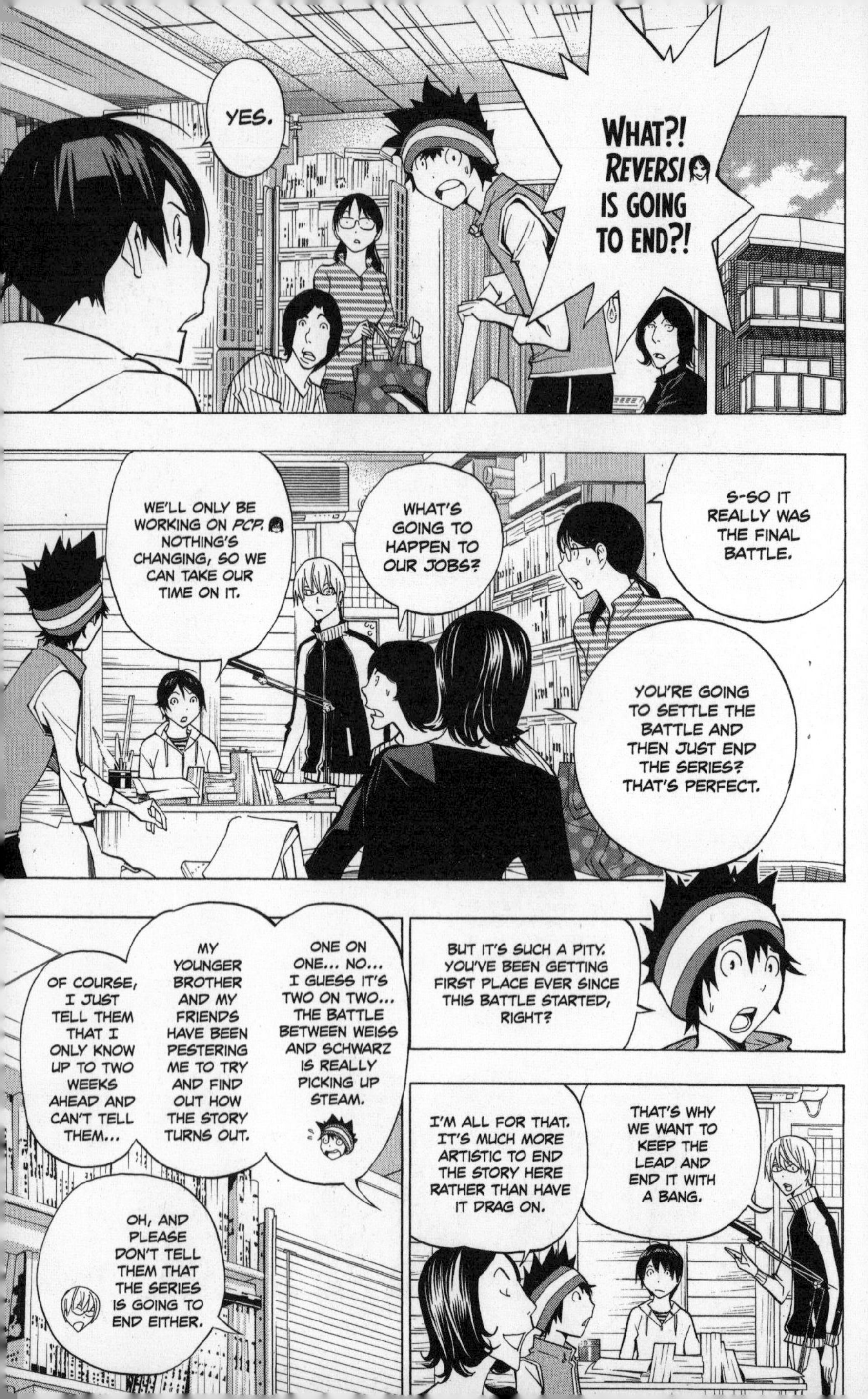
WHAT?! REVERSI IS GOING TO END?!
YES.
S-SO IT REALLY WAS THE FINAL BATTLE.
YOU'RE GOING TO SETTLE THE BATTLE AND THEN JUST END THE SERIES? THAT'S PERFECT.
WHAT'S GOING TO HAPPEN TO OUR JOBS?
WE'LL ONLY BE WORKING ON PCP. NOTHING'S CHANGING, SO WE CAN TAKE OUR TIME ON IT.
BUT IT'S SUCH A PITY. YOU'VE BEEN GETTING FIRST PLACE EVER SINCE THIS BATTLE STARTED, RIGHT?
THAT'S WHY WE WANT TO KEEP THE LEAD AND END IT WITH A BANG.
I'M ALL FOR THAT. IT'S MUCH MORE ARTISTIC TO END THE STORY HERE RATHER THAN HAVE IT DRAG ON.
ONE ON ONE... NO... I GUESS IT'S TWO ON TWO... THE BATTLE BETWEEN WEISS AND SCHWARZ IS REALLY PICKING UP STEAM.
MY YOUNGER BROTHER AND MY FRIENDS HAVE BEEN PESTERING ME TO TRY AND FIND OUT HOW THE STORY TURNS OUT.
OF COURSE, I JUST TELL THEM THAT I ONLY KNOW UP TO TWO WEEKS AHEAD AND CAN'T TELL THEM...
OH, AND PLEASE DON'T TELL THEM THAT THE SERIES IS GOING TO END EITHER.

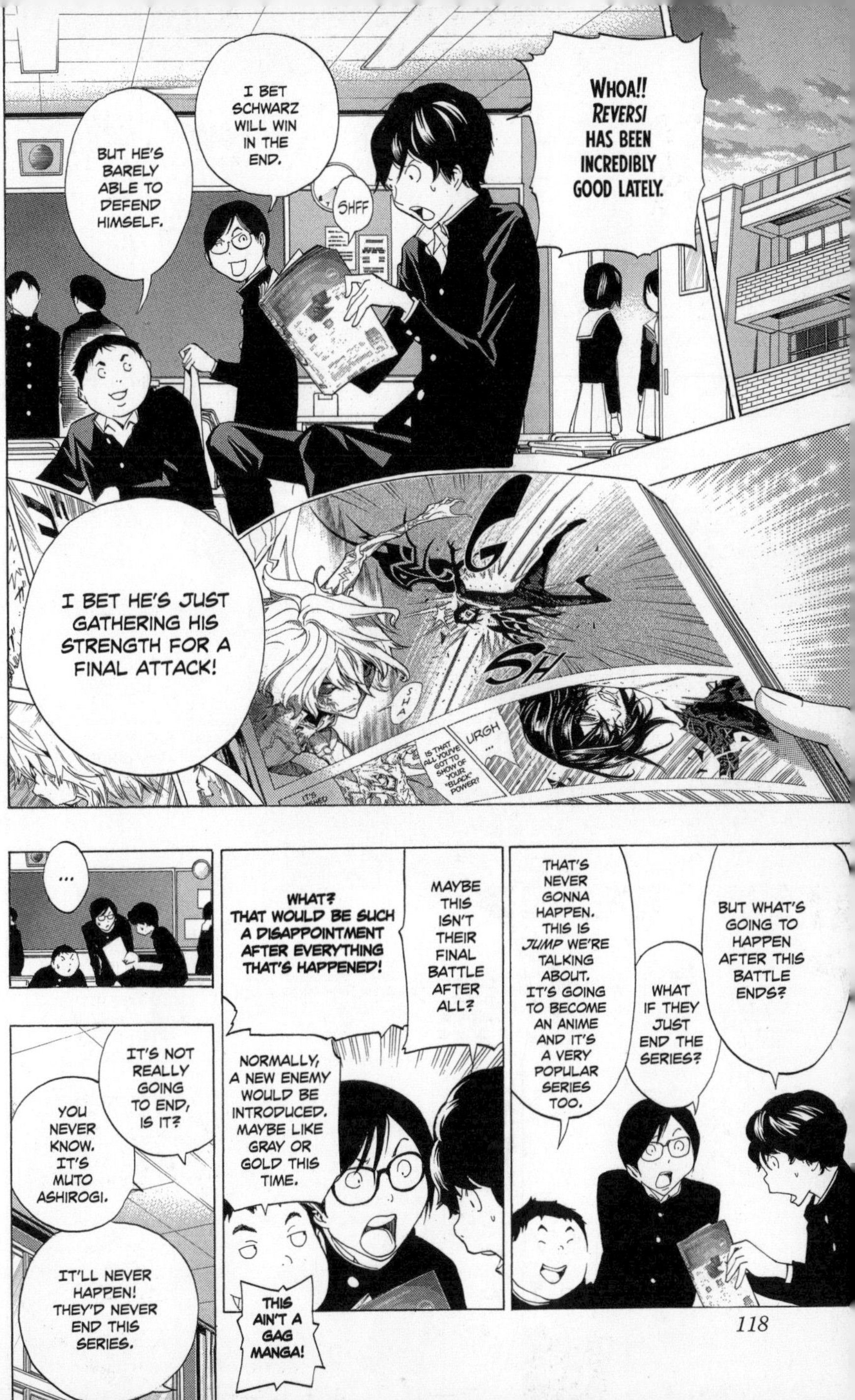
WHOA!! *REVERSI* HAS BEEN INCREDIBLY GOOD LATELY.
SHFF
I BET SCHWARZ WILL WIN IN THE END.
BUT HE'S BARELY ABLE TO DEFEND HIMSELF.
I BET HE'S JUST GATHERING HIS STRENGTH FOR A FINAL ATTACK!
SH
SHA
URGH ...
IS THAT ALL YOU'VE GOT TO SHOW OF YOUR "BLACK" POWER?
BUT WHAT'S GOING TO HAPPEN AFTER THIS BATTLE ENDS?
WHAT IF THEY JUST END THE SERIES?
THAT'S NEVER GONNA HAPPEN. THIS IS *JUMP* WE'RE TALKING ABOUT. IT'S GOING TO BECOME AN ANIME AND IT'S A VERY POPULAR SERIES TOO.
MAYBE THIS ISN'T THEIR FINAL BATTLE AFTER ALL?
WHAT? THAT WOULD BE SUCH A DISAPPOINTMENT AFTER EVERYTHING THAT'S HAPPENED!
NORMALLY, A NEW ENEMY WOULD BE INTRODUCED. MAYBE LIKE GRAY OR GOLD THIS TIME.
THIS AIN'T A GAG MANGA!
...
IT'S NOT REALLY GOING TO END, IS IT?
YOU NEVER KNOW. IT'S MUTO ASHIROGI.
IT'LL NEVER HAPPEN! THEY'D NEVER END THIS SERIES.

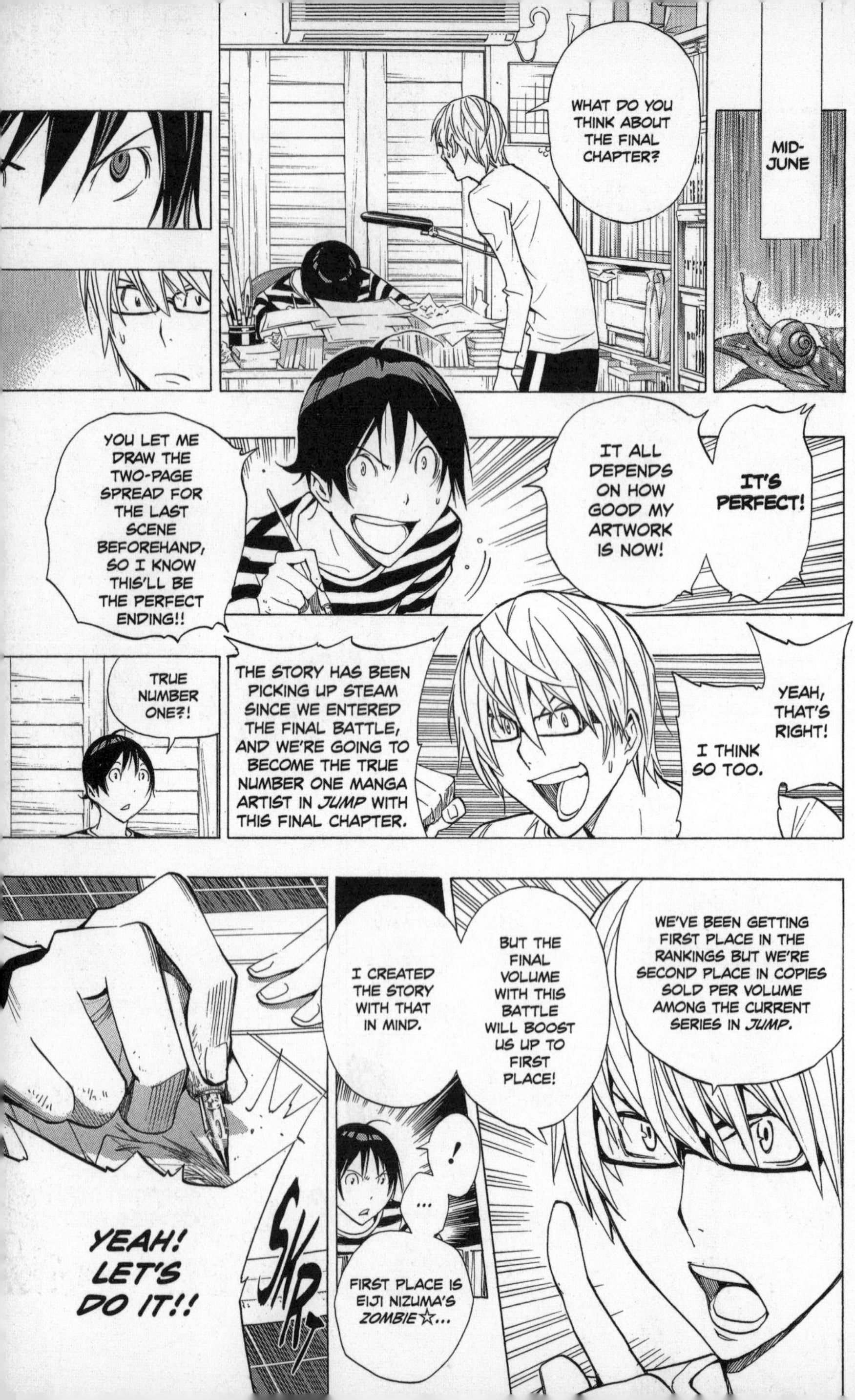
MID-JUNE
WHAT DO YOU THINK ABOUT THE FINAL CHAPTER?
IT'S PERFECT!
IT ALL DEPENDS ON HOW GOOD MY ARTWORK IS NOW!
YOU LET ME DRAW THE TWO-PAGE SPREAD FOR THE LAST SCENE BEFOREHAND, SO I KNOW THIS'LL BE THE PERFECT ENDING!!
YEAH, THAT'S RIGHT!
I THINK SO TOO.
THE STORY HAS BEEN PICKING UP STEAM SINCE WE ENTERED THE FINAL BATTLE, AND WE'RE GOING TO BECOME THE TRUE NUMBER ONE MANGA ARTIST IN *JUMP* WITH THIS FINAL CHAPTER.
TRUE NUMBER ONE?!
WE'VE BEEN GETTING FIRST PLACE IN THE RANKINGS BUT WE'RE SECOND PLACE IN COPIES SOLD PER VOLUME AMONG THE CURRENT SERIES IN *JUMP*.
BUT THE FINAL VOLUME WITH THIS BATTLE WILL BOOST US UP TO FIRST PLACE!
I CREATED THE STORY WITH THAT IN MIND.
!
...
FIRST PLACE IS EIJI NIZUMA'S *ZOMBIE☆*...
SKR
YEAH! LET'S DO IT!!

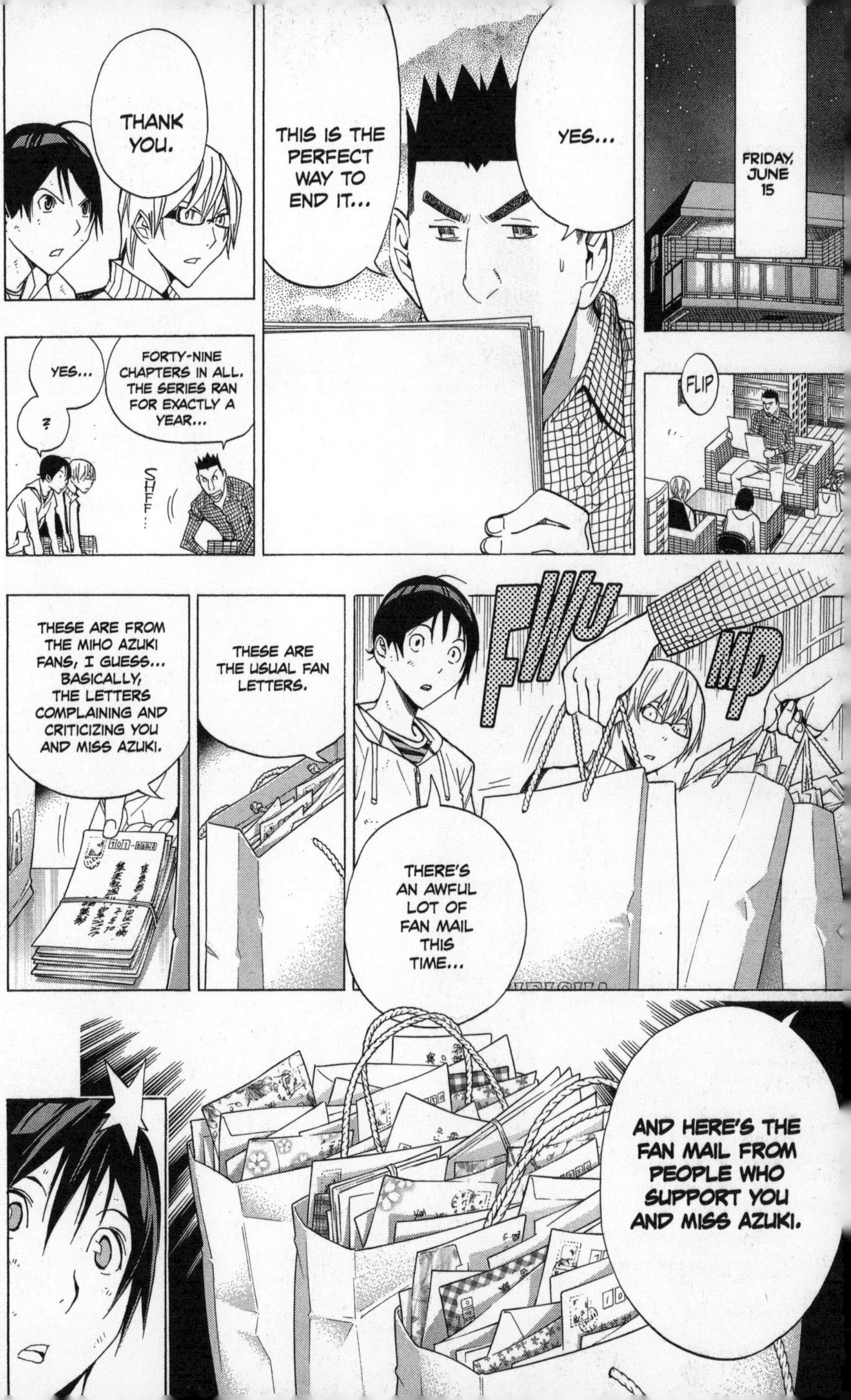
FRIDAY, JUNE 15
FLIP
YES...
THIS IS THE PERFECT WAY TO END IT...
THANK YOU.
FORTY-NINE CHAPTERS IN ALL. THE SERIES RAN FOR EXACTLY A YEAR...
YES...
?
SHFF...
FWUMP
THERE'S AN AWFUL LOT OF FAN MAIL THIS TIME...
THESE ARE THE USUAL FAN LETTERS.
THESE ARE FROM THE MIHO AZUKI FANS, I GUESS... BASICALLY, THE LETTERS COMPLAINING AND CRITICIZING YOU AND MISS AZUKI.
AND HERE'S THE FAN MAIL FROM PEOPLE WHO SUPPORT YOU AND MISS AZUKI.

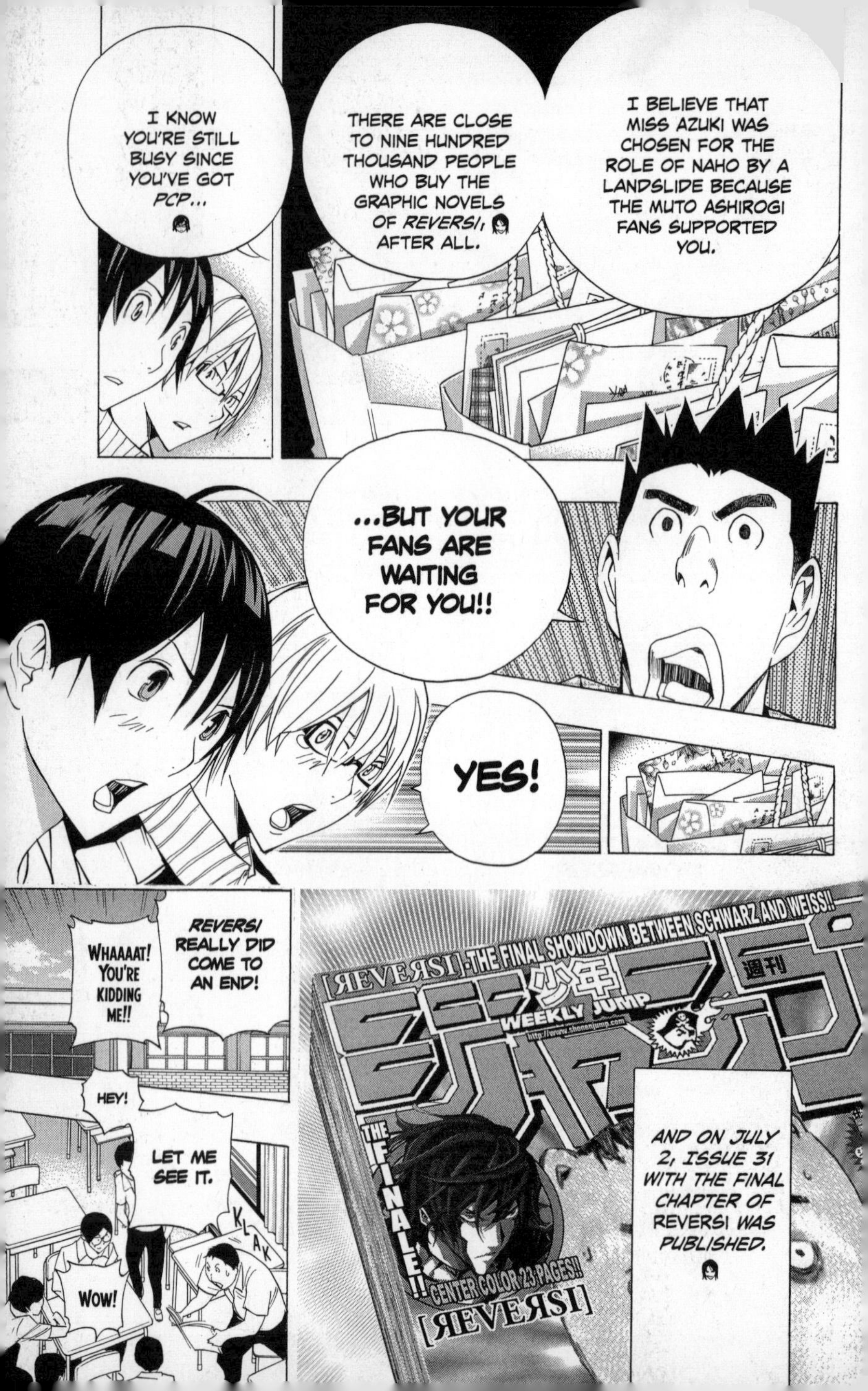
I BELIEVE THAT MISS AZUKI WAS CHOSEN FOR THE ROLE OF NAHO BY A LANDSLIDE BECAUSE THE MUTO ASHIROGI FANS SUPPORTED YOU.
THERE ARE CLOSE TO NINE HUNDRED THOUSAND PEOPLE WHO BUY THE GRAPHIC NOVELS OF *REVERSI*, AFTER ALL.
I KNOW YOU'RE STILL BUSY SINCE YOU'VE GOT *PCP*...
...BUT YOUR FANS ARE WAITING FOR YOU!!
YES!
[REVERSI] THE FINAL SHOWDOWN BETWEEN SCHWARZ AND WEISS!!
週刊
少年
WEEKLY JUMP
THE FINALE!!
CENTER COLOR 23 PAGES!!
[REVERSI]
AND ON JULY 2, ISSUE 31 WITH THE FINAL CHAPTER OF REVERSI WAS PUBLISHED.
REVERSI REALLY DID COME TO AN END!
WHAAAAT! YOU'RE KIDDING ME!!
HEY!
LET ME SEE IT.
KLAK
WOW!

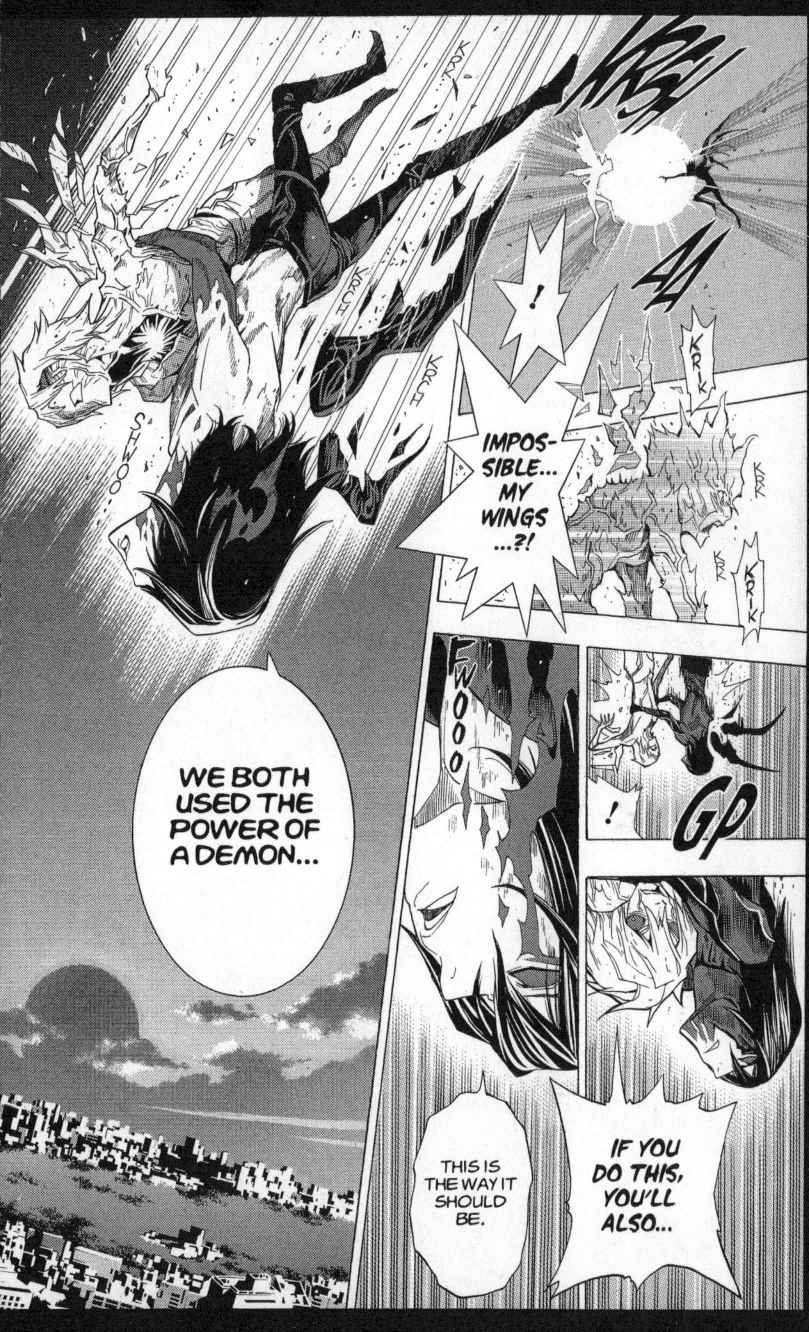

KRSH
AA
!
IMPOSSIBLE... MY WINGS ...?!
KRIK
KRK
KRK
KRIK
!
GP
FWOOO
IF YOU DO THIS, YOU'LL ALSO...
THIS IS THE WAY IT SHOULD BE.
KRK
KRCH
KRCH
SHWOO
WE BOTH USED THE POWER OF A DEMON...

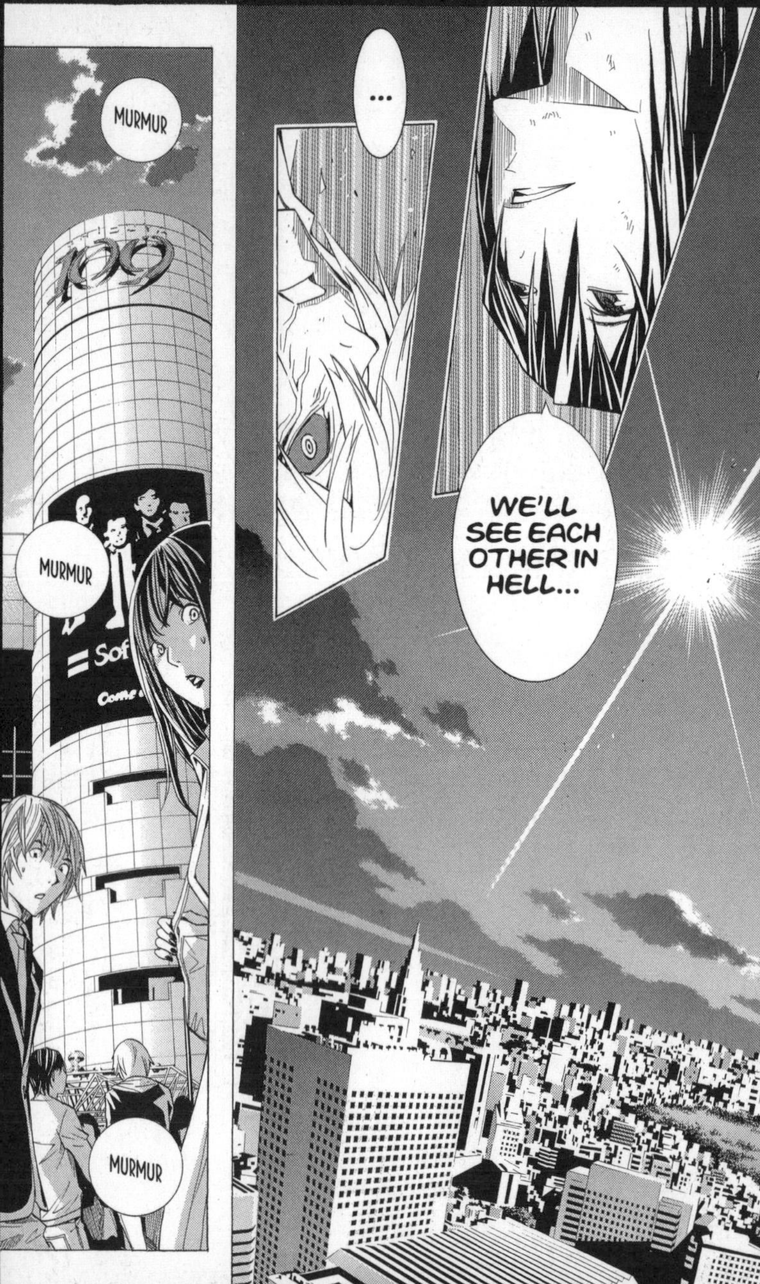
...
WE'LL SEE EACH OTHER IN HELL...
MURMUR
MURMUR
MURMUR

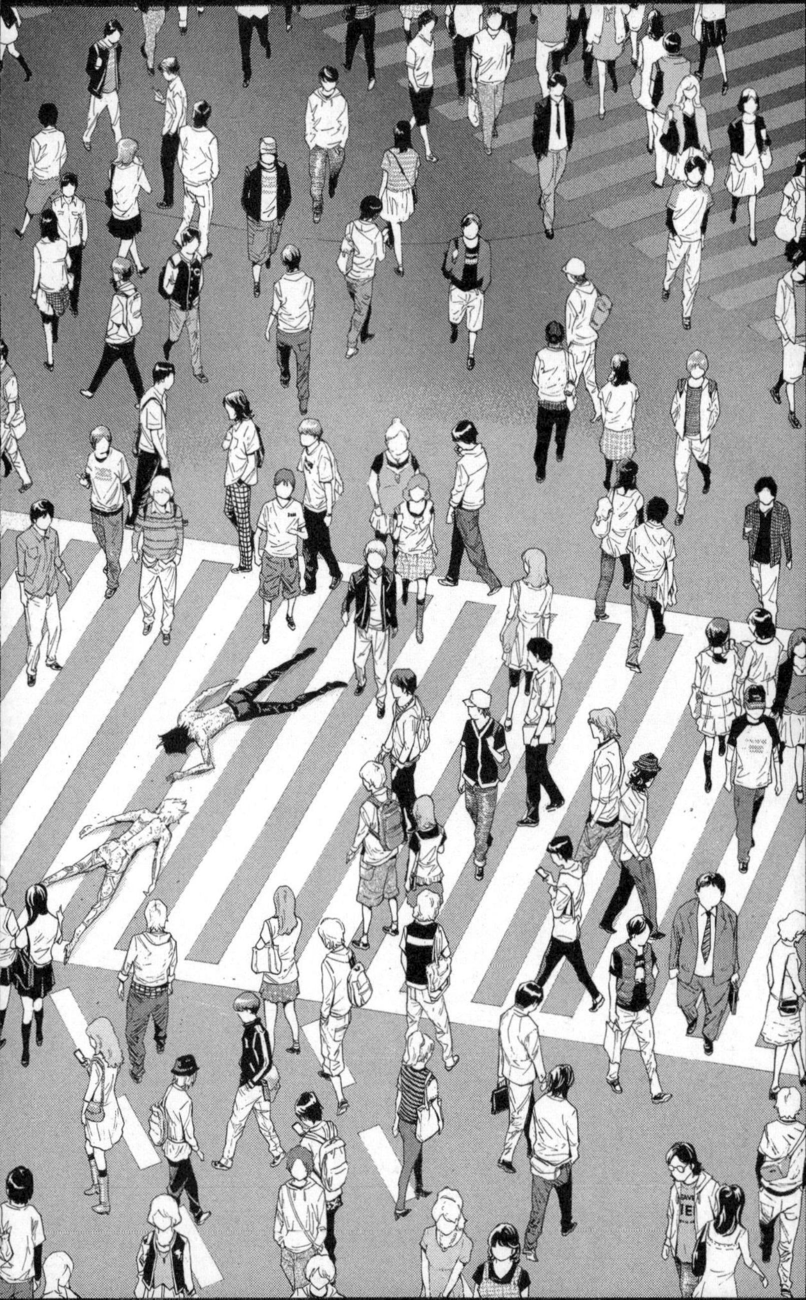

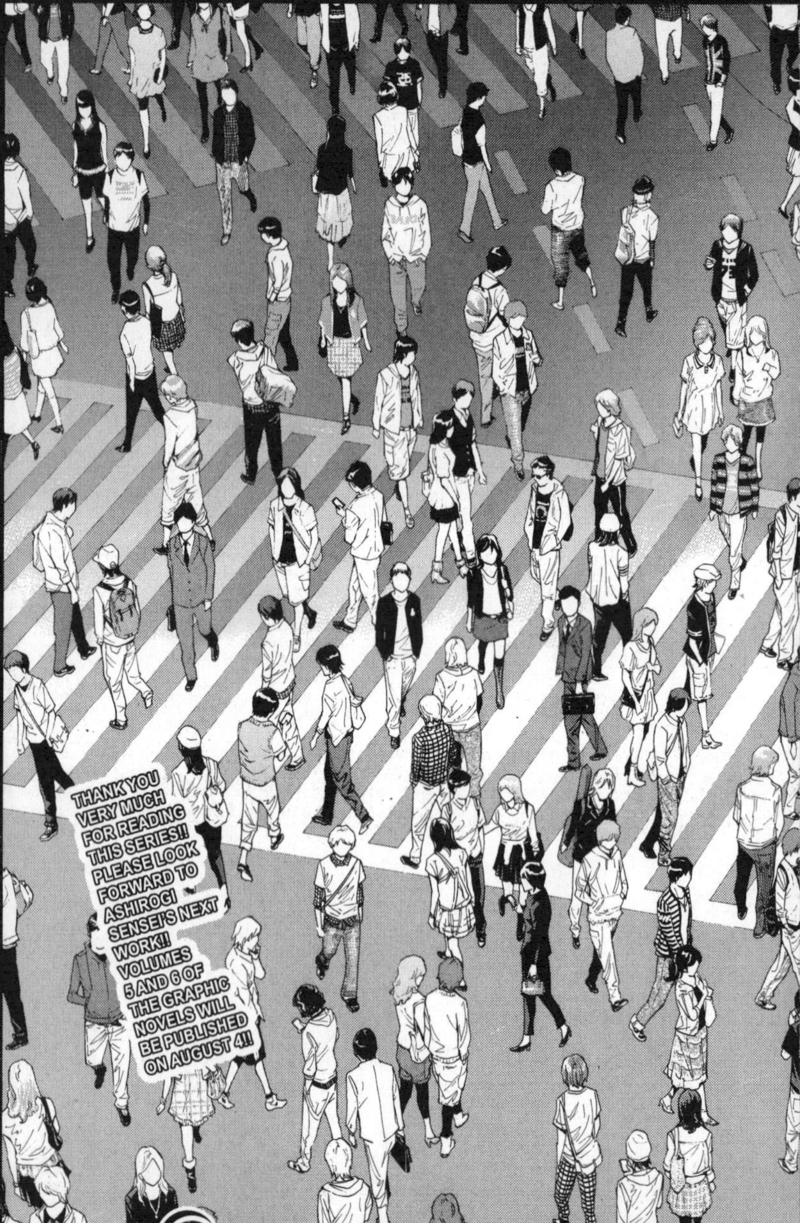
THANK YOU VERY MUCH FOR READING THIS SERIES!! PLEASE LOOK FORWARD TO ASHIROGI SENSEI'S NEXT WORK!! VOLUMES 5 AND 6 OF THE GRAPHIC NOVELS WILL BE PUBLISHED ON AUGUST 4!!
REVERSI
THE END

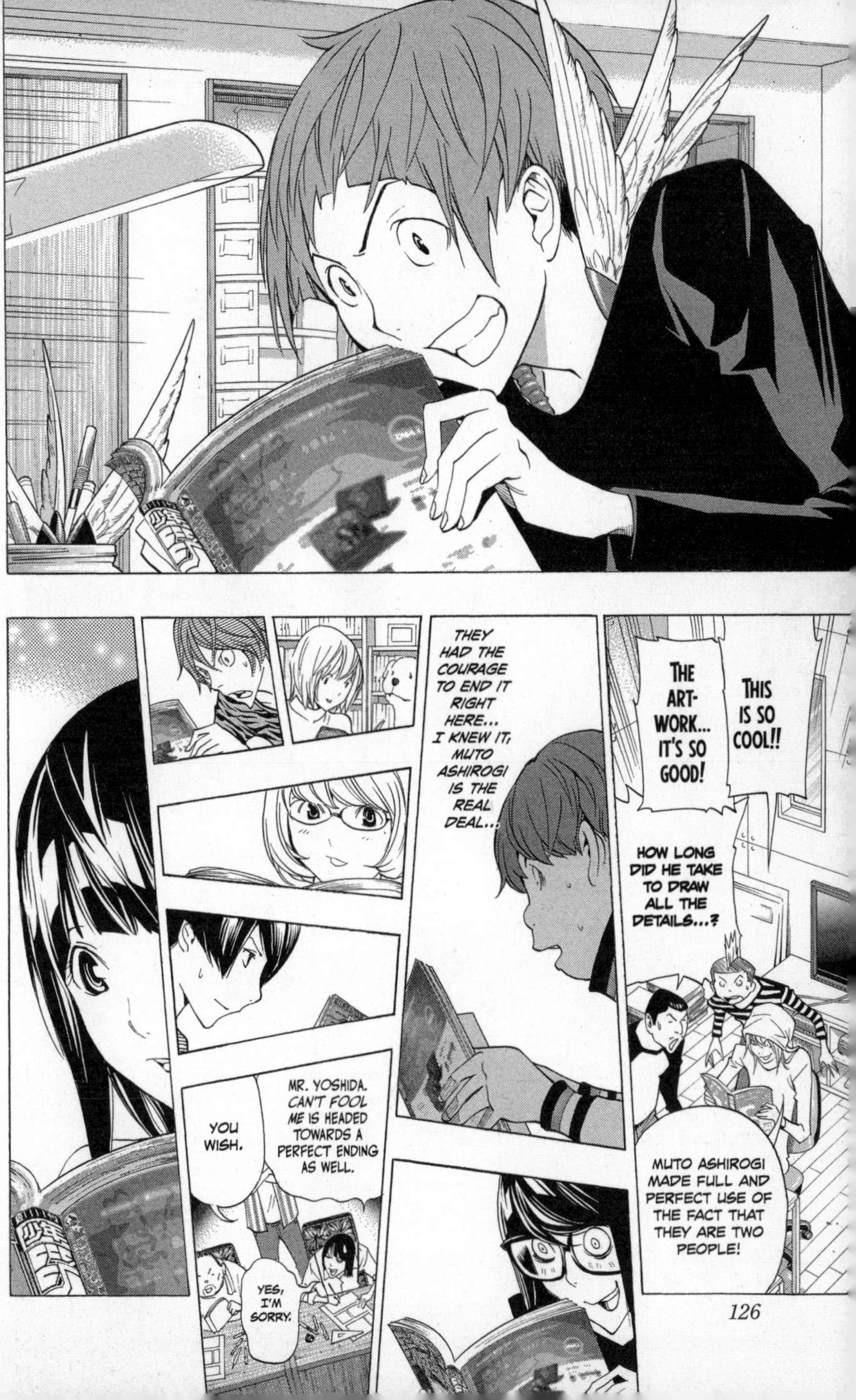

THIS IS SO COOL!!
THE ART-WORK... IT'S SO GOOD!
HOW LONG DID HE TAKE TO DRAW ALL THE DETAILS...?
MUTO ASHIROGI MADE FULL AND PERFECT USE OF THE FACT THAT THEY ARE TWO PEOPLE!
THEY HAD THE COURAGE TO END IT RIGHT HERE... I KNEW IT, MUTO ASHIROGI IS THE REAL DEAL...
MR. YOSHIDA. CAN'T FOOL ME IS HEADED TOWARDS A PERFECT ENDING AS WELL.
YOU WISH.
YES, I'M SORRY.

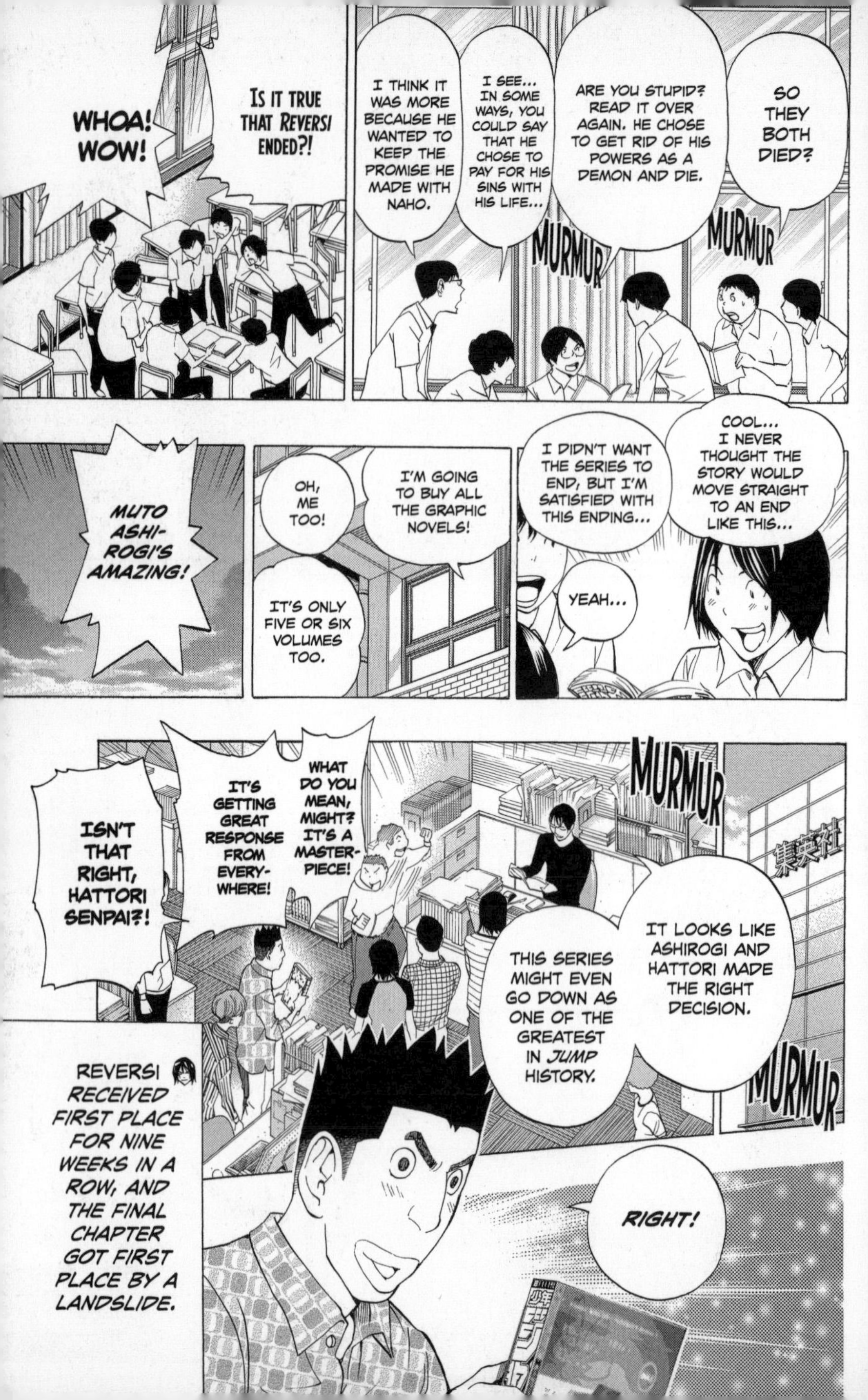
SO THEY BOTH DIED?
ARE YOU STUPID? READ IT OVER AGAIN. HE CHOSE TO GET RID OF HIS POWERS AS A DEMON AND DIE.
I SEE... IN SOME WAYS, YOU COULD SAY THAT HE CHOSE TO PAY FOR HIS SINS WITH HIS LIFE...
I THINK IT WAS MORE BECAUSE HE WANTED TO KEEP THE PROMISE HE MADE WITH NAHO.
MURMUR
MURMUR
IS IT TRUE THAT *REVERSI* ENDED?!
WHOA! WOW!
COOL... I NEVER THOUGHT THE STORY WOULD MOVE STRAIGHT TO AN END LIKE THIS...
I DIDN'T WANT THE SERIES TO END, BUT I'M SATISFIED WITH THIS ENDING...
YEAH...
I'M GOING TO BUY ALL THE GRAPHIC NOVELS!
OH, ME TOO!
IT'S ONLY FIVE OR SIX VOLUMES TOO.
MUTO ASHIROGI'S AMAZING!
MURMUR
集英社
IT LOOKS LIKE ASHIROGI AND HATTORI MADE THE RIGHT DECISION.
THIS SERIES MIGHT EVEN GO DOWN AS ONE OF THE GREATEST IN *JUMP* HISTORY.
WHAT DO YOU MEAN, MIGHT? IT'S A MASTERPIECE!
IT'S GETTING GREAT RESPONSE FROM EVERYWHERE!
ISN'T THAT RIGHT, HATTORI SENPAI?!
MURMUR
RIGHT!
REVERSI *RECEIVED FIRST PLACE FOR NINE WEEKS IN A ROW, AND THE FINAL CHAPTER GOT FIRST PLACE BY A LANDSLIDE.*

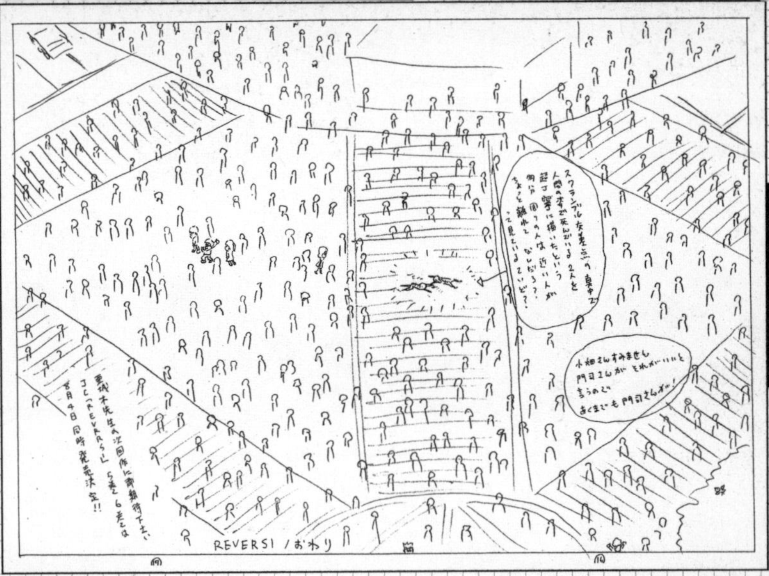
スクランブル交差点の真中で
人間の字で死んでいる２人を
超丁寧に描いたという
多分周りの人は近い人が
ちょっと離れて　なんだろう?
って見ているといいかど?
小畑さんすみません
門司さんがそれがいいと
言うので
あくまでも門司さんがッ!
亜城木先生の次回作に御期待下さい
JC「REVERSI」5巻と6巻は
8月4日同時発売決定!!
REVERSI / おわり

OHBA'S STORYBOARD

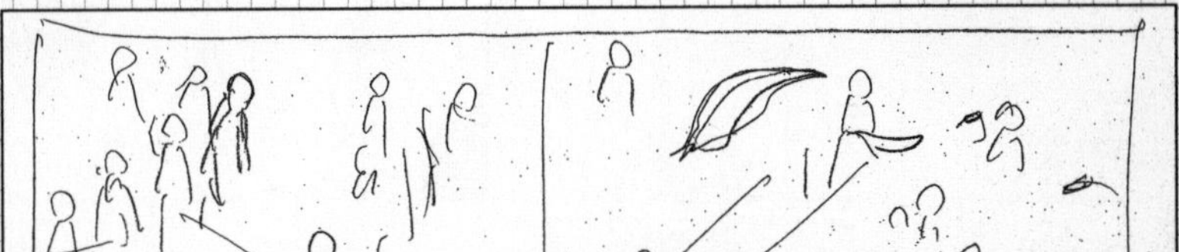
REVERSI 最後ページ②

OBATA'S STORYBOARD

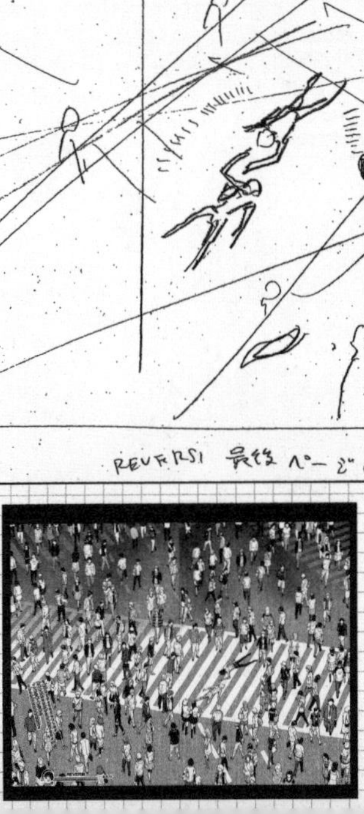

COMPLETE!

※CREATOR STORYBOARDS AND FINISHED PAGES IN JAPANESE

BAKUMAN。 vol.20

"Until the Final Draft Is Complete"

Chapter 174, pp. 128-129

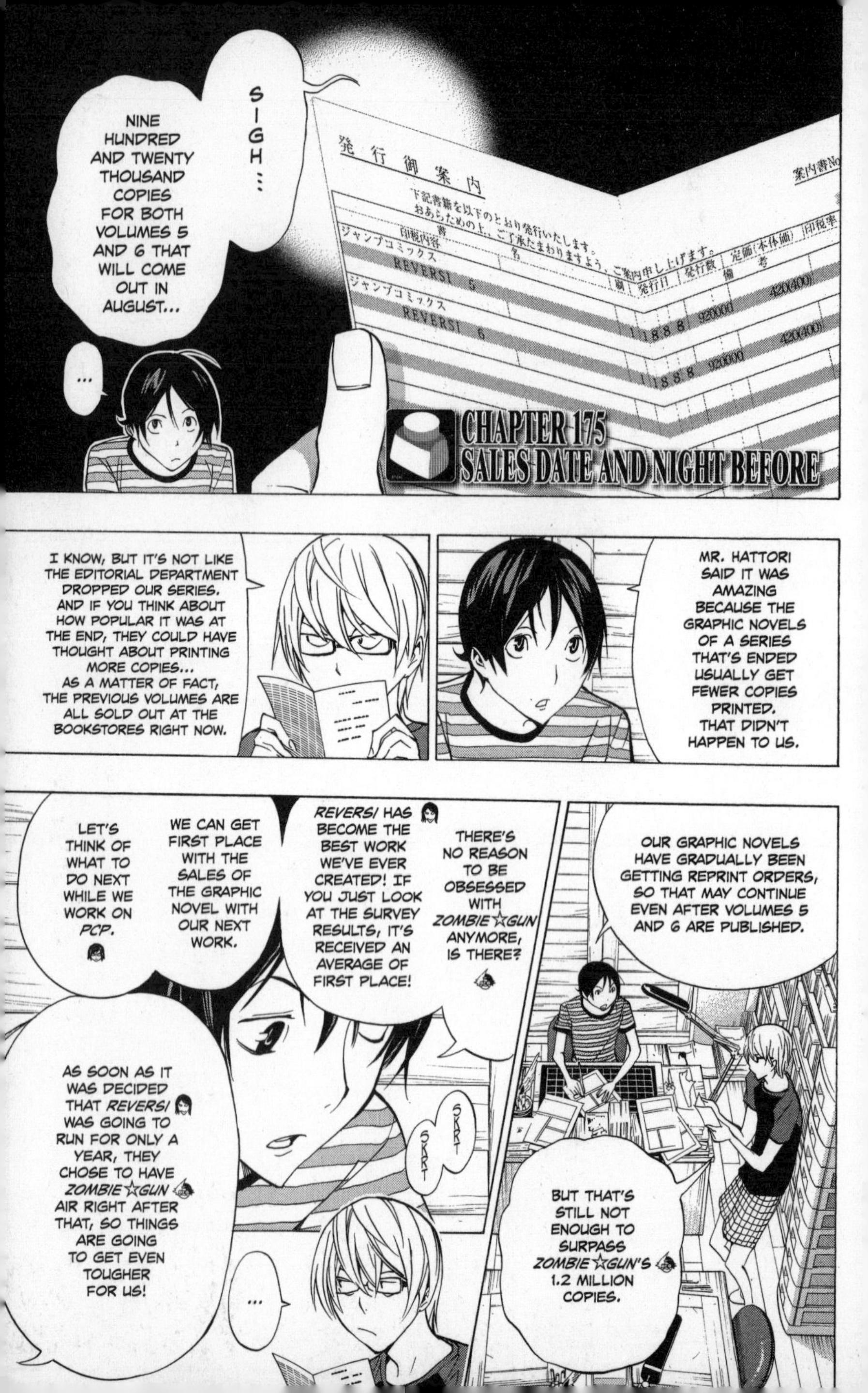
S-I-G-H...
NINE HUNDRED AND TWENTY THOUSAND COPIES FOR BOTH VOLUMES 5 AND 6 THAT WILL COME OUT IN AUGUST...
発行御案内
下記書籍を以下のとおり発行いたします。
おあらための上、ご承たまわりますよう、ご案内申し上げます。
ジャンプコミックス REVERSI 5
ジャンプコミックス REVERSI 6
920000
420(400)
...
CHAPTER 175 SALES DATE AND NIGHT BEFORE
MR. HATTORI SAID IT WAS AMAZING BECAUSE THE GRAPHIC NOVELS OF A SERIES THAT'S ENDED USUALLY GET FEWER COPIES PRINTED. THAT DIDN'T HAPPEN TO US.
I KNOW, BUT IT'S NOT LIKE THE EDITORIAL DEPARTMENT DROPPED OUR SERIES. AND IF YOU THINK ABOUT HOW POPULAR IT WAS AT THE END, THEY COULD HAVE THOUGHT ABOUT PRINTING MORE COPIES... AS A MATTER OF FACT, THE PREVIOUS VOLUMES ARE ALL SOLD OUT AT THE BOOKSTORES RIGHT NOW.
OUR GRAPHIC NOVELS HAVE GRADUALLY BEEN GETTING REPRINT ORDERS, SO THAT MAY CONTINUE EVEN AFTER VOLUMES 5 AND 6 ARE PUBLISHED.
BUT THAT'S STILL NOT ENOUGH TO SURPASS ZOMBIE☆GUN'S 1.2 MILLION COPIES.
THERE'S NO REASON TO BE OBSESSED WITH ZOMBIE☆GUN ANYMORE, IS THERE?
REVERSI HAS BECOME THE BEST WORK WE'VE EVER CREATED! IF YOU JUST LOOK AT THE SURVEY RESULTS, IT'S RECEIVED AN AVERAGE OF FIRST PLACE!
WE CAN GET FIRST PLACE WITH THE SALES OF THE GRAPHIC NOVEL WITH OUR NEXT WORK.
LET'S THINK OF WHAT TO DO NEXT WHILE WE WORK ON PCP.
SKRT
SKRT
AS SOON AS IT WAS DECIDED THAT REVERSI WAS GOING TO RUN FOR ONLY A YEAR, THEY CHOSE TO HAVE ZOMBIE☆GUN AIR RIGHT AFTER THAT, SO THINGS ARE GOING TO GET EVEN TOUGHER FOR US!
...

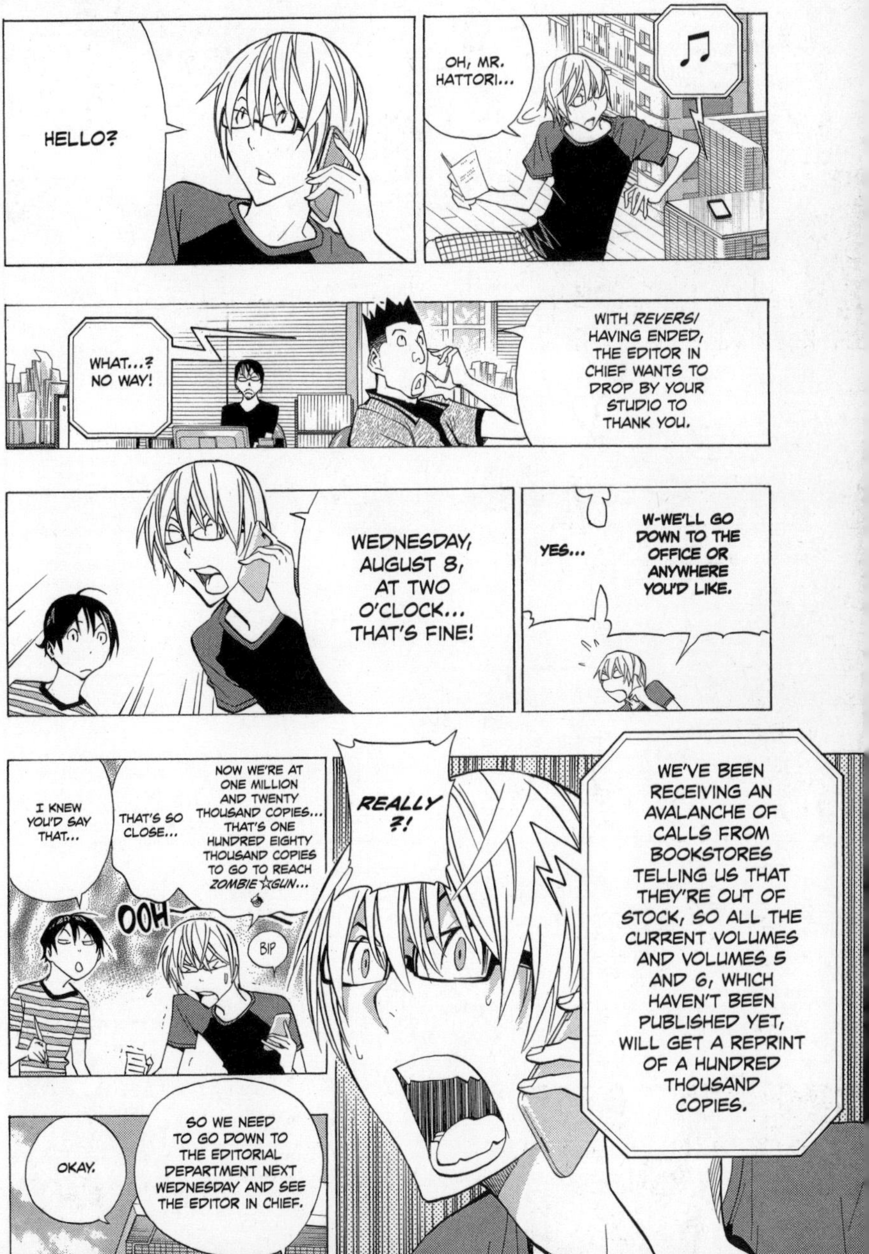
♫
OH, MR. HATTORI...
HELLO?
WITH *REVERSI* HAVING ENDED, THE EDITOR IN CHIEF WANTS TO DROP BY YOUR STUDIO TO THANK YOU.
WHAT...? NO WAY!
W-WE'LL GO DOWN TO THE OFFICE OR ANYWHERE YOU'D LIKE.
YES...
WEDNESDAY, AUGUST 8, AT TWO O'CLOCK... THAT'S FINE!
WE'VE BEEN RECEIVING AN AVALANCHE OF CALLS FROM BOOKSTORES TELLING US THAT THEY'RE OUT OF STOCK, SO ALL THE CURRENT VOLUMES AND VOLUMES 5 AND 6, WHICH HAVEN'T BEEN PUBLISHED YET, WILL GET A REPRINT OF A HUNDRED THOUSAND COPIES.
REALLY ?!
NOW WE'RE AT ONE MILLION AND TWENTY THOUSAND COPIES... THAT'S ONE HUNDRED EIGHTY THOUSAND COPIES TO GO TO REACH *ZOMBIE☆GUN*...
THAT'S SO CLOSE...
I KNEW YOU'D SAY THAT...
BIP
OOH
SO WE NEED TO GO DOWN TO THE EDITORIAL DEPARTMENT NEXT WEDNESDAY AND SEE THE EDITOR IN CHIEF.
OKAY.

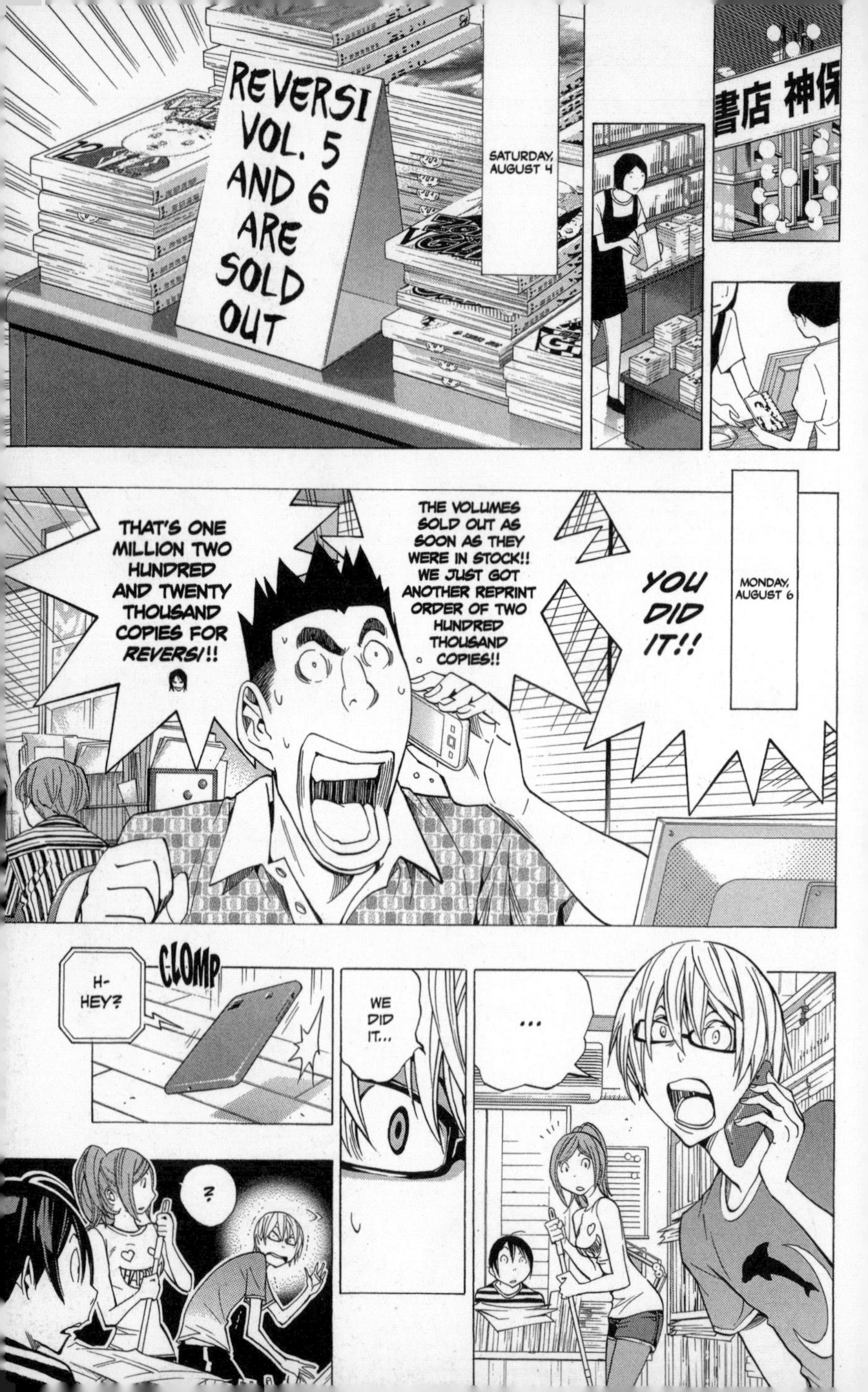
書店 神保
SATURDAY, AUGUST 4
REVERSI VOL. 5 AND 6 ARE SOLD OUT
MONDAY, AUGUST 6
YOU DID IT!!
THE VOLUMES SOLD OUT AS SOON AS THEY WERE IN STOCK!! WE JUST GOT ANOTHER REPRINT ORDER OF TWO HUNDRED THOUSAND COPIES!!
THAT'S ONE MILLION TWO HUNDRED AND TWENTY THOUSAND COPIES FOR REVERSI!!
...
WE DID IT...
CLOMP
H- HEY?
?

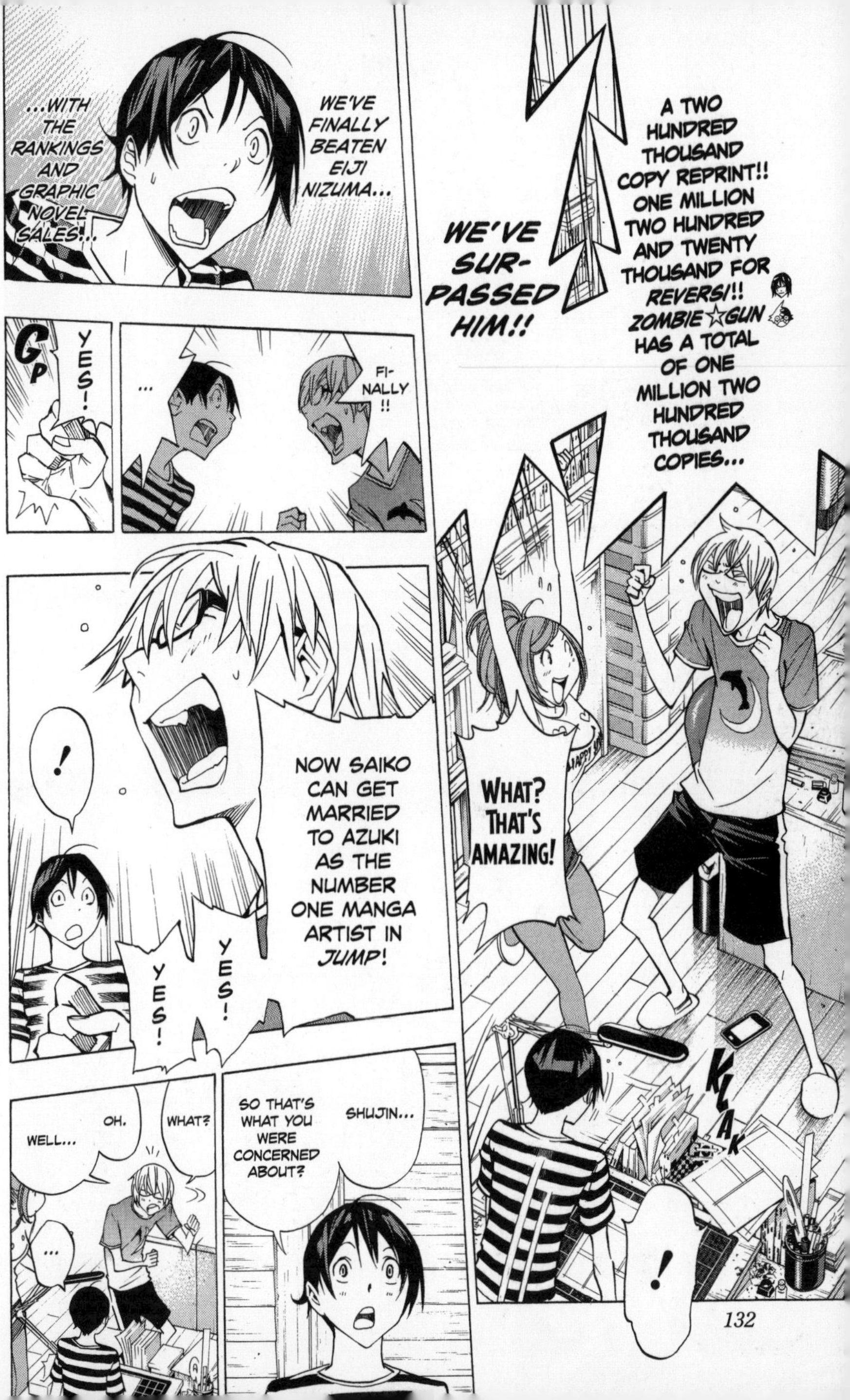
A TWO HUNDRED THOUSAND COPY REPRINT!! ONE MILLION TWO HUNDRED AND TWENTY THOUSAND FOR REVERSI!! ZOMBIE☆GUN HAS A TOTAL OF ONE MILLION TWO HUNDRED THOUSAND COPIES...
WE'VE SURPASSED HIM!!
WHAT? THAT'S AMAZING!
KLAK
!
WE'VE FINALLY BEATEN EIJI NIZUMA...
...WITH THE RANKINGS AND GRAPHIC NOVEL SALES!...
FINALLY!!
...
YES!
GP
NOW SAIKO CAN GET MARRIED TO AZUKI AS THE NUMBER ONE MANGA ARTIST IN JUMP!
YES!
YES!
!
SHUJIN...
SO THAT'S WHAT YOU WERE CONCERNED ABOUT?
WHAT?
OH.
WELL...
...

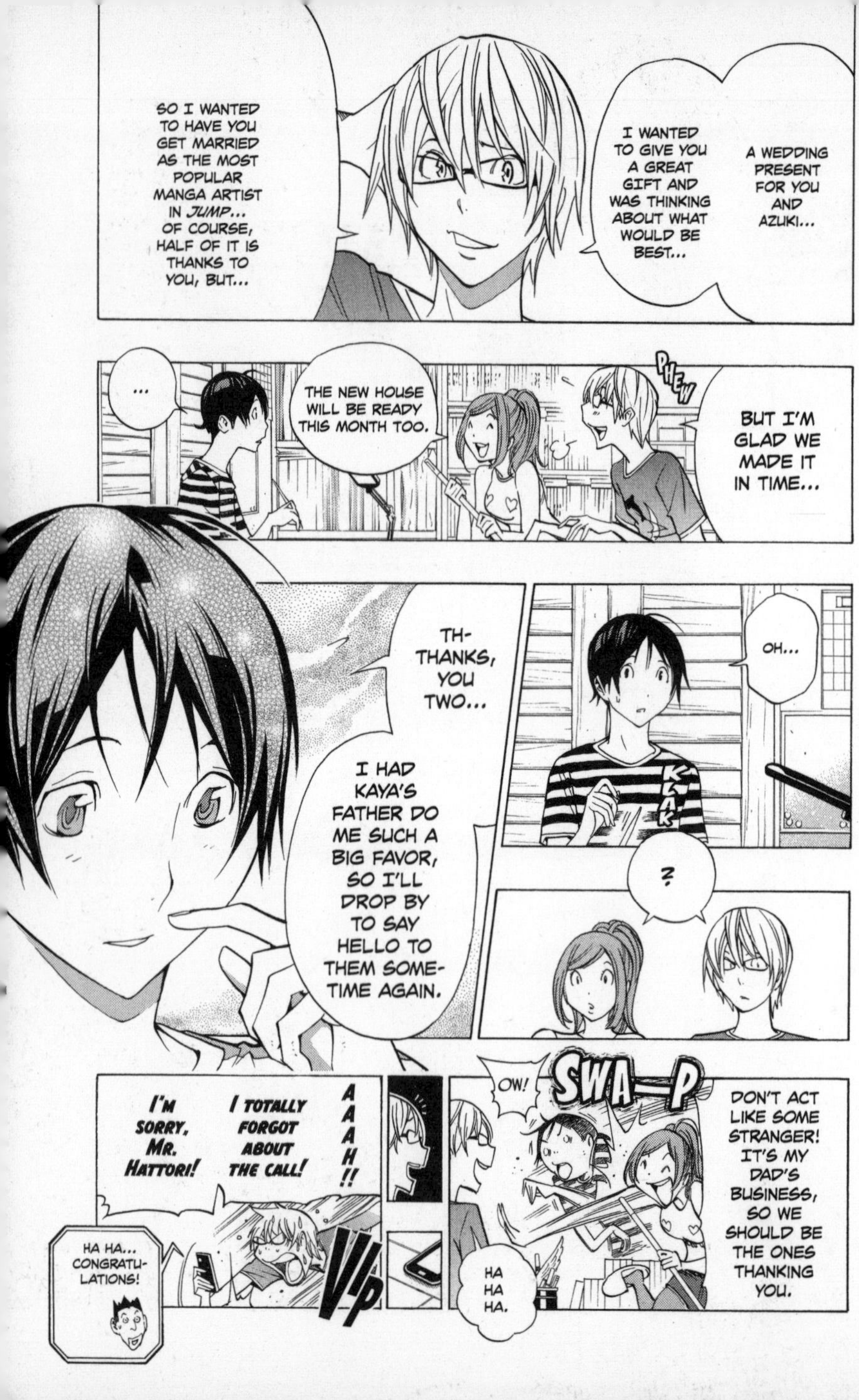
A WEDDING PRESENT FOR YOU AND AZUKI...
I WANTED TO GIVE YOU A GREAT GIFT AND WAS THINKING ABOUT WHAT WOULD BE BEST...
SO I WANTED TO HAVE YOU GET MARRIED AS THE MOST POPULAR MANGA ARTIST IN *JUMP*... OF COURSE, HALF OF IT IS THANKS TO YOU, BUT...
PHEW
BUT I'M GLAD WE MADE IT IN TIME...
THE NEW HOUSE WILL BE READY THIS MONTH TOO.
...
OH...
KLAK
?
TH-THANKS, YOU TWO...
I HAD KAYA'S FATHER DO ME SUCH A BIG FAVOR, SO I'LL DROP BY TO SAY HELLO TO THEM SOMETIME AGAIN.
SWA—P
DON'T ACT LIKE SOME STRANGER! IT'S MY DAD'S BUSINESS, SO WE SHOULD BE THE ONES THANKING YOU.
OW!
HA HA HA.
AAAAH!!
I TOTALLY FORGOT ABOUT THE CALL!
I'M SORRY, MR. HATTORI!
VIP
HA HA... CONGRATULATIONS!

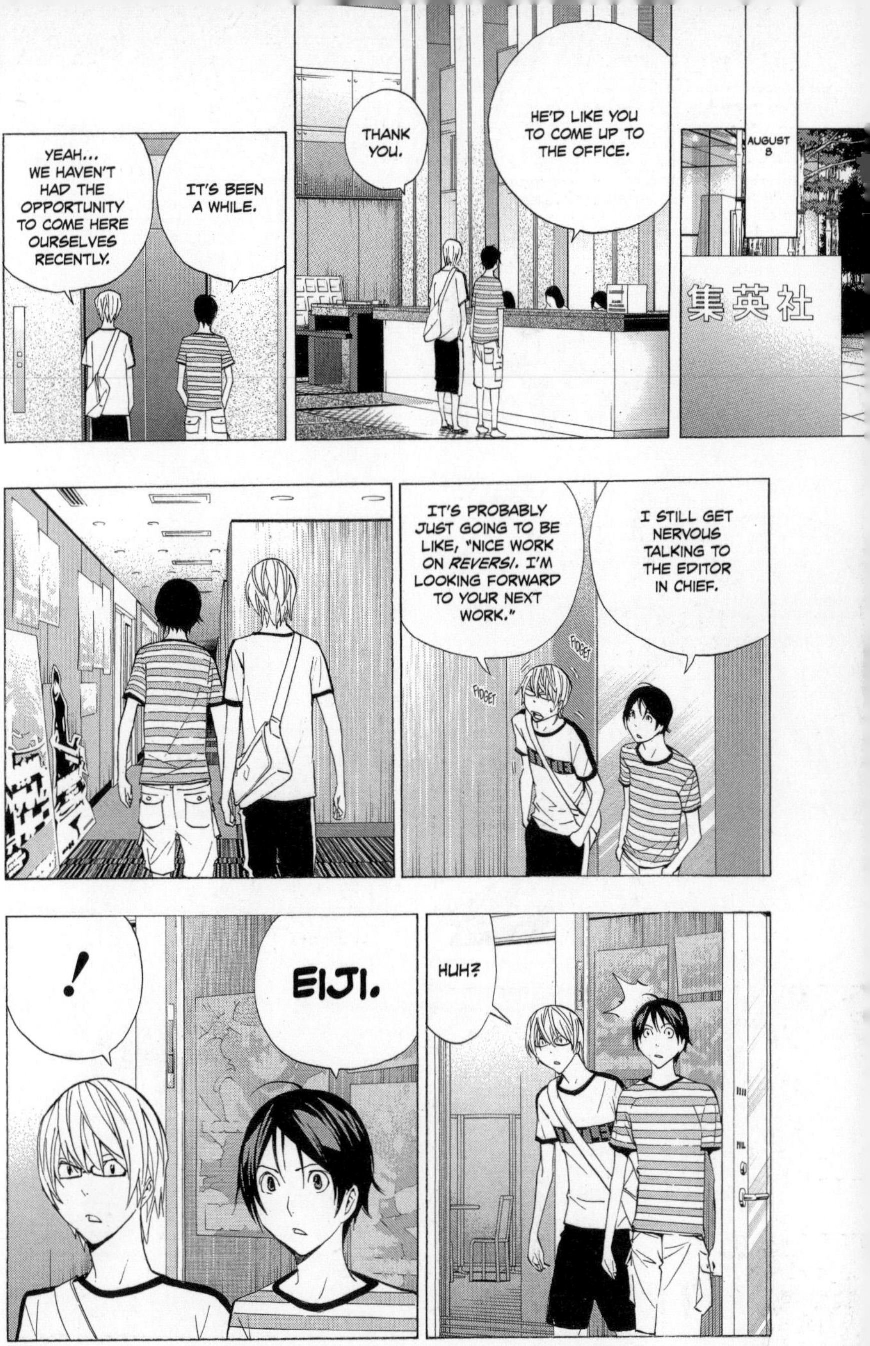

AUGUST 8
集英社
HE'D LIKE YOU TO COME UP TO THE OFFICE.
THANK YOU.
IT'S BEEN A WHILE.
YEAH... WE HAVEN'T HAD THE OPPORTUNITY TO COME HERE OURSELVES RECENTLY.
I STILL GET NERVOUS TALKING TO THE EDITOR IN CHIEF.
IT'S PROBABLY JUST GOING TO BE LIKE, "NICE WORK ON *REVERSI*. I'M LOOKING FORWARD TO YOUR NEXT WORK."
FIDGET
FIDGET
HUH?
EIJI.
!

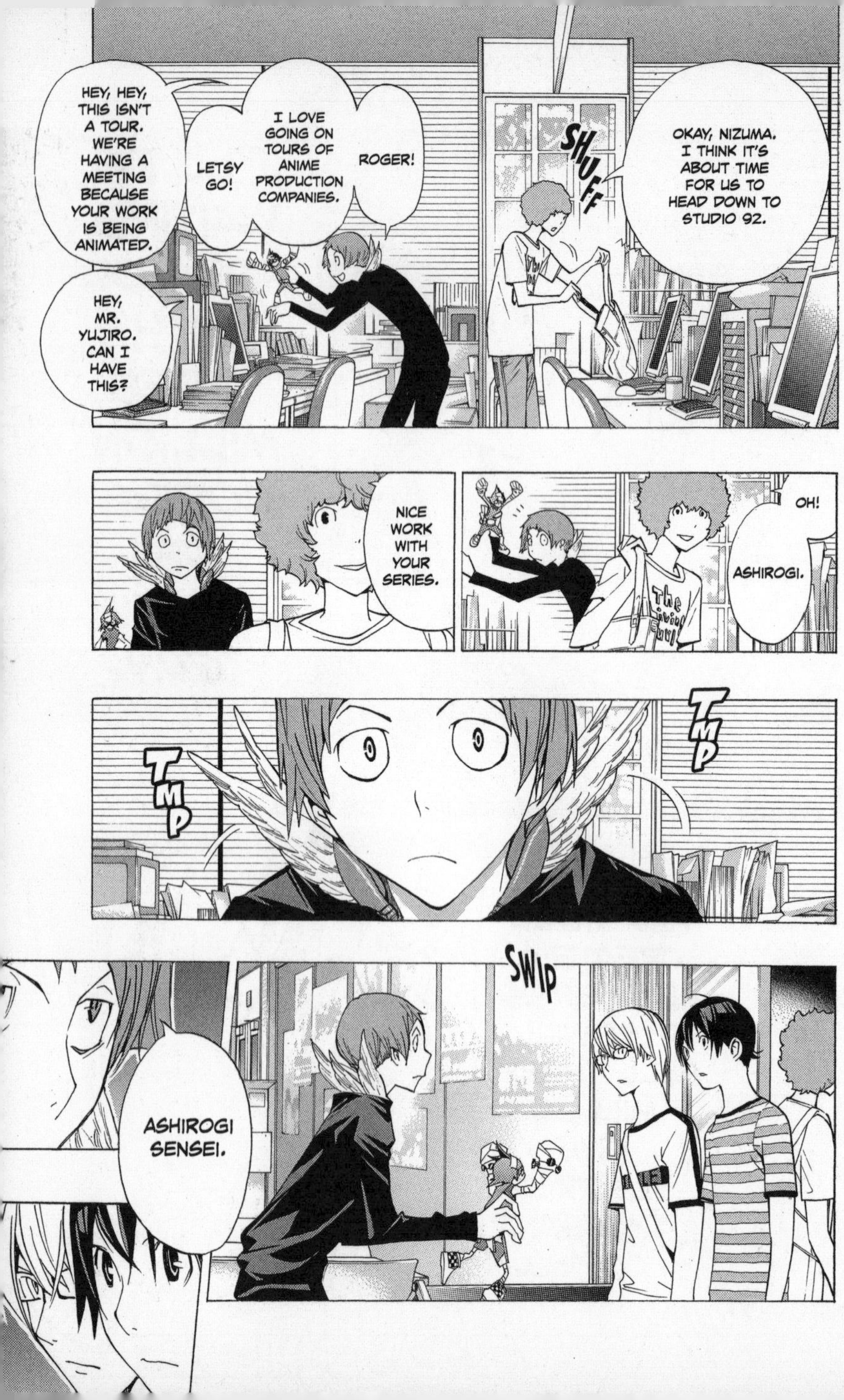
OKAY, NIZUMA. I THINK IT'S ABOUT TIME FOR US TO HEAD DOWN TO STUDIO 92.
SHUFF
ROGER!
I LOVE GOING ON TOURS OF ANIME PRODUCTION COMPANIES.
LETSY GO!
HEY, HEY, THIS ISN'T A TOUR. WE'RE HAVING A MEETING BECAUSE YOUR WORK IS BEING ANIMATED.
HEY, MR. YUJIRO. CAN I HAVE THIS?
OH!
ASHIROGI.
NICE WORK WITH YOUR SERIES.
TMP
TMP
SWIP
ASHIROGI SENSEI.

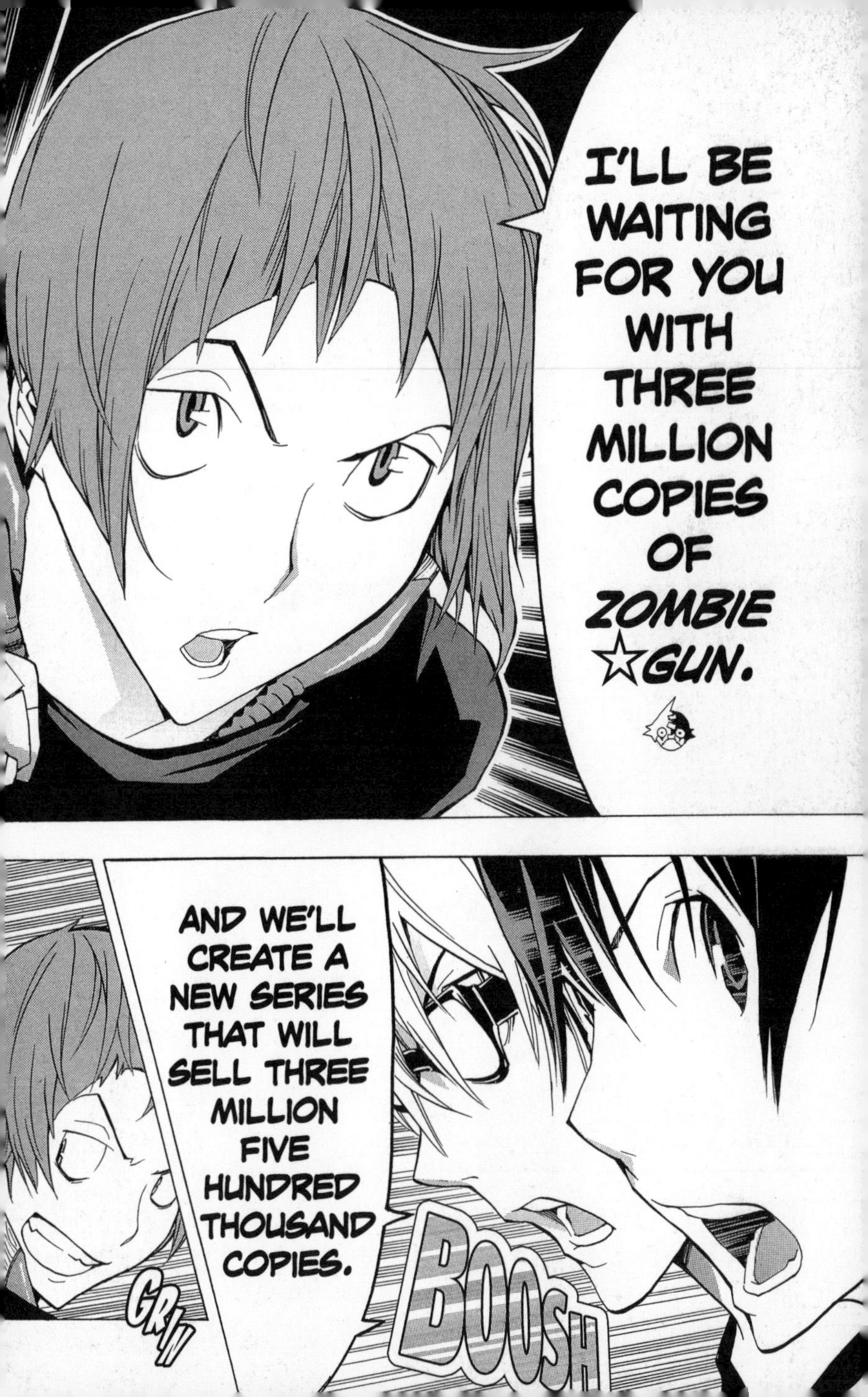
I'LL BE WAITING FOR YOU WITH THREE MILLION COPIES OF ZOMBIE☆GUN.
BOOSH
AND WE'LL CREATE A NEW SERIES THAT WILL SELL THREE MILLION FIVE HUNDRED THOUSAND COPIES.
GRIN

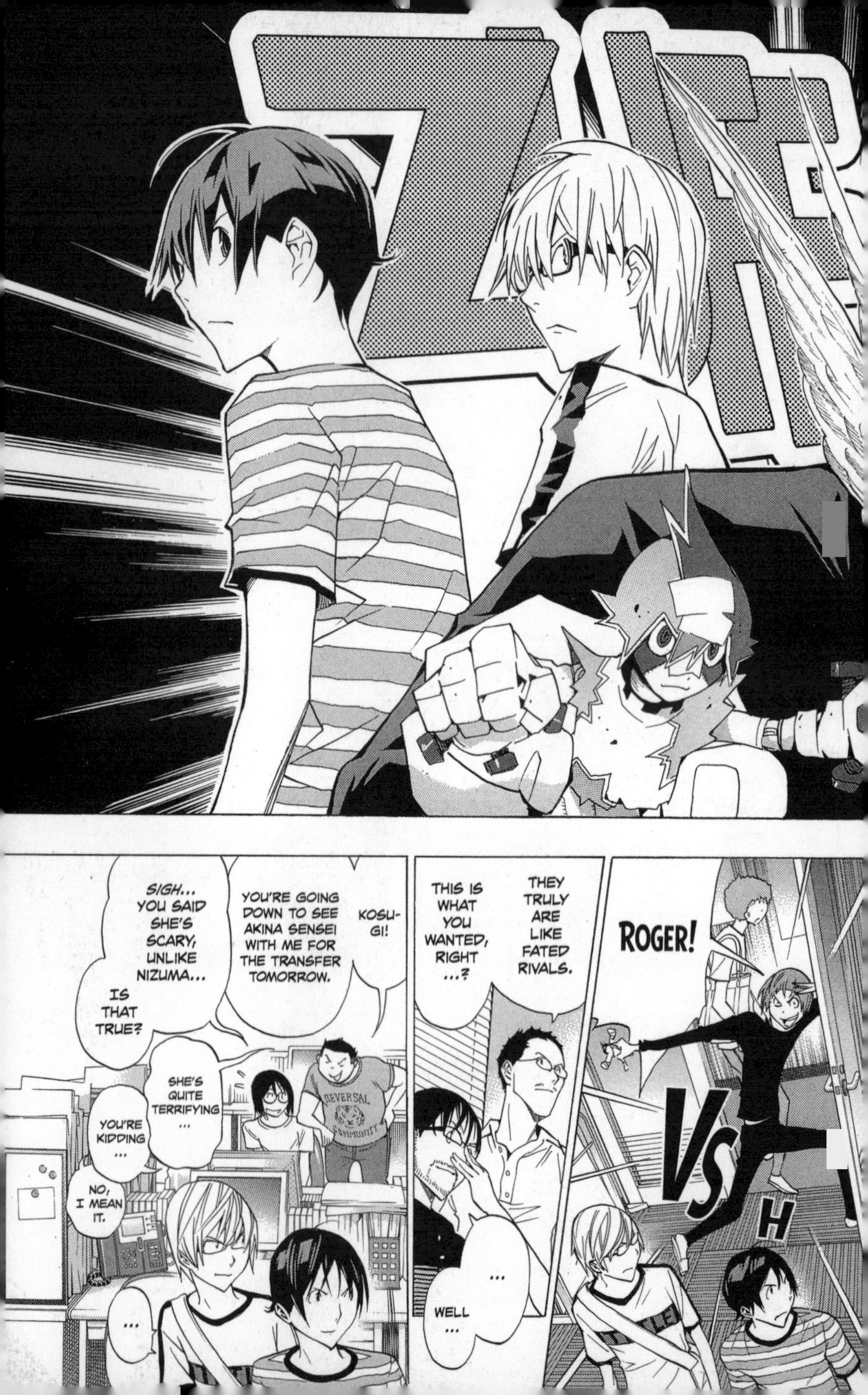
ROGER!
THEY TRULY ARE LIKE FATED RIVALS.
THIS IS WHAT YOU WANTED, RIGHT ...?
...
WELL ...
KOSU-GI!
YOU'RE GOING DOWN TO SEE AKINA SENSEI WITH ME FOR THE TRANSFER TOMORROW.
SIGH... YOU SAID SHE'S SCARY, UNLIKE NIZUMA...
IS THAT TRUE?
SHE'S QUITE TERRIFYING ...
YOU'RE KIDDING ...
NO, I MEAN IT.
...

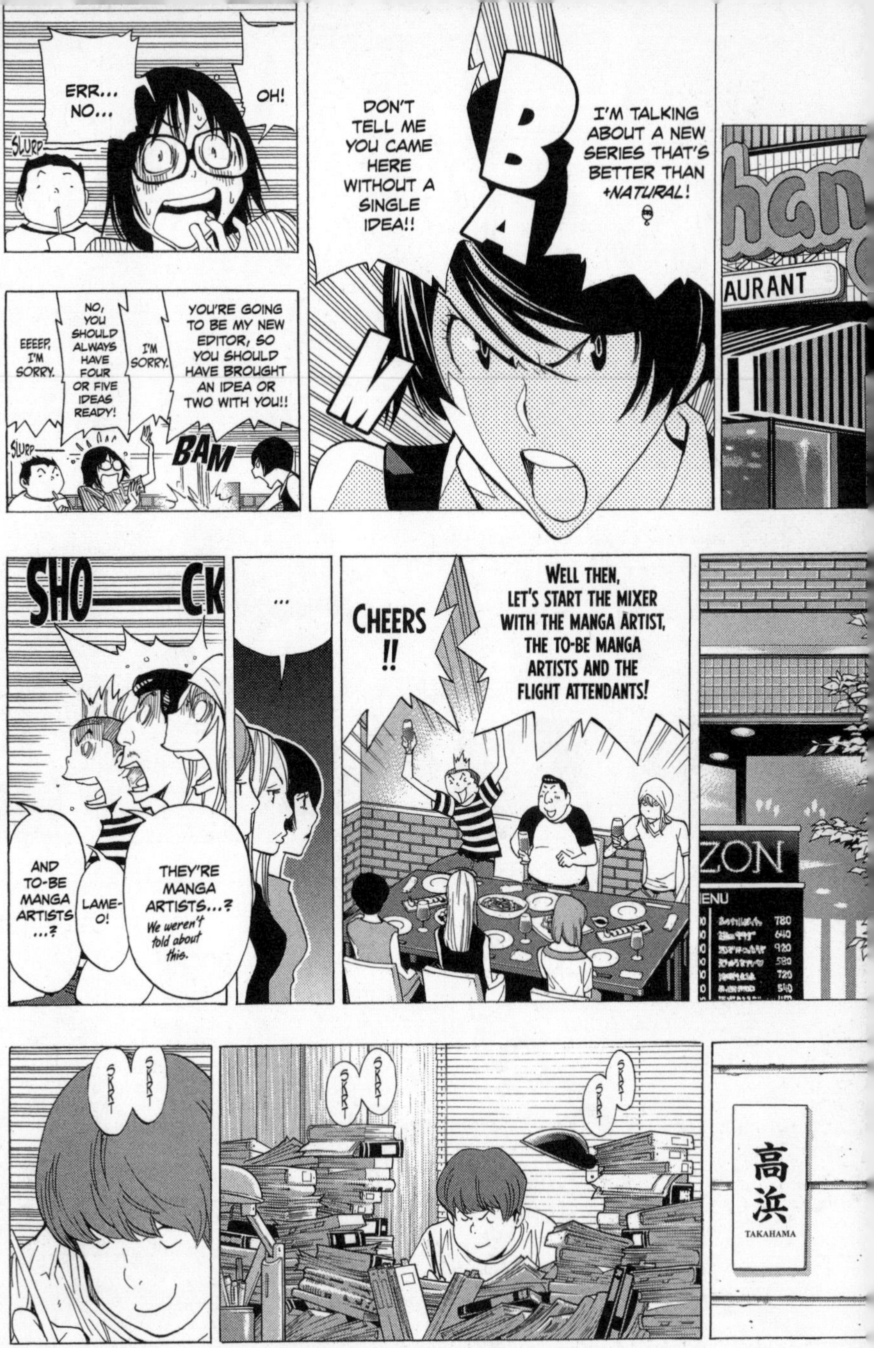

AURANT
B A M
I'M TALKING ABOUT A NEW SERIES THAT'S BETTER THAN +NATURAL!
DON'T TELL ME YOU CAME HERE WITHOUT A SINGLE IDEA!!
OH!
ERR... NO...
SLURP
YOU'RE GOING TO BE MY NEW EDITOR, SO YOU SHOULD HAVE BROUGHT AN IDEA OR TWO WITH YOU!!
I'M SORRY.
NO, YOU SHOULD ALWAYS HAVE FOUR OR FIVE IDEAS READY!
EEEEP, I'M SORRY.
BAM
SLURP
ZON
780
640
920
580
720
540
WELL THEN, LET'S START THE MIXER WITH THE MANGA ARTIST, THE TO-BE MANGA ARTISTS AND THE FLIGHT ATTENDANTS!
CHEERS!!
...
SHO——CK
THEY'RE MANGA ARTISTS...? We weren't told about this.
LAME-O!
AND TO-BE MANGA ARTISTS...?
高浜
TAKAHAMA
SKRT SKRT
SKRT SKRT
SKRT SKRT

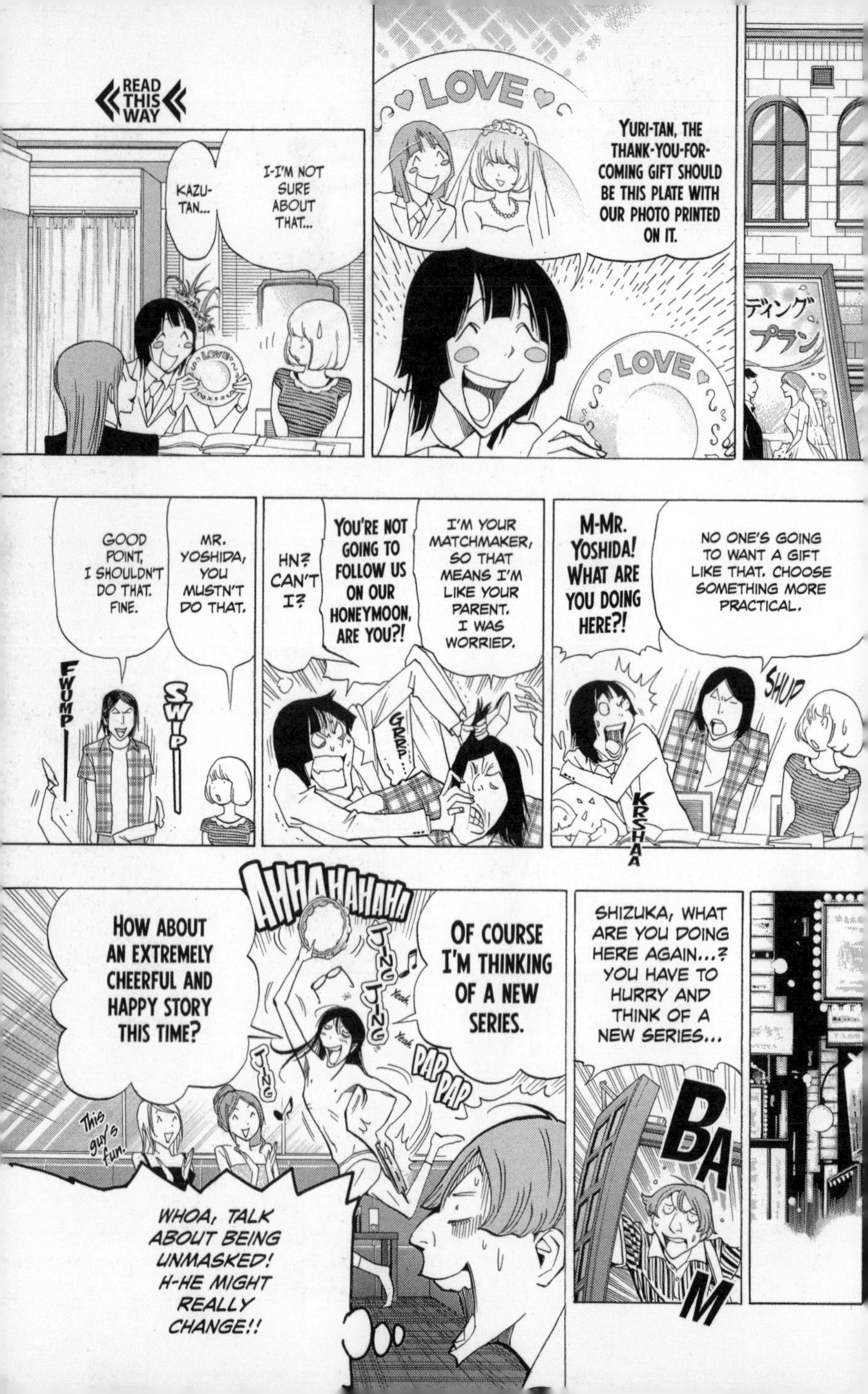
READ THIS WAY
ディング
プラン
YURI-TAN, THE THANK-YOU-FOR-COMING GIFT SHOULD BE THIS PLATE WITH OUR PHOTO PRINTED ON IT.
LOVE
LOVE
KAZU-TAN...
I-I'M NOT SURE ABOUT THAT...
LOVE
NO ONE'S GOING TO WANT A GIFT LIKE THAT. CHOOSE SOMETHING MORE PRACTICAL.
M-MR. YOSHIDA! WHAT ARE YOU DOING HERE?!
SHUP
KRSHAA
I'M YOUR MATCHMAKER, SO THAT MEANS I'M LIKE YOUR PARENT. I WAS WORRIED.
YOU'RE NOT GOING TO FOLLOW US ON OUR HONEYMOON, ARE YOU?!
HN? CAN'T I?
GRRP...
MR. YOSHIDA, YOU MUSTN'T DO THAT.
GOOD POINT, I SHOULDN'T DO THAT. FINE.
SWIP
FWUMP
SHIZUKA, WHAT ARE YOU DOING HERE AGAIN...? YOU HAVE TO HURRY AND THINK OF A NEW SERIES...
BAM
OF COURSE I'M THINKING OF A NEW SERIES.
AHHAHAHAHA
JING JING
Yeah.
Yeah.
PAP PAP
HOW ABOUT AN EXTREMELY CHEERFUL AND HAPPY STORY THIS TIME?
JING
This guy's fun.
WHOA, TALK ABOUT BEING UNMASKED! H-HE MIGHT REALLY CHANGE!!

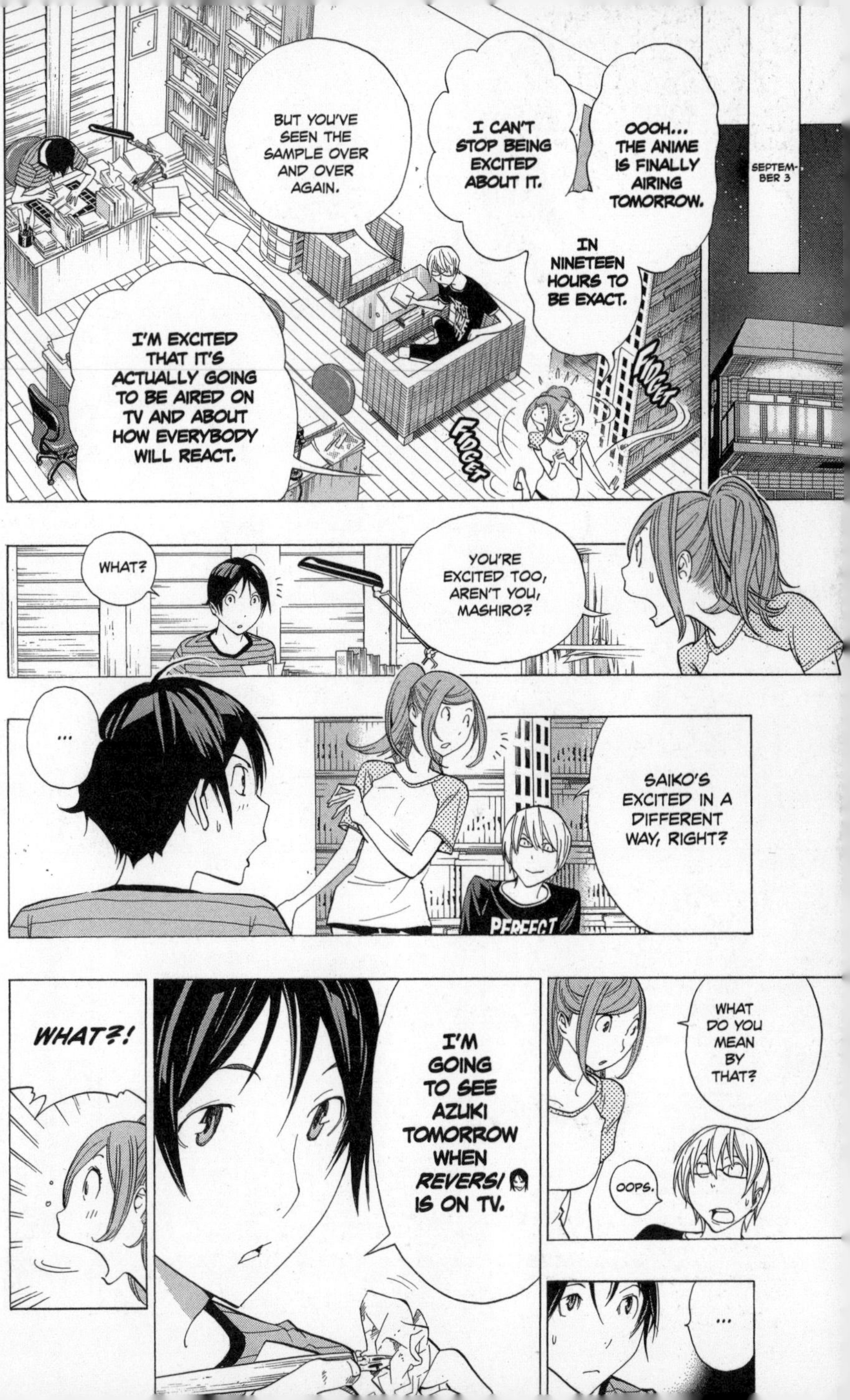
SEPTEMBER 3
OOOH... THE ANIME IS FINALLY AIRING TOMORROW.
IN NINETEEN HOURS TO BE EXACT.
FIDGET
FIDGET
I CAN'T STOP BEING EXCITED ABOUT IT.
BUT YOU'VE SEEN THE SAMPLE OVER AND OVER AGAIN.
I'M EXCITED THAT IT'S ACTUALLY GOING TO BE AIRED ON TV AND ABOUT HOW EVERYBODY WILL REACT.
YOU'RE EXCITED TOO, AREN'T YOU, MASHIRO?
WHAT?
SAIKO'S EXCITED IN A DIFFERENT WAY, RIGHT?
...
WHAT DO YOU MEAN BY THAT?
OOPS.
...
I'M GOING TO SEE AZUKI TOMORROW WHEN *REVERSI* IS ON TV.
WHAT?!

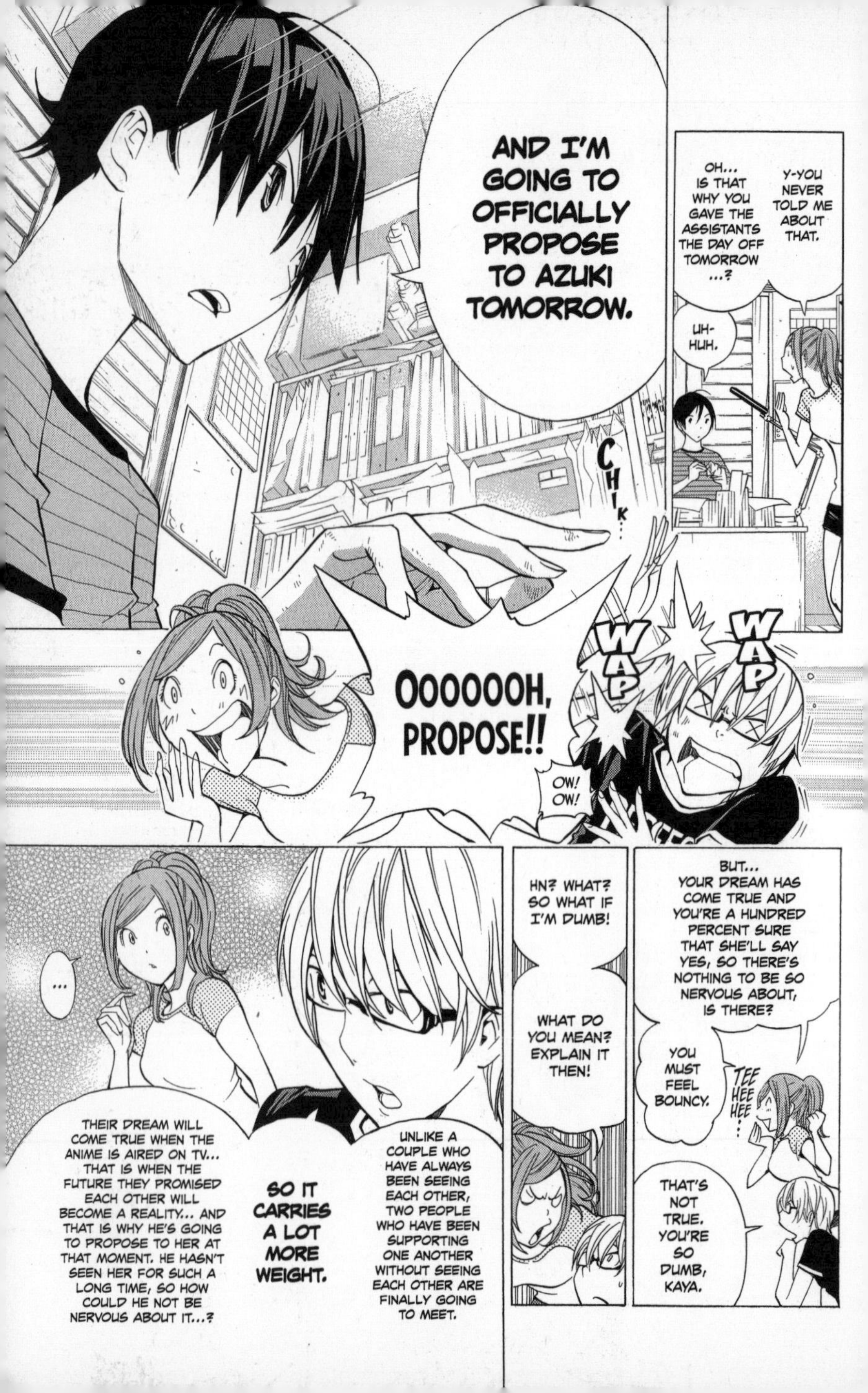

Y-YOU NEVER TOLD ME ABOUT THAT.
OH... IS THAT WHY YOU GAVE THE ASSISTANTS THE DAY OFF TOMORROW...?
UH-HUH.
AND I'M GOING TO OFFICIALLY PROPOSE TO AZUKI TOMORROW.
CHIK...
WAP
WAP
OW! OW!
OOOOOOH, PROPOSE!!
BUT... YOUR DREAM HAS COME TRUE AND YOU'RE A HUNDRED PERCENT SURE THAT SHE'LL SAY YES, SO THERE'S NOTHING TO BE SO NERVOUS ABOUT, IS THERE?
YOU MUST FEEL BOUNCY.
TEE HEE HEE
THAT'S NOT TRUE. YOU'RE SO DUMB, KAYA.
HN? WHAT? SO WHAT IF I'M DUMB!
WHAT DO YOU MEAN? EXPLAIN IT THEN!
...
UNLIKE A COUPLE WHO HAVE ALWAYS BEEN SEEING EACH OTHER, TWO PEOPLE WHO HAVE BEEN SUPPORTING ONE ANOTHER WITHOUT SEEING EACH OTHER ARE FINALLY GOING TO MEET.
SO IT CARRIES A LOT MORE WEIGHT.
THEIR DREAM WILL COME TRUE WHEN THE ANIME IS AIRED ON TV... THAT IS WHEN THE FUTURE THEY PROMISED EACH OTHER WILL BECOME A REALITY... AND THAT IS WHY HE'S GOING TO PROPOSE TO HER AT THAT MOMENT. HE HASN'T SEEN HER FOR SUCH A LONG TIME, SO HOW COULD HE NOT BE NERVOUS ABOUT IT...?

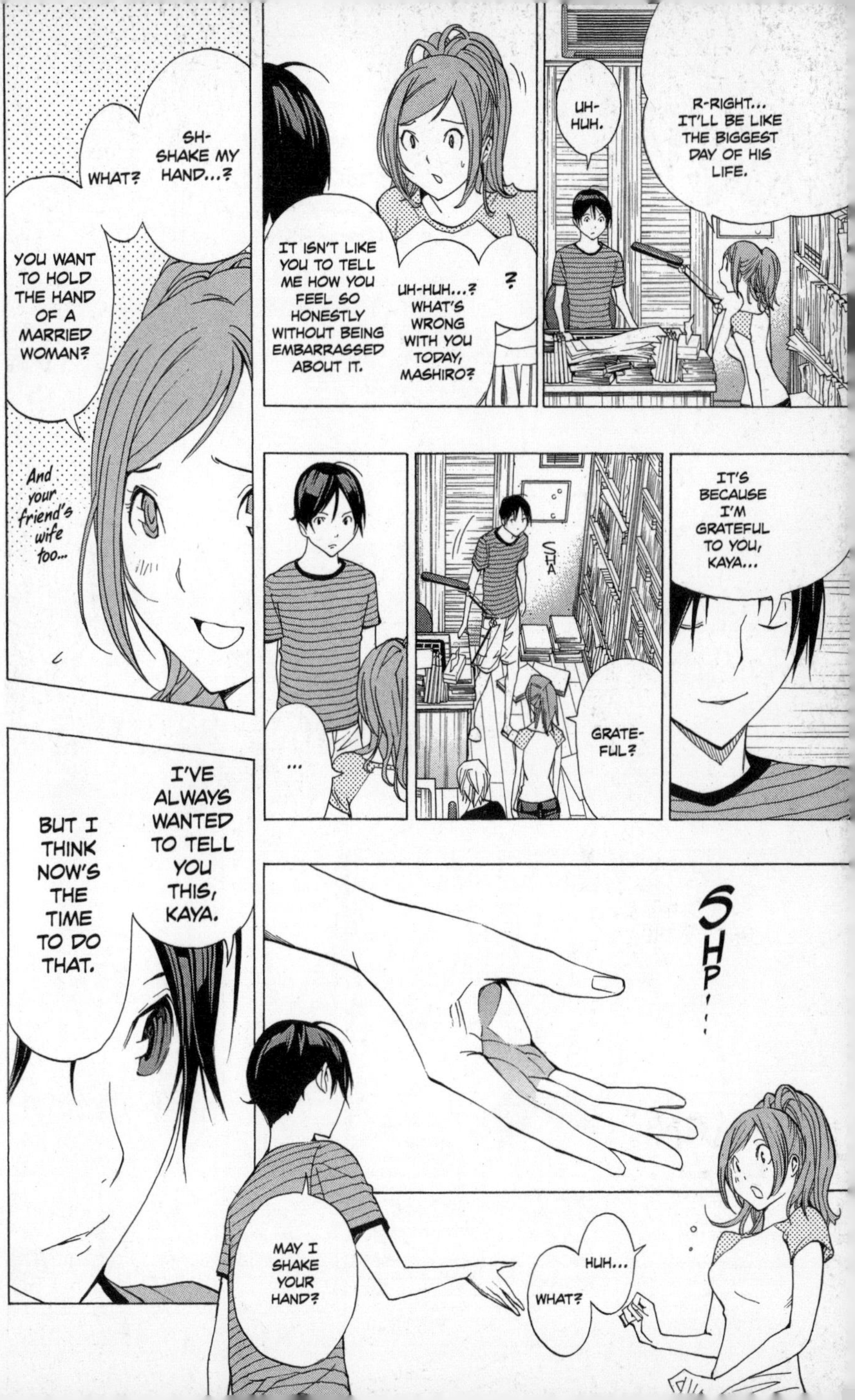
R-RIGHT... IT'LL BE LIKE THE BIGGEST DAY OF HIS LIFE.
UH-HUH.
?
UH-HUH...? WHAT'S WRONG WITH YOU TODAY, MASHIRO?
IT ISN'T LIKE YOU TO TELL ME HOW YOU FEEL SO HONESTLY WITHOUT BEING EMBARRASSED ABOUT IT.
IT'S BECAUSE I'M GRATEFUL TO YOU, KAYA...
GRATE-FUL?
SHA
...
SHP
MAY I SHAKE YOUR HAND?
HUH...
WHAT?
SH-SHAKE MY HAND...?
WHAT?
YOU WANT TO HOLD THE HAND OF A MARRIED WOMAN?
And your friend's wife too...
I'VE ALWAYS WANTED TO TELL YOU THIS, KAYA.
BUT I THINK NOW'S THE TIME TO DO THAT.

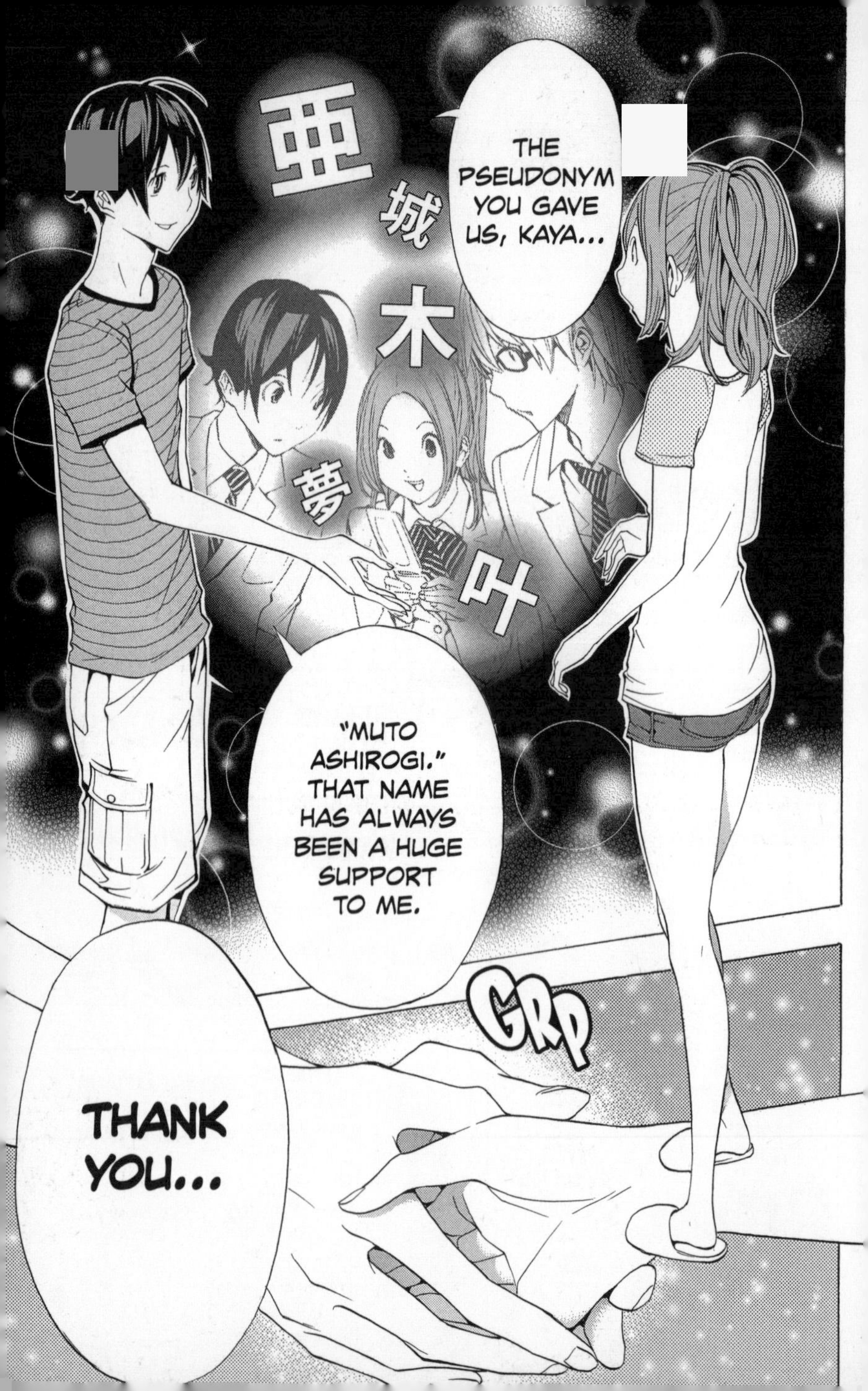
THE PSEUDONYM YOU GAVE US, KAYA...
亜城木夢叶
"MUTO ASHIROGI." THAT NAME HAS ALWAYS BEEN A HUGE SUPPORT TO ME.
GRP
THANK YOU...

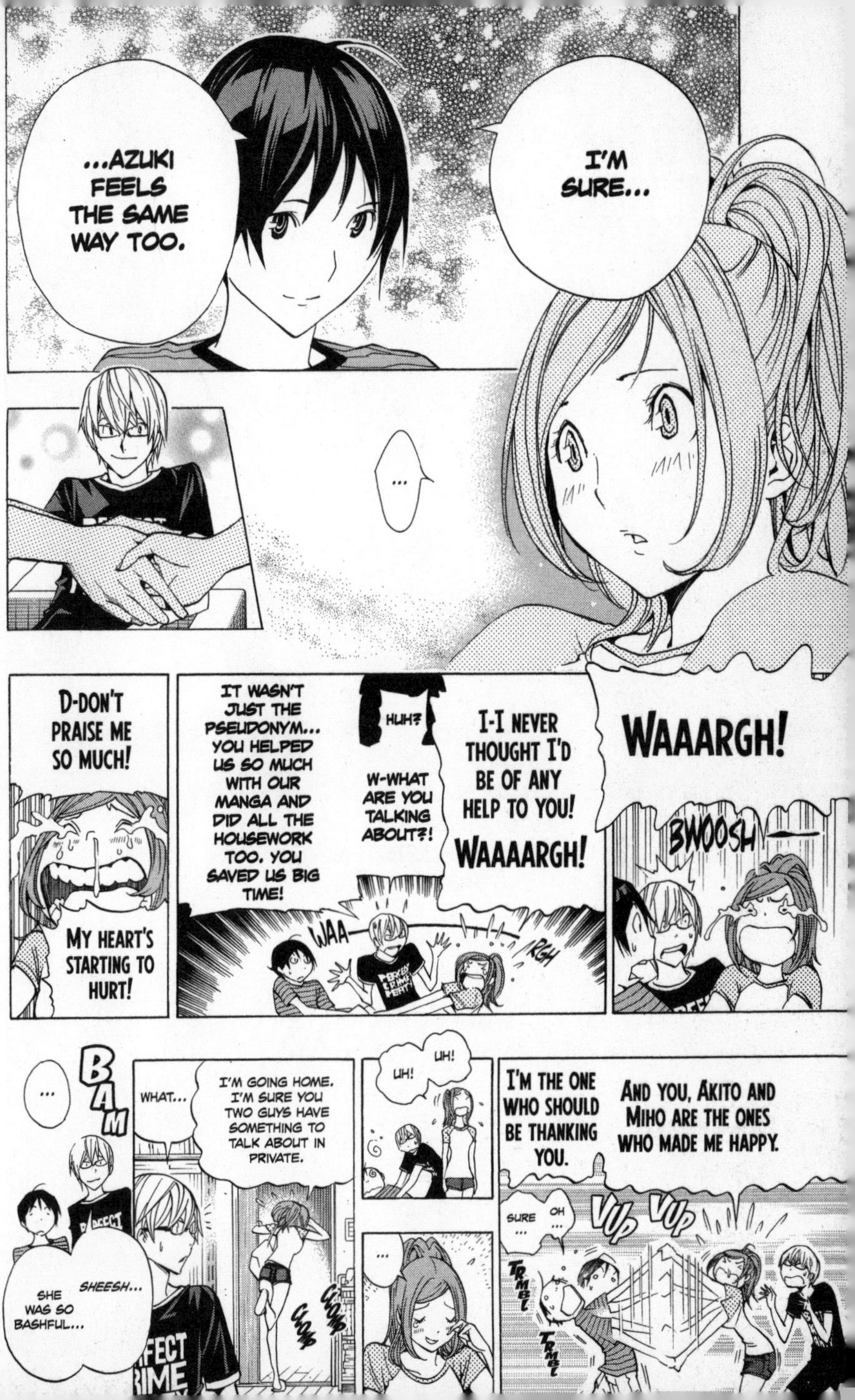
I'M SURE...
...AZUKI FEELS THE SAME WAY TOO.
...
WAAARGH!
BWOOSH
I-I NEVER THOUGHT I'D BE OF ANY HELP TO YOU!
WAAAARGH!
HUH?
W-WHAT ARE YOU TALKING ABOUT?!
IT WASN'T JUST THE PSEUDONYM... YOU HELPED US SO MUCH WITH OUR MANGA AND DID ALL THE HOUSEWORK TOO. YOU SAVED US BIG TIME!
WAA
RGH
D-DON'T PRAISE ME SO MUCH!
MY HEART'S STARTING TO HURT!
AND YOU, AKITO AND MIHO ARE THE ONES WHO MADE ME HAPPY.
I'M THE ONE WHO SHOULD BE THANKING YOU.
VUP
VUP
OH ...
SURE ...
TRMBL
TRMBL
UH!
UH!
...
I'M GOING HOME. I'M SURE YOU TWO GUYS HAVE SOMETHING TO TALK ABOUT IN PRIVATE.
WHAT...
CLOMP
CLOMP
...
BAM
SHEESH...
SHE WAS SO BASHFUL...

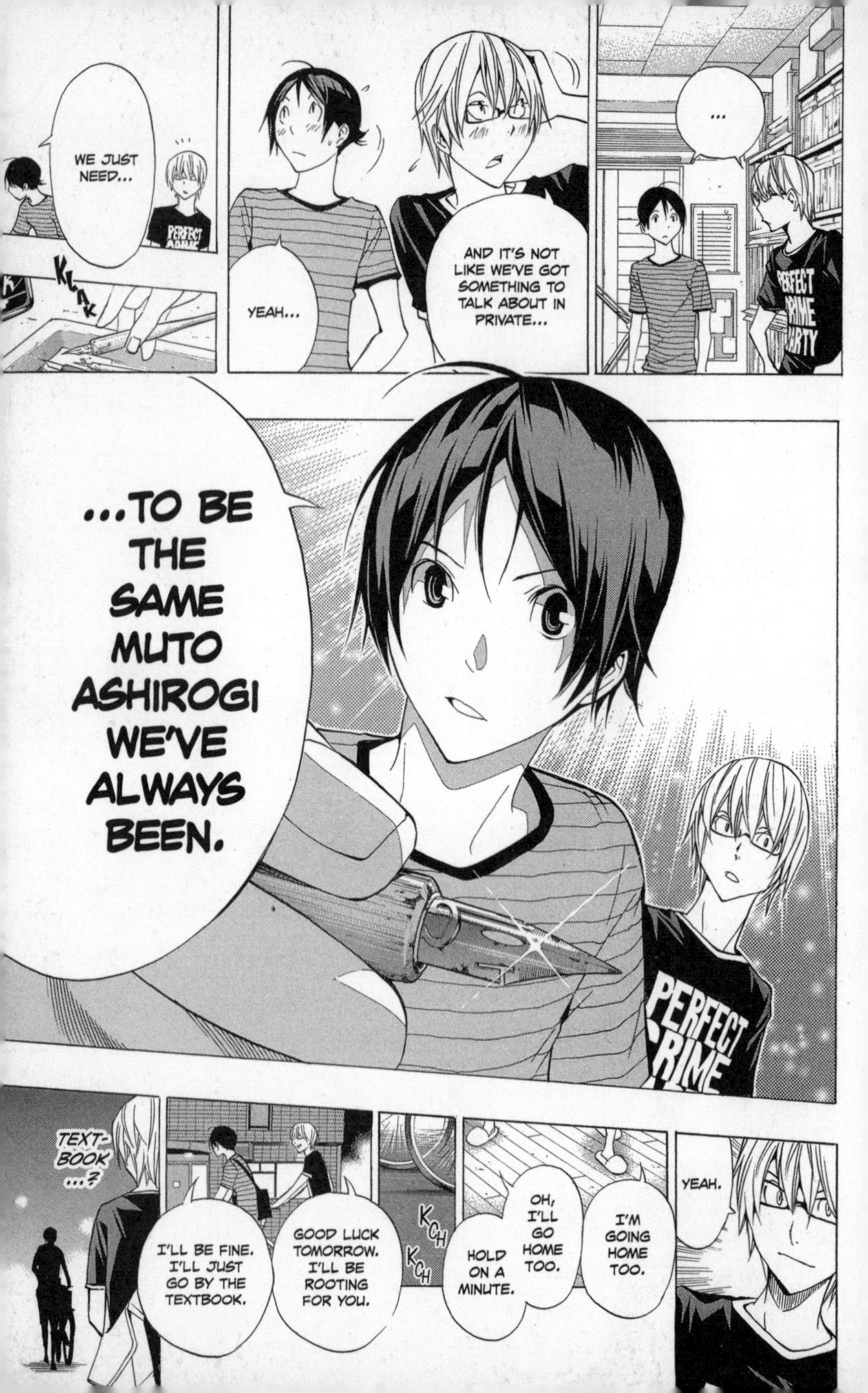
...
AND IT'S NOT LIKE WE'VE GOT SOMETHING TO TALK ABOUT IN PRIVATE...
YEAH...
WE JUST NEED...
KLAK
...TO BE THE SAME MUTO ASHIROGI WE'VE ALWAYS BEEN.
YEAH.
I'M GOING HOME TOO.
OH, I'LL GO HOME TOO.
HOLD ON A MINUTE.
KCH KCH
GOOD LUCK TOMORROW. I'LL BE ROOTING FOR YOU.
I'LL BE FINE. I'LL JUST GO BY THE TEXTBOOK.
TEXT-BOOK...?

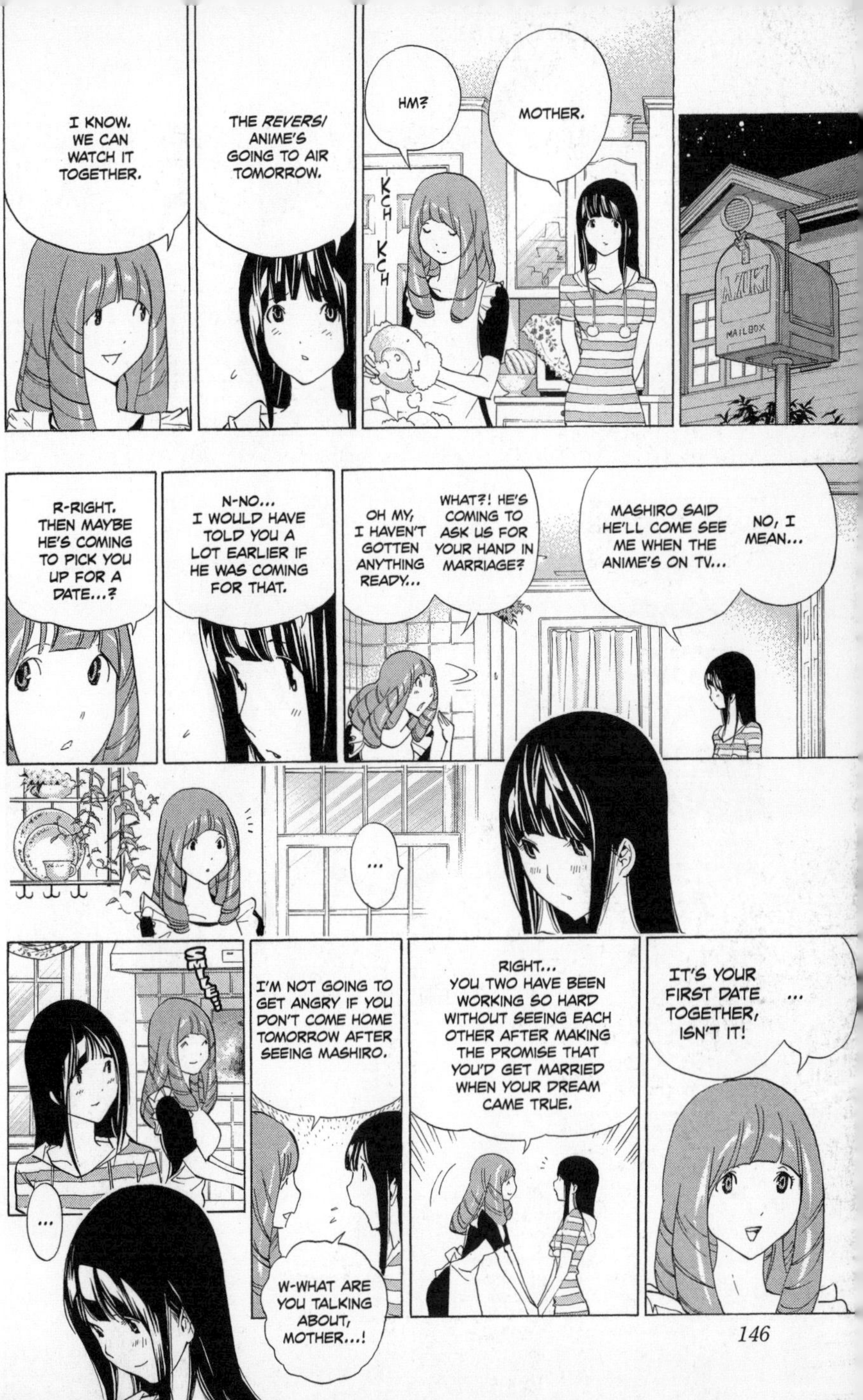
AZUKI
MAILBOX
MOTHER.
HM?
KCH KCH
THE *REVERSI* ANIME'S GOING TO AIR TOMORROW.
I KNOW. WE CAN WATCH IT TOGETHER.
MASHIRO SAID HE'LL COME SEE ME WHEN THE ANIME'S ON TV...
NO, I MEAN...
WHAT?! HE'S COMING TO ASK US FOR YOUR HAND IN MARRIAGE?
OH MY, I HAVEN'T GOTTEN ANYTHING READY...
N-NO... I WOULD HAVE TOLD YOU A LOT EARLIER IF HE WAS COMING FOR THAT.
R-RIGHT. THEN MAYBE HE'S COMING TO PICK YOU UP FOR A DATE...?
...
IT'S YOUR FIRST DATE TOGETHER, ISN'T IT!
...
RIGHT... YOU TWO HAVE BEEN WORKING SO HARD WITHOUT SEEING EACH OTHER AFTER MAKING THE PROMISE THAT YOU'D GET MARRIED WHEN YOUR DREAM CAME TRUE.
I'M NOT GOING TO GET ANGRY IF YOU DON'T COME HOME TOMORROW AFTER SEEING MASHIRO.
W-WHAT ARE YOU TALKING ABOUT, MOTHER...!
SMILE
...

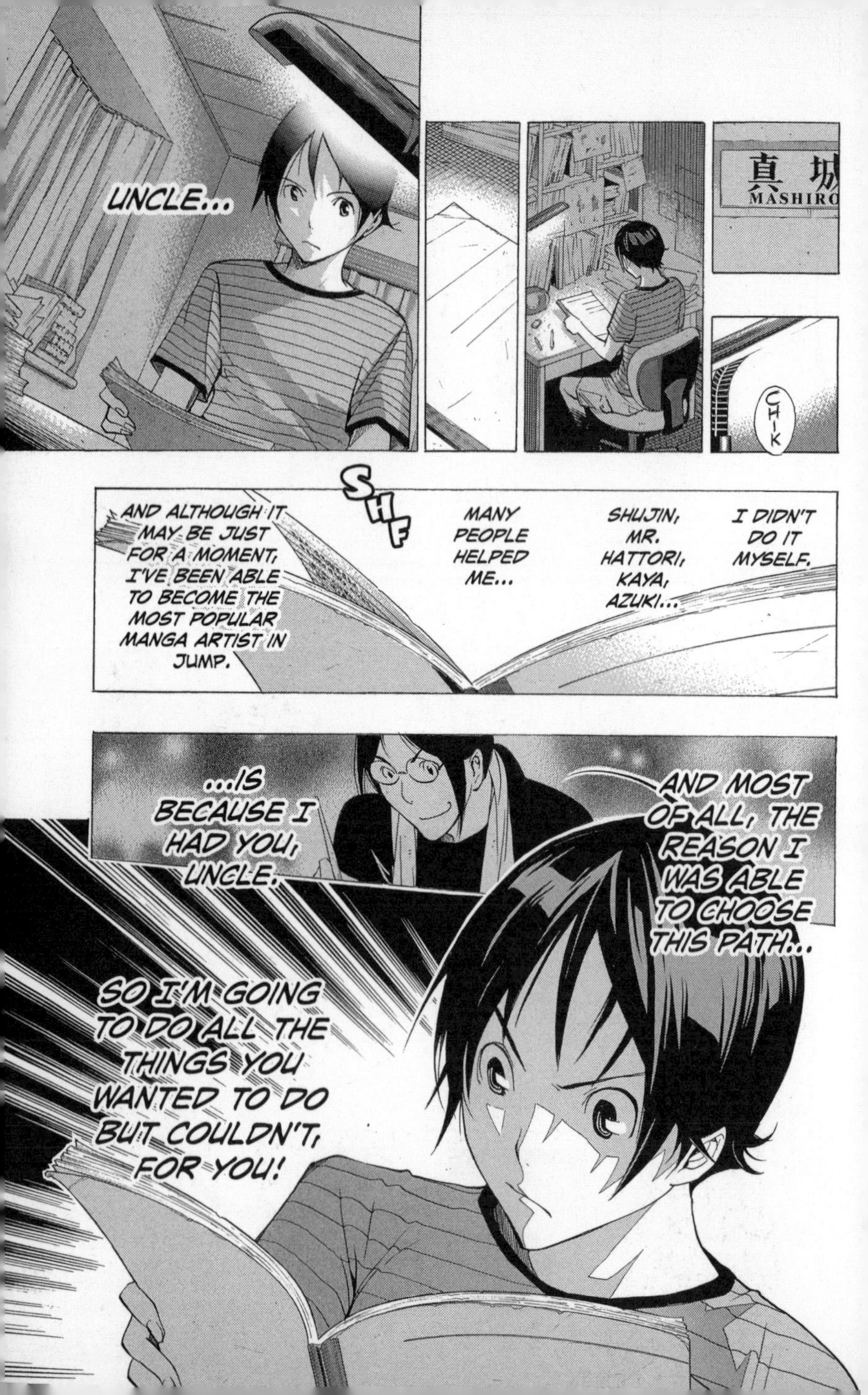
真城
MASHIRO
CHIK
UNCLE...
I DIDN'T DO IT MYSELF.
SHUJIN, MR. HATTORI, KAYA, AZUKI...
MANY PEOPLE HELPED ME...
SHF
AND ALTHOUGH IT MAY BE JUST FOR A MOMENT, I'VE BEEN ABLE TO BECOME THE MOST POPULAR MANGA ARTIST IN JUMP.
AND MOST OF ALL, THE REASON I WAS ABLE TO CHOOSE THIS PATH...
...IS BECAUSE I HAD YOU, UNCLE.
SO I'M GOING TO DO ALL THE THINGS YOU WANTED TO DO BUT COULDN'T, FOR YOU!

OHBA'S STORYBOARD

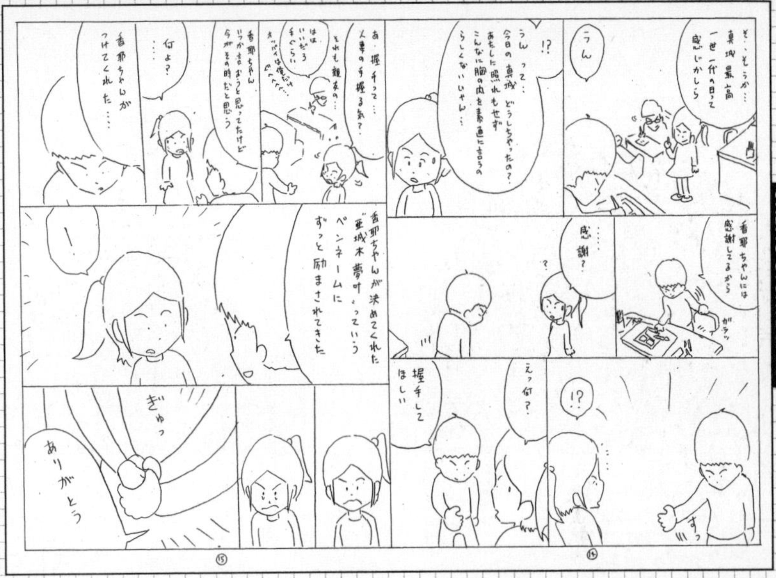

そ、そうか… 真城最高一世一代の日って感じかしら
うん
!?
うんって… 今日の真城どうしちゃったの? あたしに照れもせず こんなに胸の内を素直に言うの らしくないじゃん…
香耶ちゃんには感謝してるから
ガラッ
……
感謝?
?
!?
すっ
え、何?
握手してほしい
あ、握手って… 人妻の手握る気?
それも親友の…
ははいいだろ手ぐらい
オッパイは俺だけ ぐへへへへ…
香耶ちゃん いつか言おうと思ってたけど 今がその時だと思う
何よ? …
香耶ちゃんがつけてくれた…
香耶ちゃんが決めてくれた "亜城木夢叶"っていうペンネームにずっと励まされてきた
!
ぎゅっ
ありがとう
⑭
⑮

OBATA'S STORYBOARD

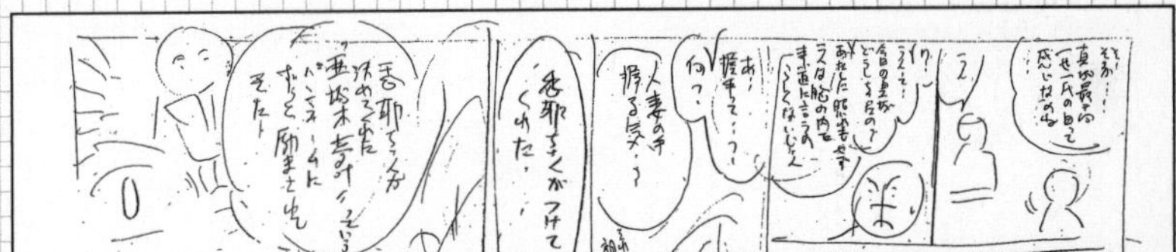

ズッ
!
ぎゅっ
ありがとう

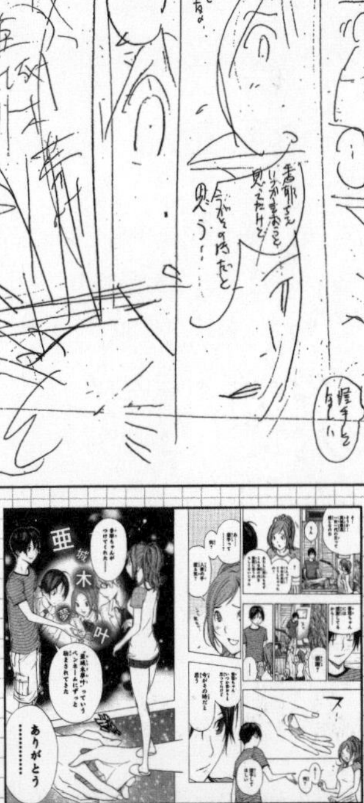

亜
城
木
夢
叶
ありがとう

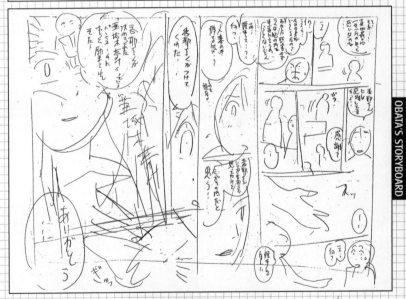

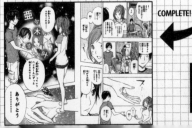

COMPLETE!

※CREATOR STORYBOARDS AND FINISHED PAGES IN JAPANESE

BAKUMAN。 vol.20

"Until the Final Draft Is Complete"

Chapter 175, pp. 146-147

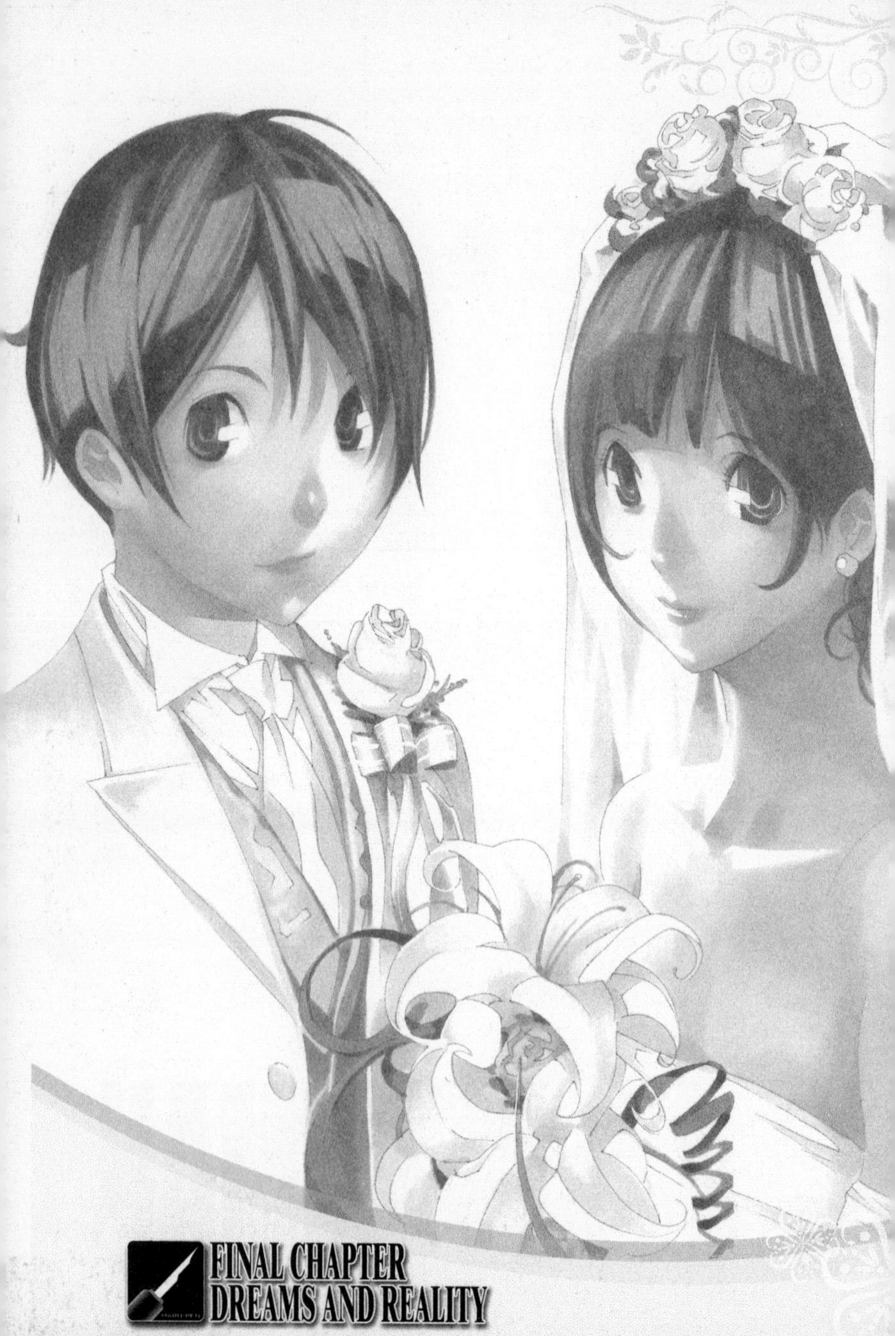

FINAL CHAPTER
DREAMS AND REALITY

BAKUMAN。

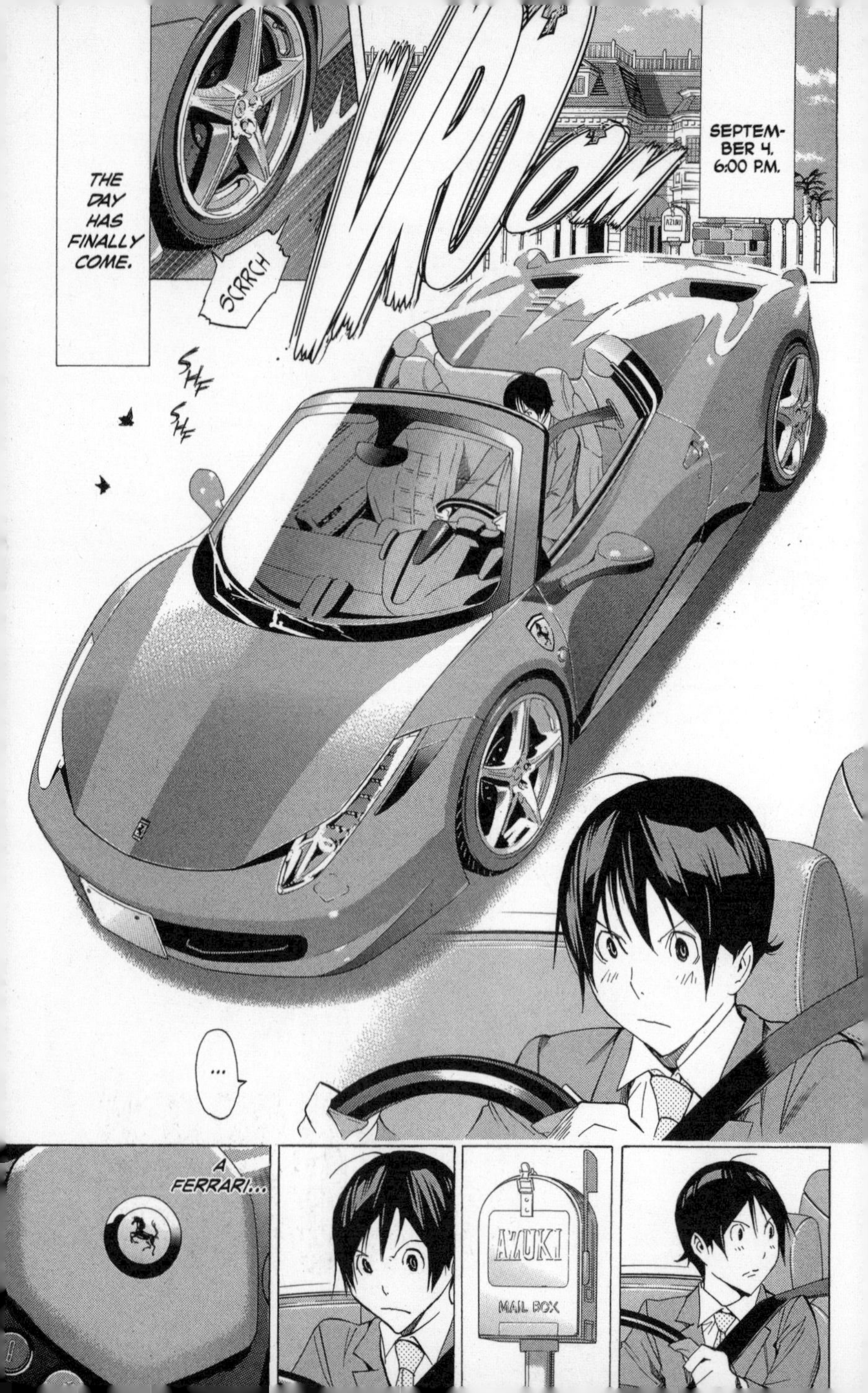
SEPTEMBER 4, 6:00 P.M.
VROOM
AZUKI
THE DAY HAS FINALLY COME.
SCRRCH
SHF SHF
...
AZUKI
MAIL BOX
A FERRARI...

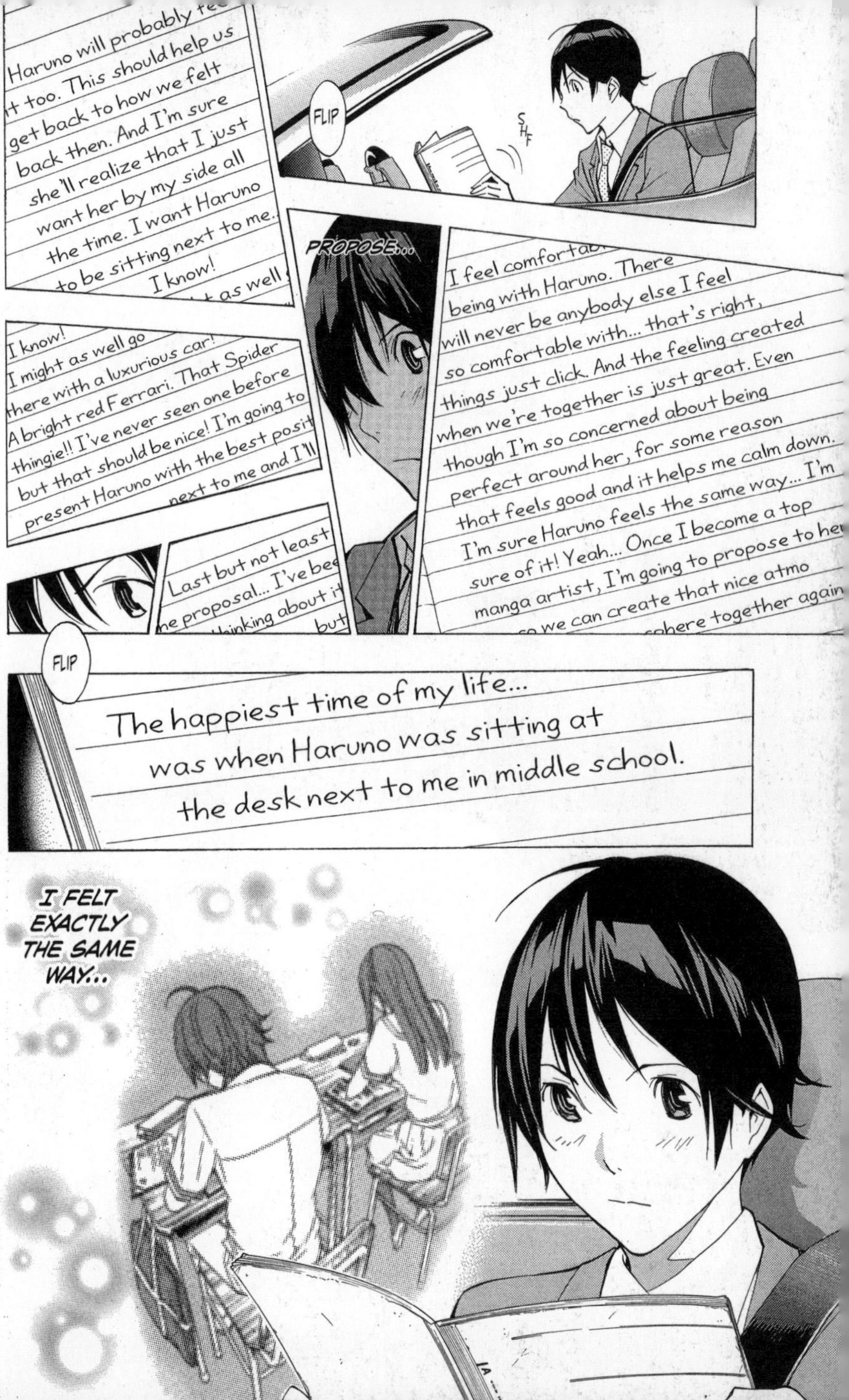

FLIP
SHF
Haruno will probably fe
it too. This should help us
get back to how we felt
back then. And I'm sure
she'll realize that I just
want her by my side all
the time. I want Haruno
to be sitting next to me.
I know!
as well
I feel comforta
being with Haruno. There
will never be anybody else I feel
so comfortable with... that's right,
things just click. And the feeling created
when we're together is just great. Even
though I'm so concerned about being
perfect around her, for some reason
that feels good and it helps me calm down.
I'm sure Haruno feels the same way... I'm
sure of it! Yeah... Once I become a top
manga artist, I'm going to propose to he
so we can create that nice atmo
sphere together agai
PROPOSE...
I know!
I might as well go
there with a luxurious car!
A bright red Ferrari. That Spider
thingie!! I've never seen one before
but that should be nice! I'm going to
present Haruno with the best posit
next to me and I'll
Last but not least
the proposal... I've bee
thinking about it
but
FLIP
The happiest time of my life...
was when Haruno was sitting at
the desk next to me in middle school.
I FELT EXACTLY THE SAME WAY...

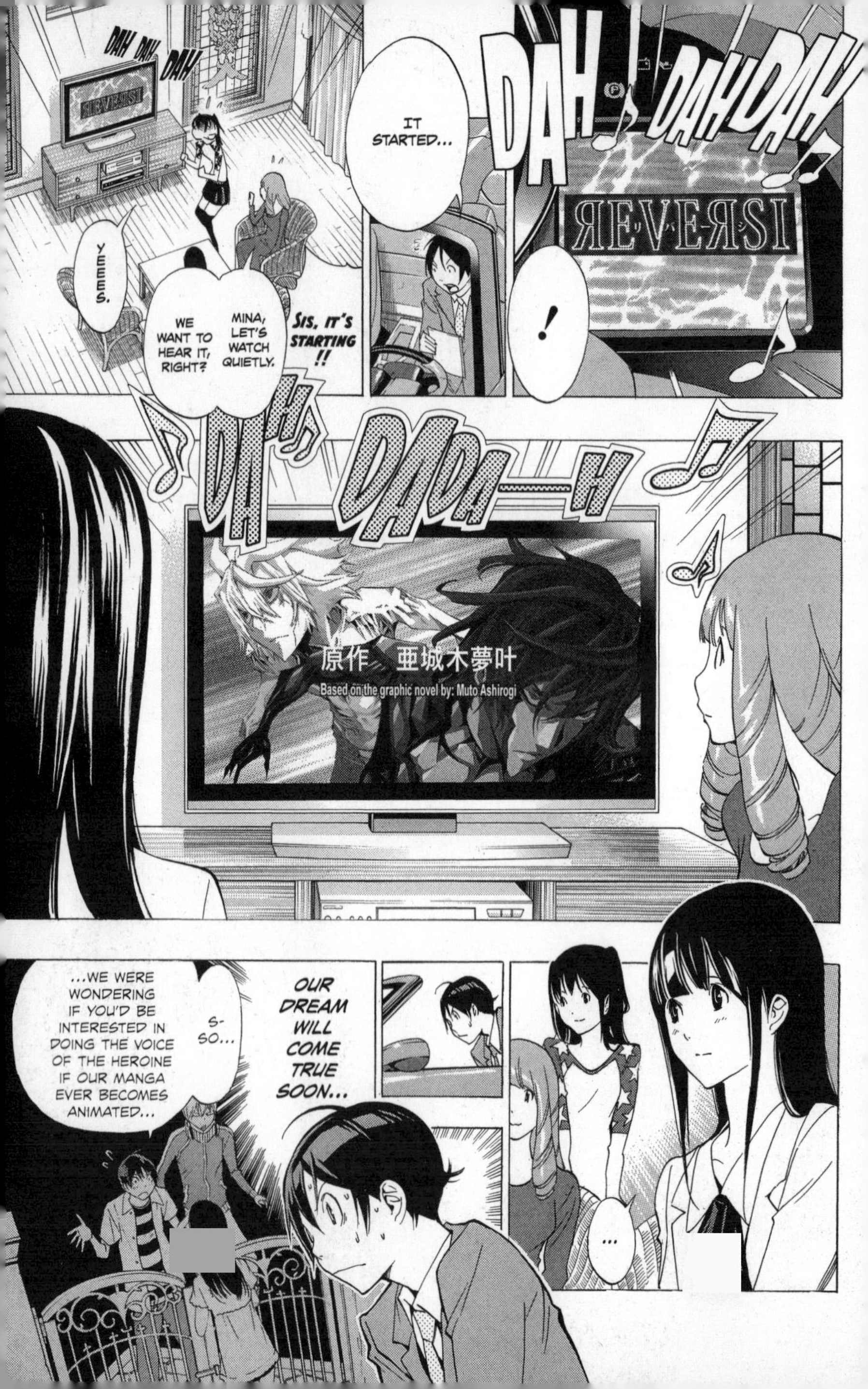
DAH DAHDAH
REVERSI
!
IT STARTED...
DAH DAH DAH
SIS, IT'S STARTING!!
MINA, LET'S WATCH QUIETLY.
WE WANT TO HEAR IT, RIGHT?
YEEES.
DAH DADA—H
原作　亜城木夢叶
Based on the graphic novel by: Muto Ashirogi
...
OUR DREAM WILL COME TRUE SOON...
S-SO...
...WE WERE WONDERING IF YOU'D BE INTERESTED IN DOING THE VOICE OF THE HEROINE IF OUR MANGA EVER BECOMES ANIMATED...

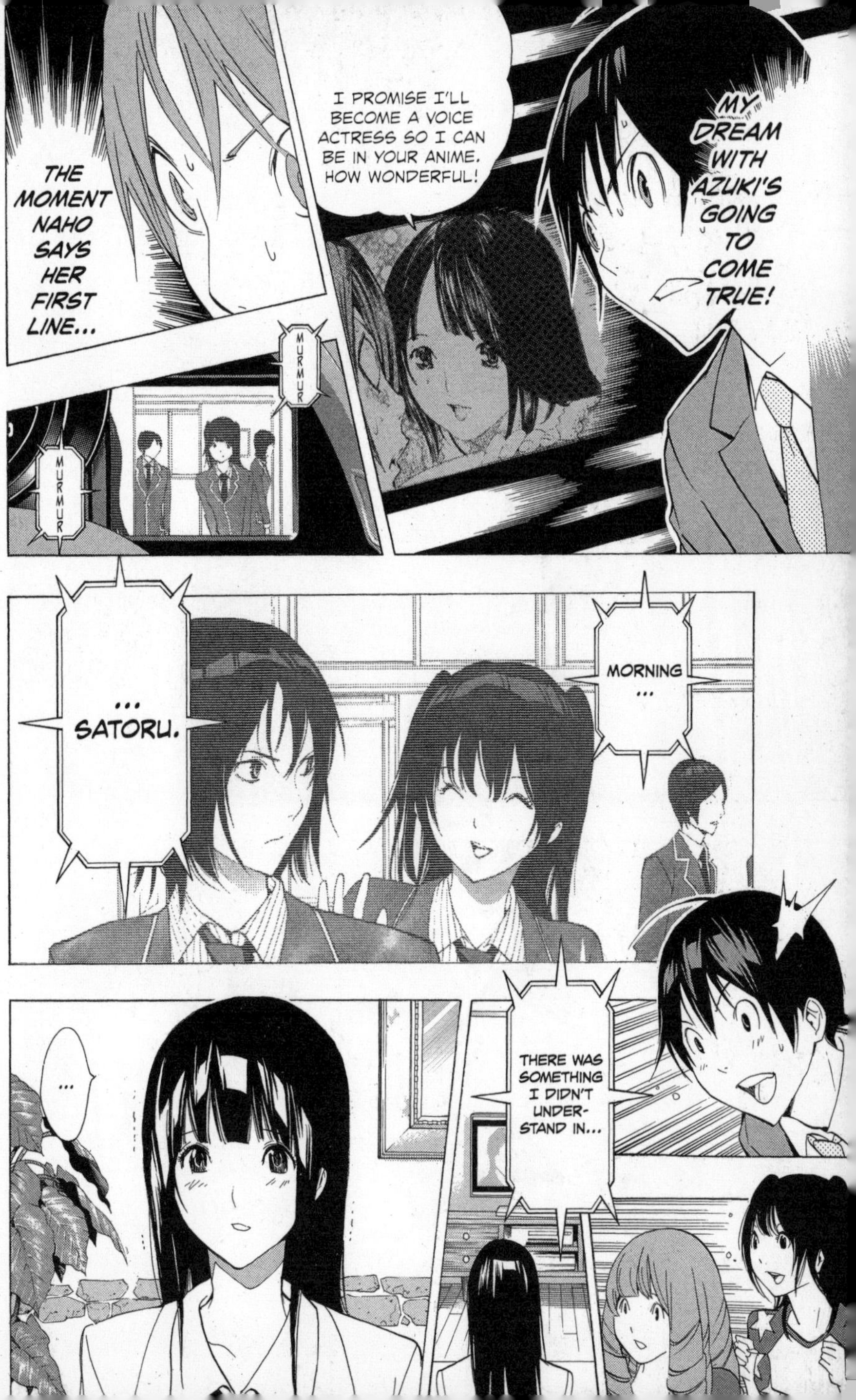
MY DREAM WITH AZUKI'S GOING TO COME TRUE!
I PROMISE I'LL BECOME A VOICE ACTRESS SO I CAN BE IN YOUR ANIME. HOW WONDERFUL!
THE MOMENT NAHO SAYS HER FIRST LINE...
MURMUR
MURMUR
MORNING...
... SATORU.
THERE WAS SOMETHING I DIDN'T UNDER-STAND IN...
...

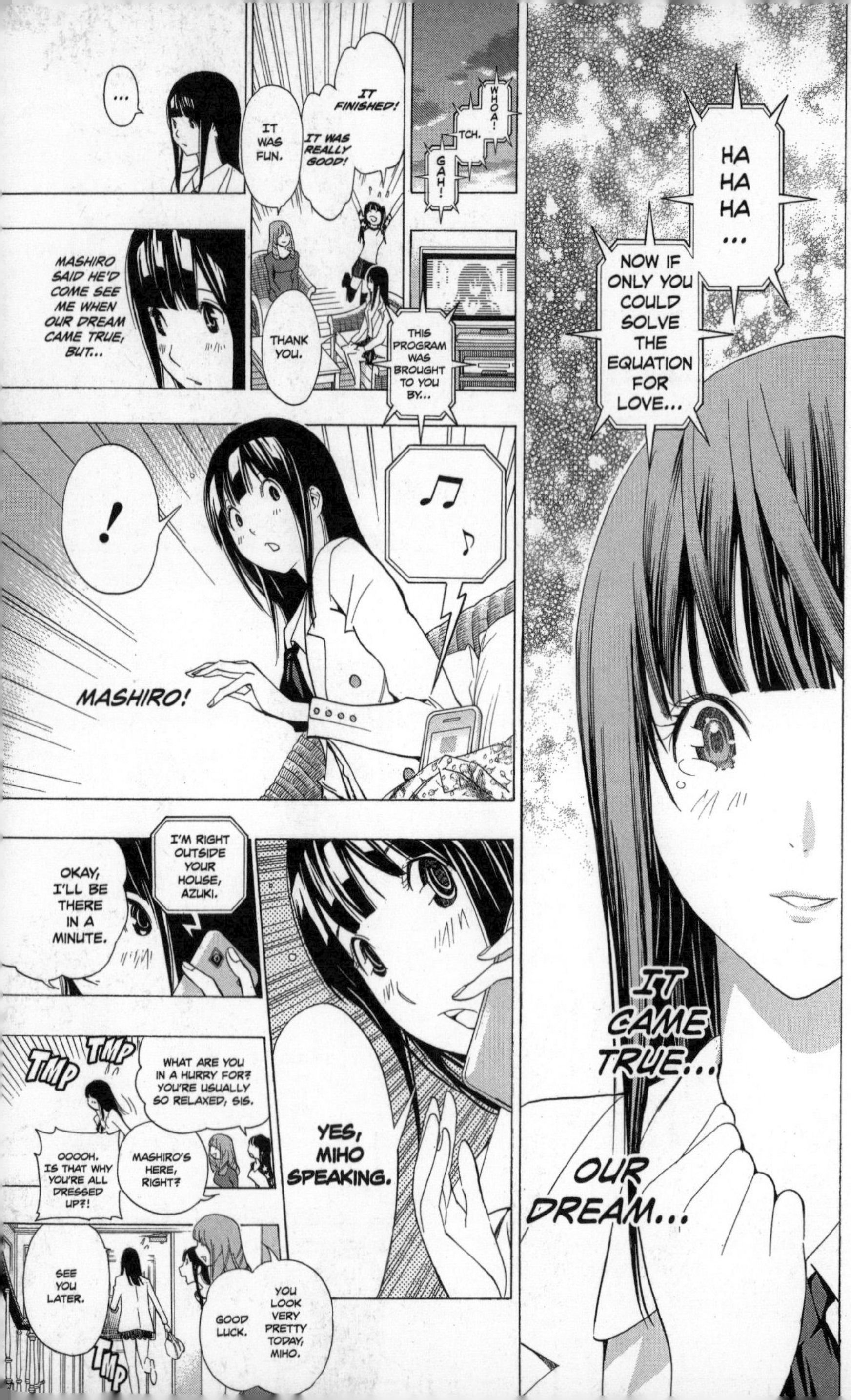
HA HA HA ...
NOW IF ONLY YOU COULD SOLVE THE EQUATION FOR LOVE...
IT CAME TRUE...
OUR DREAM...
WHOA!
TCH.
GAH!
THIS PROGRAM WAS BROUGHT TO YOU BY...
IT FINISHED!
IT WAS REALLY GOOD!
IT WAS FUN.
THANK YOU.
...
MASHIRO SAID HE'D COME SEE ME WHEN OUR DREAM CAME TRUE, BUT...
♫ ♪
!
MASHIRO!
YES, MIHO SPEAKING.
I'M RIGHT OUTSIDE YOUR HOUSE, AZUKI.
OKAY, I'LL BE THERE IN A MINUTE.
TMP
TMP
WHAT ARE YOU IN A HURRY FOR? YOU'RE USUALLY SO RELAXED, SIS.
MASHIRO'S HERE, RIGHT?
OOOOH. IS THAT WHY YOU'RE ALL DRESSED UP?!
YOU LOOK VERY PRETTY TODAY, MIHO.
GOOD LUCK.
SEE YOU LATER.
TMP

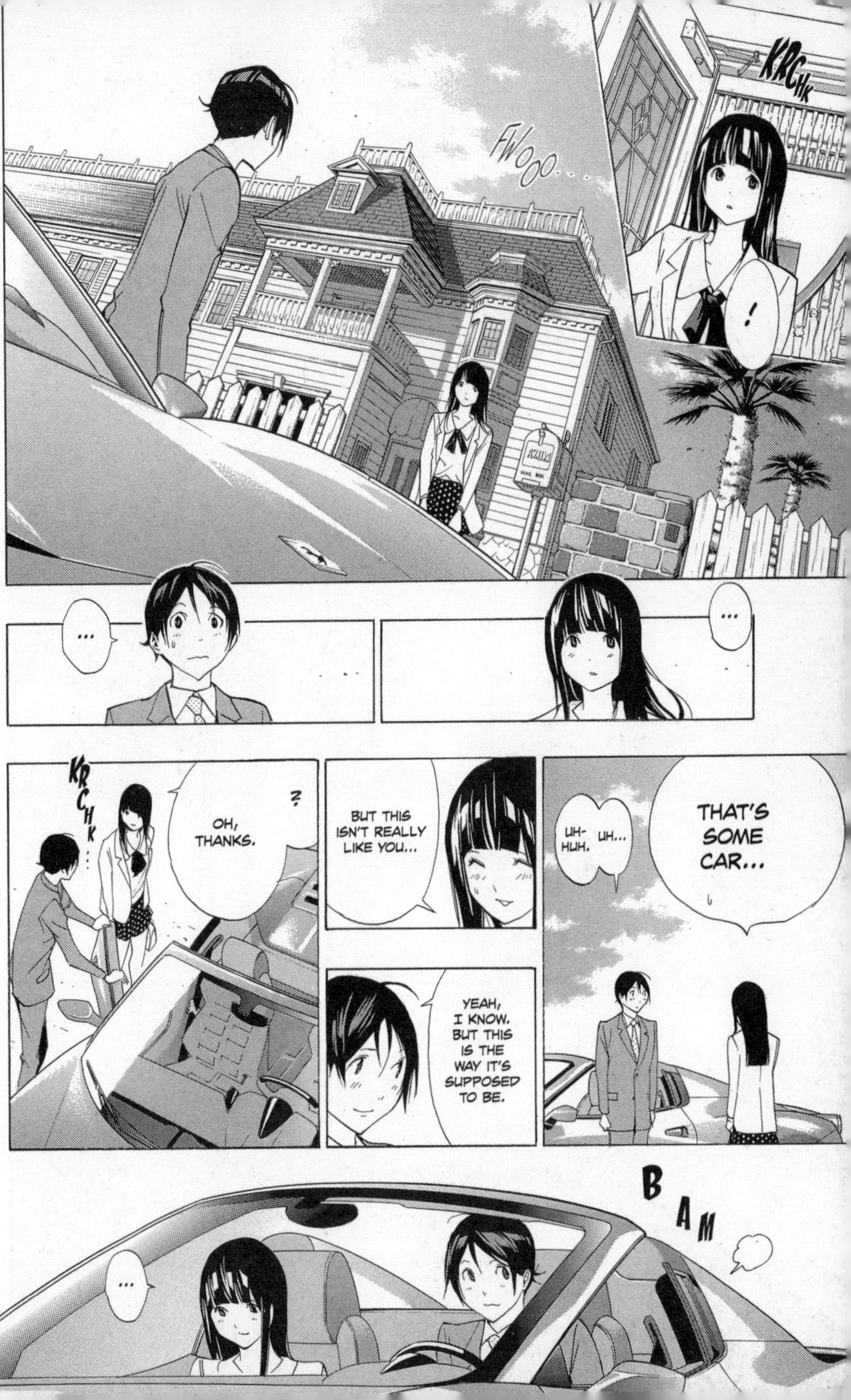
KRCHK
!
FWOOO...
AZUKI
...
...
THAT'S SOME CAR...
UH...
UH-HUH.
BUT THIS ISN'T REALLY LIKE YOU...
YEAH, I KNOW. BUT THIS IS THE WAY IT'S SUPPOSED TO BE.
?
OH, THANKS.
KRCHK...
BAM
...

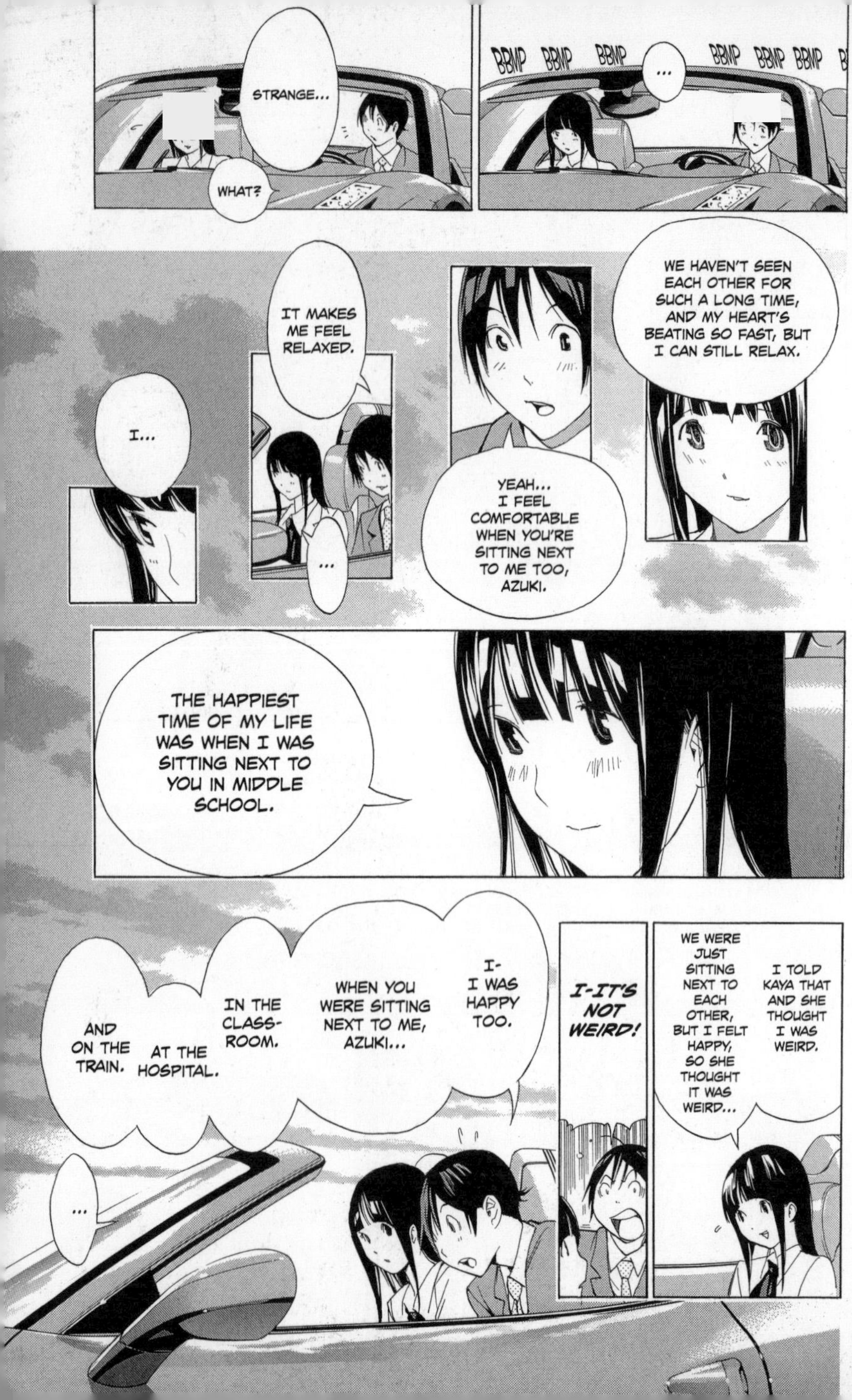
BBMP BBMP BBMP BBMP BBMP BBMP
...
STRANGE...
WHAT?
WE HAVEN'T SEEN EACH OTHER FOR SUCH A LONG TIME, AND MY HEART'S BEATING SO FAST, BUT I CAN STILL RELAX.
YEAH... I FEEL COMFORTABLE WHEN YOU'RE SITTING NEXT TO ME TOO, AZUKI.
IT MAKES ME FEEL RELAXED.
...
I...
THE HAPPIEST TIME OF MY LIFE WAS WHEN I WAS SITTING NEXT TO YOU IN MIDDLE SCHOOL.
I TOLD KAYA THAT AND SHE THOUGHT I WAS WEIRD.
WE WERE JUST SITTING NEXT TO EACH OTHER, BUT I FELT HAPPY, SO SHE THOUGHT IT WAS WEIRD...
I-IT'S NOT WEIRD!
I- I WAS HAPPY TOO.
WHEN YOU WERE SITTING NEXT TO ME, AZUKI...
IN THE CLASS-ROOM.
AT THE HOSPITAL.
AND ON THE TRAIN.
...

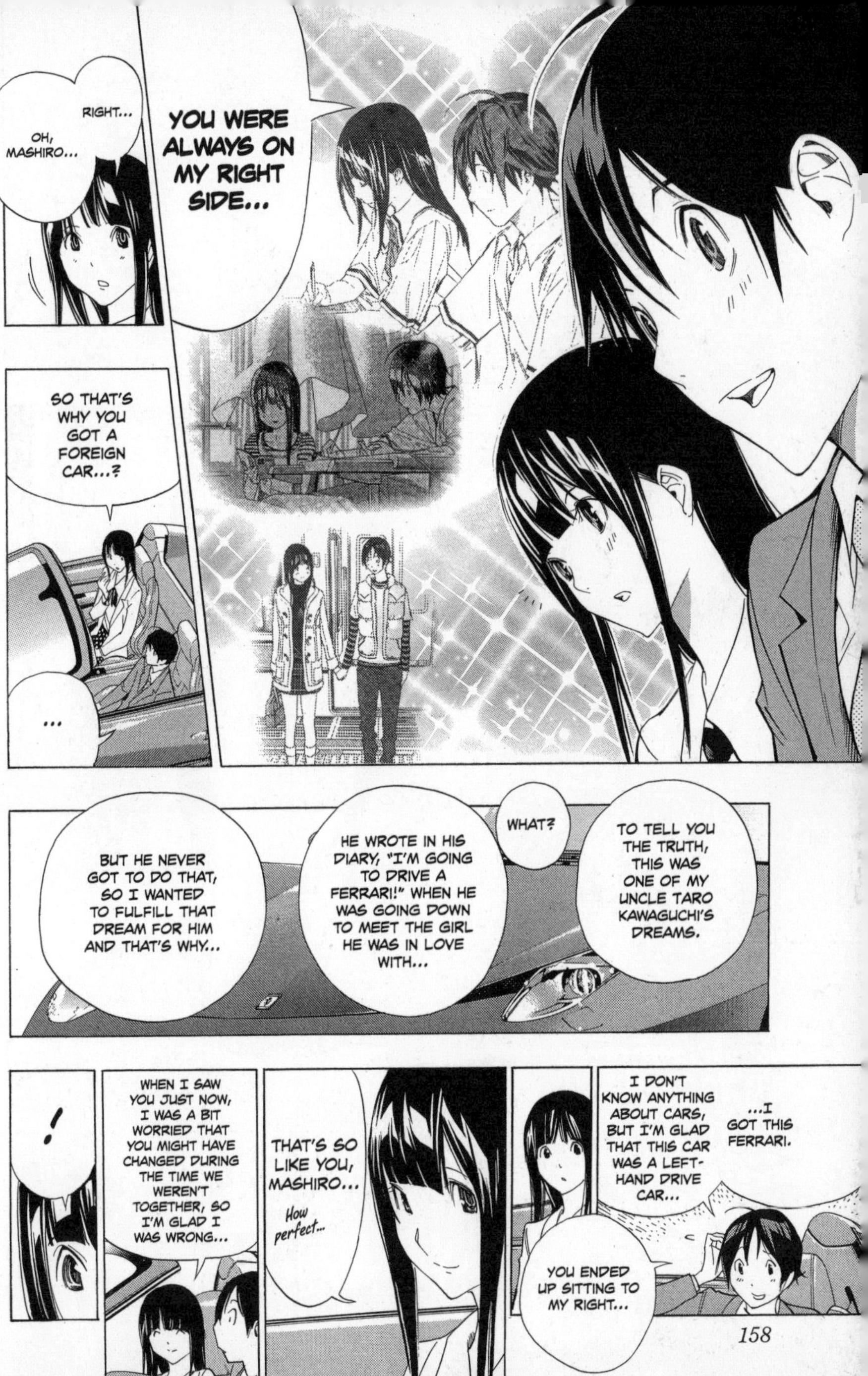
YOU WERE ALWAYS ON MY RIGHT SIDE...
RIGHT...
OH, MASHIRO...
SO THAT'S WHY YOU GOT A FOREIGN CAR...?
...
TO TELL YOU THE TRUTH, THIS WAS ONE OF MY UNCLE TARO KAWAGUCHI'S DREAMS.
WHAT?
HE WROTE IN HIS DIARY, "I'M GOING TO DRIVE A FERRARI!" WHEN HE WAS GOING DOWN TO MEET THE GIRL HE WAS IN LOVE WITH...
BUT HE NEVER GOT TO DO THAT, SO I WANTED TO FULFILL THAT DREAM FOR HIM AND THAT'S WHY...
...I GOT THIS FERRARI.
I DON'T KNOW ANYTHING ABOUT CARS, BUT I'M GLAD THAT THIS CAR WAS A LEFT-HAND DRIVE CAR...
YOU ENDED UP SITTING TO MY RIGHT...
THAT'S SO LIKE YOU, MASHIRO...
How perfect...
WHEN I SAW YOU JUST NOW, I WAS A BIT WORRIED THAT YOU MIGHT HAVE CHANGED DURING THE TIME WE WEREN'T TOGETHER, SO I'M GLAD I WAS WRONG...
!

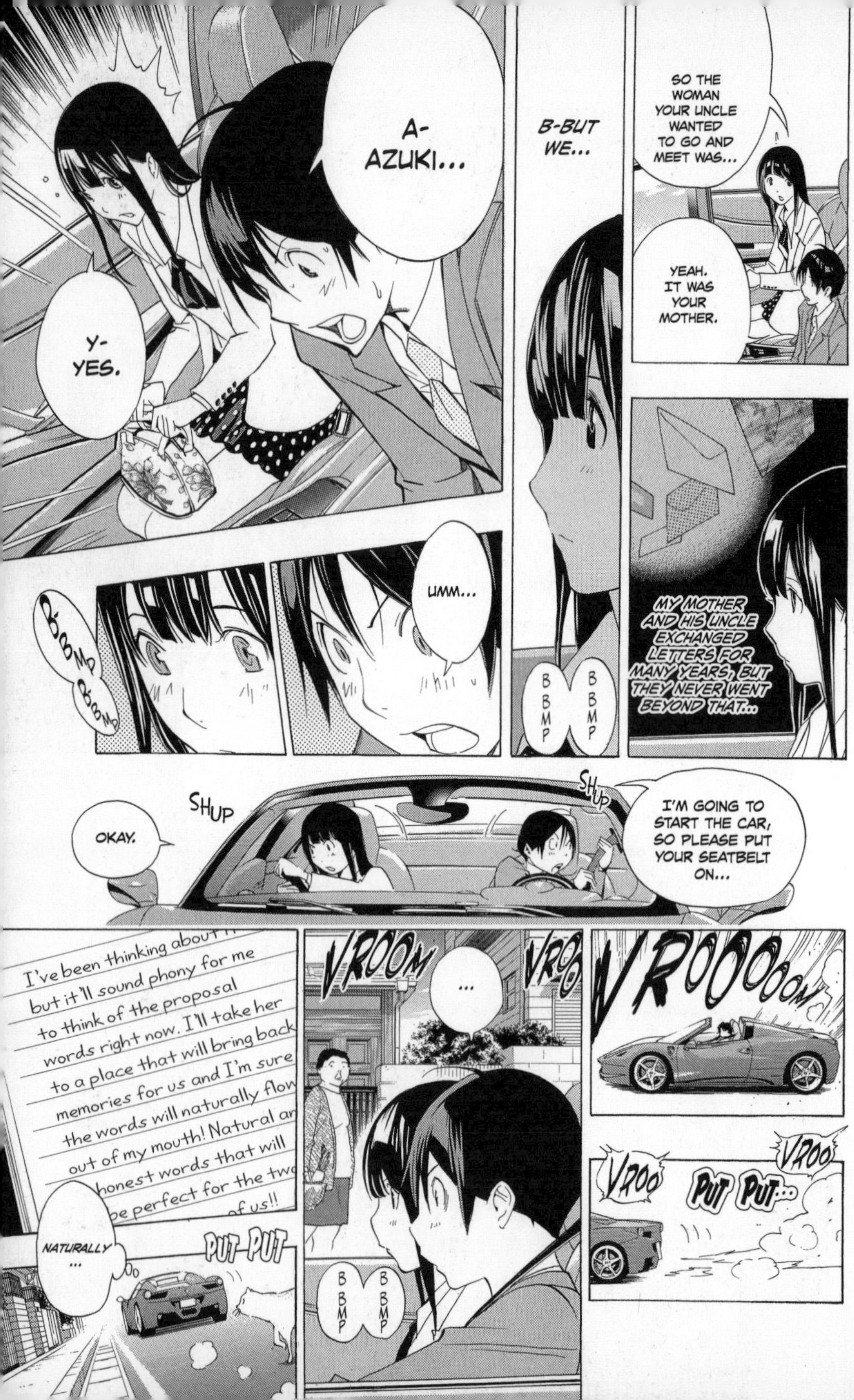
SO THE WOMAN YOUR UNCLE WANTED TO GO AND MEET WAS...
YEAH. IT WAS YOUR MOTHER.
MY MOTHER AND HIS UNCLE EXCHANGED LETTERS FOR MANY YEARS, BUT THEY NEVER WENT BEYOND THAT...
B-BUT WE...
BBMP
BBMP
A-AZUKI...
Y-YES.
UMM...
BBMP BBMP
I'M GOING TO START THE CAR, SO PLEASE PUT YOUR SEATBELT ON...
SHUP
SHUP
OKAY.
VROOOOoom
VROO
PUT PUT...
VROO
VROO
VROOM
...
BBMP
BBMP
I've been thinking about
but it'll sound phony for me
to think of the proposal
words right now. I'll take her
to a place that will bring back
memories for us and I'm sure
the words will naturally flow
out of my mouth! Natural an
honest words that will
be perfect for the two
of us!!
PUT PUT
NATURALLY...

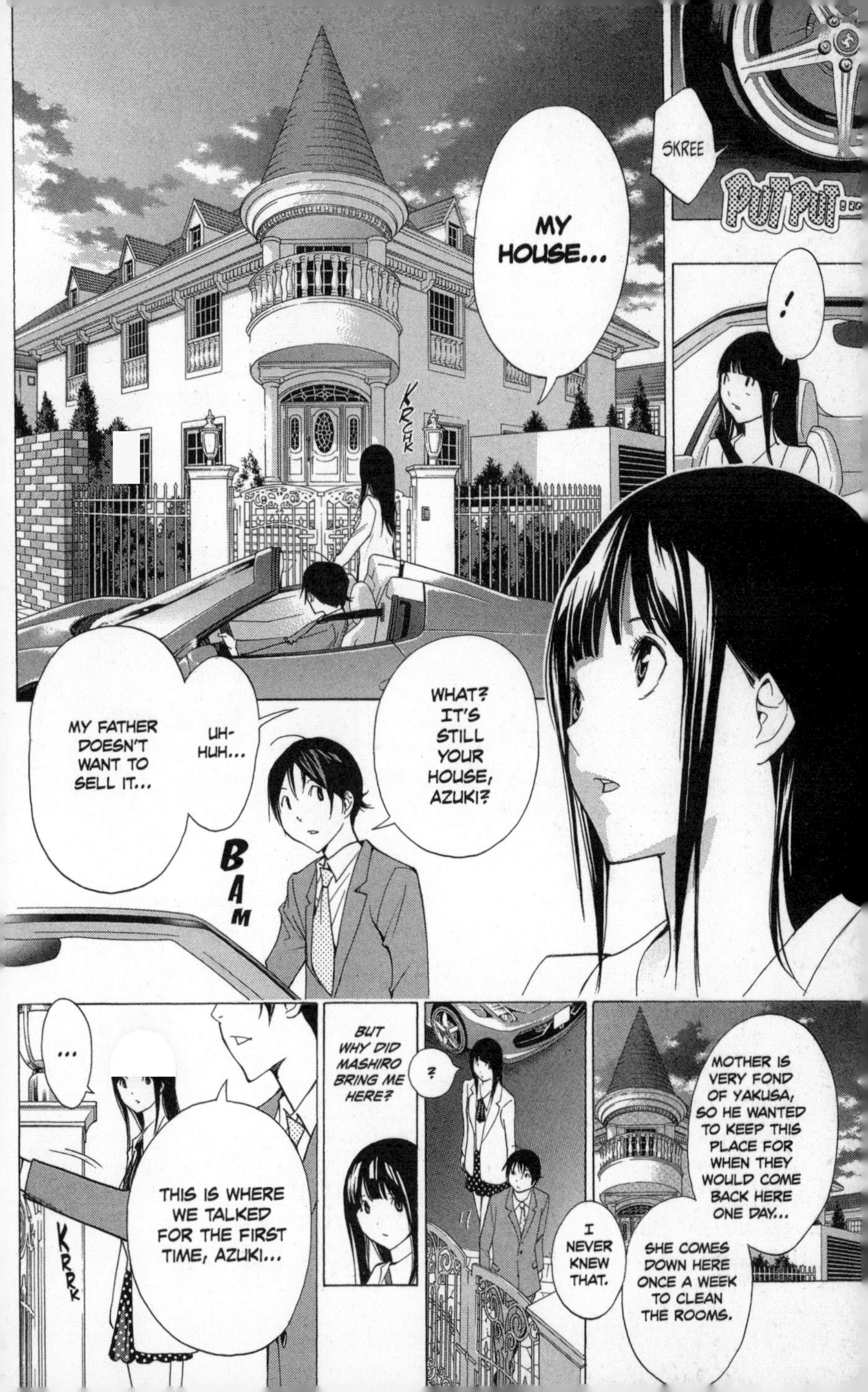
SKREE
PUTPUT...
!
MY HOUSE...
KRCHK
WHAT? IT'S STILL YOUR HOUSE, AZUKI?
UH-HUH...
MY FATHER DOESN'T WANT TO SELL IT...
BAM
MOTHER IS VERY FOND OF YAKUSA, SO HE WANTED TO KEEP THIS PLACE FOR WHEN THEY WOULD COME BACK HERE ONE DAY...
SHE COMES DOWN HERE ONCE A WEEK TO CLEAN THE ROOMS.
I NEVER KNEW THAT.
?
BUT WHY DID MASHIRO BRING ME HERE?
...
THIS IS WHERE WE TALKED FOR THE FIRST TIME, AZUKI...
KRRK

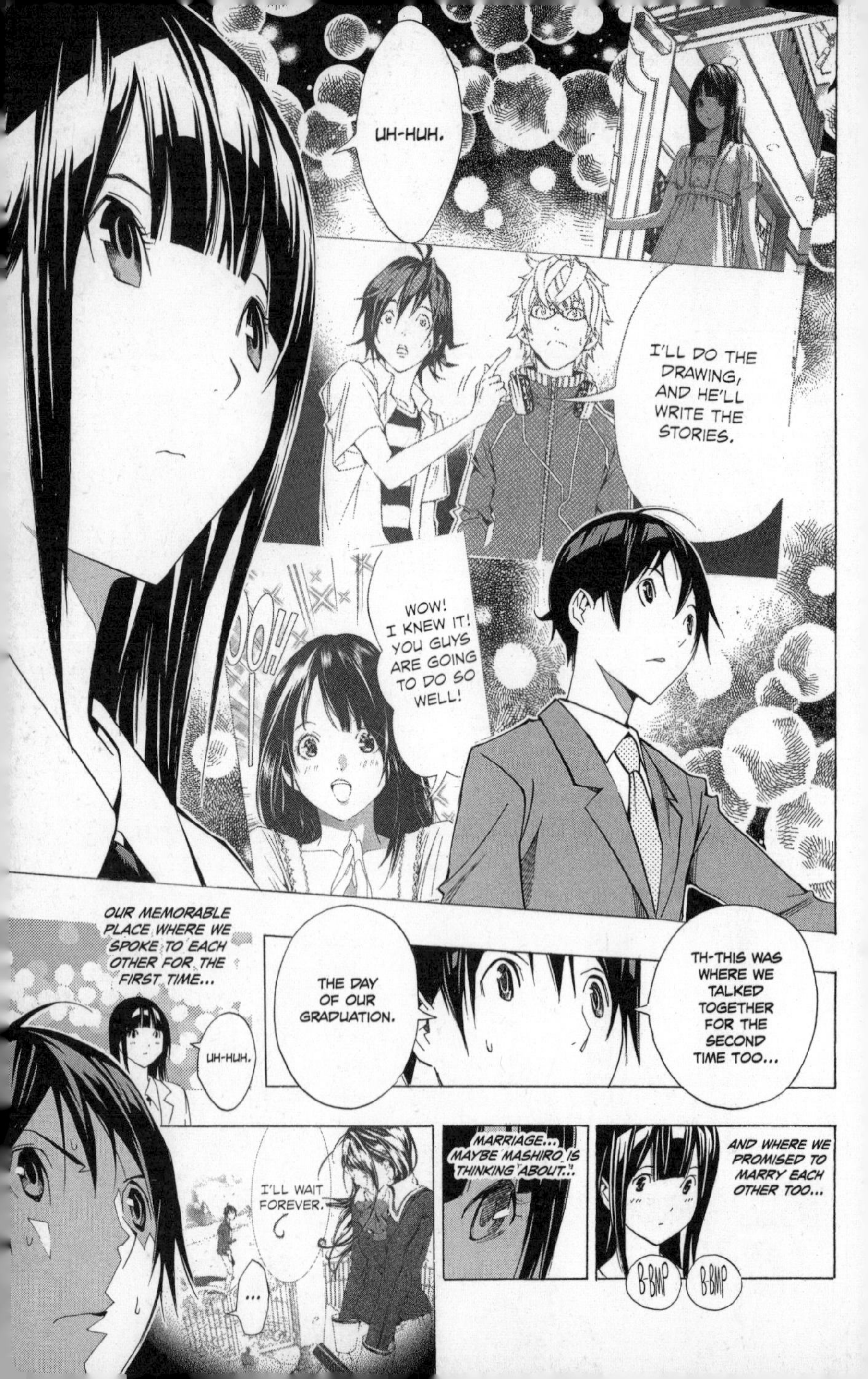
UH-HUH.
I'LL DO THE DRAWING, AND HE'LL WRITE THE STORIES.
WOW! I KNEW IT! YOU GUYS ARE GOING TO DO SO WELL!
TH-THIS WAS WHERE WE TALKED TOGETHER FOR THE SECOND TIME TOO...
THE DAY OF OUR GRADUATION.
OUR MEMORABLE PLACE WHERE WE SPOKE TO EACH OTHER FOR THE FIRST TIME...
UH-HUH.
AND WHERE WE PROMISED TO MARRY EACH OTHER TOO...
B-BMP
B-BMP
MARRIAGE... MAYBE MASHIRO IS THINKING ABOUT...
I'LL WAIT FOREVER.
...

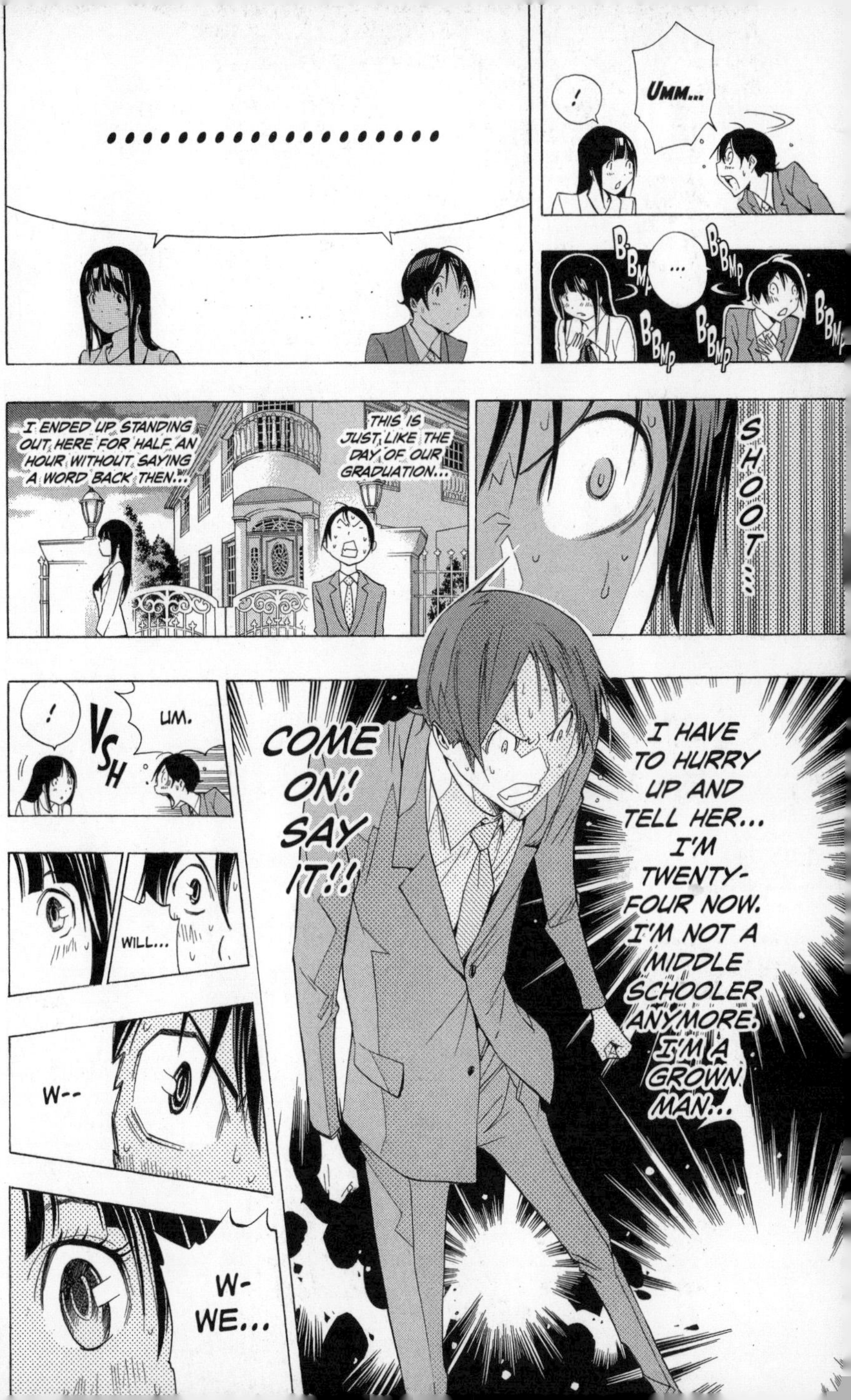
UMM...
!
B-BMP
...
B-BMP
B-BMP
B-BMP
B-BMP
....
SHOOT...
THIS IS JUST LIKE THE DAY OF OUR GRADUATION...
I ENDED UP STANDING OUT HERE FOR HALF AN HOUR WITHOUT SAYING A WORD BACK THEN...
I HAVE TO HURRY UP AND TELL HER... I'M TWENTY-FOUR NOW. I'M NOT A MIDDLE SCHOOLER ANYMORE. I'M A GROWN MAN...
COME ON! SAY IT!!
UM.
VSH
!
WILL...
W--
W-WE...

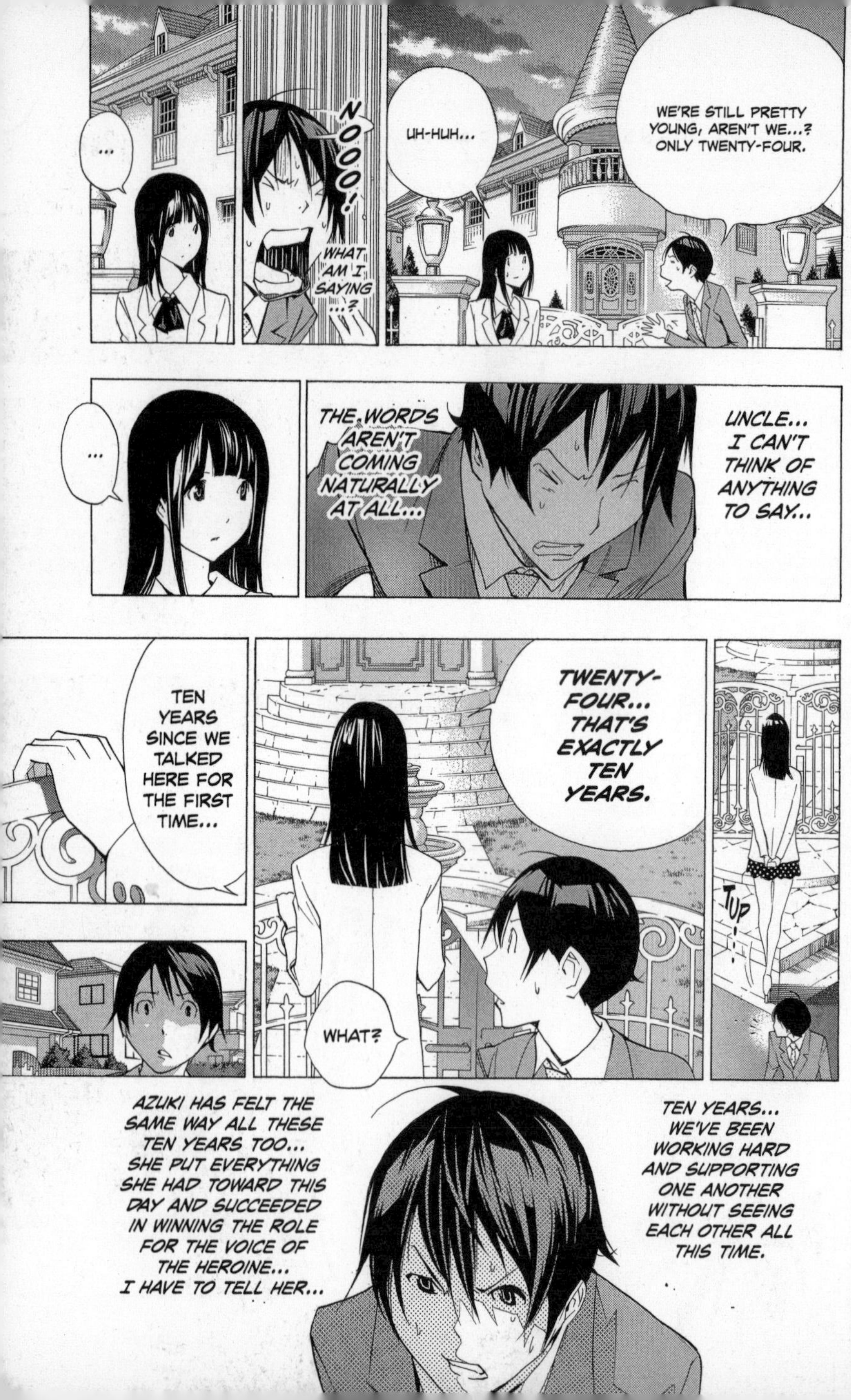
WE'RE STILL PRETTY YOUNG, AREN'T WE...? ONLY TWENTY-FOUR.
UH-HUH...
NOOOO!
WHAT AM I SAYING...?
...
UNCLE... I CAN'T THINK OF ANYTHING TO SAY...
THE WORDS AREN'T COMING NATURALLY AT ALL...
...
TUP...
TWENTY-FOUR... THAT'S EXACTLY TEN YEARS.
WHAT?
TEN YEARS SINCE WE TALKED HERE FOR THE FIRST TIME...
TEN YEARS... WE'VE BEEN WORKING HARD AND SUPPORTING ONE ANOTHER WITHOUT SEEING EACH OTHER ALL THIS TIME.
AZUKI HAS FELT THE SAME WAY ALL THESE TEN YEARS TOO... SHE PUT EVERYTHING SHE HAD TOWARD THIS DAY AND SUCCEEDED IN WINNING THE ROLE FOR THE VOICE OF THE HEROINE... I HAVE TO TELL HER...

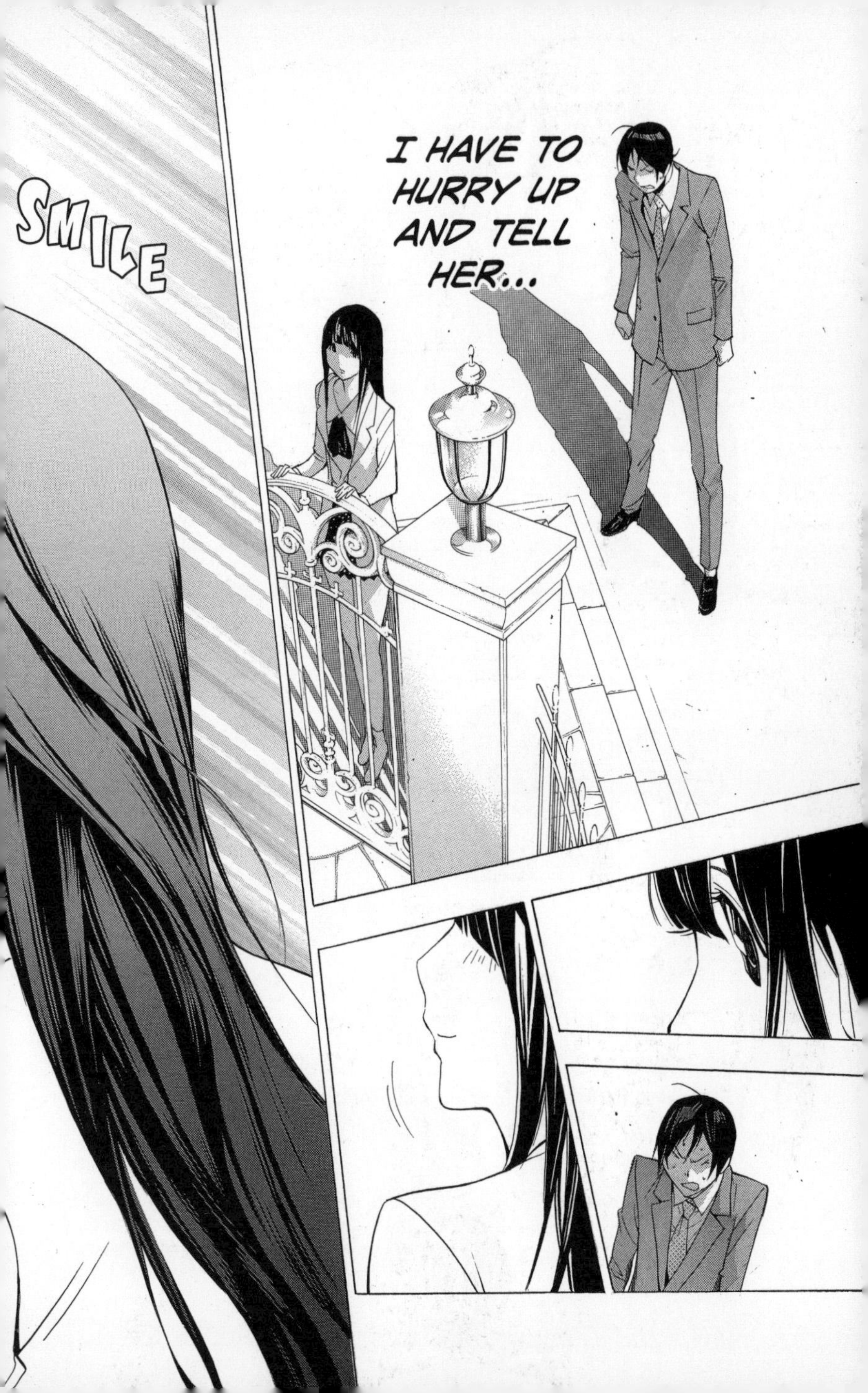
I HAVE TO HURRY UP AND TELL HER...
SMILE

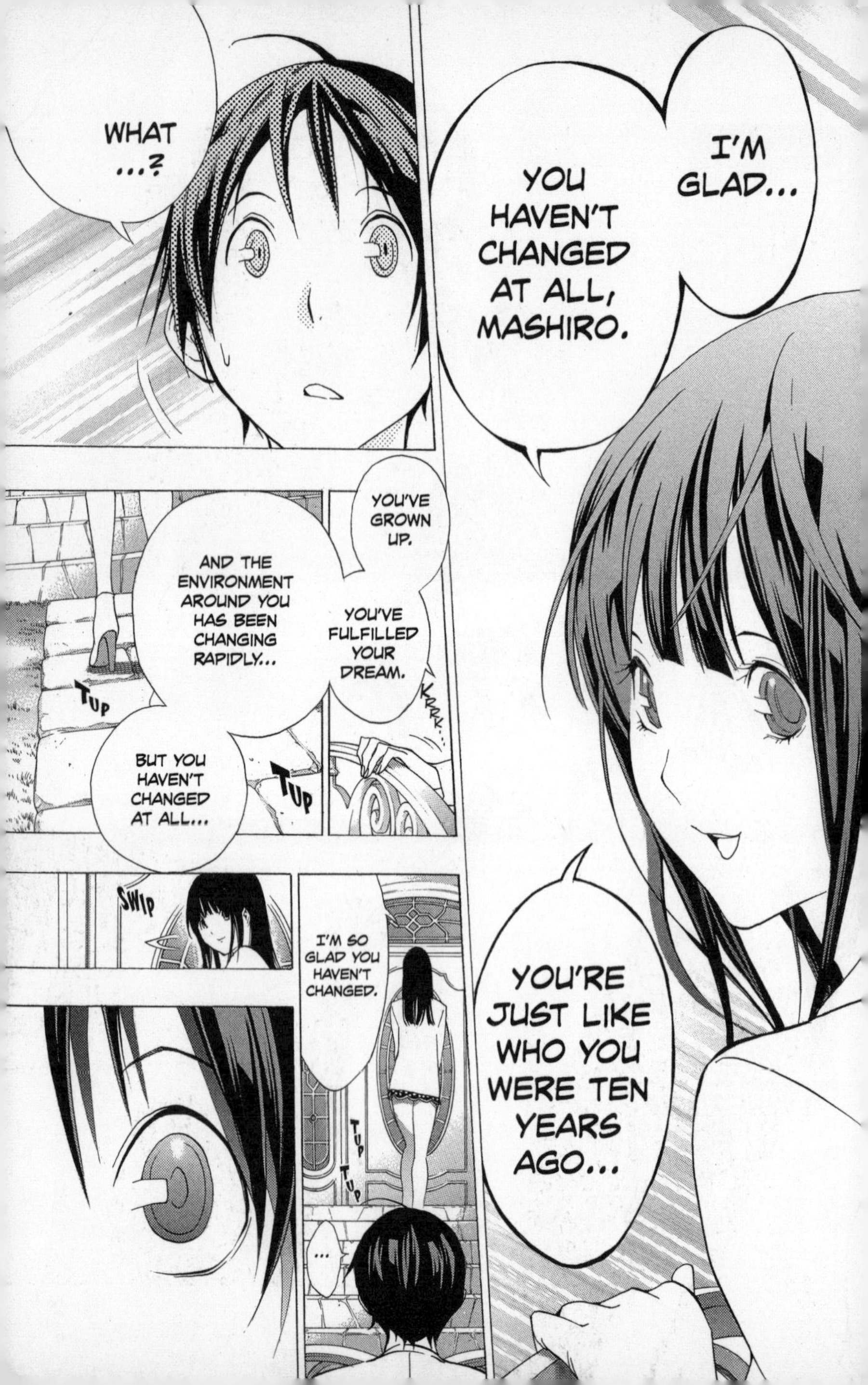
I'M GLAD...
YOU HAVEN'T CHANGED AT ALL, MASHIRO.
YOU'RE JUST LIKE WHO YOU WERE TEN YEARS AGO...
WHAT ...?
YOU'VE GROWN UP.
YOU'VE FULFILLED YOUR DREAM.
KRRK...
AND THE ENVIRONMENT AROUND YOU HAS BEEN CHANGING RAPIDLY...
BUT YOU HAVEN'T CHANGED AT ALL...
TUP
TUP
I'M SO GLAD YOU HAVEN'T CHANGED.
TUP
TUP
...
SWIP

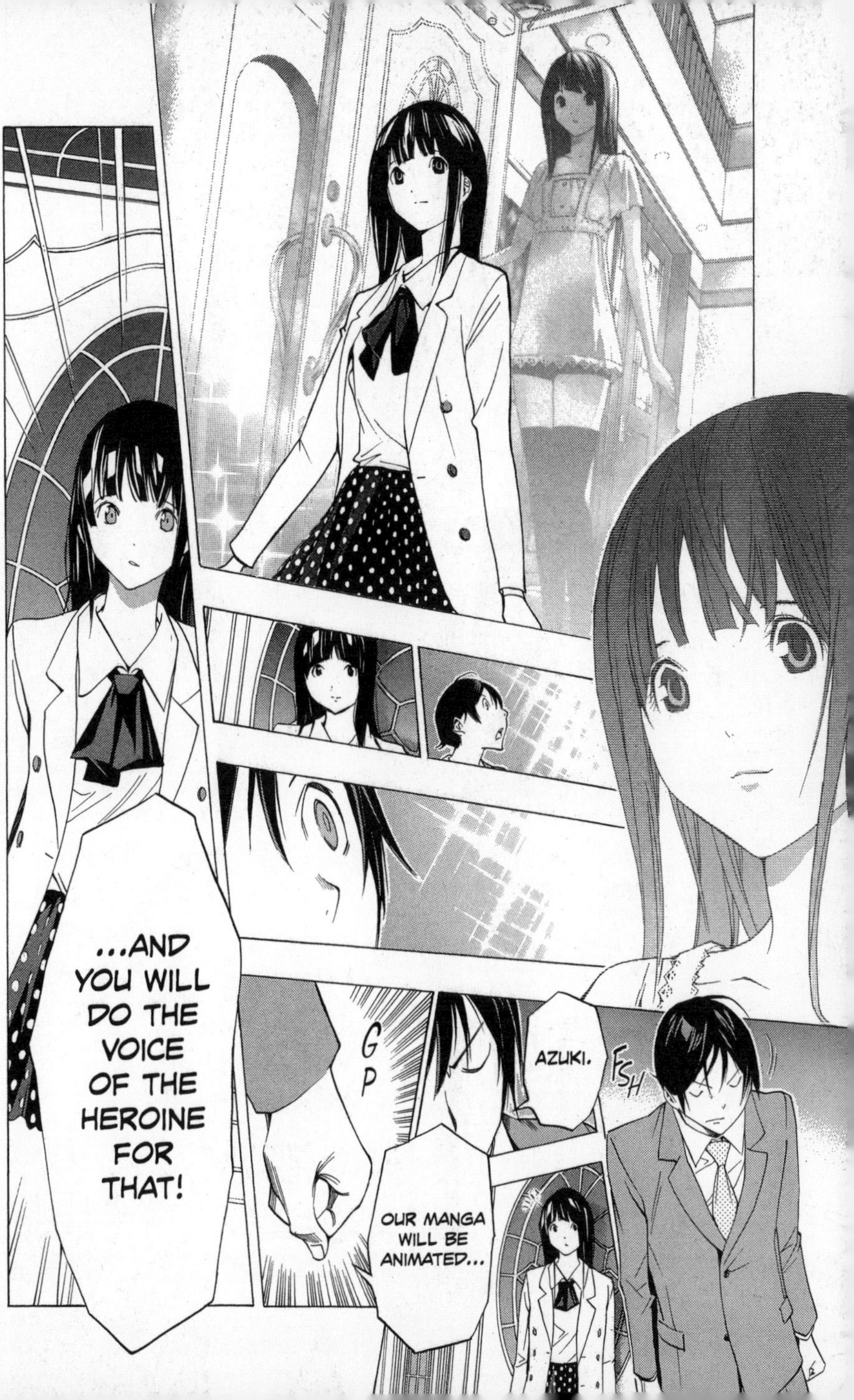
AZUKI.
FSH
OUR MANGA WILL BE ANIMATED...
GP
...AND YOU WILL DO THE VOICE OF THE HEROINE FOR THAT!

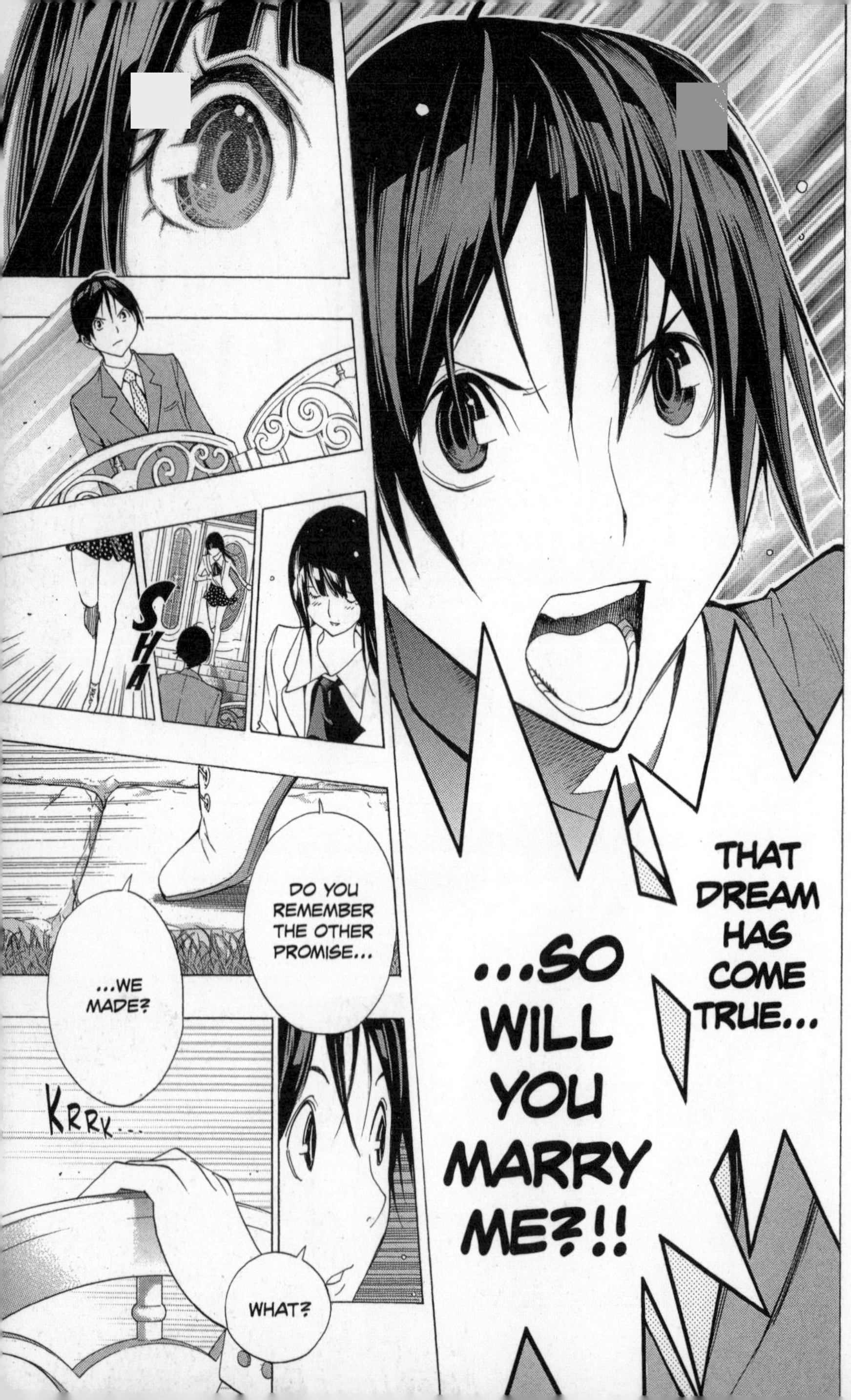
THAT DREAM HAS COME TRUE...
...SO WILL YOU MARRY ME?!!
SHA
DO YOU REMEMBER THE OTHER PROMISE...
...WE MADE?
KRRK...
WHAT?

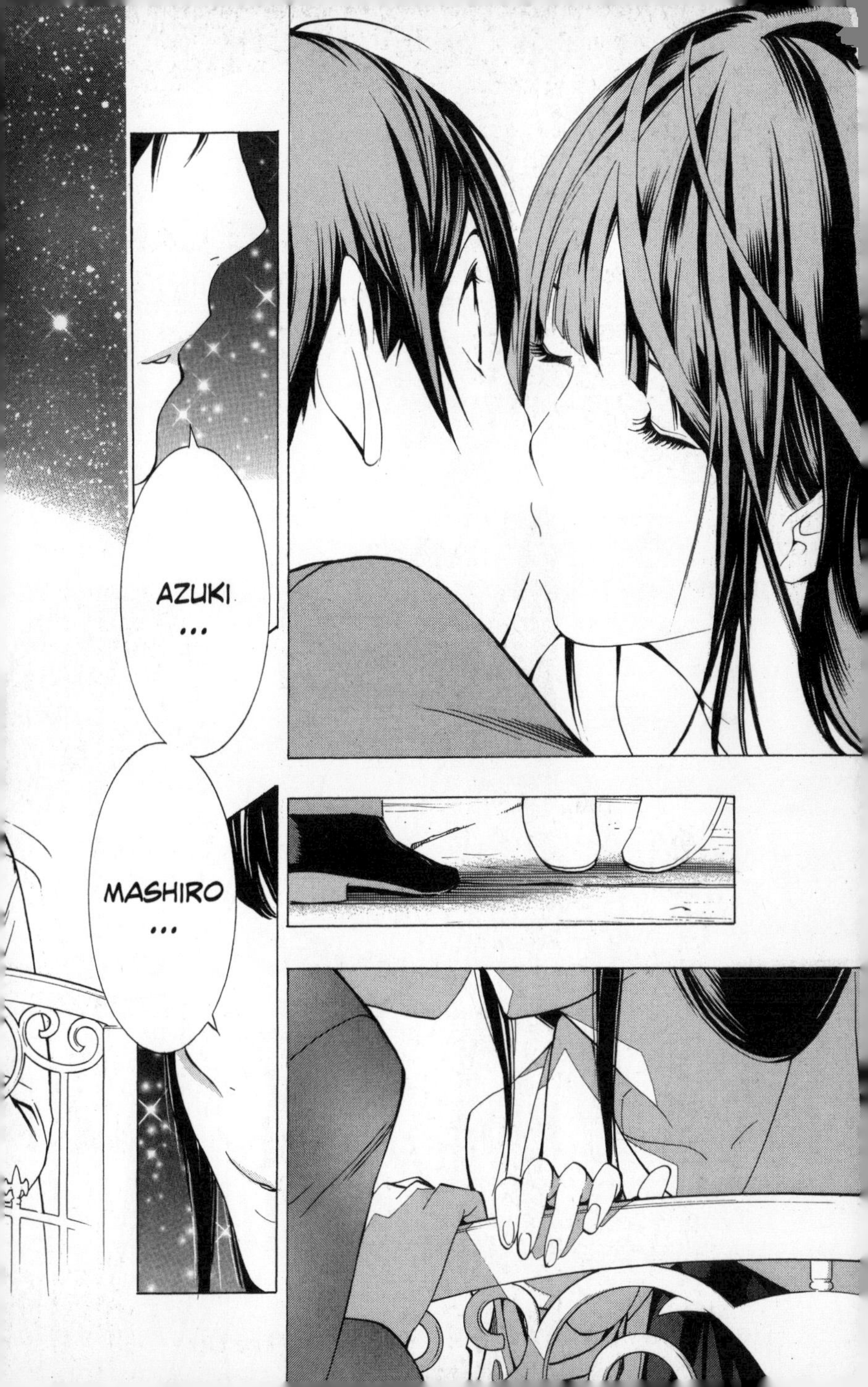
AZUKI ...
MASHIRO ...

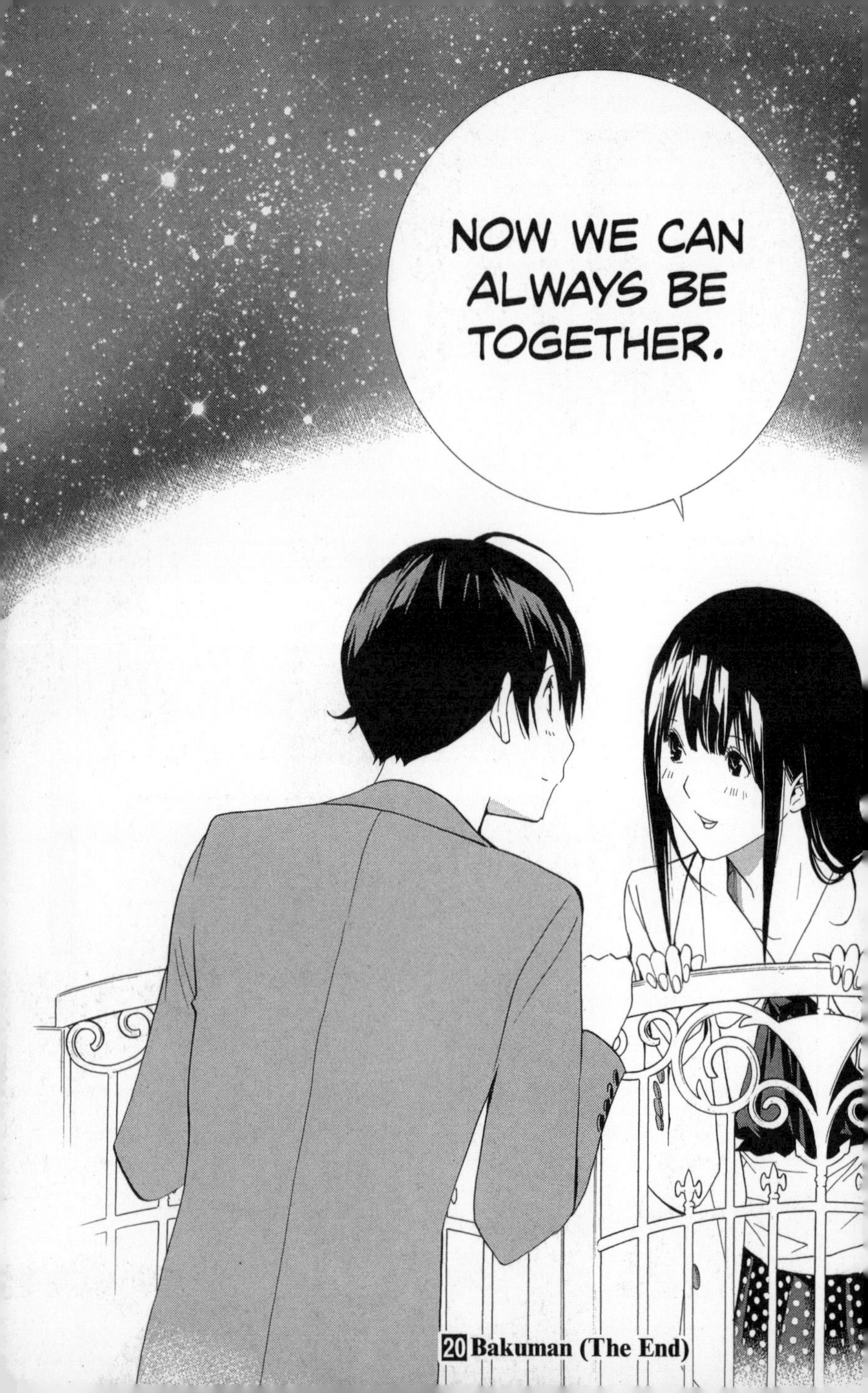
NOW WE CAN ALWAYS BE TOGETHER.
20 Bakuman (The End)

OHBA'S STORYBOARD

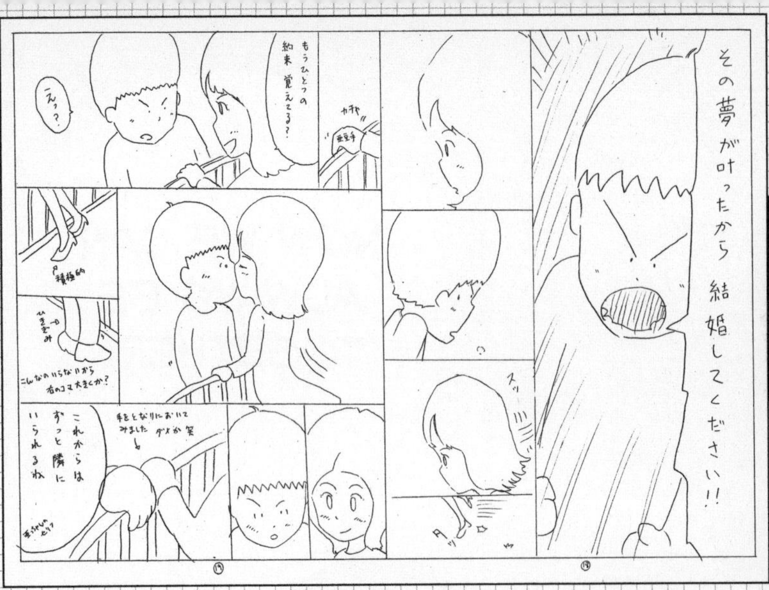
その夢が叶ったから結婚してください!!
スッ
もうひとつの約束覚えてる?
カチャ
えっ?
積極的
こんなのいらないから右のコマ大きくか?
手をとなりにおいてみました ダメか笑
これからはずっと隣にいられるね

OBATA'S STORYBOARD

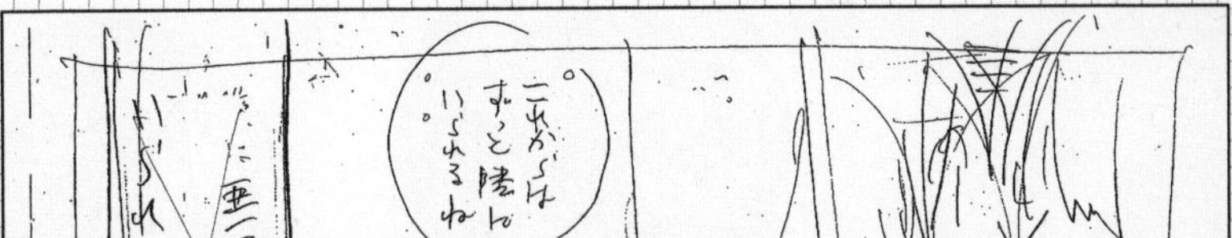
これからはずっと隣にいられるね
亜豆の隣にいられるんだ
ずっと隣に
これから僕はずっと
19
18

COMPLETE!

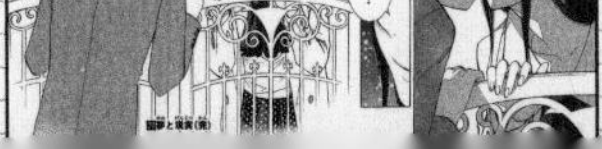
これからはずっと隣にいられるね
亜豆……
真城くん……

※CREATOR STORYBOARDS AND FINISHED PAGES IN JAPANESE

BAKUMAN。 vol.20

"Until the Final Draft Is Complete"

Last Chapter, pp. 172-173

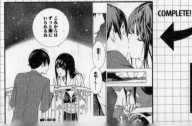

BAKUMAN。

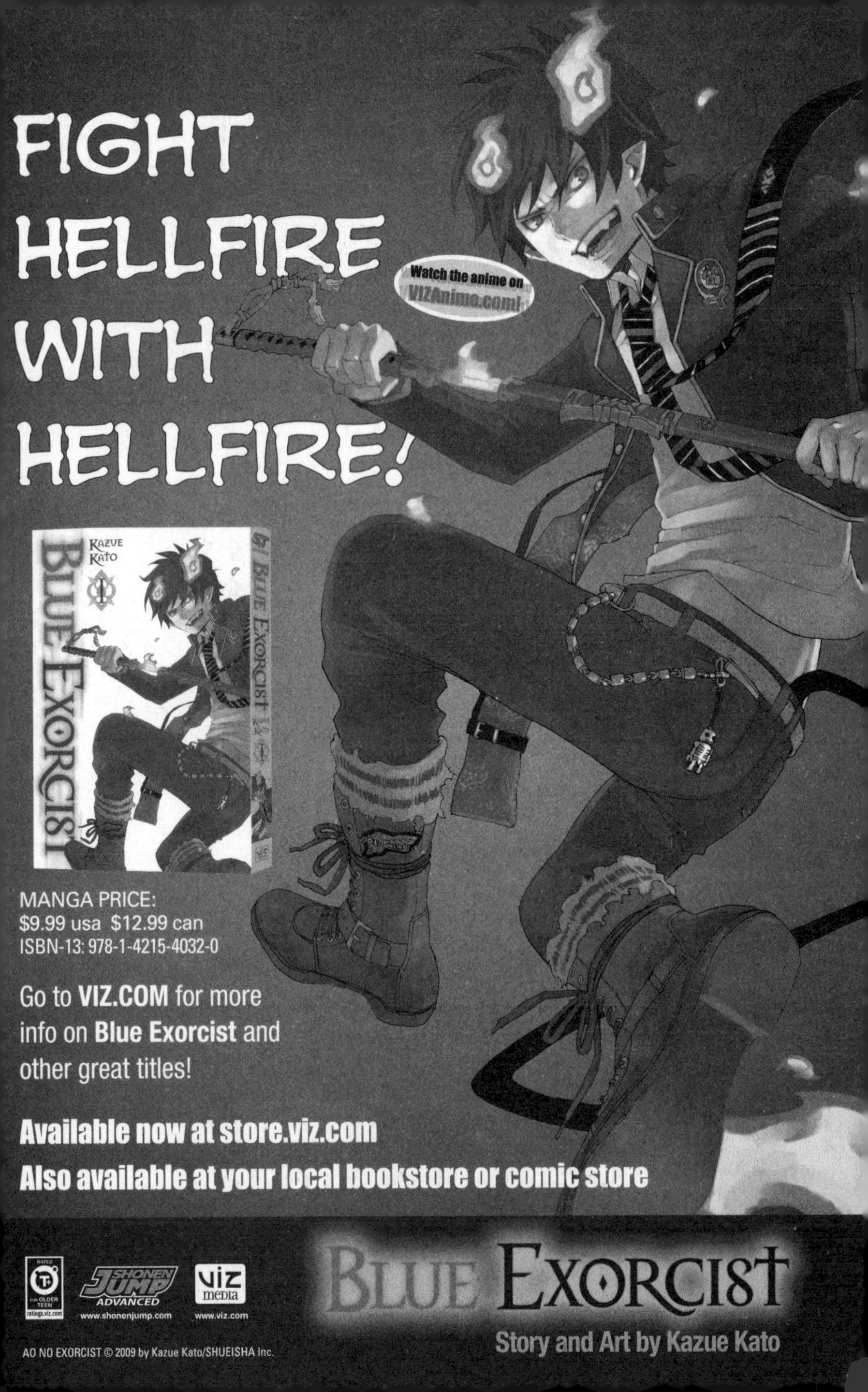
FIGHT HELLFIRE WITH HELLFIRE!
Watch the anime on VIZAnime.com!
KAZUE KATO
BLUE EXORCIST
MANGA PRICE:
$9.99 usa $12.99 can
ISBN-13: 978-1-4215-4032-0
Go to VIZ.COM for more info on Blue Exorcist and other great titles!
Available now at store.viz.com
Also available at your local bookstore or comic store
RATED T FOR OLDER TEEN ratings.viz.com
SHONEN JUMP ADVANCED
www.shonenjump.com
viz media
www.viz.com
BLUE EXORCIST
Story and Art by Kazue Kato
AO NO EXORCIST © 2009 by Kazue Kato/SHUEISHA Inc.

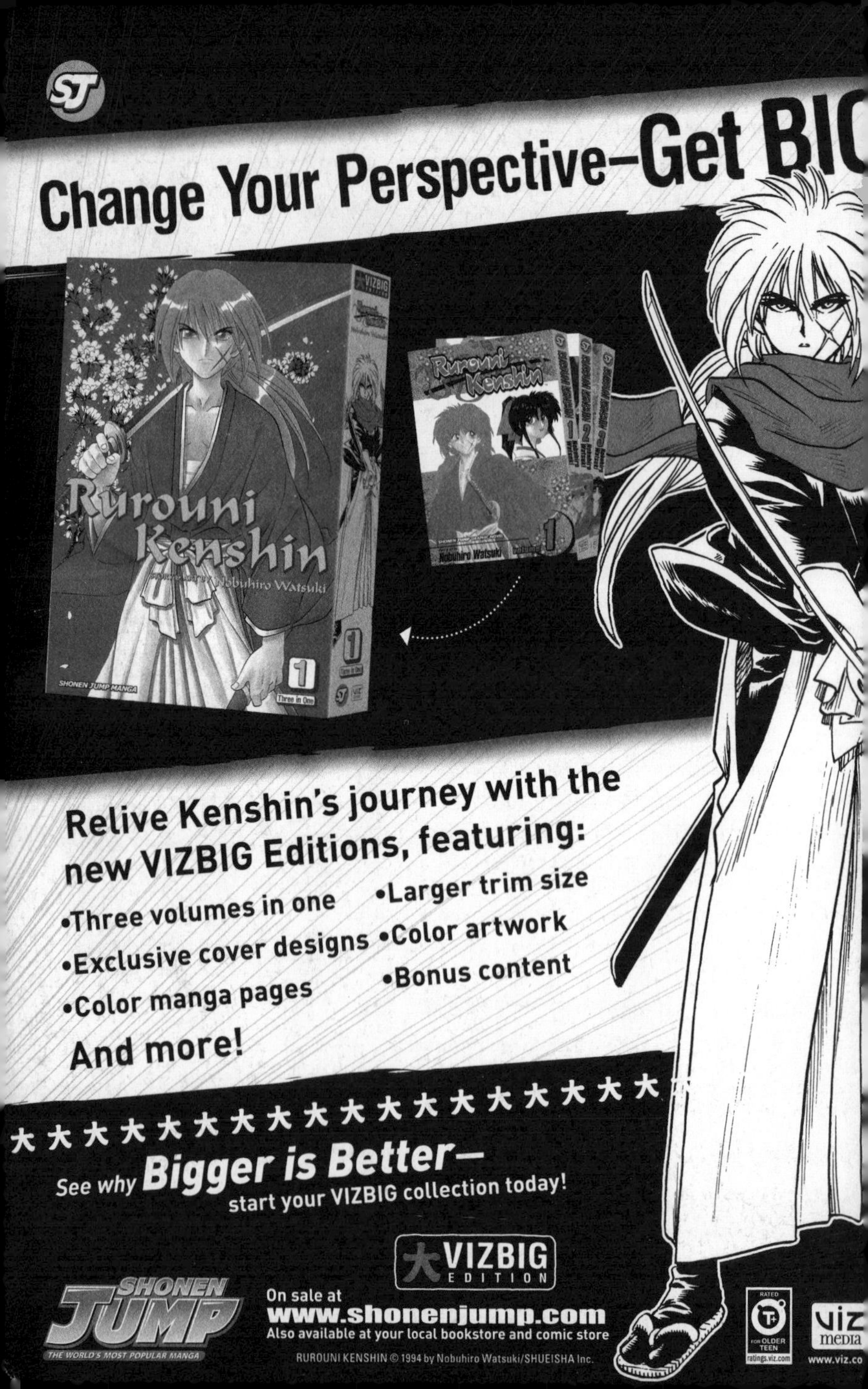
SJ
Change Your Perspective—Get BIG
Rurouni Kenshin
Nobuhiro Watsuki
SHONEN JUMP MANGA
1
Three in One
Relive Kenshin's journey with the new VIZBIG Editions, featuring:
•Three volumes in one
•Larger trim size
•Exclusive cover designs
•Color artwork
•Color manga pages
•Bonus content
And more!
See why Bigger is Better—
start your VIZBIG collection today!
大 VIZBIG EDITION
SHONEN JUMP
THE WORLD'S MOST POPULAR MANGA
On sale at
www.shonenjump.com
Also available at your local bookstore and comic store
RUROUNI KENSHIN © 1994 by Nobuhiro Watsuki/SHUEISHA Inc.
RATED T+ FOR OLDER TEEN ratings.viz.com
viz media
www.viz.co

UIZMANGA

Read manga anytime, anywhere!

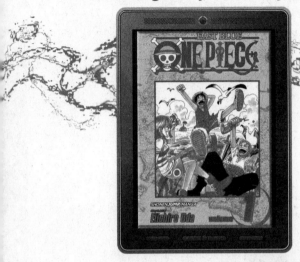

From our newest hit series to the classics you know and love, the best manga in the world is now available digitally. Buy a volume* of digital manga for your:

- iOS device (**iPad®, iPhone®, iPod® touch**) through the **VIZ Manga** app
- Android-powered device (**phone or tablet**) with a browser by visiting **VIZManga.com**
- **Mac or PC computer** by visiting **VIZManga.com**

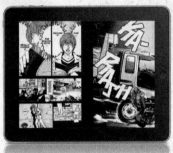

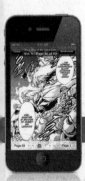

VIZ Digital has loads to offer:

- 500+ ready-to-read volumes
- New volumes each week
- FREE previews
- Access on multiple devices! Create a log-in through the app so you buy a book once, and read it on your device of choice!*

To learn more, visit www.viz.com/apps

* Some series may not be available for multiple devices.
 Check the app on your device to find out what's available.

DEATH NOTE © 2003 by Tsugumi Ohba, Takeshi Obata/SHUEISHA Inc.
NURARIHYON NO MAGO © 2008 by Hiroshi Shiibashi/SHUEISHA Inc.
ONE PIECE © 1997 by Eiichiro Oda/SHUEISHA Inc.

RATED
T
FOR OLDER
TEEN
ratings.viz.com

UIZ
media
viz.com/apps

This is the LAST PAGE.

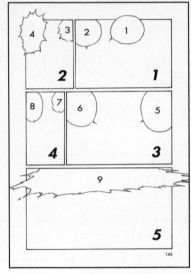

← Follow the action this way.

BAKUMAN。 has been printed in the original Japanese format in order to preserve the orientation of the original artwork.

Please turn it around and begin reading from right to left. Unlike English, Japanese is read right to left, so Japanese comics are read in reverse order from the way English comics are typically read. Have fun with it!

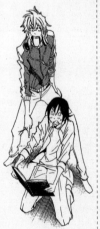

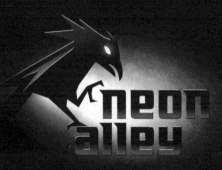
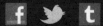